HOW TO KILL

HOW TO KILL

The Definitive History of the Assassin

KRIS HOLLINGTON

arrow books

Published by Arrow 2008

2 4 6 8 10 9 7 5 3 1

First published in Great Britain in 2007 by
Century
Random House, 20 Vauxhall Bridge Road,
London, SW1V 2SA

www.randomhouse.co.uk

Addresses for companies within The Random House Group Limited can be found at: www.randomhouse.co.uk

The Random House Group Limited Reg. No. 954009

A CIP catalogue record for this book is available from the British Library

ISBN 9780099502463

Graphic Design © Jonathan Holgate

The Random House Group Limited supports The Forest Stewardship Council (FSC), the leading international forest certification organisation. All our titles that are printed on Greenpeace approved FSC certified paper carry the FSC logo. Our paper procurement policy can be found at: www.rbooks.co.uk/environment

Typeset by SX Composing DTP, Rayleigh, Essex
Printed in the UK by CPI Cox & Wyman, Reading, RG1 8EX

Contents

Acknowledgements

I'd like to thank everyone who helped with the writing of this book. Particular thanks go to Andrew Lownie (www.andrewlownie.co.uk), the hardest-working literary agent in the business, for his unstinting support, optimism, enthusiasm and for getting straight to the point in the most wonderfully concise emails.

My editor, Timothy Andrews at Century, to whom I owe the best chapter heading in *How to Kill* (not to mention the very existence of this book), is a master of the editorial scissors. His judicial snipping and shuffling has meant that far more material, not less, has ended up going into *How to Kill* than I could have hoped. Thanks are also due to his team, who have patiently steered me through each stage of the editorial process.

To those who have given me shelter as I travelled, wrote and investigated – in particular Gus and Janet, James and Lucy, Sian and Mum – I thank you all for saving me from cheap hotels and nights spent sleeping in my car.

I must also acknowledge all the researchers and writers who have gone before me (a full list of sources for this book can be found on my website www.assassinology.org). Special thanks must go to the witnesses, the would-be victims and the assassins themselves (in particular the London hit-man whom I hope to never see again) who were prepared to relive their brushes with death.

And finally, this book is dedicated to Nina Kollmann, a woman of infinite patience, who has given 'that damn book' and me the space we needed. Thank you for being my ruthless test audience, translator of Russian, German and Spanish and for your subediting wizardry (especially for helping me understand the mysteries of the semicolon); will you marry me?

Introduction

On the day this introduction was written a senior Georgian politician was blown to smithereens by a car bomb, a popular Shia cleric in Pakistan was stabbed *and* shot to death, a senior member of the National Union of Mineworkers in Cape Town was beaten and then executed by a single gunshot to the head, Sri Lanka's third-highest-ranking general was blasted at point-blank range by a man wielding a home-made sawn-off shotgun and a 'protected' witness about to give evidence against those accused of the assassination of Serbian Prime Minister Zoran Djindjic was found dead in a side street with his throat slit. In other assassination news a former MI6 agent who claimed that Princess Diana was assassinated was arrested, there was a demand for a new inquiry into the 1993 slaying of South African Communist Party leader Chris Hani, an apology from a Tamil Tiger leader for the assassination of former Indian Prime Minister Rajiv Gandhi, it was revealed that the current ruler of Iran was once a professional assassin, and Papua New Guinea's police released the details of a plot to assassinate the country's president. There was nothing particularly special about this day: just another typical twenty-four hours in world affairs.

Assassination is an often-employed tool used by governments, terrorist groups and lone crackpots; its effectiveness and sizeable role in everyday world affairs remains largely underestimated. Between 1950 and 2000, over four thousand assassinations have played a defining role in most of the world's key events. Assassination has been used in attempts to change the regimes of the Philippines, Cuba, Egypt, Iran, Iraq, China, Russia, America, Spain, the United Kingdom, Sweden, Saudi Arabia, South Korea, India, Pakistan, the Democratic Republic of the Congo, Uganda and South Africa – to name but a few (and in many cases more than once). Assassination has also played a role in German reunification; the collapse of Communism; the ending of apartheid in South Africa; the fight over Northern Ireland; the American Civil Rights Movement; the campaigns for democracy in Poland and Bulgaria; the nuclear arms race; various countries' battles against organised crime; and, in one instance, an assassination sparked the worst genocide since the Holocaust. Assassinations have featured in, started, ended, shortened or prolonged dozens of wars including those fought in Korea, Vietnam, Afghanistan, Algeria, the former Yugoslavia, Lebanon, and most of the South American countries as well as Russia and the former Soviet states. As this book will show, politics involves a lot more dagger – as distinct from cloak – than most politicians will admit.

Before going any further, it is of course necessary to define the act of 'assassination'. The *word* 'assassination' is straightforward enough. It derives from the name of the *Hashishin*, a secretive Iranian sect that existed between 1090 and 1256 in the Elburz Mountains of north-west Iran, just south of the Caspian Sea. They pioneered the use of selective murder instead of war to acquire wealth and power. They did not take hashish before murdering someone as many have written. (Some scholars have speculated that *Hashishin* means 'hashish eater' but eating hashish leads to confusion, forgetfulness, in some cases paranoia and the removal of violent tendencies – not a good idea if you're planning to sneak into an enemy fortress, creep past the guards, silently murder your victim and escape back to your hideout six thousand feet up a mountain.)

As for the act of assassination, this occurs when someone important is murdered for one of three reasons:

1. Political beliefs: the selective killing of an individual enemy in the hope that their policies will die with them.
2. Power: committed simply to take the place of a VIP, or to transfer their power to someone else. As international terrorist Carlos the Jackal put it: 'To get anywhere, you have to walk over corpses.'
3. Notoriety: disturbed individuals who want to achieve fame through the elimination of a VIP. Sirhan Sirhan told his interrogators: 'They can gas me, but I am famous; I have achieved in one day what it took Robert Kennedy all his life to do.'

The motive of the assassin is almost never personal: they are killing what the target represents, be it their power or fame, ideology, religious practice or economic system. The victim may be killed by a variety of means; anything from exploding clams to poisoned toilet paper, from guided missiles to falling lifts, involving a planned – or occasionally unplanned – violent or subtle surprise attack. The attack may sometimes, however, take the form of an abuse of the justice system – beginning with a false accusation and leading to a speedy conviction and execution, as happened to Lavrenti Beria, Chief of the Soviet Police, himself an expert assassin and master of the cover-up, who once boasted: 'Any fool can commit a murder, but only an artist can make murder look like suicide.'

Assassins can be divided into two groups, professional and amateur. In the 1970s, the CIA produced a remarkable book called *How to Kill* which provided guidelines for agents training to be professional assassins. (Naturally, the KGB produced their own version, *The KGB Alpha Team Training Manual.*) It states: 'The will to kill, the complete lack of sympathy and compassion, and no hesitation in killing the subject, is paramount. You must take his life as detachedly as you might swat a fly or crush an ant . . . the morally squeamish should not attempt it.' This statement makes clear the difference between the two groups. While the professional is usually a calm psychopathic killer who murders for money, the amateur is typically an emotional character whose will to kill is driven by passion.

The professional assassin holds immense psychological power. A former American army sniper who worked for the CIA in the 1990s understood this perfectly: 'There's a moment when you have a man dead in your sights, when you decide whether or not to pull the trigger. It's like being God when you realise that the person you're making life-and-death decisions over doesn't even know you're there. *That's real power.*'

The professional hit man commands a tremendous amount of respect brought about by people's fear of what he is capable of doing. There is something very unsettling about meeting a man who kills for money and knowing that if someone paid him enough he'd kill you. A London-based hit man described the reaction of fellow criminals when they learned who he was: 'They change. They respect you but at the same time they're afraid of you – you can tell, you know? They think you're different, not human or something. They have this picture of you as this cold-blooded killer who never smiles. But then they see you are human and you do smile and you're pretty much like them. But it still puts them off. They don't know how to act around you, so they end up avoiding you altogether. I guess they can't get over that picture they have of you out there squeezing the trigger on some poor, hopeless bastard who doesn't have a chance . . . they know that one day it might be them.'

Non-governmental, untrained assassins are hot-blooded individuals driven by passionate beliefs (however misplaced), some of whom only discover they are 'morally squeamish' when they come face to face with their intended target. They are ordinary, unremarkable people, often failures: the antithesis of the men and women they try to kill. This is what makes the amateur assassin particularly unnerving. Anyone, absolutely anyone, could wake up one morning and decide to do something extraordinary with their lives: to immortalise themselves and change the course of history.

It is quite remarkable just how many people actually take this step and the rise of the lone-nut assassin – the madmen and -women who kill for no reason other than a lust for notoriety – is almost exclusively a post-1960 phenomenon. These assassins toss bombs inexpertly, aim guns poorly or strike with a knife without any genuine knowledge of anatomy – whether their target lives or dies is down to chance.

For example, in 2005 twenty-seven-year-old Vladimir Arutyunian threw a live Russian-made RDG-5 hand grenade at President George W. Bush while the President was on a state visit to the former Soviet state of Georgia. It landed 18.6 metres from the President, well within its killing range of twenty-five metres. But when the assassin had pulled the pin, his scarf had become caught in the firing mechanism and it had failed to strike the fuse hard enough to ignite it. It was an extraordinarily close call.

When police searched Arutyunian's mother's garden shed they found a copy of *The Day of the Jackal*[1] and enough chemicals and grenades to kill thousands of people. Arutyunian had links to Chechen rebels who were hiding out in a forbidding place called the Pankisi Gorge just one hundred miles east of Tblisi, a terrorist hot spot that has also played host to al-Qaeda. The Chechens were annoyed that the United States was sending its special forces to root them out of their hideouts and so Bush's visit to Georgia seemed like an ideal chance to strike back. Had Vladimir Arutyunian succeeded, no doubt America's War on Terror would have come to Georgia and, perhaps more worryingly, to Chechnya.

Incidentally, since Bush became President his elite protection officers, the Secret Service, have been kept very busy. In 1974 President Richard Nixon received three hundred death threats. In 2004, President George Bush received five hundred – a month. While playing a Presidential round of golf with his dad in 2005 at

[1] Frederick Forsyth's seminal assassination novel has been found in the possession of an extraordinary number of assassins – one group of Spanish terrorists even went to see the newly released film of the book a few days before they had a pop at the Prime Minister of Spain.

the world-famous Augusta course, Bush Jr's face creased in a frown as he looked down the fairway to see dozens of Secret Service agents looking up trees, darting in and out of bushes, waving guns and hollering while pressing their earpieces. One man with a gun had been spotted wandering around checking out bunkers. 'Amazing how this job follows you everywhere,' Bush told reporters matter-of-factly before shouting 'Fore!' and teeing off.

Despite its title, this book is not a guide on how to kill, although assassins do tend to study the literature. Unbelievably, such a guide was published by the Paladin Press in 1983. *Hit Man: A Technical Manual for Independent Contractors* by Rex Feral was described as 'a step-by-step murder manual, a training book for assassins' by the US Circuit Court of Appeals shortly before they banned it in 1999. The book had checklists and related detailed killing techniques. It recommended particular weapons, had illustrative photographs, discussed surveillance, floor plans, chemical formulas, how to dispose of evidence, even how to mentally prepare yourself to kill. The one thing it didn't tell you was to throw away the book after you had completed your hit. It was found in the possession of two murderers (one of whom killed an eight-year-old disabled boy, his carer and his mother for life-insurance money) who had used its 'step-by-step' instructions to the letter. The discovery of the book formed part of the prosecution case that saw them sent to death row (one can only wonder at how many others might have used the book successfully). Paladin Press were not too worried about the ban as their most popular publications such as *Be Your Own Undertaker: How to Dispose of a Dead Body*, *Silencers for Hand Firearms* and *Contingency Cannibalism: Superhardcore Survivalism's Dirty Little Secret* are all still available and selling well.

This book is the first to study in detail not only the causes and surprising consequences of assassination but also the crucial seconds of the act itself and the psychology of the assassin in an effort to understand why some assassinations succeed where others fail – and what might be done to prevent them. It is also the first book to examine the fascinating facts and figures of assassination, revealing everything from the success rate by type of weapon and the escape and survival rates of assassins to the most popular time of year and location for assassination. For the first time, too, it provides the definitive answer to the most important question of all: Can one murder really change the world?

One

The Truman Show

Allen Dulles, the first director of America's Central Intelligence Agency (the CIA, formed in 1947), once described the Russian State Security Committee (the KGB, formed in 1954) as: 'A multi-purpose, clandestine arm of power . . . more than a secret police organisation, more than an intelligence and counter-intelligence organisation. It is an instrument for subversion, manipulation and violence, for secret intervention in the affairs of other countries.' With hindsight, it is obvious to most observers that Dulles's description encapsulates *both* agencies perfectly. The second half of the twentieth century saw the beginning of a new war, the Cold War, that frosty tension between the two superpowers each of whom had a limitless budget to devote to the sneaky practice of espionage (i.e. subversion, manipulation and assassination) without having to blow each other to bits using increasingly powerful weapons that, by 1980, could destroy the world a hundred times over. With limitless resources, both countries devoted a lot of time to learning the arts of assassination. The Americans had the wonderfully – if not too subtly – named Health Alteration Committee and the Russians the slightly more mysterious Alpha Squad.

The first major assassination attack in the post-1950s world was neither Russian- nor US-backed, however, but came from a little Caribbean island. It was a direct assault on the United States President, unheard of today for, in a sign of things to come, the attempt was covered up and played down by the American Secret Service with the line that the 'President was never in any danger'. In reality, it was far more dramatic than anything that Hollywood would ever dare to produce.

'Mr President, my husband is dead.' On 12 April 1945, with one of the most succinct sentences in history, Mrs Eleanor Roosevelt informed Vice-President Harry S. Truman of her misfortune and his sudden elevation. Franklin D. Roosevelt had died from a massive stroke, a result of hypertension which, at the crucial end stages of the war, had left him an ineffective leader, easily fatigued and suffering constant headaches.

Truman had no time to ease himself into the job. One of his first acts as President of the United States was to authorise the use of atomic bombs against Japan. On 24 July 1945, Truman noted in his diary that he had given instructions to 'use it so that military objectives and soldiers and sailors are the target and not women and children . . . we will issue a warning statement'. No warning was given to the women and children of Hiroshima who far outnumbered any military personnel there. On 6 August the atom bomb was dropped and about 150,000 people died or were wounded. A second bomb was meant to be dropped on 9 August on the industrial town of Kokura but the area was obscured by smog so the pilot, whose orders were to drop the bomb on a visual target, flew ninety miles south-west into clearer skies and dropped the bomb on the town of Nagasaki, killing about 75,000 people.

Truman also supported the Marshall Plan to help countries devastated by the Second World War, established the CIA and began the Fair Deal programme of social reforms. Despite this, he was not expected to defeat the popular Thomas E. Dewey in the 1948 presidential election. The *Chicago Times* was so confident that Dewey would win that they ran their morning edition with the headline 'Dewey Defeats Truman' without waiting for the election result. The next morning, a delighted President Truman posed holding up the newspaper for photographers after one of the greatest election upsets in history. His inauguration ceremony in early 1949 was broadcast live on television, reaching ten million Americans. A further one hundred million were listening on radios across the world, then a record audience. Truman took this opportunity to draw the battle lines for the Cold War: 'The actions resulting from Communist philosophy are a threat to the efforts of free nations to bring about world recovery and lasting peace.' Two days after Truman's speech, Communist forces marched into Peking. By the end of the year, Mao Tse-tung had proclaimed the People's Republic of China and agreed a thirty-year pact of friendship with Stalin, whose scientists had recently successfully tested their own atom bomb. Truman authorised the American boffins (with a little assistance from German scientists captured at the end of the Second World War) to get on with producing a much more powerful device – the hydrogen bomb. He also worked rapidly towards consolidating the North Atlantic Treaty Organisation (NATO), established by twelve countries in April that year, the aim of which was mutual military assistance in the event of aggression.

On 25 June 1950 North Korea invaded the South. After North Korea refused to obey the United Nations Security Council's demands to withdraw, America intervened. Truman made a note in his diary: 'Must be careful not to cause a general Asiatic War.' By the end of 1950, Chinese troops had joined the fray on the side of the North and General MacArthur, the Supreme Commander of all the United Nations forces in South Korea, asked Truman for permission to drop thirty to fifty atom bombs on the Chinese. In Washington, Senator Joseph McCarthy launched a ruthless anti-communist purge, despite opposition from the President. The Cold War was hotting up.

Despite living with the constant threat of assassination, Truman made life difficult for his Secret Service agents. He would stay up late into the night playing poker (his adviser, Clark Gifford, once lost three thousand dollars to Truman in a single hand – when the President dealt him his losing card, Gifford couldn't help himself: 'You son of a bitch!') and then arose every morning at five-thirty a.m. By six a.m. he was walking around Washington at a strict 120 paces per minute. Truman tipped his hat to passers-by as his agents huffed and puffed to keep up. He would also walk from the White House to Blair House and back again, refusing to be driven the short distance in 'one of those damn limousines'.

Puerto Rico was possibly the last country from which Truman would have expected an assassin to come. Shortly after becoming President, he had sent a special message to Congress recommending that four proposals for changing the status of Puerto Rico (the Caribbean island and its one million inhabitants had been under US control since 1898), including independence, should be submitted to the Puerto Ricans for their choice. In 1946, he appointed Jesus T. Pinero as the country's first native governor, and in 1949 he made provision for the island to write its own constitution.

The first sign of trouble came on 29 October 1950 when a nationalist coup began in southern Puerto Rico, rapidly spreading from town to town across the island. It was led by the charismatic Harvard graduate Pedro Albizu Campos, President of the Nationalist Party, whose exposure to racism in the American army during the First World War had left him an embittered advocate of independence through revolution. In the capital, San Juan, there was particularly fierce fighting. The presidential palace was fired upon and, although efforts to assassinate Governor Muñoz Marín failed, twenty-seven people were killed and a further ninety suffered gunshot wounds. The coup was all but quelled by the next day: Albizu Campos was captured in a jeep packed full of assault rifles. He had been struggling to find nationalists inspired by his actions to give them to and discovered too late that there simply wasn't enough popular support to sustain the rebels against the better-equipped army. In the aftermath of the failed revolt, thousands of pro-independence Puerto Ricans were arrested by the nervous government without explanation, even if they had not supported the uprising.

Oscar Collazo, a thirty-four-year-old Puerto Rican and ardent nationalist, was appalled that his innocent countrymen were being imprisoned. Collazo came to America as a teenager at the height of the Depression, managed to find work and supported his family in Puerto Rico. He also selflessly donated his time and money to other Puerto Rican nationalists who were trying to settle in America. At his last job, as a metal polisher in a large machine factory, his employer rated him as one of his best employees and his co-workers had elected Collazo as their union representative. He was also the Secretary of the New York City Junta of the (Puerto Rican) Nationalist Party and a devoted follower of Albizu Campos. Collazo divorced his first wife after she was unfaithful and he then married a fellow metalworker who had two daughters. The daughters became so fond of Collazo that they officially changed their surname to his.

Twenty-five-year-old Griselio Torresola's radicalism was genetic; his family had participated in every Puerto Rican revolution for a century. He and his brother Elio and two sisters, Angelina and Doris, were devoted to Albizu Campos from childhood. One of Torresola's sisters had been wounded in the coup, and his brother was eventually sentenced to life imprisonment for killing a policeman. Although he was married, Torresola had a reputation for being a gigolo. After being fired from his job in a stationery office, he relied on the generosity of fellow Puerto Ricans for his welfare while in New York.

Collazo and Torresola were frustrated and angered by their inability to assist in the coup or die for the cause. After an impassioned discussion of their helplessness Collazo suddenly suggested that they should assassinate President Truman. Torresola, who longed to do something important, agreed immediately. Their decision was not born out of personal hatred: they only wanted to draw America's attention to the plight of the nationalists in Puerto Rico at this critical time. The plan would have been completely absurd except for two things: the two men's utter determination and the fact that Torresola had one vital talent – he was a deadly shot with a pistol. It was to be the first-ever assault on the White House and it led to one of the bloodiest, most dramatic shoot-outs in American history.

1 November 1950 was an exceptionally warm day in Washington DC and the front door of Blair House (the Trumans were living at Blair House while the White House was undergoing renovation) was open with only a locked screen door blocking the way. Unlike the White House, which stood protected behind iron fences that enclosed an enormous expanse of lawn, Blair House was separated from the pavement – where hundreds of people passed every hour – by just a five-foot-wide front garden and a low hedge. The Secret Service agents wanted to at least rope off the main area in front of the house but Truman dismissed the idea: 'Nobody wants to shoot me.' At two p.m. Truman decided to take an afternoon nap, got undressed and went to bed.

Meanwhile, the two amateur assassins were asking a taxi driver to point out Blair House for them (they hadn't been able to find it using a map). If they'd read the newspapers they'd have known that Truman was due to give a speech at Arlington Cemetery that afternoon, and would have walked out of Blair House at 2.50 p.m.; or if they'd bothered to research Truman's routine they would have known that he was most vulnerable on his morning walks.

Six of the usual seven-man detail stood guard; the seventh handled other duties as and when they arose. Three men guarded the three entrances to the building; another was stationed just inside the front door; and two, including the officer in charge, moved around wherever they were needed. In one of the two sentry boxes was forty-year-old White House Police officer Leslie Coffelt, a quiet, good-humoured man. He was due to take some leave because his seriously ill wife Chessie was about to undergo a life-saving operation. In the other box was White House Police officer Joseph Davidson, at thirty-seven the group's only bachelor. Thirty-five-year-old Secret Service Agent Floyd Boring was standing to the side of the main entrance, not far from a small guardhouse with Secret Service agent Vincent Mroz. Donald Birdzell, forty-one, guarded the stairway to the all-important front door to Blair House, while Pennsylvania State Police veteran Stewart Stout stood just inside that door, the last man between an assassin and the President.

At 2.19 p.m., Oscar Collazo made his move. He approached Blair House from the east, and stopped when he was five feet behind the uniformed Donald Birdzell. Collazo pointed his Walther P38 at Birdzell's back and pulled the trigger. Nothing happened. As the officer sensed some activity behind him, he started to turn. Callazo desperately pounded his pistol with his left hand; suddenly it fired. The bullet hit Birdzell in the right knee and he dropped to the ground. Collazo ran towards Blair House.

White House Police officer Joseph Davidson and Secret Service Agent Floyd Boring were standing outside a nearby guardhouse when they heard the shot and saw Birdzell go down. They drew their weapons and started firing at Collazo. To their intense frustration, their bullets repeatedly ricocheted off a wrought-iron fence that separated them from the assassin. Collazo returned fire with his 9mm while Birdzell, fighting the intense pain, hauled himself to his feet and dragged his crippled leg behind him as he hobbled after Collazo, firing his own Police Special.

Boring, who was one of the top marksmen on the White House squad, took his time directing his sights at Collazo's head before firing. The bullet grazed Collazo's skull and blew off his hat, leaving a bloody but superficial wound. Davidson fired a second later; his bullet, travelling at a sharp angle, tore through Collazo's pectoral muscle before burying itself in his right arm.

Secret Service agent Vincent Mroz rushed towards the sound of the guns and fired his first shot as he spotted Collazo, but because he was still too far away and approaching from too wide an angle, his bullet passed well wide of its target. Mroz dived through a door into a corridor, and sprinted through Blair House, looking for another exit from where he would have a better shot.

Collazo, meanwhile, had emptied his first clip. As blood poured over his face, he slumped down on the front steps of Blair House, retrieved a fresh magazine from his pocket and reloaded.

Then the real shooter joined the fight. Torresola was armed with a mint-condition Luger, and he was just aching to use it. Their plan had worked: Collazo had drawn the fire of all of the White House guards, giving Torresola a clear run as he approached the small guardhouse from the west, from Pennsylvania Avenue. White House policeman Leslie Coffelt was drawing his gun ready to take on Collazo when Torresola whipped out his 9mm and, holding it professionally in a two-hand 'isosceles position', opened fire. Coffelt, a life-long lover of guns and a member of a pistol team, turned to face Torresola but it was too late. The attacker fired off four fast shots while moving steadily forward until the final bullet was fired about a foot and a half away from the uniformed officer. Three full-metal-jacket bullets pounded into Coffelt's body; a fourth tore the sleeve of his coat. He slumped backward into the chair in the guard booth, fatally injured. Torresola pressed on, towards Blair House.

Joe Downs, a White House policeman working plain-clothes was on an errand to buy food for that night's Blair House dinner and almost stumbled straight into Torresola as he emerged from a basement door on the west side of Blair House. Downs went for his gun but, like Coffelt, he was too late. Torresola's first slug struck his hip, causing Downs to reel back and drop his gun Torresola shot him twice more, hitting his chest and neck. Downs staggered back through the open basement door and locked it behind him as he collapsed, denying Torresola an entry point. Undeterred, Torresola pressed on towards the front entrance.

Torresola looked across and spotted Donald Birdzell (the uniformed officer whom Collazo had wounded with his opening shot) in the middle of the street, his service revolver aimed at Collazo. He was forty feet away. Torresola raised the Luger in his two-handed grip, carefully aimed and pressed the trigger. His shot struck Birdzell square in the left knee. Shot in both knees, in agonising pain, Birdzell dropped his gun and tumbled to the pavement; helpless, he watched as the assassin moved forward to finish him off. As Torresola lifted his gun, he realised that he was out of ammunition. He decided not to waste time and bullets on the downed officer and moved on, reloading as he went. He was at the edge of the Blair House front entrance, now only thirty feet from the President of the United States and with just one man between him and his target.

They should never have made it this far but, thanks to Torresola, the two men were shockingly close to realising their aim. Truman was now in genuine danger. And it was about to get worse. Startled out of his nap by the gunfire, clad only in his underwear, the President of the United States suddenly appeared at the bedroom window on the second floor of Blair House and looked down to see Torresola reloading. Davidson realised that as soon as Torresola looked up he would be able to see Truman – and there was no way he would miss from that distance. Torresola looked up. Inside Blair House, State Police veteran Stewart Stout, now armed with a tommy-gun, charged through the bedroom door, screaming at the President to get down.

A gunshot. The agents outside Blair House froze. Griselio Torresola's body jerked as a 38 slug blew his head wide open. He toppled over, dead before he hit the ground. Behind him, some twenty feet away, skin white, clothes soaked in his own blood, stood the dying Leslie Coffelt, gripping his revolver with one hand. He stumbled back into the guard shack and collapsed in his chair. Despite his fatal injuries, Coffelt had somehow made a superhuman effort; he came back from the dead to kill his own murderer and to save the life of the President of the United States, the man he had sworn to protect.

Meanwhile, his Walther reloaded, Oscar Collazo was still standing. He turned, as if to rejoin the battle, but instead of raising his gun and opening fire, he swayed unsteadily and fell forwards, landing with a heavy thud right at the bottom of the Blair House steps.

The battle had lasted forty seconds.

Truman left half an hour later than planned to attend the ceremony at Arlington Cemetery. The next day he told friends that 'a President has to expect these things'. His courage was undeniable; he had risked his life many times as a soldier in the First World War.

Despite this, one can't help but wonder what compelled the President of the United States to behave like a B-movie horror actress, investigating a strange noise, in this case gunshots, instead of leaving that job to the Secret Service.

Fortunately, from that day forth Truman vowed that he would cooperate with his guards in every way possible, which included not going to investigate any unusual noises; that would be left to the Secret Service, who had earned his undying appreciation. He would do this, he said, not because he was personally afraid but because he had learned the hard way the extent of his own responsibility for the safety of the men who were assigned to protect him. He wrote: 'Since the assault . . . I ride across the street in a car which will stop a grenade, the windows will turn a bullet and the floor will stop a landmine! Behind me in an open car ride six or seven men with automatics and machine guns.' The official line was that 'the President was never in any danger' but the truth was quite different – he had been less than a second from being fired upon when Coffelt's bullet struck Torresola.

Leslie Coffelt's wife was seriously ill and scheduled to have a kidney removed only four days after her husband died. Although she was still in shock, presidential aides persuaded her to postpone the surgery and to travel to Puerto Rico. For three days she received the condolences of various Puerto Rican leaders in front of thousands of people. She gave a series of speeches in which she said that she did not blame Puerto Rico for the actions of two fanatics. Local school children collected pennies to help pay for Mrs Coffelt's hospital bills; they raised two hundred dollars. Her visit undoubtedly eased the tensions created by the coup attempt.

Collazo's wounds were not life-threatening – he had simply fainted. Davidson's bullet was probably slowed by striking the wrought-iron fence as it didn't actually enter Collazo's chest. At his trial in 1951, Collazo scorned his attorney's advice that he plead insanity and delivered an impassioned oration from the witness stand decrying the brutal exploitation of Puerto Rico by the United States. Many of his facts were dated or inaccurate, and neither the

American public nor the people of Puerto Rico paid much attention. The island was already well on the way to becoming a self-governing commonwealth.

Collazo was found guilty of murder, attempted assassination, and assault with intent to kill. Judge T. Alan Goldsborough sentenced Collazo to death and set his execution date for August 1, 1952. One week before he was due to face the electric chair, Truman denied Collazo martyrdom by commuting the sentence to life imprisonment.

In September 1979 President Jimmy Carter commuted Collazo's life sentence and Collazo returned to Puerto Rico where he died on 20 February 1994 at the age of eighty. On 1 November 1990, the fortieth anniversary of the attack, the day room of the Secret Service Uniformed Division in the basement of Blair House was renamed the Leslie W. Coffelt Memorial Room, honouring the man who came back from the dead to save the life of President Harry Truman who died peacefully aged eighty-eight on 26 December 1972.

Two

Stalin's Last Supper

Assassinations are sometimes disguised as death by 'natural causes' and accidents – the truth may often never emerge. In the case of the following assassination, which had previously been assumed to have been death from natural causes, the truth came out more than fifty years later, thanks to the diligent detective work of American and Russian historical academics. This assassination ranks as perhaps one of the most audacious and important ever undertaken and it can be argued that the world owes the assassin (an exceptionally unpleasant character) a debt of thanks, for not only did he save millions of lives but quite possibly prevented a Third World War – a nuclear one.

On the dark snowy morning of 23 December 1953 the temperature in central Moscow was about minus 12°C. It was a shade warmer in the secret bunker thirty feet below Osipenko Street where Lavrenti Pavlovich Beria, the former head of the Soviet Security Police and Deputy Prime Minister, who had formerly held the title of the Marshal of the USSR for outstanding services along with five Orders of Lenin among many other honours, was about to face a firing squad. Above ground, while the five soldiers charged and cocked their smoking rifles, an officer administered the *coup de grâce* to the head of the condemned man who preceded Beria. He was hauled away on a stretcher. All around the execution post the snow was stained bright red.

Beria was marched out to the point of death by Major Hizhnyak Gurevich, his prison guard for the past six months. Gurevich had done everything for Beria, from tasting his food to cutting his hair. They had become friends but now Gurevich's orders were to be part of the firing squad. Beria stood limply as his greatcoat was removed and his hands were roughly bound behind the post to a metal ring. Now he was ready to face the fate to which he himself had condemned tens of thousands. Perhaps mindful of this he paled and his left cheek began to tremble. 'Tell my son what happened,' he told Gurevich. 'Tell him I was innocent.' Gurevich said nothing. Beria's wife and son, whom he had fought so hard to protect, languished in one of the Gulags he had ordered to be constructed and filled with his countrymen.

Beria had asked the court many times to spare his life, but he was steadfastly ignored by those who wanted their once powerful rival dead and who had produced fifty volumes of evidence of his crimes, including a list of women he had supposedly raped. Gurevich placed a blindfold over Beria's eyes, a prelude to the eternal darkness that would soon follow. The last words he heard were the short barks of Major-General Pavel Batitskii, chief of staff of the air force, as the soldiers took careful aim and fired. Beria hung against the execution stake, his body twitching as Gurevich strode over, held a pistol to his heart and fired.

Such was the fate of the assassin who saved the world.

Eight months earlier, in March 1953, Lavrenti Beria had been a worried man. Pushed to the point of exhaustion, his once lively face was grey and strained. Too much scheming and double-crossing, imprisonment, torture and execution of the innocent had aged the head of Russia's secret police beyond his fifty-three years. Two dark smudges seemed to have taken up permanent residence under his eyes and his hair barely had time to turn grey before it fell out.

Beria knew that his career had reached its zenith; unless seventy-three-year-old Joseph Stalin suddenly died, Beria knew the only direction he could go was downwards. In Stalinist Russia, that generally meant the Gulag or the firing squad. Unfortunately for Beria, Stalin was in rude health and was planning his latest paranoid purge; his previous efforts had cost the lives of twenty million people in twenty-three years (some historians argue that the true figure is as high as forty million). On 13 January 1953 *Pravda*, Russia's leading newspaper, had announced the arrest of a number of Kremlin doctors, most of them Jews. They were accused of plotting to poison Soviet leaders, including Stalin. The 'conspiracy' became known as the 'Doctors' Plot'. By the end of February, Stalin had ordered Beria to build vast new prison camps.

The main reason for Beria's worry was that Stalin had accused him to his face of insufficient vigilance, i.e. failing to spot the Doctors' Plot (which of course both men knew to be fictional; a testament to the power of Stalin's endless paradoxes). Stalin had said that some of the leadership thought they could get by on their past merits, adding 'they are mistaken'. Secretly, the Soviet leader was rightly concerned that Beria's influence was becoming too great, so much so that it was on the verge of threatening his own. Beria, along with six loyal deputies, controlled the secret police of the Soviet Union. With some fifteen divisions of elite troops, and informers in every department, he wielded practically unlimited power.

Beria had started out in counter-intelligence work before working his way up to head of the secret police in Georgia in 1921 and taking personal charge of Stalin's purges in the 1930s. He was a natural for the job, a deviant murderer devoid of conscience who would do anything for more power. He was summoned to Moscow in 1938 to serve as deputy to Nikolay Yezhov, Head of the Soviet Secret Police. Beria soon discovered Yezhov's homosexuality and passed on the news to a displeased Stalin who ordered Yezhov's execution. Beria, who kept sex toys and ladies' underwear in his desk, personally 'tried' Yezhov in his office and urged him to confess to a plot to kill Stalin. Yezhov refused, stating 'it is better to leave this earth an honourable man' – which he did, in front of a firing squad a few days later.

Beria took Yezhov's place and ruthlessly purged his own department. He also set up a network of labour camps to receive the hundreds of thousands of Russians being sent by Stalin into internal exile. Soon he was the dictator's golden boy, and became a hero during the Second World War by working the internees of the labour camps to death, producing vital supplies for the desperate war effort.

Because Beria had more effective instruments in his hands for extracting resources from the economy than anyone else, he was chosen to organise Russia's post-war race for the hydrogen bomb. US President Harry Truman had already declared in 1950 that the United States was to proceed with 'work on all forms of atomic weapons, including the so-called hydrogen or superbomb', adding 'we will never use it if we can possibly help it. But I know the Russians would use it if they had it.' The hydrogen bomb would be one thousand times more powerful than the atomic bombs dropped on Nagasaki and Hiroshima.

Using data recovered by a spy working on the Manhattan Project in Los Alamos (the spy, Klaus Fuchs, handed over the details to his contact in a London pub) the Soviets had already managed to build and successfully test a copy of America's atomic bomb in 1949. But they didn't yet have the resources to build enough to take on the United States who by then had a clutch of B-50 Superfortress bombers with 133 atomic bombs (just enough to destroy Russia) on permanent standby on the airfields of West Germany. The worry that Russia would attack the US as soon as it had the technology increased as time went on. Some US government scientists suggested that America should strike first while it held the upper hand. Harold M. Agnew, a physicist who worked on the Manhattan Project, recalled: 'Some of us even advocated that we should go to Russia and just bomb them, just keep doing it to keep them from developing anything.'

With this in mind, Beria worked night and day to make sure that the labour camps were full with tens of thousands of prisoners labouring on H-bomb-related projects. Whole regions in the Urals and Siberia were left without electricity for weeks as energy was diverted to the project. But now, as the H-bomb neared completion, Beria felt for a number of reasons that this might well be his last project. First, Joseph Stalin had admonished his previously trusted friend. Second, Beria believed that once Russia had the bomb Stalin would be prepared to destroy the world if the world was not prepared to capitulate to the aged dictator. Beria had seen drafts of speeches in which Stalin quoted fabricated evidence to accuse the United States and Russian Jews of planning a nuclear attack on the Soviet Union. Stalin was just waiting for the H-bomb to be ready before he confronted the US over the war in Korea. Beria had to do something.

On 28 February 1953 Stalin invited Beria, along with fellow Politburo members Georgi Malenkov, Nikolai Bulganin and Nikita Khrushchev, to dinner. Beria, weary from driving the H-bomb project forward in an attempt to meet Stalin's impossible demands, knew that Stalin would drag the dinner into a night-long lecture. Indeed, it was four a.m. on 1 March before the weary ministers left Stalin's room.

Stalin had given orders to his guards that he was not to be disturbed. Although they thought it odd that he did not rise at his usual time the next day, they knew that disobeying a direct order meant certain death. They finally dared to enter at eleven p.m. that night and found Stalin on the floor, conscious but unable to speak. The guards helped him into bed and summoned Beria – who took his time, eventually arriving at three the following morning. After a brief inspection, Beria claimed that Stalin was only sleeping and said that no doctors should be called. Beria returned at nine a.m. the following day when it was clear to all that something was terribly wrong with the Soviet leader, and only then were doctors summoned. They immediately realised that Stalin had had a stroke.

As Stalin slipped into unconsciousness, a delighted Beria couldn't contain himself any longer. He jumped a short distance into the air and shook his fist. Then, as he paced furiously up and down Stalin's bedroom floor, he let the tyrant have it – using every curse he knew, he mocked the great dictator and spat at his feet. Nikita Khrushchev and Aliluyeva, Stalin's daughter, watched in astonishment, unable to believe their eyes.

Suddenly, Stalin regained partial consciousness and pointed to something on the wall. Beria froze in the middle of an air-punch and then, lightning fast, he grabbed Stalin's hand and stared into his eyes lovingly, anxious to convince the dictator that he was the most loyal and devoted of them all, as he had always tried with every ounce of his strength to appear to be. He kissed Stalin's hand, much to the disgust of Khrushchev. As Stalin lost consciousness again, Beria stood up, spat once more and resumed cursing.

The next day Stalin's head started to loll and his left arm went into spasm. At midday he vomited blood. Beria, Khrushchev and Malenkov had received the Politburo's permission to ensure that Stalin's 'documents and papers, both current and archival, are put in proper order'. Leaving the other two at the bedside, Beria sped to the Kremlin to begin the process of searching Stalin's files for documents that might incriminate him. If Stalin had ever made a will or kept a diary, Beria destroyed them. Beria discovered files filled with denunciations and evidence against all members of the Politburo, including himself: clearly Stalin had been planning the mother of all purges of his Politburo.

On 5 March, as Stalin's condition worsened, his ministers and family lined up to say goodbye to their leader. Beria and Malenkov went first, and both of them shook his hand. Malenkov later said that Stalin squeezed his fingers as he went past, passing him the succession. Stalin held out until nine p.m. when he started to sweat, his pulse faded and his lips turned blue. At 9.40 p.m. his doctors gave Stalin oxygen. His pulse had all but disappeared. The doctors suggested an injection of camphor and adrenalin to stimulate his heart. Stalin gave a shiver after the injection and became increasingly breathless as he started to drown in his own fluids.

'Take Svetalana away,' commanded Beria, who wanted to prevent her seeing her father's slow, painful death – but no one moved. 'His face was discoloured,' she wrote later, 'his features becoming unrecognisable . . . He literally choked to death as we watched. The death agony was terrible . . . At the last minute, he opened his eyes. It was a terrible look, either mad or angry and full of the fear of death.'

Stalin was buried on 9 March. Officially, the cause of death was listed as a cerebral haemorrhage but Beria later boasted to Vyacheslav Molotov that: 'I did him in! I saved you all!' At the time, Molotov mistakenly thought that Beria was referring to his not calling the doctors for a day after the stroke. Beria was quite capable of poisoning; he had previously 'done in' the ruler of Abkhazia, Nestor Lakoba, a trusted friend of Stalin's, and had then sent a firing squad for his son. He also made the famous boast: 'Any fool can commit murder but only an artist can make it look like suicide.' Beria certainly had the motive: Stalin's demise arrived at a convenient time for Beria and all the others who were expecting to be swept away in the purge that would follow the Doctors' Plot.

In 2003, Yale University history professor Jonathan Brent, also the director of the Yale University Press and the editor of a twenty-five-volume series on the contents of the Soviet Union's secret archives, conducted an investigation into Stalin's death with Vladimir Naumov, a historian who works in Russia and specialises in Soviet records. They discovered a copy of Stalin's original death certificate, which shows that he fell ill shortly after dinner on 1 March, vomited blood that night and suffered a brain haemorrhage on the morning of 2 March, shortly after doctors arrived. The 'official' death certificate shows him falling ill on the night of 2 March, and doctors arriving shortly afterward. They also recovered Stalin's original medical file (which contains thirty years' worth of the dictator's medical reports) which revealed that results of blood and urine tests indicated warfarin poisoning between 28 February and 1 March. Warfarin is a powerful rat poison that thins the blood vessels and causes strokes and haemorrhages. Both odourless and tasteless, it is the perfect assassination poison.

Stalin's doctors had a quick conference and decided not to tell Beria or try and treat Stalin for poisoning as they were certain that they would be charged with being part of the Doctors' Plot. Stalin's paranoia had been the death of him.

After Stalin's death, Beria tried to become dictator of the Soviet Union but was defeated by a coalition of Nikita Khrushchev, Vyacheslav Molotov and Georgy Malenkov. After Khrushchev became Premier he appointed Beria Head of the Ministry of Internal Affairs. Beria's first act was to 'abolish' the Doctors' Plot. The trials were cancelled, the doctors exonerated and the prison camps were never built. In the wake of Stalin's death, Beria practically became a liberal: he wound down the affairs of the secret police and released hundreds of political prisoners.

A few months later, ever-fearful of Beria's power and ambition, Khrushchev launched a carefully planned public attack on Beria, accusing him of being in the pay of British intelligence. Beria was taken completely by surprise. He asked, 'What's going on, Nikita Sergeyevich?' Molotov (Beria had just freed his Jewish wife from prison) and others then also spoke against Beria, and Khrushchev put forward a motion for his instant dismissal. Malenkov then pressed a button on his desk as the pre-arranged signal to a group of armed officers in a nearby room. They immediately burst in and confronted Beria. His arrest was kept secret until his principal lieutenants could be rounded up.

The NKVD troops in Moscow which had been under Beria's command were disarmed by regular Red Army units. Beria's wife and son were sent to a labour camp, but survived and were later released: his wife Nina died in 1991 in exile in the Ukraine; his son Sergo died in October 2000. Shortly before his death he told a CNN news reporter that: 'Stalin had . . . plans [to use the nuclear bomb] and my father was very much afraid of these plans . . . My father was even against the preparation of this bomb, and he understood that if the Soviet Union got this bomb, nothing would be able to stop Stalin in his wish to conquer the whole world . . . And if he hadn't died in 1953, it seems to me that he would have killed all the members of the Politburo.'

A few weeks after Beria's execution, subscribers to the *Great Soviet Encyclopaedia* received an essay on 'the Bering Sea', along with instructions to cut out the entry 'Beria, L.' and replace it with the new – and perfectly fitting – article. Lavrenti Pavlovich Beria, the assassin who saved the world, was carefully erased from Soviet history.

Although that was the end of Beria and Stalin, it was by no means the end of the nuclear crisis. At Bermuda in December 1953, Prime Minister Winston Churchill, who had been re-elected in 1951, urged President Dwight Eisenhower to begin talks with the Russians. (The Korean War had ended on 27 July 1953 and, as had been the case before the start of the war three years earlier, North and South Korea were once again symbols of the East–West divide.) Eisenhower disagreed. According to the top-secret minutes of the meeting, Eisenhower said that if there were a 'deliberate breach' of the Korean armistice then the United States 'would expect to strike back with atomic weapons at military targets'.

On 1 March 1954, almost one year to the day from Stalin's death, a Japanese fishing vessel called the *Lucky Dragon* was fishing east of Bikini Atoll, twenty miles outside the bomb-testing area that had been declared a 'danger zone' by the United States. As the boat fished, there was a vast explosion and the fishermen were subsequently covered in a cloud of ash. They developed radiation sickness. As the Japanese government demanded seven million dollars in compensation from the United States, Japanese meteorologists reported that radioactive rain caused by a hydrogen bomb had fallen in Japan. The source was not an atomic test conducted by the United States but a series of hydrogen bombs detonated by the Soviet Union.

America no longer held the upper hand. It was now nuclear stalemate: the Cold War was well and truly under way.

Three

Saddam's First Kill

In the 1950s South America was rocked by three assassinations: Venezuela's President Colonel Delgado Chalbaud, Panama's dictator Jose Antonio 'Chichi' Remón, and Nicaragua's strongman, seventeen-stone Anastasio 'Tacho' Somoza were all shot to death. One failure linked all three assassinations, and that was the inability of the targets' bodyguards to limit the amount of distance between themselves and their paymaster. In each case, the assassins were able to walk within point-blank range of their target.

Many people would consider that these men, all cruel dictators, deserved to die. Each of them regularly ordered their citizens tortured and executed while they themselves exploited the natural resources of their countries for their own personal gain. So it was just as well that their guards did a bad job, some may think. But in each case the people who replaced these rulers (and in two cases had planned the assassinations) turned out to be far worse and cost the lives of thousands of innocent people while plunging their countries into insurmountable debt.

If a few well-trained bodyguards had been kept close by at all times, then thousands of lives and billions of dollars might not have been squandered. All too often the unnecessary gaps left between targets and their protectors have been exploited by professional assassins and such was the case in Iraq, in an attack that would eventually prove to be a defining moment in the history of the world.

*

Even in autumn, the temperature in Iraq soars to the unpleasantly dry high thirties Celsius. Across the sweltering capital, those of Baghdad's citizens who were fortunate enough not to have to make their living on the teeming streets hid away from the sun in the city's many coffee shops. It was 7 October 1959, the day that a small group of men had decided that the leader of Iraq, Brigadier General Abdul Karim Kassem, would die.

Outside the Defence Ministry the afternoon sun scorched the leather seats of the premier's specially modified Chevrolet station wagon. As well as the Chevy, about half a dozen American and British cars were parked in the courtyard, poorly shaded by palm trees. Their drivers, lurking wherever the shadows had arrived first, smoked and exchanged the idle banter of those who spend their working lives waiting on their masters' whims. At two p.m. the Ministry's doors were pulled open and Iraq's Cabinet ministers emerged from their extended meeting with General Kassem. They trotted down the steps as the chauffeurs returned to their cars and started the engines. The guards at the enormous iron gates straightened and saluted as the convoy accelerated out of the grounds past a collection of rotting bodies hanging from lamp-posts, into Al-Rashid Street and the city centre.

General Kassem, Iraq's ruthless new military strongman, who had been in power for just fifteen months, emerged from his office later than usual, at 3.30 p.m. The General typically worked every day from nine a.m. until two p.m. but a recent failed uprising demanded that he met with his cabinet three times each day as troops hunted for the plotters, so his schedule was slightly off. He climbed into the middle seat of his brand new desert-brown and armour-plated Chevy, with armed aides in front and behind. A Land Rover full of troops followed.

The son of a carpenter, Kassem had been born in Baghdad in 1914. As soon as he was old enough he joined the Iraqi Army where he rose through the ranks quickly and was sent to a senior officers' school at Devizes in south-west England. (Iraq was then a friend of the British who had wrested control of the country from the Turks during the First World War.) Although inordinately and naively suspicious, cursed by shyness and with a weak high-pitched voice, his classmates nicknamed him 'the snake charmer' because of his extraordinary ability to win improbable arguments. (Once, while on army exercises, he persuaded his classmates to send their tanks into a deep swamp.) A British instructor accurately summed up Kassem as 'sincere, hard-working, completely unbalanced'. A small, slight man, with a tiny mouth and large teeth, the front two of which were a rotten-looking dirty brown, Kassem was not handsome but his appearance was nonetheless fearsome, what with his large permanent-marker-thick eyebrows that darkened his eye sockets and his black Hitler-style moustache. His army uniform with three stars on the shoulders and the crown of a brigadier served as a constant reminder of his long and successful career in the army.

After the Jewish state of Israel was established on 14 May 1948, when the British mandate over Palestine came to an end, the neighbouring Arab states, including Iraq, refused to recognise Israel and invaded the country on 15 May. During the war, Kassem showed outstanding bravery and won several medals, eventually reaching the rank of brigadier. Fiercely nationalist and anti-Western, Kassem, with the full support of his army, decided to take power from Iraq's British-installed monarchy. He struck at the height of the dry season, on 14 July 1958.

That morning, twenty-three-year-old King Faisal and his uncle, Crown Prince Abdul Illah, forty-six, were preparing to catch a breakfast flight to Istanbul for an emergency meeting of the Muslim members of the Baghdad Pact, an anti-communist alliance signed by Iraq, Turkey, Pakistan and the UK which formed a line of defence against the Soviet Union. The King and Crown Prince's preparations were interrupted when a mortar shell flew over the palace wall and exploded in the courtyard. The Crown Prince ran downstairs, closely followed by the young King. As they darted through the front door they found Kassem waiting, along with several hundred soldiers.

The Palace Guard opened fire, cutting down fourteen of the

General's men before they themselves were obliterated by bullets and shells. When the smoke cleared, the King and the Crown Prince were dead. An hour later the country was in the hands of Kassem and only one thing remained to be done: find Iraq's Prime Minister for the last twenty-seven years, the seventy-year-old pro-Western Nuri asSaid who had lived up to his nickname of 'The Fox' by managing to escape. He was spotted the next day by a sergeant, in the suburbs of Baghdad. Nuri asSaid was disguised as a woman, veiled and accompanied by two female allies.

The old man was captured after a short battle, stripped of his disguise, and impaled alive on a stake driven through his stomach. He died squirming in public view before his corpse was left for a week in the rotting heat.

Thousands of British residents living and working in Iraq were told to get out of the country. Television reporters gathered at RAF Hendon as the first refugees arrived home. The wife of a British major, Carol Magee, who lived near the palace described how quickly the coup took place: 'I was woken by gunfire, but went back to sleep again because I thought they were shooting dogs . . . which they do periodically.' The next morning she looked out of her window just in time to see a mob pulling the unpopular Prince Regent's body literally limb from limb.

Kassem became Prime Minister and Minister of Defence in the new republican government and immediately rejected the Baghdad Pact, lifted a ban on the Communist Party in Iraq and established friendly relations with the Soviet Union. Iraq had gone from being a conservative pro-Western country to a hotbed of radical nationalism and communism.

One year later, the first anniversary of the 14 July revolution, Baghdad was all holiday celebration. Down the hot, dusty streets, clowns danced, balloons bobbed, Girl Scouts marched, and a giant papier-mâché fist rolled by on a float, clutching the 'Viper of Imperialism'. Under the crisp salute of Kassem, Soviet T-54 and British Centurion tanks rumbled by in a two-hour parade of military might while the army band played British marches. (Oddly enough, the General deemed this music suitable for his anniversary.)

But beneath this happy public façade, Iraq had become a place of terror, plot and counterplot. Kassem's main opposition, the Baath Party, had been outlawed and decimated. The jails were jammed with an estimated five thousand political prisoners, ex-officials and once-eminent citizens. In March 1959, an abortive Baathist uprising led by former primary-school teacher General Ahmed Hassan al-Bakr had taken place in Mosul. While al-Bakr had escaped, his second in command, Brigadier Nadhem Tabakchali, had been captured.

Kassem's vengeance was prompt and ruthless, leading to one of the bloodiest episodes in Iraq's modern history. He allowed his militia to run amok. Rapes, murders, lootings, summary trials and executions in front of cheering mobs followed. Hundreds of army officers were butchered. The extremely popular Brigadier Nadhem Tabakchali, one of the army's most distinguished soldiers, was tried publicly by a top judge, the notorious Colonel Fadhil Abbas Mahdawi. The trial was transmitted live on Iraq Radio. Mahdawi rambled, typically, through twenty minutes of invective against the 'gangsters and robbers' and then praised Kassem, the 'leader of the whole Arab nation'. During the broadcasts, Tabakchali remained calm and dignified in complete contrast to the rabid Mahdawi and the Brigadier won the hearts and minds of most of the Arab world, not least Abdel Nasser, the leader of Egypt and sworn enemy of Kassem. Nasser tasked his secret service to eliminate the principal witness against Tabakchali.

Ostensibly assisting the military attaché in the Egyptian embassy in Baghdad, Syrian-born Muhammad Mahmoud Jamil had been a trusted Egyptian intelligence agent and as such had been privy to the part that the Egyptians had played in setting up the Mosul revolt. Jamil was in fact a double agent introduced into the Egyptian embassy by the Iraqi espionage service – to whom he had given invaluable warning of the Mosul coup. Mahdawi had recalled him from his new assignment in Lebanon to give evidence against Tabakchali.

Nasser's assassins caught up with the pallid long-haired witness at Beirut's International Airport. As Jamil waited at the Middle East Airlines ticket desk, he was confronted by two men in yellow sports shirts. The ticket clerk later gave a detailed eyewitness report to journalists. Jamil's bride of two months plucked at her husband's sleeve and pointed at them. Jamil hissed back: 'Don't look over there.'

At that, the two men began to move in. One touched Jamil's elbow with his hand and asked him to come with them. Jamil refused, and for a moment the two men squared off against each other wordlessly. Then the thug seized Jamil by the hair, pulled his head down and, steadying it, struck him with two jarring punches. As Jamil's body sagged and the airport crowd surged in to break up what looked like a personal quarrel, the second tough fired four shots into Jamil's body. Simultaneously, two other men loitering near the terminal exit opened fire at the ceiling. As the crowd scattered in panic, and as Jamil's wife held her dying husband, the assassins made their getaway.

The assassination didn't help Tabakchali – Mahdawi sentenced him to death by firing squad without hearing from a single witness. This, combined with Tabakchali's dignified conduct during the trial, inspired for the first time open criticism of Kassem in Baghdad. Much of the public anger was focused on Mahdawi, so Kassem sent him on a six-week trip to Peking in the hope that things would cool down in his absence.

The massacres of his fellow officers convinced General al-Bakr that it was essential to assassinate Kassem as soon as possible. Not an easy task, for Kassem kept thousands of his most loyal troops close by. General al-Bakr decided to seek professional assistance and approached the Americans, who were appalled at Kassem's anti-Western stance. Previously, America had seen Iraq as a key buffer and strategic asset in the Cold War with the Soviet Union. Now, as Kassem bought weapons from the Soviets and embraced communism, CIA Director Allen Dulles publicly declared that Iraq was 'the most dangerous spot in the world'. This was a clear message, as far as General al-Bakr was concerned, that he had a friend on the

CIA. He was right. Roger Morris, a former National Security Council staffer in the 1970s, confirmed that the CIA had chosen the authoritarian and anti-communist Baath Party as its instrument for regime change in Iraq. General al-Bakr's contact was Captain Abdel Maquid Farid, the assistant military attaché at the Egyptian Embassy. (In the 1950s the Egyptian Intelligence Service worked closely with the CIA.)

Captain Farid recommended that General al-Bakr should search outside Iraq for a professional assassin because his previous attempt had been scuppered thanks to Kassem's well-placed double agents. As well as the problem with moles infiltrating the Baathists, the government of Iraq ran a vast, paranoid and efficient bureaucracy. Every soldier and policeman in the country had easy access to names, descriptions, photographs and family histories of all Baathist members. Therefore, Farid told al-Bakr, the assassin should not be a member of the Baathists, and should not be on any government file. In Iraq, what was not on the files did not exist. This way the assassin would be an unknown quantity and would be free to plan an attack secretly with a high chance of success. He also advised General al-Bakr not to let anyone else know about their plans: after all, the more people who know a secret the less secret it becomes. The authoritarian Baathist leadership was only slightly less bureaucratic than Kassem's administration and would want detailed reports at each stage of the planning process. Finally, Captain Farid warned General al-Bakr that professionals didn't come cheap and that he must be prepared to pay a high financial price. General al-Bakr accepted the Captain's advice.

Obviously, professional assassins are not easy to find: they do not advertise their services. Fortunately the secret services of most nations, thanks to the nature of their clandestine security work, are better than most at finding assassins, and the resourceful Captain Farid contacted Syria's tough Interior Minister, Colonel Abdel Hamid Serraj, who had presided at a clandestine meeting in the Syrian town of El Haseke with General al-Bakr, to discuss plans for Iraq should Kassem be overthrown.

Serraj knew just the man, a mercenary who had been killing to order for more than twenty years. A Palestinian once employed by the Grand Mufti of Jerusalem, the assassin counted among his successes the shooting of an Arab sheikh who had agreed to sell land to Jews, the murder of a British official on the steps of a church in Nazareth and, most importantly perhaps, the audacious airport shooting of the double agent Jamil. Known only as Tariq, he slipped into the country via Syria, met with Captain Farik and General al-Bakr and agreed to take out Kassem for a significant sum. General al-Bakr put him in touch with a loyal Baathist agent close to the Defence Ministry, a local dentist, who would get him everything he needed for the attempt.

Tariq spent a few days watching Kassem, following his route, examining side streets for their suitability for getaway vehicles or a multi-vehicle ambush, likely windows from which a grenade might be thrown or rifles fired and so on. Eventually, he asked the dentist to provide him with half a dozen reliable men who were expert shots.

One of the men the dentist found was twenty-one-year-old Saddam Hussein, the son of a shepherd and a relatively new, enthusiastic and radical member of the Baath Party. Even then the future ruler of Iraq had a reputation as a thug more than capable of killing. The dentist installed Saddam in an apartment in Baghdad on Al-Rashid Street (paid for by Captain Farid) directly opposite Kassem's office in Iraq's Ministry of Defence and told him to observe and record the General's movements.

Saddam learned that Kassem, a teetotaller and non-smoker, almost never left Baghdad and slept on a sofa in his office where he worked from about nine a.m. to two p.m. and then had lunch, which he took on a tin tray in a nearby council room. At three p.m. he typically drove out from the Ministry for a tour through the city. At the city gate crowds usually swarmed around his car to thrust petitions – for jobs, for property claims, or simply for money – at his open window. Then the convoy headed for the small house in the outskirts where Kassem had lived until the revolution. At the house,

Kassem would play briefly with his eight dogs (all of whom he called 'Lassie') and have a bath. By eight p.m. he was back at the office, and at nine p.m. Cabinet meetings started, finishing at around two or three a.m.

Tariq soon realised that their main opportunities would come when Kassem was in transit. An assassin would have to sacrifice his own life if he struck at the city gate, perhaps pretending to petition the General, and even then the jostling crowds and the bullet-proof car would make success only a fleeting possibility. Besides, the Baathists had made it quite clear to the assassin that failure was not an option. If the attempt was botched, then Kassem's revenge would be bloody and absolute. To be certain, Tariq decided on a lightning-fast street ambush in central Baghdad. Speed was the key: make sure that Kassem was dead before the troops in the Land Rover had time to react.

Kassem's bodyguards gave Tariq plenty of room in which to strike. The soldiers were packed tightly into the Land Rover, which travelled a few metres behind the Chevy, and although they carried rifles their proximity to each other would interfere with their aim. Tariq believed that Kassem would be dead and the assassination squad would have fled into the teeming alleyways before the soldiers knew the attack was over.

Eventually Tariq chose an area in Al-Rashid Street as the site of the assassination. Al-Rashid Street, the spiritual and intellectual centre of the city, was at the heart of Baghdad. It was full of famous cafés such as the Al Braziliyya, the favourite of intellectuals who studied at the nearby thirteenth-century Al-Mustansiriyya College which housed eighty thousand ancient manuscripts as well as of those journalists who worked for one of the twelve newspapers based nearby. Most of the street's buildings had been haphazardly constructed in the 1920s, giving rise to a warren of alleyways and side streets, often no more than a few feet wide. They zigzagged drunkenly through the Old City and joined several other busy streets in which it would be easy for an assassin to shake off pursuers. Even in the late 1950s Al-Rashid Street was congested with vehicles, including the occasional British-built red double-decker bus as well as donkey-drawn carts. The congestion would prevent Kassem's driver from trying to escape by accelerating away and would also stop the Land Rover engaging in a pursuit.

The plan was for five marksmen to hide behind a row of thick pillars near the Al Braziliyya café and to open fire on the front and sides of the General's slow-moving car while a sixth member of the squad would fire on the following Land Rover from behind. In this way he would confuse and, with luck, incapacitate some of the soldiers, buying the other five shooters more time. Saddam Hussein drew the short straw and agreed to fire upon the soldiers.

On 7 October, as Kassem's convoy turned along Al-Rashid Street, little knots of surprised pedestrians stopped to wave or cheer, and some trotted alongside the waving General. His bodyguards watched the pavements anxiously as the Chevy slowed in the heavy traffic, much to the apparent delight of the locals who pressed in closely.

Saddam watched the convoy from where he was sitting in the Umm Kulthoum Café, an unfashionable joint where elderly patrons chewed the fat about nothing in particular. While the young assassin sipped his coffee, the five marksmen lounged under the colonnaded roof that shielded them from the afternoon sun, their loaded guns concealed in cloth bags, grenades in their coat pockets.

With Kassem now less then fifty metres away, Saddam Hussein got up from the table, felt for his gun in its holster under his jacket and slipped his hand over its butt. Fifty metres ahead of him, the assassins collected their bags, left their pavement café seats, and took cover behind the nearby Corinthian-style columns.

As the Chevy approached within ten metres of Saddam it was forced to brake suddenly as a taxi pulled out in front of it. Then the taxi almost ran into a car coming the other way, juddered to a halt and stalled. The Chevy drew alongside Saddam and stopped.

Staring straight at his target and unable to contain himself, Saddam seized what he saw as a golden opportunity to assassinate Kassem. There was almost no distance between him and the target, after all. But unlike the five gunmen waiting behind the pillars, Saddam was exposed and still had to draw his gun in full view of the crowd and Kassem. Tariq and the other four gunmen watched in horror from behind the colonnade's pillars as Saddam began firing through the Chevy window.

Kassem threw himself to the floor taking cover behind the driver's seat as the bullets bounced around the car's interior. The first of Saddam's slugs blew a hole in the driver's head, spraying the car's cream interior with blood, brain and bone. A ricochet caught Kassem in the arm. Fifty metres away, Tariq and the five other assassins broke cover and ran towards the Chevy, opening fire with a deafening clatter while the soldiers in the Land Rover scrambled out of the vehicle.

The hit was further complicated as the crowd started to react. Although most of them dived and ran for cover, a teenage boy sprang from the pavement and hurled himself in front of Kassem's window. He was immediately cut down by Tariq who already knew that the distance between him and his target was too great. He could only pray that the hot-headed fool Saddam had mortally wounded Kassem.

Then the taxi driver who had complicated the assault in the first place reversed in an effort to block off the Chevy from the running gunmen. The driver ducked as bullets zinged through his windscreen. One of Kassem's aides threw himself over the General while the other opened the passenger door and reached for his pistol.

Tariq leaped onto the bonnet of the taxi, crouched and emptied his clip through the front windscreen into the bodyguard lying on Kassem; one of his bullets tore through Kassem's hand, another blasted through the General's torso and came out of his side, hitting his right arm. Another assassin, a landowner called Fatiq al Sail, shot the second bodyguard before he could aim his pistol.

By now the guards were firing back. Tariq's plan was turning into a disaster as the assassins became entangled in a full-on gun battle. Saddam, caught in the crossfire, dived towards an alleyway in an effort to escape but was hit in the calf by one of his own team. One of the assassins had a hand grenade in his coat pocket which he had planned to throw through Kassem's window. Now, in full panic, as he tried to extract the bulky grenade which had become entangled in his pocket, he was shot in the back by al Sail, who was trying to provide covering fire. Another assassin had brought the wrong bullets for his gun and couldn't reload. Tariq, meanwhile, had rapidly backed up Al-Rashid Street. He dropped his gun, ran into an alleyway and, in a few seconds, had melted into the crowd, vanishing with the practised finesse of the professional.

Saddam and al Sail also escaped into the surrounding alleyways. The remaining three, two of whom were incapacitated, were quickly captured. Inside the bloody bullet-ridden interior of the Chevy, the driver and the bodyguard were dead; Kassem was alive, albeit seriously wounded; the bones in his right arm and hand were shattered and there was a gaping hole in his shoulder and back. While the Land Rover full of heavily armed soldiers had been rendered ineffective by their distance, one of the lightly armed men sitting close to Kassem had saved the General's life, albeit at the cost of his own.

First results of the shooting were the arrest of hundreds of Iraqis, the establishment of military and police blockades throughout Baghdad and the imposition of a dusk-to-dawn curfew on the city. Airline flights were cancelled and international telephone and telegraph connections were cut as the search for the gunmen continued. From Peking, Colonel Fadhil Mahdawi announced that he was returning home immediately – an indication that a new wave of executions was on its way.

Somehow, Saddam escaped. The details remain unknown and Saddam's own account, which would eventually become an essential part of the Iraqi President's legend, was somewhat dubious. Saddam's version was dramatised and repeated endlessly in Iraqi cinemas and on television. It went something like this: 'Escaping the mêlée, the brave young warrior seeks medical help but is refused on the grounds that he is a well-known revolutionary. Instead, he removes the bullet in his leg with a knife and gallops through the desert on his horse, resourcefully escaping numerous pursuing military patrols. Finally, the fugitive warrior swims to freedom, crossing the mighty Tigris, his knife clenched between his teeth.'

While Saddam was 'swimming the Tigris', Kassem was recuperating in hospital and it wasn't long before TV cameras were allowed in to film the General smiling and waving from his hospital bed. The newsreader announced that Kassem would soon leave the hospital and on that happy day Iraqi citizens were promised free admission to movie theatres, half-fare on trains, and free circumcision for their newborn sons.

By the time Kassem was discharged eight weeks later, more than fifty Baathists were scheduled to stand trial. Seventeen were sentenced to death; the others were given long prison sentences. The court condemned Saddam Hussein to death *in absentia*. General Ahmed Hassan al-Bakr escaped. Thanks to the wise words from Captain Farid, nobody knew who was behind the plot. The General discreetly retired from the army and set up home in Baghdad from where he regularly met and plotted with other retired officers. The next attempt on Kassem's life, however, came directly from the Americans. It was orchestrated by a man who was perhaps one of the most unhinged employees the CIA ever had the misfortune to hire.

Four

The Black Sorcerer

American scientist Dr Sidney Gottlieb enjoyed overcoming problems. Despite having a club foot he was a passionate folk dancer and his lifelong stutter didn't prevent him from winning a Master's degree in speech therapy. Gottlieb had joined the CIA in 1951 as a poisons expert and his enthusiasm for nerve-frazzling toxins soon earned him two nicknames: 'the Black Sorcerer' and 'the Dirty Trickster'. He was the ideal man for the very difficult task that the CIA had in mind – updating the infamous cyanide L-pill, the suicide capsule used in the Second World War. Contrary to popular movie myth, cyanide takes up to fifteen minutes to work and causes an agonisingly painful death by asphyxiation. Understandably, agents didn't want to take that kind of pill and generally preferred to risk capture and torture rather than face a certain agonising death.

Working on what became known as 'Project MK Naomi' at the US Army's laboratory at Fort Detrick, Maryland, Gottlieb came up with a lethal toxin derived from shellfish (it took forty-five kilos of shellfish to produce one gram of poison). After receiving the toxin orally or by pinprick, a victim first feels a tingling sensation in the fingers and lips and dies ten seconds later from a painless paralysis. U-2 pilot Francis Gary Powers carried the toxin contained in the grooves of a tiny drill bit that was concealed in a silver dollar when he was shot down over Russia in 1960. But he chose not to use it – the slim chance of survival after capture, torture and humiliation still remained more appealing than the certainty of a quick and painless death.

Project MK Naomi was partly funded to find countermeasures to chemical and biological weapons that might be used by the KGB. A Russian agent had recently used poison darts and poison spray to assassinate two Ukrainian-liberation leaders in West Germany and this was enough to spook the CIA into action. They formed the wonderfully (if not too subtly) named Health Alteration Committee (HAC), which formed part of the CIA's Technical Services Division.

Fort Detrick was home to an array of extraordinary biological experiments. More than two thousand volunteers, nicknamed 'the White Coats', passed through its checkpoints between 1954 and 1973, where they worked as lab technicians as well as offering up their bodies for science. Many were Seventh Day Adventists who were conscientious objectors to the Vietnam War. It was decided that in return for being guinea pigs the Adventists would be free from the draft.

The room in which experiments were carried out was a mad scientist's wet dream. About thirty metres square, at its centre was a giant metal sphere known as the 'eight ball'. Connected to the sphere by a series of metal tubes were eight telephone boxes, arranged in a circle. Volunteers stepped into the boxes, the doors were vacuum-sealed and gas masks with long breathing tubes were lowered to the subjects who then breathed in a toxic substance released from the eight ball. After the white coats had been infected with a virus or poison, the scientists tried to cure them with a selection of antidotes and antibiotics.

Gottlieb and his fellow researchers also came up with an array of James Bond-type weaponry that could use the shellfish toxin and other poisons as ammunition. A pistol resembling a Colt .45 and equipped with a fat telescopic sight fired a toxin-tipped dart, almost silently and up to two hundred and fifty feet. Moreover, the dart was so tiny – the width of a human hair and a quarter of an inch long – as to be almost undetectable, and the poison left no trace in a victim's body.

Gottlieb's gadgets had a habit of not working (the poison dart was alarmingly susceptible to small breezes) and, as we shall see, field agents often rejected them, preferring instead to rely on the eight-cent option (the price of a single bullet) which made for a much more certain death. (The stats bear this out: see the final chapter for the success rates of various methods of assassination.) The inventiveness of the HAC was never matched by the practicality of their inventions. Despite this, the agency developed two other dart-launching pistols, as well as a poisoned-dart-firing fountain pen and an automobile engine-head bolt that released a toxic substance when heated. Dart launchers that were disguised as walking canes and umbrellas were also designed. (An idea that the Soviet Union would later steal and use to great effect – some conspiracy theorists believe that Gottlieb's umbrella was used on JFK – see page 100.) There was also an ingenious device that fitted into a fluorescent bulb and slowly spread a biological poison when the light was turned on. The CIA always claimed that none of these weapons and poisons were ever used. This wasn't for lack of trying or enthusiasm on Gottlieb's part, however, and in 1960 he was given a golden opportunity to put his mad methods into practice in Iraq.

From 1958 to 1960, despite General Abdul Kassem's harsh repression of his own people, the Eisenhower administration allowed him to continue to rule so as not to antagonise Russia. The fact that Kassem was against Nasser of Egypt – then a sworn enemy of the US – was a bonus. But Kassem's decision to nationalise the British-controlled Iraq Petroleum Company, along with his resurrection of a long-standing Iraqi claim to Kuwait and a sudden drastic accumulation of Soviet weaponry, was all too much for America to bear and in 1961 the CIA, by then under the command of President John F. Kennedy, decided that it was time for Kassem to go. It became one of the most elaborate CIA operations in the history of the Middle East. Washington's role in the coup went unreported at the time and has been little noted since but the reality of the intrigue has since been widely substantiated in disclosures by the Senate Committee on Intelligence.

In a top-secret operation, Richard Bissell, the CIA's Deputy Director of Plans (responsible for what became known as the CIA's 'Black' Operations, including Executive Action – the removal of troublesome leaders using assassination as a last resort) authorised the HAC to come up with a plan to assassinate General Kassem. Gottlieb soon had the answer: a monogrammed handkerchief infected with a lethal poison. The only snag was that it relied on the unreliable Iraqi postal service to get the item concerned to the Iraqi dictator. In addition, it was not known if Kassem ever had cause to use a handkerchief – typically he dressed in his army uniform and so wouldn't have any need for top-pocket decoration. Nevertheless, Bissell gave Gottlieb the go-ahead and the handkerchiefs were flown to the US Embassy in Egypt and posted to Kassem's home.

If the handkerchief plan was going to work then it was necessary for there to be a US-friendly replacement ready to take the poisoned general's place. For a while the Kurds, located in northern Iraq, seemed likely candidates; they revolted and demanded independence from Baghdad. They had already contacted the United States, asking for help in overthrowing Kassem and offering a pro-American government in return. President Kennedy declined the offer, stating with emphatic hypocrisy that to do so would be 'interfering with the internal affairs of Iraq'. Instead, America had already chosen the authoritarian and anti-communist Baath Party, which was still a relatively small political faction but had great influence in the Iraqi army. In exchange for CIA help in the coup, Baath Party leaders agreed to eliminate all the communists they could find, which meant that hundreds if not thousands of professionals would be assassinated. Roger Morris, serving on the staff of the National Security Council under first Lyndon Johnson and then Richard Nixon in the late 1960s, often heard CIA officers – including Archibald Roosevelt, grandson of Theodore Roosevelt, and a ranking CIA official for the Near East and Africa at the time – speak openly about their close relations with the Iraqi Baathists.

The CIA had decided that Saddam Hussein would play a key part in the hunt for the communists in Iraq. From his hideout in Syria he was transferred by Egyptian intelligence agents to Beirut where the CIA paid for an apartment and put him through a brief training course in espionage, sabotage and interrogation. The agency then helped him get to Cairo where he was installed in another apartment in the upper-class neighbourhood of Dukki where he was given a monthly allowance by the Egyptian Secret Service.

Saddam spent his time playing dominoes in the Indiana Café, a local dive, and made frequent visits to the American Embassy where CIA agent Miles Copeland and CIA Station Chief Jim Eichelberger became his new handlers. Together, they compiled assassination lists of suspected communists which were sent, along with lists from other CIA stations throughout the Middle East and with the help of other Iraqi exiles, to William Lakeland, the US assistant military attaché in Baghdad, who was the coup's main organiser. The American agent who produced the most names was William McHale, who operated under the cover of a news correspondent for the Beirut bureau of *Time* magazine. When the time came, the lists would be passed to Baathist assassins who would wear green armbands for identification.

Disaster almost struck when one of the coup leaders, Colonel Saleh Mahdi Ammash, a former Iraqi assistant military attaché in Washington, was arrested after the Iraqi police discovered that he was in touch with Lakeland in Baghdad. But his arrest simply prompted the conspirators to move earlier than they had planned.

Washington set up a base of operations in Kuwait, intercepting Iraqi communications and radioing orders to the rebels. On 8 February 1963, the conspirators staged a coup, led by the army, in Baghdad. Kassem, surprised by a dawn raid at his home, was machine-gunned to death as he lay in bed; his bullet-riddled body, like that of King Faisal whom he had assassinated five years earlier, was dragged through the streets and displayed to TV cameras. Washington immediately befriended the successor regime. 'Almost certainly a gain for our side,' Robert Komer, a National Security Council aide, wrote to Kennedy on the day of the takeover.

At a press conference at the Baghdad Hotel, a swarm of more than one hundred foreign correspondents pushed past machine-gun-toting guards, crowded around rebel President Abdul Salam Aref, Iraq's new ruler, and shouted their questions. The new President kept quiet about his mysterious revolutionary backers and spoke briefly about the aims and purposes of the new government, announcing an end to one-man rule, friendship with all Arab states, and the 'overcoming of all the difficulties facing the Iraqi people'. But he remained silent about the size or membership of the all-powerful National Council of the Revolutionary Command, which had organised and led the revolt against Kassem: 'This is a secret which must remain a secret for many reasons.' Asked why, the English-speaking Aref snapped out a reply in Arabic. Pressed again for an answer, Aref suddenly announced: 'The conference is closed' and departed, surrounded by his guards.

But the answer was clear to those who could read between the lines. As Ali Saleh Al Sa'adi, Iraq's Minister of the Interior and Deputy Prime Minister, put it many years later: 'We came to power on a CIA train.' Most Western observers praised the new twenty-one-man Cabinet. Said one: 'In general, they're a top-notch bunch of responsible, eager, exceptionally well-educated people.' Many of the ministers had lived or been educated in the West, ranging from Foreign Minister Talib Hussein Shabib, who graduated from London University and married an Englishwoman, to Finance Minister Salih Kubba, who attended the University of California and had an international reputation as an economist. Seven of the new Cabinet ministers were in Kassem's concentration camp at Rashid military base when the rebels broke down the gates during the coup.

Meanwhile, Saddam Hussein rushed back to Iraq from exile in Cairo and became personally involved in the torture of communists in the separate detention centres for *fellaheen* (peasants) and the *muthaqafeen* (educated classes). Hundreds of dogged men with green armbands, carrying lists of communist supporters complete with home addresses and car-licence numbers, methodically hunted them down. With twenty-four-hour tank and armoured-car patrols there was little chance of escape.

Within a week, the new regime had killed or jailed nearly two and a half thousand people. The final tally is unknown but as the weeks passed the Baathists continued to murder untold numbers of Iraq's educated elite. The victims included thousands of doctors, teachers, technicians, lawyers and other professionals as well as military and political figures who were buried in mass graves[2]. Thousands more were jailed and interrogated before being summarily gunned down in mass executions. These massacres were presided over by Saddam and took place at Qasr al-Nehayat – literally, the 'Palace of the End'. A former senior US State Department official said: 'We were frankly glad to be rid of them. You ask that they get a fair trial? You have to be kidding. This was serious business.' A US intelligence operative said: 'We weren't sorry to see the communists go at all. Hey, we were playing for keeps.' Saddam, in the meantime, became head of *Al-Jihaz a-Khas*, the secret intelligence apparatus of the Baath Party.

Soon Western corporations like Mobil, Bechtel and British Petroleum were doing business with Baghdad – for American firms this was their first major involvement in Iraq. But it wasn't long before there was infighting among Iraq's new rulers. Five years later, in 1968, the CIA encouraged a palace revolt among Baath Party elements led by long-time Saddam mentor – and relative – Ahmed Hassan al-Bakr. The CIA plot ultimately failed – Al-Bakr quickly nationalised the Iraq Petroleum Company while introducing wide-ranging social and economic reforms. He established friendly relations with the Soviet Union in 1972 and in 1979 turned over the reins of power to his ambitious Vice-President, Saddam Hussein.

And the poisoned handkerchief? It must have got lost in the post. But in 1960 Gottlieb was given another chance to put his ideas into action.

*

[2] These burials were the result of the CIA giving lists of names of suspected communists to the incoming Baath Party. In 2003, after the earlier reasons for invading Iraq proved false, US President George W. Bush sought to justify the invasion of Iraq on the basis of the mass graves resulting from Saddam Hussein's reign of terror.

At 3.10 p.m. on 4 March 1960 Che Guevara was on his way to the National Bank of Cuba, of which he was president, when a massive explosion rocked Havana. As Che looked out of the car window, he saw an enormous mushroom cloud rise over the harbour and ordered his driver to head for the source. At the harbour, he was confronted with a scene straight out of the bloodiest battle. The freighter *La Coubre*, a 4,310-tonne French vessel carrying seventy-six tonnes of Belgian munitions bound for Castro's army, had exploded while being unloaded.

Among the dead and dying lay hundreds of other terribly injured people, many of whom had lost limbs; the medically trained revolutionary got to work and spent the next few hours trying to save the lives of scores of ship-workers. Then, thirty minutes after the first explosion, a second and even more powerful blast rocked the harbour, injuring most of the rescue team. By evening at least seventy-five were dead and over two hundred were seriously injured.

The next day Cuba's radio stations screamed 'Imperialist beast! Bandit, hypocrite, thief!', denouncing the United States. 'The US wants to prepare public opinion for military action,' raved *Revolution*, Fidel's mouthpiece newspaper. The Cuban leader said: 'Those who committed this sabotage are those who were interested in our not getting these arms – officials of the United States Government.' The US denied any involvement – the blasts were most likely caused by the careless unloading of explosives.

This was the lowest point in Cuban–US relations since Castro had taken power from General Fulgencio Batista in the Battle of Yaguajay – in which Che Guevara had played a key role – in December 1958. A US government spokesperson told the press that they were 'holding their temper' but despite this US Secretary of State Christian Herter summoned Enrique Patterson, Cuba's chargé d'affaires, to the State Department to make America's denial of the unfounded accusations perfectly clear. By then, communist Cuba already had the look of a nation at war with America. Black-bereted militia drilled in Havana's parks and along the seaside drives; the last remaining US companies were packing up hurriedly as Castro demanded that they leave 'Free Cuba'. Castro finished every speech with the phrase: 'Homeland or death. We shall prevail.'

Time magazine wrote: 'The virtue of the US policy of forbearance is that it demonstrates once again that the days of unilateral US intervention in the affairs of its smaller Latin neighbours are past.' They couldn't have been more wrong. Castro's accusations of murder and sabotage were the final straws for the US administration.

The CIA had advocated the elimination of Fidel Castro as early as December 1959, and the matter was brought up again at a meeting in January 1960 and again in March the same year when President Eisenhower finally signed an authorisation for covert action by the CIA to overthrow Castro. According to Ray Cline, a former Deputy of Intelligence at the CIA: 'At an NSC [National Security Council] meeting on 10 March 1960, terminology was used suggesting that the assassination of Castro, his brother Raoul and Che Guevara was at least theoretically considered.' High officials clearly thought 'they had been authorised to plan Castro's assassination'. Cline added the caveat that 'whether President Eisenhower or Dulles or President Kennedy had actually intended to authorise Castro's murder is simply not clear from the records'.

The attempt by the CIA to assassinate Cuba's Fidel Castro not only provides several examples of how *not* to kill someone but is one of the most bizarre state-sponsored assassination plans ever put into action. Few plots to kill a government leader have received more publicity than the supposedly super-secret Operation Mongoose.

To start with, the plan was not to assassinate Castro but to debilitate, incapacitate and humiliate him. This was considered to be more effective than actual martyrdom. Gottlieb and the Health Alteration Committee got to work once more on a variety of hare-brained schemes; although the methods of assassination had elements of genius, their impracticality made them well-nigh impossible to carry out. For a while the monkeys at the CIA's Technical Services Division ran around without their fur as Gottlieb tested his idea to dust Fidel's shoes with thallium, a powerful depilatory which would cause his beard to fall out; Castro had often remarked that his beard was like a 'badge of honour' (Gottlieb hoped to contaminate Castro's shoes while he was on a foreign trip, the idea being that he would place his boots outside his hotel door for cleaning). Next, the unfortunate primates lost their minds as smoke from cigars laced with LSD was pumped into their glass cages (it was hoped that Castro could be induced to smoke one before or while giving a speech)[3].

The monkeys finally met their end after the CIA changed tack and decided that the assassination of Castro was the only way to create the possibility of a US-friendly regime change. In October 1960 a box of Castro's favourite cigars was laced with botulinum toxin, a substance so lethal that one cigar placed against the lips would cause death. They were passed on to a Cuban exile the following February who promised to deliver them to Castro – but the exile and the cigars promptly disappeared.

The main problem the CIA faced was that, for all its intelligence capabilities and resources, it lacked any method of penetrating Castro's Cuba. Occasionally an anti-Castro Cuban would approach the CIA – for example, a man promised J.C. King, the Chief of the Western Hemisphere Division of the CIA, to arrange an 'accident' for Raoul Castro in return for ten thousand dollars and US college educations for his sons. This mishap failed to materialise and no money was ever paid.

In August 1960, the agency embarked on a bizarre recruitment programme. J.C. King and the Chief of the Directorate for Plans, Richard Bissell, contacted Colonel Sheffield Edwards, Director of the Office for Security. They asked Edwards to find someone to assassinate Castro and he suggested that they should try the Mafia, knowing that their former Havana gambling empire gave them some contacts to work with. An assassination carried out by a Mafia hood

[3] When Castro learned of this plan he gave up smoking, which, ironically, probably contributed to his longevity.

would make it easy for the American government to distance itself from any such operation. The contract on Castro's life was set at one hundred and fifty thousand dollars, enough to tempt most hit men.

Edwards recruited Robert Maheu, an ex-FBI agent who had forged a successful career as a private detective from 1954. He had already been used in several sensitive covert operations in which the CIA didn't want to risk one of their agents getting caught. At the end of August 1960 the two men met and Edwards asked Maheu to contact the mobster John Rosselli who had gambling contacts in Las Vegas to see if he would be prepared to take part in a plan to 'dispose of' Castro. Maheu resisted at first as he had just won a contract to work for the tycoon Howard Hughes and didn't want to jeopardise their relationship. Edwards reminded Maheu that the CIA had paid him a monthly five-hundred-dollar retainer which had kept him going when times had been harder. Maheu agreed that he owed the agency: he told Edwards that he had known Rosselli for a number of years and thought he would be the man who could organise such a thing. He arranged a meeting with Rosselli in a Beverly Hills restaurant in September 1960.

Rosselli sat stunned as Maheu told him that 'high government officials' needed his cooperation in getting rid of Castro and asked if he could recruit some Cubans interested in doing the job. The mobster was hesitant at first, but on or around 14 September 1960, at the Plaza Hotel in New York, the CIA and the mob agreed to work together to eliminate Castro. Rosselli said he would do it because he felt he owed the country which had been so good to him (plus, in his line of work, it paid to have friends in the CIA).

The following year he went on to recruit Salvatore Giancana, a Chicago-based gangster, and Santos Trafficante, Cuba's Cosa Nostra chieftain who lived in Tampa. Both men were on US Attorney-General Robert F. Kennedy's ten-most-wanted list. No doubt they thought that they would earn a degree of protection for helping out the CIA. When Sheffield Edwards found out who Rosselli had involved, he moaned: 'We're up to our ears in it.'

When the CIA suggested a simple Mafia machine-gun ambush,

Rosselli patiently pointed out that the chances of any of his team surviving such an ambush were pretty much nil – the survival instincts of paid hit men are rather more highly developed than those of fanatical political assassins. They agreed on a poisoned pill instead and Gottlieb went back to his monkeys and set about producing something tailor-made for Castro. Rosselli came back to Maheu, telling him that he had arranged for a lady friend of Castro's to administer the poison.

Maheu became concerned at this point when he received a cable from FBI chief J. Edgar Hoover, telling him that Rosselli had been boasting about the assassination plot to a variety of criminal associates, including his girlfriend whom Rosselli told Maheu he suspected of having an affair. Worried that Rosselli's girlfriend would blab to her lover, Maheu had her followed and her hotel room bugged. Unfortunately the detective who bugged the room was caught out when a maid accidentally found the device after he had popped out for a sandwich midway through the installation. She called the police who arrested the detective and an embarrassed Maheu had to get his CIA contacts to call off the FBI. The decision went all the way up to the Attorney General's office. Giancana almost 'swallowed his cigar' from laughing when he heard this, according to Rosselli.

Meanwhile, Gottlieb's first batch of pills were rejected because they failed to dissolve in liquid. The next batch, however, were completely soluble, devastatingly effective (the lab was by this point running short of monkeys) and were considered perfect for the job. Rosselli passed the pills on to his contact who came back with cold feet a few weeks later, having had a change of heart.

The pills were later passed on to Marita Lorenz, the daughter of an American cruise-ship captain and a German ex-spy. Back in February 1959 she had accompanied her father on a trip to Cuba on his luxury cruise ship, the MS *Berlin*. She didn't recognise the bearded *comandante* who invited himself on board. Marita Lorenz and Fidel Castro flirted, and later in the evening drank Cuba Libres together at the ship's bar.

That night there was a knock on Marita's cabin door. Shutting the door behind him, Castro took the toothpaste cup from her bathroom and filled it from a bottle of Cuban rum. The next day she returned to New York, but she kept thinking about her new 'boyfriend'. Not long afterwards, Castro sent a private plane to fly her back to Cuba and she lived with Fidel for a few months.[4] It is not clear exactly what happened next but Marita later claimed (she has given different versions of this story over the years) that she gave birth to Castro's baby but the child was taken from her while she was drugged.

After this, Marita returned to the USA where the CIA picked her up and convinced her that her baby had been killed on Castro's orders. When they felt that she harboured enough hatred for her ex-lover, her 'friends' presented her with a plan; one that, as a bonus, would help protect the American way. With two of Gottlieb's capsules hidden inside a jar of face cream, Lorenz flew back to Havana to meet Fidel Castro in the suite that had been their home for seven months. She searched for the pills concealed in her cream while waiting for her ex-lover but they had disintegrated. Marita threw the jar's contents down the toilet. When Castro finally joined her he lay down on the bed, fully dressed, chewed on a cigar, and said, 'You come to kill me?'

'Yes,' Marita replied.

'You can't kill me. Nobody can kill me.' Castro took out his .45 and handed it to Marita. She checked the clip. It was loaded. But she couldn't bring herself to shoot. Marita left Cuba shortly afterwards, much to the frustration of her handlers, but later settled down with Marcos Pérez Jímenez, the wily former dictator of Venezuela.[5]

Rosselli next found a Cuban associate of Santos Trafficante who

[4]Although clueless about politics and as to who exactly Fidel was, Marita Lorenz later remarked that he must have been 'pretty important' because he 'slept with a bazooka under the bed'.

[5]Jímenez had taken power in 1950 after arranging the assassination of the former President, Colonel Delgado Chalbaud. He quickly befriended America, awarded them ridiculously generous oil-drilling concessions and squirrelled away $200m of the country's money before fleeing to the USA in 1958.

was prepared to do the job in return for arms and communications equipment. J.C. King authorised the hit to go ahead, and gave Rosselli fifty thousand dollars in cash, ten thousand of which was to be paid in advance to the assassin whose plan was to poison Castro as he ate at his favourite restaurant. In an extraordinary meeting on 12 March 1961 Maheu, Rosselli, Trafficante and the assassin met at the Boom-Boom Room of the Fontainebleau Hotel in Miami. The hotel was packed with fight fans, there for the Patterson–Johansson World Heavyweight Championship. Maheu passed the pills to the assassin and then the men went to watch the big fight. Sadly for the conspirators, Castro had grown bored of his favourite restaurant by the time the assassin got back to Cuba.

Towards the end of 1961 there was a shake-up at the CIA and the elimination of AMTHUG (Castro's CIA code name) became the responsibility of William Harvey – who was also tasked by Richard Bissell, shortly before he was replaced by Richard Helms, with establishing a general 'capability' within the CIA for neutralising uncooperative foreign leaders with assassination as a last resort. The capability was called Executive Action and was later referred to under the cryptonym ZR/RIFLE.

Harvey arrived in Miami with four poison pills on 21 April 1962 and gave them to Rosselli, telling him that they would 'work anywhere and at any time with anything'. Rosselli passed them on to a small team of Cuban assassins who disappeared with a weapons cache that had also been supplied by the CIA. Rosselli came back to his CIA handlers with thrilling tales of derring-do as the assassins sneaked into Cuba and put together the hit – but they, like the others before them, vanished.

Eventually the CIA had had enough and they pulled out of Operation Mongoose. There are several who believe that the 1975 murder of Giancana (just prior to his scheduled appearance before the State Committee headed by Frank Church that was inquiring into alleged government assassination plots) and the 1976 killing of Rosselli were the work of the CIA. The alleged motive was to keep secret the more embarrassing details of Operation Mongoose, but no evidence was ever produced to support this theory.

Fabian Escalante, who for a time had the job of keeping *El Comandante* alive, has calculated that there have been in total 638 attempts on Castro's life. This is a slight exaggeration, even when one includes those plans that never made it past the CIA's suggestion box – including the exploding clam. Knowing of Castro's fascination with scuba-diving off the coast of Cuba, the CIA at one time invested in a large quantity of Caribbean molluscs. The idea was to find a shell big enough to contain a lethal amount of explosive, which would then be painted in colours lurid and bright enough to attract Castro's attention when he was underwater. The idea was rejected by the Technical Services Division as being 'impractical'.

An idea deemed to be more workable was for James Donovan (a chief negotiator of prisoner exchanges after the CIA-led failed Bay of Pigs invasion of Cuba) to present Castro with a contaminated diving suit in January 1963. The boffins at HAC beavered away on lining a diving suit with a fungus that would cause a chronic skin disease and they also contaminated the breathing apparatus with tubercle bacillus. Sadly, nobody thought to warn Donovan of the plan and he presented an uncontaminated suit as a goodwill gesture shortly before the HAC's version was ready.

In other plots, one of Castro's old classmates planned to shoot him dead in the street in broad daylight, much in the manner of a Mafia hit. One would-be sniper at the University of Havana was caught by security men. But the shooters were no more successful than the poisoners and bombers. Jokes about Castro's apparent indestructibility became commonplace in Cuba. One tells of him being given a present of a Galapagos turtle. Castro declines it after he learns that it is likely to live only one hundred years. 'That's the problem with pets,' he says. 'You get attached to them and then they die on you.'

But although the CIA had given up on Operation Mongoose, they still persisted with plans for the assassination of Castro. In 1963 Desmond Fitzgerald, Chief of the CIA's Special Affairs Staff, with the backing of CIA Director Richard Helms and Robert Kennedy, met with Rolando Cubela, a senior Cuban government official who was prepared to assassinate Fidel Castro. But instead of presenting the assassin with the high-powered rifle with telescopic sights that he had asked for, Fitzgerald presented Cubela, code-named AM/LASH, with a hypodermic syringe disguised as a pen. Fitzgerald suggested that Cubela should use the deadly poison Blackleaf-40. Cubela wasn't impressed and replied that the CIA should be able to come up with something better than that. Fitzgerald assured him that whatever the method Cubela would have the backing of the United States. The two men left the meeting shortly before noon. The date was 22 November 1963.

Five

Hearts of Darkness

Sometimes it's what a leader says in a single angry moment that seals their end. For the Congo's Patrice Lumumba, it was a case of angering just about everybody who had an interest in his country, so much so that it became an extraordinary race between the Americans, the English, the Belgians and the Congolese to see who could get to him first – until they realised that cooperation was the way forward.

Larry Devlin, the CIA station chief in Léopoldville, had received orders from Washington to pick up 'Joe from Paris' (also known by the code name QJ/WIN) from the airport. Devlin recognised the thin bespectacled figure as soon as he emerged from the plane's doorway and tried to suppress a groan. 'Joe from Paris' was the CIA's chief technical officer, Dr Sidney Gottlieb. True to form, he had brought with him a tube of poisoned toothpaste. Gottlieb told Devlin that his job was to get the toothpaste into Congolese Prime Minister Patrice Lumumba's bathroom. Devlin didn't think much of Gottlieb's plan (apparently Lumumba didn't even use toothpaste) and threw the poison into the Congo River. He made sure that the Black Sorcerer got on the next plane out of the Congo.

Meanwhile, Devlin cabled his CIA bosses in Washington DC using loosely coded language, no doubt an effort to avoid any more nonsense: *Recommend . . . high-powered foreign-make rifle with telescopic scope and silencer. Hunting good here when lights right. However, as hunting rifles now forbidden would keep rifle in office pending opening of hunting season.*

Devlin had asked for the rifle to be sent via diplomatic bag (an illegal use of diplomatic immunity, also used by the USA in the case of Rafael Trujillo).[6]

Patrice Lumumba's rise had been truly meteoric. In four years he had gone from post office clerk to Prime Minister, negotiating the Congo's independence from Belgium along the way. He was an *evolue*, one of the Congo's tiny black middle class, a beer salesman and a convicted prisoner – twice: once for embezzlement, though he claimed his motivation was political, and once for his political activities and inciting unrest. He was certainly charismatic and often displayed too much confidence in his own abilities. Although Lumumba's share of the vote in the May 1960 elections could hardly be described as a majority (his party, the Congolese National Movement, won forty-one of the 137 seats), his was the largest single block and so he took control of the country. Within a month of his rule, Lumumba somehow managed to annoy every single major Western power with an interest in his country, so much so that assassination soon became an attractive option.

On the day of his country's Independence Day celebrations, held in the presence of the Belgian King Baudouin, Lumumba told him in an impromptu speech that: 'From today, we are no longer your monkeys!' The final straw for the Belgians came when shortly afterwards Lumumba stated that he wanted to nationalise the copper industry, an act that would never be allowed by the Belgians – the

[6]Generalissimo Doctor Rafael Leónidas Trujillo Molina, Benefactor of the Fatherland, Rebuilder of the Financial Independence of the Republic, Father of the New Fatherland, Chief Protector of the Dominican Working Class, Genius of Peace, was the model for every tinpot medal-jingling dictator that ever rifled a Latin American treasury. His subjects referred to him as 'The Goat' because of his many revolting excesses, including the sick enjoyment he got from having his subjects tortured. He was shot to death in 1961 in a roadside ambush by a team of assassins led by a disgruntled General.

Congo's copper mines, the largest in the world, were run and controlled by Belgian companies.

A few days after Lumumba's impromptu speech, sections of his army rebelled against the continued presence of a Belgian commander. While this was taking place, the tribal region of Katanga declared that it had seceded from the Democratic Republic of the Congo under the leadership of Moise Tshombe who was known to be close to the Belgian companies which mined the copper, gold and uranium and whose wealth had flowed back to Brussels for decades. Without Katanga, the Congo would be an impoverished economy. The Belgians gratefully provided secret financial and military backing for Tshombe who continued to threaten Lumumba with war.

Within one short week all but a hundred of the 1,200 Belgian doctors in the country hastily packed their bags and fled from the Congo – some of them alarmed by the breakdown of order and the rumours of the rape of white nuns. Their departure left just six of the fledgling nation's four hundred hospitals, manned by nurses and semi-trained 'medical assistants'. The result was both inevitable and catastrophic: reports began filtering back to Léopoldville, the capital (today known as Kinshasha) of eruptions of bubonic and pneumonic plague, outbreaks of smallpox and widespread increases in serious but less spectacular diseases such as malaria, meningitis and pneumonia.

By now the Belgian government had the excuse they were waiting for. They sent their troops back to Katanga and the Congo, arguing that they had to protect Belgian nationals still resident in the area when all they were really doing was offering covert support to Moise Tshombe. Appeals by Lumumba to the United Nations Secretary-General Dag Hammarskjöld for help to expel the Belgians from the new, supposedly independent country of the Congo fell on deaf ears.

In retaliation, Lumumba expelled Belgian diplomats and called again on the United Nations to defend the newly independent state, this time hinting that it might be necessary to ask the Soviet Union for assistance. That set alarm bells ringing in the West. A multinational UN peacekeeping force was deployed; troops were provided with the not very reassuring instructions that 'if [poison] arrows are removed within two seconds, they cause only temporary discomfort'.

But the UN was rendered impotent by the lack of cooperation from the Belgians who did their best to make it impossible for the UN's representatives to work properly. The Belgians did this by spreading misinformation and burying the UN people in paperwork. Finally, reluctantly, Lumumba looked to the Eastern Bloc for help against Tshombe and accepted a consignment of Soviet transport planes, military trucks and guns. Although Lumumba was no communist, he was nonetheless interested in getting aid from wherever he could. In 1960 the Cold War was powering ahead at full throttle: if any previously friendly or unaligned country established trade links with the Soviet Union it led to intense warlike conferences in both Whitehall and the White House.

In London, one MI6 desk man, H.F.T. 'Howard' Smith who later became head of the British internal security service MI5, opined that order could be restored and the threat of Communism in the Congo could be removed by 'ensuring Lumumba's removal from the scene by killing him'. On 19 September the US Republican President General Dwight David Eisenhower told the British Foreign Minister Lord Home that it would be most convenient if Lumumba fell 'into a river full of crocodiles'. Eisenhower, now in the twilight weeks of his final term as President, mistakenly saw Lumumba as a potential African Fidel Castro.

He was also concerned about Lumumba's behaviour towards American businesses. In 1959 Lumumba had visited businessmen in New York where he had stated: 'The exploitation of the mineral riches of the Congo should be primarily for the profit of our own people and other Africans.' There were several significant American investors in copper and uranium in the Congo at that time, including the Rockefellers, the Guggenheims and C. Douglas Dillon. Dillon was at many of the government's National Security

Council (NSC) secret meetings that discussed the 'Lumumba problem'.

Robert Johnson, a member of the NSC staff, later testified that sometime during the summer of 1960, at an NSC meeting, he heard President Eisenhower make a comment that sounded to him like a direct order to assassinate Lumumba: 'At some time during that discussion, President Eisenhower said something – I can no longer remember his words – that came across to me as an order for the assassination of Lumumba.' Johnson said that Eisenhower made the statement while 'looking toward the Director of Central Intelligence'. With or without direct authorisation, on 26 August 1960 CIA Director Allen Dulles initiated Project Wizard and cabled Devlin the following message:

> *In high quarters here it is the clear-cut conclusion that if [Lumumba] continues to hold high office, the inevitable result will at best be chaos and at worst pave the way to Communist takeover of the Congo with disastrous consequences for the prestige of the UN and for the interests of the free world generally. Consequently we conclude that his removal must be an urgent and prime objective and that under existing conditions this should be a high priority of our covert action.*

As the conflict between Tshombe and Lumumba, between West and East escalated, Devlin realised that assassinating Lumumba wasn't going to be that straightforward. Shooting him or poisoning him would only intensify the Soviets' interest in the Congo and give them the right – as they would see it – to try and take control of the mineral-rich country by using Tshombe. It would be much better for the United States if Lumumba was seen to have been eliminated by his own people. Devlin set about joining forces with the Belgians and anti-Lumumban Congolese strongmen to eliminate the thirty-five-year-old Prime Minister.

Sixty-seven days after he came to power, on 5 September 1960, Patrice Lumumba was sacked by his State President Joseph

Kasavubu (installed by the Belgians as a stooge for British, Belgian and American interests). In response Lumumba tried to fire Kasavubu but the President was supported by the army and it was Lumumba who was placed under informal house arrest at the Prime Minister's residence, surrounded by UN guards who were there to protect him.

A month later, as Lumumba tried to rally his supporters, the Belgians agreed with the CIA that if they wanted to secure their continued access to the Congo's minerals, then Lumumba would have to go. On 6 October the Belgian Minister for African Affairs, Count d'Aspremont Lynden, sent a cable to Katanga's capital, Elizabethville, stating clearly that policy was now directed at the 'definitive elimination' of Patrice Lumumba. Joseph Mobutu, a former newspaper editor, at that time Chief of Staff of the Congolese army, was given the task of getting past the UN soldiers to Lumumba.

By now, the only man able to save Lumumba's life was the incoming US President, forty-three-year-old John F. Kennedy. While Kennedy had pledged to meet 'the Communist challenge', he wanted the Congolese Prime Minister alive. Unlike Eisenhower, JFK saw Lumumba as a potential leader of a Western stronghold in Africa. If Lumumba had waited long enough in his safe house, protected by the United Nations, then Kennedy could have stopped the assassination once he was in the White House. Instead, Lumumba made the worst decision of his life.

Receiving CIA misinformation that his supporters had established an independent state in Stanleyville, Lumumba decided to try and escape. Smuggled out of his residence at night in a visiting diplomat's car, he began the long journey with Mobutu's troops in hot pursuit. Finally, trapped on the banks of the impassable Sankuru River, he was captured. He appealed to local UN troops to save him but they refused on direct orders from their headquarters in New York.

Lumumba could have been killed there and then but the Belgians and the CIA demanded a more decisive ending – they wanted

Lumumba delivered into the hands of his sworn enemy, President Tshombe of Katanga. On 15 January the Belgian Minister for African Affairs informed Tshombe that he must accept and deal with Lumumba without delay. After a moment's hesitation, Tshombe agreed.

Lumumba was savagely beaten before being put on a plane bound for Katanga with two of his former ministers. As the circling DC-4 bounced through a tropical thunderstorm over Elisabethville, the pilot relayed a cryptic message down to the tower: 'I've got a big parcel for you fellows.' Minutes later, the 'parcel' stumbled down the plane ramp into the eager hands of the tough Katanga gendarmes. Lumumba was blindfolded and shackled to two of his government lieutenants. The Katanga cops fell on all three and dropped them to the ground in a hail of swinging rifle butts, in full view of journalists and UN soldiers. Then they flung the bloody and dishevelled Lumumba into a waiting jeep. With four gendarmes sitting on him, he was whisked off to a secret jail.

A few nights later, the Prime Minister was hustled on board a chartered Air Congo plane and delivered to Tshombe. En route, the guards pummelled Lumumba so severely that the alarmed pilot went back to the cabin to warn them against damaging the plane.

On the day when the executions were to take place, President Tshombe travelled to the remote area in the bush that had been chosen as the kill site to watch. It was January 17, three days before Kennedy was to assume the United States presidency. Ludo de Witte, the author of *The Assassination of Lumumba*, pieced together the final minutes of Lumumba's life using official Belgian archives. The executioners were a mixture of Belgian–Katangan police: Belgian officers Captain Julien Gat, Liutenant Gabriel Michels, Commissioner Frans Verscheure and Sergeant François Son, plus a nine-member firing squad made up of local men. The prisoners were barefoot, and dressed only in their trousers and vests. At about 9.40 p.m., as the men walked across the scrub to a large, lone tree, Lumumba asked Verscheure: 'You are going to kill us, aren't you?'

'Yes,' Verscheure answered. Lumumba simply nodded.

As the condemned men reached the tree, hemmed in by policemen and soldiers, Verscheure announced that they were going to be executed; that they should prepare themselves and pray. Lumumba declined and told them to get it over with.

There were three firing squads, one for each victim. The first, made up of two soldiers and two policemen, got ready to shoot Joseph Okito, Lumumba's former deputy. According to de Witte, Okito's last words were: 'I want my wife and children in Leopoldville to be taken care of.' As soon as he turned to face the firing squad they fired. Soldiers collected his body and threw it into a pre-dug grave.

Next, Maurice Mpolo, the huge former Minister for Youth, was marched to the tree. As the bullets struck their large target he was slammed him back against the trunk and his bulky frame hit the earth with a thud.

Finally, the firing squad turned to watch as Verscheure escorted Lumumba past his grave to the tree, now scarred with bullet holes. Lumumba was shaking, but with tears in his eyes, he pulled himself together and stared the firing squad down. The soldiers raised their weapons, took aim and unleashed a tremendous fusillade, emptying every last clip. After the execution, the Belgians picked up half a kilo of spent bullet casings.

The following day Katanga's Interior Minister called Belgo-Katangan police commander Gerard Soete into his office with orders to conceal the killings. 'Destroy the bodies, make them disappear. How you do it doesn't interest me.' Soete, along with his brother, exhumed the bodies from their shallow graves, hacked them into pieces and dissolved them in sulphuric acid brought from some Belgian-run mines nearby. It took them two days, drinking whisky the entire time in an attempt to obliterate the unpleasant task from their minds. When they ran out of acid, they made a fire for the last remains. They kept a couple of teeth for souvenirs.

Three weeks later, President Kennedy was working from his country estate when he got the call telling him that Congolese ex-Premier

Patrice Lumumba was dead. It was, the President knew, a serious crisis, the first one he would face as leader of his country. The Soviets knew full well that the Americans had done for Lumumba and were considering their reaction; they could use Lumumba's murder as an excuse to support forces loyal to the former Prime Minister in an effort to take control of the Congo. It was tempting: if successful, such a move would hurt the West financially and Russia could use the African state's precious natural resources.

Kennedy issued a moderate statement expressing his 'shock' at the news and waited anxiously for the Russian response. It came quickly, as expected. The Soviet Union threatened military intervention on behalf of Lumumba's Deputy Prime Minister, Antoine Gizenga, whose forces commanded Stanleyville. It denounced the authority of UN Secretary-General Dag Hammarskjöld whom it held directly responsible for the UN's failure to protect Lumumba, and accused the UN of failing in its duty to keep order and maintain its neutrality.

The world turned to Washington for a sign of the new administration's reaction to its first full-blown crisis. In his fourth presidential press conference, John Kennedy had an ideal forum for his answer. The conference was shown live on television, at seven p.m., a prime-time viewing hour. More than three hundred and fifty newsmen, photographers and technicians gathered in the room to hear what Kennedy had to say. The President's youthful vigour and serious demeanour served him well as he made it clear that:

1. The US could 'take care of itself'.
2. The US intended to support and defend the UN for the sake of smaller independent nations who needed it more than the US did.
3. The Russians would be in trouble if they tried to intervene in the Congo.

Kennedy was quite willing to risk a showdown in calling the Soviet bluff. Unlike the battlegrounds of Korea and Laos – where the problem of supply was simple for the Communists but difficult for the US – the Congo was a Russian strategic nightmare. Lacking the ability to mount a serious airlift to the embattled Congo, the Soviet Union could not, if the US and the UN took a vigorous stand, intervene militarily without risking either a big defeat or the kind of all-out global war that Russian Premier Nikita Khrushchev did not want. Russia backed down and Kennedy passed his first serious test in world affairs.

Sadly, however, the assassination of Lumumba would not prove to be enough to safeguard Western interests. It simply proved to be a prelude to another murder, the killing of a world leader that appalled the world and the truth about which would not be learned until almost forty years later.

At close to midnight on 18 September 1961, United Nations Secretary-General Dag Hammarskjöld climbed into the *Albertina*, a DC-6 aircraft that could hold up to one hundred passengers. The plane was to take Hammarskjöld and fifteen others to Ndola airport in British-controlled Rhodesia, close to the border of the Congo. He was to meet with Moise Tshombe to broker a ceasefire agreement. The pilot of the *Albertina* filed a fake flight plan in an attempt to keep Hammarskjöld's ultimate destination hidden. Dag had received several threats; he was unpopular with the communists who accused him of siding with the colonialists, and Western interests were worried that he was too eager to give the country's government control of their mines.

Dag Hammarskjöld's family had served the Swedish government for generations as soldiers and statesmen. It was only natural that Hammarskjöld, the son of a prime minister, would be drawn to a life of governmental service. He was an intensely private man who had never married. Because of this, many assumed that he must have been a homosexual.

An agile negotiator who spoke four languages, Hammarskjöld made a highly successful career in international politics at the Swedish Foreign Office. He was an obvious choice for leader of the

United Nations and after his appointment in 1953 he travelled the world, seeking peace and reconciliation among warring factions in Israel and China. In 1957 he intervened in the aftermath of the Suez Crisis. He felt that dispatching UN troops on peacekeeping missions was a necessary, if poor, substitute for failed political negotiations, although many had criticised him for what they thought had been his slow reaction to the crisis in the Congo. Nonetheless, Hammarskjöld was an internationally known figure, popular across the globe. He appeared on the cover of *Time* twice and was hardly ever out of TV news reports.

In 1958, Hammarskjöld was unanimously re-elected to a second five-year term as UN Secretary-General. By far the biggest challenge of this second term was the Congo. The struggle for power had intensified following the assassination of Patrice Lumumba. In Katanga, forces loyal to Lumumba took control of Bakuvu and most of the northern province in Stanleyville. Antoine Gizenga, who had been trained in Prague, proclaimed a separate regime and prepared to defend it with seven thousand armed men.

A resolution adopted by the Security Council on 21 February 1961 began a concerted effort by the United Nations to avert civil war, restore parliamentary institutions to the Congo, and supervise the withdrawal of all Belgian military personnel and all foreign mercenaries serving with Tshombe's army in Katanga. But a mob loyal to Tshombe attacked UN personnel at Elizabethville airport and on 13 September UN forces were attacked by jet aircraft flown by mercenaries. Kennedy announced US support for forceful UN military action. In an attempt to avert an imminent war, Hammarskjöld flew from Léopoldville for talks with the Katangese.

British and American intelligence believed that the only way to stop Hammarskjöld handing back the Congo to the Congolese was to blow up his plane. The British had already sided with Tshombe by sending food and medical supplies to Katanga via British-controlled Rhodesia and Rhodesia's Prime Minister Roy Welensky often served as a supportive media conduit for Tshombe. As far as the British were concerned Hammarskjöld stood in the way of

Katanga's independence which they, along with their Belgian and American allies, covertly supported. In a meeting between the CIA and British intelligence, CIA Director Allen Dulles agreed that 'Dag is becoming troublesome . . . and should be removed'. Dulles promised 'full cooperation from his people . . . I want his removal to be handled more efficiently than was Patrice [Lumumba].'

The plan for Hammarskjöld's elimination was given the code name Operation Celeste. A bomb supplied by Union Minière, the powerful Belgian mining conglomerate operating in the Katanga province, was placed in the undercarriage of Hammarskjöld's plane and was set to detonate shortly after take-off. Fortunately, it failed to explode. But the assassins had a back-up plan – it was just a lot more bloody.

As the DC-6 approached Ndola airport at 10.10 p.m., the pilot radioed that he could see their lights and was then given permission to descend from 16,000 to 6,000 feet. What he couldn't see was the fighter jet rapidly closing in on him from behind. What happened next exactly is unclear (although the evidence suggests that the fighter was flown by a long-time CIA and Special Ops mercenary) but three explosions suddenly lit the night sky and the *Albertina* plummeted down. The pilot managed to pull the aircraft's nose up shortly before impact and the plane belly-flopped onto rough ground some eight miles from the airport.

Amazingly, Hammarskjöld and five others survived the crash, although they were badly injured. The UN chief struggled to crawl away from the aircraft as two Land Rovers raced away from the airport towards the plane, reaching the site about fifteen minutes after the crash. A dozen or so armed men leaped out and started looking for survivors. One of the gunmen called out to his companions: he had found one. His commander walked over, took out his pistol and shot the man in the head.

When they eventually found the still-conscious but badly injured Hammarskjöld he was executed with a single shot fired between his eyes. Then his body was raked with a dozen more bullets. The hit men then placed a large box of ammunition in the plane's hold and set it on fire. The idea was to make it look as if the ammo had exploded on the plane during the crash, killing the survivors.

Meanwhile, the airport's controller sent the airport personnel home, claiming that the *Albertina*'s occupants must have simply 'changed their mind' and decided not to land there. No official search-and-rescue operation was launched until well into the following morning. When the wreckage was found, members of the UN search team were amazed to find that the bodies were riddled with bullets. Despite the assassination squad's efforts, they had missed one man, a UN security guard and former US Marine. He had survived but he lost consciousness shortly after his rescuers arrived and he died five days later.

The next day, the Swedish prime minister travelled to collect Hammarskjöld's body. Outraged, he told reporters that the UN chief had a bullet hole 'precisely in the centre of his forehead'. The British (who controlled Rhodesia) launched an inquiry into Hammarskjöld's death. Dozens of witnesses came forward with information that implied the plane had been shot down.

But the British exhibited a strange tendency to ignore eye-witness testimony and this, coupled with the fact that the airport had been chosen for Hammarskjöld by the British Foreign Secretary Lord Lansdowne, led many commentators to accuse them of complicity in Hammarskjöld's murder. The *Indian Express*, India's largest daily, wrote: 'Never have Britain's hands been so bloodstained as they are now.' The *Ghanaian Times* ran an editorial headed 'Britain: The Murderer'. The journalist didn't hold back: 'Britain stands alone in facing responsibility for history's No. 1 international murder – the murder of United Nations Secretary-General Dag Hammarskjöld.'

Several English and American ex-pats living nearby, including two police officers, came forward claiming to have seen the plane shot down. UN investigators recovered 201 live rounds, 342 spent bullets and 362 cartridge cases from both the crash site and the bodies. Bullets were found in the bodies of six people, two of whom were Swedish guards. The British Rhodesian authorities concluded that the ammunition had simply exploded in the intense heat of the fire, and happened to shoot into some of the plane's passengers. But this was refuted by Major C. F. Westell, an authority on ballistics, who said: 'I can certainly describe as sheer nonsense the statement that cartridges of machine guns or pistols detonated in a fire can penetrate a human body.' Other experts filmed tests showing that bullets heated to the point of explosion did not achieve sufficient velocity to penetrate their container box.

In their final report the Rhodesian commission concluded that the incident was the result of pilot error, and denied any possibility that the plane was in any way sabotaged or attacked. The UN was unable to pinpoint the cause, and refused to rule out the possibility of sabotage or attack. In contrast, the Swedish government held fast to their firm opinion that the plane had been hit by shots from the ground or the air, or had been blown up by a bomb.

After Hammarskjöld's death, violence again spread throughout the Congo. On 11 November troops of the regular Congolese Army, nominally under UN supervision, looted a UN base and murdered thirteen Italian aircrew members. Another Security Council resolution authorised the United Nations' new Burmese Secretary-General, U Thant, to take 'vigorous action, including the use of the requisite measure of force' to restore the rule of law and the non-violent ascendancy of the Congolese authorities. Tshombe agreed to begin talks with the central government on 20 December and accepted Katanga's subordinate status within the Congo. A short time later, with a little help from his friends, Tshombe was in control of the entire country, although this power would prove to be short-lived.

Had he been wiser, or at least more cautious, Patrice Lumumba, the only leader ever democratically elected in the Congo, might have helped his country to become a nation with no more than the normal ration of African problems instead of a blood-spattered land of corruption and anarchy – which was largely what it became. Since his assassination, the Congo has been looted by the US-supported regime of the despot Mobutu Sese Seko[7] and racked by regional and civil wars. In 1997, after the Mobutu regime fell, the Congolese democratic opposition pleaded in vain for American and international support. Since then, almost four million lives have been lost as a result of civil and regional wars. The mineral resources of the Congo, from diamonds to coltan, a material used in the manufacture of mobile phones, continue to be reaped by wealthy foreign industries.

[7] When Mobutu took power in 1965 after defeating Tshombe, he sat through a two-day CIA briefing, after which he ordered all Soviet Bloc embassy staff to leave the country within forty-eight hours.

Six

The Mississippi Conspiracy

1963 began with the now-forgotten assassination of Sylvanus Olympio, President of the handkerchief-sized West African country of Togo. Chief architect of Togo's 1960 independence from French control, London-educated Olympio practised stern austerity at home, rejected demagoguery, and sided openly with the West (he visited President Kennedy in March 1962).

His nightmare began shortly after midnight on 15 January. Disturbed by strange sounds in his comfortable house in Togo's capital city of Lomé, Olympio grabbed a pistol and went to the head of the stairs. There, to his consternation, he saw a crowd of mutinous soldiers crowding the floor below. Barefoot, clad in shorts and sports shirt, Olympio leaped through a window onto the soft, sandy earth of his garden. He made it to the US embassy compound next door where, in a case of mistaken identity, he was turned away by the night guards. In the gravelled courtyard, Olympio found a parked Plymouth belonging to the embassy and crawled in.

The next morning, in the early sunlight, he was spotted huddled beneath the steering wheel by one of the mutineers. Crying 'All right, you have me!' Olympio surrendered and, prodded by rifle butts, was hustled down the driveway, past a mango tree and through the green gate. But he refused to go any further. Sergeant Etienne Eyadema, commander of the rebel detachment, became frustrated at

Olympio's refusal to move and warned the President that he was leaving him no choice.

At seven o'clock that morning US Ambassador Leon Poullada drove up to the embassy building and found Olympio lying in a pool of his own blood just outside the compound. There were red finger smears on the gate, as if he had struggled to rise. As embassy aides carried the corpse into the courtyard, fat lizards scuttled away across the gravel and lounging Togolese soldiers watched silently from a nearby street corner.

The trouble stemmed from Olympio's refusal, for economic reasons, to expand Togo's fly-speck army beyond its standing strength of two hundred and fifty men. A tough ex-sergeant, Emmanuel Bodjolle, thirty-five, jobless and with a family to support, organised a conspiracy with thirty other non-coms. After Olympio tore up a final plea to take into the service at least sixty of the most qualified veterans, Bodjolle snapped: '*Bon. Ça va.*' That midnight his battle-tough insurgents struck, easily occupying the capital.

The rebels declared that free elections would soon follow. But, as so often happens in such circumstances, they decided it would be best to dissolve parliament and rule militarily, at least until things settled down. Olympio's assassin, Sergeant Etienne Eyadema, took the presidency in a coup in 1967 and ruled Togo as a dictatorship until his death in 2005.

The assassination of Sylvanus Olympio was a small piece of drama that heralded the start of one of the most dramatic years of the twentieth century. It was the year when forty-six-year-old Nelson Mandela was sentenced to life imprisonment on Robben Island and seventy thousand young people marched in England in a protest against nuclear weapons. It was the year of the Great Train Robbery and the Profumo Affair, a government-ending scandal. The Beatles' first album *Please Please Me* was released in March and pop artist Andy Warhol exhibited an attention-grabbing show in New York which set him on the road to superstardom. It was also the year of the Cold War film satire *Dr Strangelove* about a group of incompetent military men and politicians who 'accidentally' end the world in a nuclear war. Thankfully, the reality was somewhat different. By 1963, President John F. Kennedy had made good progress in easing tensions between America and Russia after the Cuban Missile Crisis of the year before. On 5 April Khrushchev and the US President agreed to set up a 'hot line' via which the two world leaders could talk directly in the event of a renewed crisis. More importantly, both sides agreed to end nuclear testing. Meanwhile, in America itself in 1963, no single issue was more pressing than civil rights.

The previous year Medgar Evers, the thirty-seven-year-old civil rights leader, had been instrumental in desegregating the University of Mississippi, forcing the faculty to enrol black student James Meredith on 1 October. The local Governor, Ross Barnett, was opposed to the desegregation, and the ensuing riots left two people dead and thirty US Marshals injured. (Meredith obtained his law degree in 1968.) Barnett's belief, which he quoted during his election campaign, that 'the Negro is different because God made him different to punish him' helped earn him the endorsement of the notorious White Citizens' Council, known as 'the upmarket Klan', an organisation which attacked blacks economically by denying them employment and opportunity. He also headed Mississippi's State Sovereignty Commission, a semi-secret Masonic-style organisation dedicated to the obstruction of civil rights. He was Evers's strongest and most bitter enemy.

But by getting Meredith into university, Evers had found a chink in the segregationist armour: it was a story the media loved and Evers became a household name. Soon black students from all over the USA were applying for a university education. The fight for desegregated universities peaked the following year, on 11 June 1963. That afternoon in Alabama, Governor George Wallace (see page 155) who had previously refused two black students the right to register at the University of Alabama (he physically blocked their entry into the university), suddenly backed down. (President

John F. Kennedy had sent the National Guard to 'persuade' the newly elected Governor to stand aside.) With Kennedy's support, the chink was slowly widening.

Then, at seven p.m. the same day, Kennedy gave one of his most famous speeches, often referred to as his 'moral crisis' speech, live on television. Inspired by Evers's and Martin Luther King Jr's dignified and intelligent campaigning, Kennedy demanded not only changes in the law but also in 'all our daily lives' and outlined the Civil Rights Bill that would make racial equality enforceable by law.

The night Kennedy gave his speech, Evers drove home in his old blue Buick through the torrid hundred-degree heat to the city of Jackson's black quarter. The day had been a triumph but Evers was nervous and he anxiously checked his rear-view mirror – a police car was following him. The previous Saturday, as Evers had been crossing the street, a police officer had fired shots at him from a car and had then almost run him down. As Evers had jumped out of the way, the two officers inside the car had shouted racist abuse at him.

As the National Association for the Advancement of Coloured People's (NAACP) only full-time worker in Mississippi, Evers was a constant target of racist and violent abuse, but the Second World War veteran, who had fought bravely on the beaches of Normandy, was never going to give up the good fight. He had recently directed a big civil-rights rally in Jackson and told friends the next day: 'I've had a number of threatening calls. People calling me saying they were going to kill me, saying they were going to blow my home up, that I only had a few hours to live. I remember one individual calling with a pistol on the other end, and he hit the cylinder, and of course you could hear that it was a revolver. He said, "This is for you." And I said, "Well, whenever my time comes, I'm ready."' Evers was, however, afraid for his family: he had taught his three young children to dive for the floor if they heard gunshots and he called his wife Myrlie three times during the day to tell her that he loved her and to talk to his children. No doubt to his great relief, the police car that had been following him pulled over and parked.

Meanwhile, at the family home, Myrlie Evers couldn't wait for

Medgar to get home so that they could celebrate; this was a historic day. As a special treat, she let the two eldest children, Darrell and Reena, wait up for their father; they sat watching a late-night film on TV while Myrlie dozed in bed next to her youngest child, Van. When they heard their father's car pull up outside, the Evers children cried 'There's Daddy!'

Outside, Evers parked behind his wife's estate car. Fifty metres away, hidden in a honeysuckle thicket, lay forty-two-year-old Byron de la Beckwith. He adjusted the brand new Golden Hawk telescopic sight which was mounted on his Enfield 30.06 rifle while Evers, illuminated by the parking lights mounted on the side of his house, climbed out of his car and retrieved a stack of campaign T-shirts from the boot.

Beckwith, aka 'Delay' (after the middle words of his name), appeared to be a typical Southern gentleman. The small, neat man wore glasses and had dark wavy hair, dressed carefully, bowed deeply and punctuated his drawl with soft 'suhs' – his neighbours would have been extremely surprised to learn that he was planning to become one of America's most infamous assassins. But his gracious smile was the façade of a twisted, troubled personality. Family was everything to Beckwith. He never tired of noting that his great-grandfather, Judge Hunter Holmes Southworth, had owned vast spreads of rich Delta cotton land in pre-Civil War days. The judge's daughter, Mrs Susie Southworth Yerger, moved in the highest social circles of the Confederacy and was a close friend of President Jefferson Davis's wife Varina.

When Beckwith was five, his father died of what the death certificate termed 'pneumonia and alcoholism'. His mother suffered from schizophrenia and was hospitalised several times before dying of cancer at the age of forty-seven. Beckwith, then twelve, was sent to be raised by his eccentric uncle, William Green Yerger, who stuffed freshly caught catfish into chests of drawers and left them there to rot. The family home rotted too. The premises were cluttered with mementos of the family's better days, including a letter to Beckwith's grandmother from President Davis.

As soon as he was old enough, Beckwith joined the Marine Corps, where he was a machine-gunner in the invasions of Guadalcanal and Tarawa. Wounded in the chest by Japanese shrapnel before reaching the beach at Tarawa, he saved himself by swimming half a mile to a reef. He married a Navy WAVE, Mary Louise Williams, a descendant of Rhode Island's Founding Father Roger Williams. Beckwith returned to Greenwood, where he worked for ten years as a tobacco salesman. He and his wife were divorced, remarried, then separated – and Beckwith lived alone in the tumbledown family house. In January 1962 he became a fertiliser salesman. He was good at selling but, as one employer put it, he was 'overly enthusiastic about things not concerned with his job'.

He was referring to Beckwith's segregationist obsessions. He attended Greenwood's Episcopal Church of the Nativity where he tried to inject racism into everything. If the preacher talked about Noah and the Ark, Beckwith would ask him if there were any Negroes in the Ark. Beckwith passed out racist pamphlets that he wrote himself and launched such an aggressive recruiting drive for the local White Citizens' Council that its officers finally asked him to desist. He also stood in the doorway of Greenwood's bus terminal, blocking black Americans who were trying to overcome segregation. Beckwith had also joined the Ku Klux Klan; he had taken part in an attack on a white man's house 'for hiring the wrong nigger' to paint his house and had hurled petrol bombs through the windows of black people's homes.

He had found out Medgar's home address after approaching two Jackson cab drivers who were only too happy to share their knowledge of the famous campaigner's address. Beckwith had simply told them, 'I've got to find where he lives in a couple of days.' Beckwith had waited four hours in the thicket for his target to arrive, plenty of time to practise his aim on passers-by and Evers's wife as she took out the rubbish.

Evers grabbed a pile of paperwork from the front seat of his car, slammed the vehicle's door shut and took a few steps. Inside the house Myrlie and the children heard the car door slam. Immediately after, Beckwith pulled his trigger; the bullet exploded from the chamber and ripped into Evers's back, barrelled through his body, shattered a window, pierced a wall in the house, and came to rest on the kitchen counter. Myrlie and her three small children dived to the floor as they had practised. Myrlie told them to wait and ran outside. Medgar had crawled as far as the doorstep and lay in a pool of his own blood which already covered the T-shirts and paperwork scattered around him.

After a few moments, the children followed their mother to the front door. Gazing out, they saw their father lying face down with a large hole in his back, his house keys clenched in his fist. Blood was spattered all over the driveway. Hysterical, Myrlie started screaming. Evers, still conscious, was trying to drag himself inside. Darrell and Reena, terrified, yelled at their daddy to get up.

The Everses' neighbours, Houston and Jean Wells, heard the shot. They looked out of their front window and saw Evers pulling himself along the driveway, leaving a thick trail of blood in his wake. Houston grabbed his gun, stepped outside and blasted a series of shots into the night to scare off the assassin. He then ran back inside and came out with a thin mattress. With the help of other neighbours, Wells lifted Evers onto the mattress. The police car that had been following Evers arrived on the scene. The two white officers sat in their car and watched as Evers's black neighbours placed him in Myrlie Evers's estate car before fighting their way through the traffic and red lights without the aid of a siren to the University of Mississippi Hospital. During the journey, Evers muttered and struggled to sit up. He told his wife, 'Turn me loose.'

As soon as he heard the news Albert Britton, the Everses' family doctor, went to the hospital where Evers had been taken. Dr Britton found him in the emergency room where doctors were trying to revive him. Frustrated that the doctors weren't working quickly enough, he tried to intervene to help treat his friend but he couldn't: this was a white man's hospital – and Dr Britton was black.

As Dr Britton struggled to get to his friend and patient, he called out to him, 'Medgar!' Evers turned his head and made a horrible gulping noise. Then he died.

Soon state and local police, along with FBI agents, were scouring Mississippi for clues. They found the assassin's weapon almost immediately. Beckwith had left it at the scene. President Kennedy called the assassination 'appalling'. Even Governor Ross Barnett, the avowed enemy of Evers, denounced the crime but turned a strange phrase in the process, calling the assassination an 'apparently dastardly act'. Rewards totalling twenty-one thousand dollars were posted for information leading to the arrest of the killer.

Locals were furious but, resisting the impulse to protest violently, they bottled up their anger and marched. Thirteen black ministers began a silent walk, one by one and at widely spaced intervals, towards City Hall. To Jackson's police, this was just another protest – and so they simply hauled the marchers off. The next day the police rushed a group of black and white youths standing on a porch and beat them up. The day after that, black youngsters walked down the street towards City Hall in ones and twos, carrying tiny American flags. They too were blocked by the police, who relieved them of their flags and carried the youths off to a barbed-wire compound. Jackson's black community was seething.

Evers's funeral was spectacular. It was held in the boiling inferno (thanks to the lack of air-conditioning and electric fans) that was the Masonic Hall in the black quarter in Jackson, Mississippi. The four thousand locals – who had squeezed into every seat, into every bit of floor space on the stage, in the aisles, along the walls – turned their faces to the war veteran's flag-draped coffin. Trumpeters arose and began to play. The people sang: 'Be not dismayed, God will take care of you.' When it was over, they lined up to form a cortège behind the coffin and walked two miles to a funeral home. It was the one march for which the white authorities had given black people permission.

Standing in front of the funeral home, a small group began to sing. 'Before I'll be a slave,' they chanted, 'I'll be buried in my grave and go home to my Lord.' Others soon joined in. 'No more killin' here, no more killin' over here.' Soon a whole chorus of swaying, hand-clapping people was sobbing: 'No more Jim Crow over here, over here; I'm dead before I'd be a slave.' As they sang, the police walked towards them, ready to break up the chanting crowd that was preparing to march on City Hall.

They didn't get very far. At the next junction, police with dogs, tear gas and rifles were waiting. Fire engines were there too, their hoses ready. As the mob's momentum carried them towards the police line, some dared the police to fire, chanting, 'Shoot! Shoot! Shoot!' Instead, the police rushed the crowd, nightsticks raised. One police dog jumped and clamped its jaws around a woman's arm. She was grabbed by two policemen who dragged her screaming down the street. (Next day the newspapers said the brave policemen had rescued her from being trampled by the mob.) More screams tore through the air as the police set about breaking bones and spirits. From every direction, patrol cars with wailing sirens poured into the area. Fire engines turned on their hoses. The streets were barricaded. Pushing, clubbing, shoving, cursing, the police beat their way through the throngs and filled their vans. An hour later the riot was over but Jackson still seethed.

Evers's assassination lit a short fuse among the black people of America and rioting spread from town to city. The police upped their readiness at every peace rally in the country and didn't hesitate to quell unrest. In Savannah, Georgia, fighting led to almost a hundred arrests; in Alabama four hundred demonstrators were arrested during a freedom march; in Cambridge, Maryland, National Guardsmen with fixed bayonets patrolled the streets to enforce martial law and a ten p.m. curfew; in Boston more than eight thousand high-school students of all races skipped classes after civil-rights leaders urged a student 'stay out for freedom' protest against segregation in schools. There were riots in St Louis, New York, Atlanta, Charleston (after forty-seven black people were arrested for trespassing after trying to gain access to whites-only cinemas). Three hundred National Guardsmen paraded around Alabama University. In Birmingham, Alabama, Martin Luther King Jr, imprisoned for his part in a peaceful protest, wrote the now famous *Letter from Birmingham Jail*, a defining treatise in his battle against segregation. In the same city later that year, four black girls were killed by a bomb planted at a Baptist Church.

In early July FBI agents arrested Beckwith for the murder of Evers. FBI Director J. Edgar Hoover said that the Golden Hawk telescopic sight had been traced to Beckwith, whose fingerprints matched those on the murder weapon, which had been left at the scene of the crime. His local mayor, Charles E. Sampson, was dismayed: 'We are just stunned. I don't think he's the type. He would always greet you with a smile.' Beckwith still had his defenders in Greenwood, his home town. A community fund drive to pay his legal expenses was started. A businessman said: 'I say the shooting of Evers was a patriotic act. If Delay pulled the trigger that night, he must have felt he was doing it for the South and the State.' A friend of Beckwith's added: 'Beckwith is a Joan of Arc, and his cause is to destroy the evil of forced integration. I don't think he is fit mentally. But Joan of Arc was a little abnormal too.'

Six weeks after Evers's assassination, on 28 August, while Kennedy's Civil Rights Bill was being blocked by the Republicans in Congress, Martin Luther King Jr led more than a quarter of a million people through Washington to the steps of the Lincoln Memorial where he made his iconic 'I have a dream' speech. He told the cheering and emotional crowd: 'I have a dream that one day this nation will rise up and live out the true meaning of its creed: "We hold these truths to be self-evident, that all men are created equal." '

King knew that dream was a long way from becoming reality in the 1960s. The following year, Beckwith was tried before an all-white, all-male jury. It should have been what US lawyers describe as a 'slam-dunk' case. A fingerprint of Beckwith's was found on his rifle's telescopic sight. Prosecution witnesses identified the rifle as Beckwith's. One told of handing over to Beckwith a Japanese-made sight identical to the one on the Enfield in return for a revolver. An FBI expert swore that the fingerprint belonged to Beckwith and to 'no one else in the world'. Both of the Jackson cab drivers told how Beckwith had asked directions to Evers's home. A young woman said that she had seen a car similar to Beckwith's parked near Evers's house fifty minutes before the shooting. In all, thirty-six witnesses gave the prosecution a watertight case.

But for the eleven days of his trial, Beckwith did not seem at all worried. He performed more like a circus clown than a defendant in a first-degree murder case. He propped his feet up on a nearby chair, swigged Coca-Cola, glowered at black newsmen, 'hallooed' to white spectators, was once restrained by a bailiff from sauntering over to the jury box to chat with his peers, and with the exaggerated Southern courtliness upon which he prided himself even offered cigars to Prosecutor William L. Waller.

When the defence's turn came, Chief Counsel Hardy Lott, a former president of Greenwood's White Citizens' Council, which had solicited funds for Beckwith's defence, called twenty witnesses. Two were Greenwood policemen who claimed they had seen Beckwith in Greenwood, a fast ninety-minute drive from Jackson, shortly before and after the killing. The star witness for the defence was Beckwith himself, who punctuated his testimony with soft 'suhs'. 'Did you kill Medgar Evers?' asked Lott. 'No, suh.' Was Beckwith in Jackson on the night of the murder? 'No, suh.' At one point, Lott handed Beckwith the Enfield to examine. Beckwith leaned forward in the witness chair, aimed the gun over the jury's heads and pulled the trigger. He said: 'I couldn't say this is my scope or my gun.' Anyway, Beckwith added pleasantly, his Enfield with a telescopic sight had been stolen from his car two days before Evers was murdered. On cross-examination, Waller brought out Beckwith's militant segregationist sentiments. Beckwith admitted writing a letter to a Jackson newspaper in which he had said: 'I shall bend every effort to rid the US of integrationists, whoever and wherever they may be.'

The prosecution might as well have called Mickey Mouse for all the good it would have done. The trial was rigged. Governor Ross Barnett, formerly Mississippi's best and most expensive lawyer, had long donated his services for free to white-supremacist groups, and he made regular supportive visits to Beckwith in jail. He was also the chairman of the government-funded Mississippi State Sovereignty Commission (MSSC). The commission was created to 'protect the sovereignty of the State of Mississippi and her sister states' from federal government interference. It openly worked to preserve a segregated society and to oppose school integration. In secret, the commission harassed and spied on activists, branding many of them racial agitators and communist infiltrators, and sought to disrupt civil-rights organisations.

The truth about the commission is told here for the first time as its files were only recently declassified.[8] Its first investigators were a former chief of the Mississippi Highway Patrol and a former FBI agent. The commission, which had a yearly budget of a quarter of a million dollars (an extraordinary amount of cash in 1963), collected information through its own agents, a network of spies (which included a bank manager who gave information concerning his black clients), through information exchanges with law enforcement agencies and by working with the white-supremacist Citizens' Council (a private organisation which received $190,000 of taxpayers' money via the MSSC between 1960 and 1964).

One of the most important parts of the trial of Beckwith involved jury selection. The defence team wanted to make sure they had a good selection of white male Protestants who were preferably racist. As the prosecution fought for several days to narrow the choice from 103 possible jurors to fourteen (a jury is made up of twelve people with two 'substitutes' in case one or more of the twelve should fall ill). On 6 April 1964, Stanney Saunders, Beckwith's defence lawyer, contacted A.L. Hopkins, an investigator for the MSSC, passed him the details of the potential jurors and asked him to check their backgrounds – an illegal act which would have seen Saunders struck off and jailed had he been caught. Hopkins worked fast and came

[8] On the night before the release, the building they were being stored in caught fire, which is suggestive of just how sensitive these files are.

back to Saunders on 9 April with his report on which Hopkins based his jury selection. Six or more racist jurors would have been more than enough to bias the trial in Beckwith's favour. Saunders's plan worked. Twice.

The judge, Leon Hendrick, futilely begged the jury: 'Look at this case as if the defendant and the dead man were one and the same race.' But after the all-white, all-male jury had been out for twenty-two hours, they returned to say that they could not agree. They had been split seven to five for acquittal. Judge Hendrick declared a mistrial. Beckwith remained quiet and expressionless as he was returned to his cell, while his lawyers prepared to file a motion to get him out of prison on bail while he awaited a new trial. A second trial also produced a hung jury (all white, all male) and Beckwith was freed. Bob Dylan wrote the song 'Only a Pawn in Their Game' about Evers and a furious Nina Simone released her take on the story with 'Mississippi Goddam'.

It is unlikely that the case of Medgar Evers was the only case where this kind of racial bias occurred. An examination of the records kept by the MSSC dated March 1965 revealed that out of thirty-three racially motivated murders of black people (there are many more where motive has not been clearly established) committed in Mississippi between April 1963 and February 1965, there was only one conviction. Virgil Ware, aged thirteen, was riding his bicycle when he was shot to death by two teenage white boys. They were given a suspended sentence.

The other thirty-two cases weren't short of witnesses or suspects. For example, fifty-two-year-old Frank Norris burned to death in his shop after a group of white men covered him in petrol and barricaded him inside after setting him on fire in full view of passing cars and shoppers. During this period policemen killed at least ten black people. These included the cases of unarmed black teenager James Robinson, aged sixteen, shot in the back by a State Trooper who claimed he was acting in self-defence, and eighteen-year-old Ollie Shelby, beaten and shot to death by police officers while in jail in Jackson.

By 1989 Myrlie Evers-Williams (she remarried in 1975) had become a key member of the US Civil Rights movement, eventually becoming the NAACP's first full-time female Chairperson. She asked Assistant District Attorney Bobby DeLaughter to reopen Medgar Evers's case. DeLaughter and his officers soon came across new evidence, including 'lost' negatives of photos of the crime scene and new witnesses who testified that Beckwith had bragged to them about 'beating the system'. DeLaughter was given the go-ahead to retry Beckwith for the third time in 1990.

Beckwith, who had spent most of his life since Evers's murder living in a trailer park, was seventy-three and in poor health by the time the trial got under way in Jackson in late January 1994. The Klansman's views on race had not changed with age. He said 'I'm proud of my enemies. They're every colour but white, every creed but Christian,' and he defiantly wore a Confederate flag throughout the trial.

This time the MSSC wasn't able to 'help' with jury selection – eight of the twelve jurors were black. The trial severely tested the emotions of the Evers family who were present every day. (Medgar Evers's body was exhumed for a new autopsy; it had been embalmed and was in surprisingly good condition.) When the jury announced their verdict of guilty, Beckwith showed no emotion. But Evers's widow Myrlie and two of their children, Reena Denise and James Van, cheered and embraced in the courtroom. Reporters described a roar that thundered from spectators in a hallway outside. Myrlie said afterwards: 'All I want to say is yeah, Medgar, yeah! I don't have to say "accused assassin" any more.'

Beckwith was given a life sentence. His appeal was rejected by the Mississippi Supreme Court in 1997 and he died in prison of a heart-related illness in 2001. Myrlie, whose eldest son Darrell died of colon cancer that same year, said that Beckwith 'now faces the ultimate judge . . . Beckwith was the epitome of evil, who forever embraced racism and hatred, and who caused so much pain and suffering of so many people.'

*

On 19 June 1963 Kennedy presented his Civil Rights Bill to Congress, urging senators that policies based on race and racial discrimination had no place in American life. But the shared dream of JFK, Medgar Evers and Martin Luther King was still as far away as ever. The Republicans blocked the bill in the Senate, along with Kennedy's tax-reduction and medical-care bills. The Civil Rights Bill would eventually pass the Senate, but this was only thanks to the actions of an assassin.

Seven

JFK Reloaded

At about nine p.m. on 10 April 1963, twenty-three-year-old Lee Harvey Oswald stared through the four-power sight of his twenty-seven-dollar mail-order Mannlicher-Carcano rifle. The young Marxist was crouched in the back garden of the home of avowed commie-hater and pro-segregationist Major General Edwin A. Walker on Turtle Creek Boulevard, a quiet Dallas street. It was Wednesday and the local church round the side of Walker's house was holding its usual midweek services; Oswald was able to approach the house using the crowds as cover and they would, if necessary, help him make his escape. The General, only thirty metres in front of him, was bent over his desk, working on his income-tax returns. All that separated them was the window through which Oswald had a clear view of Walker in his brightly lit room.

Walker was a long-time supporter of pro-segregationist Governors Ross Barnett and George Wallace and joined them in attempts to prevent Medgar Evers from helping twenty-nine-year-old James Meredith to become Mississippi's first-ever coloured student in 1962. Walker had appealed to Americans 'from every state' to march to Barnett's aid which led Attorney General Robert Kennedy to issue a warrant for Walker's arrest on charges of seditious conspiracy, insurrection, and rebellion (he escaped arrest). The lean six-foot-three-inch General, who had seen action in the Second World War and Korea, used the word 'check' whenever he understood or agreed with something. Despite being considered a 'good catch' by high-society women, the General remained a bachelor.[9] Based in Dallas, he gave many speeches around the country denouncing communism and liberalism. In February 1962 Walker stood for governor of Texas. He finished last; John Connally won the race.

Lee Harvey Oswald had selected Walker because he was a nationally known right-wing politician, an enemy of communism and, most importantly, of Oswald's hero, Fidel Castro. (It also helped that he lived locally.) At the time Walker was making front-page news by joining forces with an evangelist in an anti-communist tour called Operation Midnight Ride. Oswald spent a few days staking out Walker's home, taking pictures of the house and nearby railroad tracks, a possible escape route. He used the same camera that his Russian wife Marina used to take photos of him posing in his back garden with his sniper's rifle.

Oswald pulled the trigger. The bullet zipped towards Walker's head but on its way through the window it clipped the frame, changing its trajectory just enough so that it missed the General by a couple of inches and hit the wall in front of him. Walker spun round in his chair. At first, he thought someone had thrown a firecracker through his window as a joke. But the window screen was in place. He got up, walked around the desk and froze as he spotted the bullet hole in the wall in front of him. Walker ran upstairs, got his pistol, dashed back down and out of his back door just in time to see Oswald's car turn a corner and disappear from view. It was only then that the General realised his arm was bleeding from a small wound caused by bullet fragments.

Oswald returned home, not knowing whether his single shot had killed Walker or not. His wife Marina asked him where he had been, and Oswald proudly told her that he had tried to shoot General Walker. Marina, furious, asked him how he dared to take

[9] In 1976 Walker was arrested for public lewdness in a Dallas park toilet and accused of fondling an undercover policeman; he pleaded no contest and was fined $1,000.

somebody's life. Oswald replied, 'Well, what would you say if somebody got rid of Hitler at the right time? So if you don't know about General Walker, how can you speak up on his behalf?'

At the time, the police had no idea who'd attempted to kill Walker. The General had some suspects but they all turned out to have alibis. Marina saw Oswald burn most of his plans for the assassination in the bath, though she hid the note he left her in a cookbook. The note had been meant for her if her husband were killed or captured and she intended to give it to the police should Oswald attempt again to kill Walker or anyone else.

Two years before the attempted assassination of Walker, Operation Zapata (also known as the Bay of Pigs), the US-led invasion of Cuba, had taken place. It was aborted after Kennedy decided not to send in the US Marines and Air Force to support the Cuban exile rebels fighting on the ground. Thousands of Cubans lost their lives but Fidel Castro remained in control of the country. The badly planned raid, led by the CIA, was deeply embarrassing for President Kennedy. CIA director Allen Dulles, Deputy CIA Director Charles Cabell and Deputy Director of Operations Richard Bissell were all forced to resign. Lee Harvey Oswald, meanwhile, saw Castro as a hero, and swore that if he ever had the chance he would strike out at Kennedy as the President had done at the embattled Cuban leader.

Lee Harvey Oswald was small, wiry and ugly, a failure both financially and emotionally, rejected by every organisation he ever tried to join. Fatherless, he was raised in a series of chaotic homes by his mother and attended twelve different schools before he was eighteen. The constant moving affected both his mental health and his schooling; he was close to being dyslexic and was once diagnosed with some symptoms of schizophrenia. Despite this, Oswald's mother insisted that he was a man with a great destiny. He became a committed Marxist at the age of fifteen, something that didn't go down too well with his Marine 'comrades' after he signed up when he was seventeen. His military record is less than impressive – on one occasion he accidentally shot himself in the elbow with a small, unauthorised handgun. After being punished for this infraction he started a fight with the sergeant he held responsible for his unjust treatment. Another time, while on sentry duty, he was caught firing his rifle into the night for no reason.

After leaving the Marines, Oswald sought sanctuary by defecting to Russia where he assumed that the Russians would welcome him as a communist hero. Instead they did their best to reject the young wannabe revolutionary until Oswald made a poor attempt at slitting his wrists; fearful of the bad press if he should try again and succeed, they let him stay. Oswald met his future wife in Minsk. Marina was a pretty but troubled nineteen-year-old who had been forced to live with her uncle and aunt after her parents' traumatic break-up. After a year, bored with Russia, Oswald returned to the USA where he alternately beat his wife and begged her forgiveness. In turn, she rejected and taunted him.

Oswald had tried to assassinate Walker ten days after being fired from a dead-end factory job. With only enough money for the family for two weeks, he needed to find another job fast. Then, at the end of the two weeks, a friend of Marina's found him work at the Texas School Book Depository as an order-filler. By now, Dallas newspapers were reporting almost daily about the impending visit of President Kennedy. On 19 November the *Times-Herald* described the precise route that President Kennedy would take through downtown Dallas. Shortly after noon, the motorcade was going to pass by the building where Oswald had by then been working for a month.

Oswald suddenly found himself confronted with the great destiny he had always believed was his. This was his chance to show his family, friends, enemies, the Russians, the commie-haters that he was a revolutionary capable of carrying out the most daring of political acts. All his life had been a rehearsal for this opportunity, this moment. The same fantasist who had gone to the Soviet Union expecting to be accepted as a hero now thought that he would become a hero in Cuba as the assassin of Castro's number one enemy.

On 21 November 1963, Oswald went to bed early. Marina followed a few hours later without speaking to him, although she suspected that he was awake. The next morning Oswald arose first, leaving his wedding ring in a cup on the chest of drawers and placing a hundred and seventy dollars in a wallet in one of the drawers. As he left the house he picked up a brown package about four feet long. He walked the short distance to co-worker Wesley Frazier's house and they got into Frazier's car. When asked about the package, Oswald replied simply, 'Curtain rods.' At the book depository, Oswald was seen several times looking down from the windows onto Dealey Plaza. He asked a co-worker why crowds were gathering in the area and when told that President Kennedy's motorcade would be passing by in a couple of hours, Oswald replied, 'Oh, I see.'

John F. Kennedy was in Dallas for two reasons. First, he had lost the state of Texas to the Republican candidate Richard Nixon in the close-fought campaign of 1960. With an election due in 1964, Kennedy wanted to win over the Texans. He was also there to fund-raise.

When Air Force One landed at Dallas's Love Field, the President and the First Lady stepped off into the brilliant crisp sunshine and greeted the crowd before everyone proceeded to their assigned vehicles, each of which was marked with a number indicating its position in the upcoming parade. The Kennedys were supposed to be in the number seven position, in the middle of the motorcade, but due to a mix-up they got into the number one car which placed them up front – journalists and photographers were annoyed to discover they had been placed in number fourteen, the last car in the procession.

JFK climbed into his car's right-rear seat with Jackie on his left. In the middle seats, Texas Governor John B. Connally sat directly in front of the President, with his wife next to him. Up front, the driver, veteran Secret Service Agent Bill Greer, had thirty-five years of experience. During the planning of the trip, there had been much discussion about whether the President's car should have the bubble-top in place. The President went against the Secret Service's wishes and asked that the car should be left open in the glorious sunshine.

Conservative Dallas was supposed to be downright dangerous for JFK and the possibility of a rooftop sniper had been the subject of a discussion between the President and his agents. But he had just come from a warm airport welcome and Kennedy was relieved to see that along much of his motorcade route in the downtown district he had basked in waves of applause from huge crowds.

The motorcade, flanked by motorcycle outriders, drove for more than thirty minutes from Love Field to the centre of Dallas; a quarter of a million people were standing in a line thirty deep along the route. An eight-year-old girl was holding a placard that said: 'President Kennedy . . . will you shake hands with me?' Kennedy ordered the car to stop and shook hands with the little girl; the car was mobbed by well-wishers.

As the procession neared Main Street, a man ran towards the presidential limousine and a Secret Service agent immediately wrestled him to the ground – the indignant man had just wanted to shake the President's hand.

At the corner of Elm and Houston Streets, the motorcade almost stopped as it negotiated a 120-degree left turn onto Elm Street, where the road heads down an incline toward an underpass. The crowds were thinner at this point but still enthusiastic as, at twelve-thirty p.m., the motorcade entered Dealey Plaza. Even though the crowds had thinned, Kennedy continued to smile and wave, as Mrs Connally, shielding her eyes from the bright sunlight, turned and said: 'Mr President, you can't say that Dallas doesn't love you.' JFK replied: 'That is very obvious.'

There was a crack. A full-metal-jacket bullet, specifically designed to pass through the human body and travelling at about 518m/s, pierced President Kennedy's back and exited via his throat, just below his Adam's apple. He started to choke and lifted his hands to his neck.

Almost at the same moment, John Connally jerked to his right.

The bullet that had ripped through Kennedy was still travelling at 457m/s and blasted into the senator's back just below his right armpit. It completely shattered his fifth right rib bone and exited just below his right nipple, leaving a gaping wound that hissed as air blew out from his lung. Now travelling at 274m/s the bullet passed through the senator's right wrist, shattering the bones, and hit his left thigh at 122m/s where it sat just below the skin.

Jackie leaned forward to see what had happened to her husband. 'Jack!' his wife cried. 'Oh, no! No!' Greer slowed the car, anxious not to drive into an ambush. A woman close by at the kerb saw what had happened. 'My God!' she screamed. 'He's shot.'

As soon as he heard gunfire, Secret Serviceman Clint Hill, riding in the car immediately behind Kennedy's, jumped out and started sprinting towards the presidential limo. There was another crack. The bullet had missed. Hill knew he had maybe two seconds to cover the President before the assassin had time to re-aim. He reached for the small handrail by the boot, put there specifically for bodyguards to use to climb onto the car.

At that moment, there was another crack, and the right side of Kennedy's head exploded in a cloud of blood. Officer Hargis, riding on a motorcycle behind and slightly to the left of Kennedy, was splattered with brain matter.

Connally cried, 'Oh God! They are going to kill us all!' His wife Nellie pulled her husband back onto her lap, out of the line of fire, and then bent down over him, covering him with her body. Jackie Kennedy, clearly in shock, climbed onto the boot of the limo, frantically trying to retrieve pieces of her husband's skull and brain while Hill desperately scrabbled aboard. He pushed Mrs Kennedy back into the seat, and then covered both her and the President with his body.

A photographer looked up at the Texas School Book Depository and caught a glimpse of a rifle barrel being withdrawn from a window on the sixth floor.

There was a shocked, momentary stillness, a frozen tableau. Then Hill shouted, 'To the hospital! To the hospital!' Kennedy's driver cried: 'Let's get out of here quick!' He automatically pulled out of the motorcade – the set procedure in emergencies. The Secret Service agent next to him grabbed the radio telephone, called ahead to the police escorts, and ordered them to make for the nearest hospital.

Jackie bent low, cradling her husband's head in her lap, 'Jack, Jack, can you hear me? I love you, Jack.' She tried to press his skull back into place, to keep the brains in. The Lincoln bolted ahead as if the shots themselves had gunned the engine into life. Accelerating to seventy miles an hour it fled down the highway, rounding curves on two wheels.

Hill, in his anger and frustration, pounded the car repeatedly with his fist. He could clearly see a large piece of Kennedy's brain lying below him on the back seat. Jackie Kennedy was coated in blood. The next car in line, an open touring sedan containing agents bristling with weapons, followed swiftly. In the third car, an open convertible carrying Lyndon and Lady Bird Johnson and Texas's Democratic Senator Ralph Yarborough, security agents yelled for the passengers to duck low, and that car followed in wild pursuit.

At 12.36 p.m. the President's car came to a halt in front of the emergency entrance at Parkland Memorial Hospital. Connally struggled to his feet to make way for the President and collapsed on the floor. Jacqueline Kennedy, proving that she had courage enough for a dozen, calmly continued to cradle her husband. Stretchers were brought out. Jackie, her pink skirt and stockings soaked with blood, helped get the President out of the car and, her hand on his chest, walked into the hospital beside him as he was wheeled inside.

Policemen surrounded the hospital entrance as the crowds thickened. A guard was set up around the Lincoln as Secret Service men got a pail of water and tried to wash the blood from the car. The sprays of red roses and asters that Jackie Kennedy and Nellie Connally had been given at the airport lay forlorn on the floor. Vice-President Lyndon Johnson walked into the emergency clinic holding his hand over his heart, giving rise briefly to rumours that he had either been wounded or was suffering from a heart attack. Neither was the case: Lyndon was simply profoundly stunned.

Meanwhile, at the assassination scene, that first moment of stillness gave way to frantic, confused movement. At the sound of the gunfire, bystanders grabbed children and fell over them to blanket them. Newsmen aboard the press bus far back in the procession yelled for the driver to stop, while others told him to keep moving. The bus jolted ahead, past horrified faces, frantically running figures, huddling women. A cop dropped to the ground and drew his revolver. A man fell on a grassy knoll, beating the earth with both fists in mindless fury. A heavy-set policeman began running, tripped, fell, scrambled to his feet, lumbered on. Motorcycle patrolmen and police cars stopped dead in their tracks. Officers got out, guns drawn, searching for anything that would lead them to the assassin.

Just after the presidential car sped off, the Schoolbook Warehouse Superintendent Roy Truly, who had just stepped outside his building into the crush of well-wishers on Elm Street, saw a motorcycle cop running through the crowd, knocking people out of the way as he made for the door of his warehouse. Truly joined him and led him to the elevator. An upstairs elevator gate was open, immobilising the whole system.

Truly bounded up a staircase with the cop behind him, his revolver drawn. Off the second-floor landing the cop saw a lunch room. He ran inside and saw a man standing next to a Coke machine. It was Lee Harvey Oswald. The cop asked Truly: 'This boy work here?' Truly said yes. At that the officer wheeled and ran up the steps, somehow convinced that any sniper in the building must be a stranger and not an employee.

Carrying his Coke, Oswald ambled into a nearby office. A switchboard operator said, 'Wasn't that terrible – the President being shot?' Oswald mumbled something unintelligible, went out of the office, walked down the steps and slipped through the crowd outside. He walked for several blocks, doubled back to Elm Street, approached a bus, rapped on the door and was admitted by the driver even though it was not a regular stop. The bus soon got snarled in a traffic jam caused by the excitement of the shooting. A motorist who was stalled in front of the bus got out and went back to tell the driver what had happened. Oswald took the opportunity to get out.

Meanwhile, the police had surrounded the schoolbook warehouse. Dozens of them poured inside carrying shotguns and began a room-to-room search. And near the fifth-floor landing, half-hidden behind crates of textbooks, they found an Italian-made 6.5mm rifle fitted with a four-power telescopic sight. One flight above, near a sixth-floor window only seventy-five yards from the point where Kennedy and Connally had been shot, they discovered the remnants of a chicken dinner in a bag, an empty bottle, and three spent cartridge cases. The assassin was gone.

Back at the hospital, Connally was quiet and calm in his pain as surgeons prepared to operate. His aide, Bill Stinson, blurted, 'How did it happen?' Connally said: 'I don't know.'

'Where'd they get you?'

'I think they shot me from the back. They shot the President too. Take care of Nellie.' For four hours the doctors worked, cleaning the wounds, removing bone splinters from the Governor's chest cavity, stitching a hole in one lung, treating the wounds in his thigh and wrist. He would survive. Outside, on the stretcher that had been used to wheel the senator in, was a single bullet, its tip squashed blunt. It was picked up by hospital engineer Darrell Tomlinson.

In emergency room number one, a team of surgeons was hastily assembled to save the President's life. Dr Paul Peters recalled: 'My first thought was "My God, he is dead". A considerable portion of the skull, of the brain was gone.' The President was not breathing and there was no heartbeat. The wound in his throat was small and neat, with blood running out of it. At the back of his head a huge flap of loose skull bone exposed his brain; blood flowed out and onto the floor. As soon as Dr Kemp Clark, the thirty-eight-year-old chief neurosurgeon, arrived, he saw that there was no hope.

At 12.45 p.m. two Roman Catholic priests went swiftly into the emergency room. A policeman came out. 'How is he?' a reporter asked. 'He's dead,' came the reply. Assistant Press Secretary Malcolm Kilduff appeared. In answer to a deluge of questions he screamed, 'I can't say, I just can't say!'

At one p.m., after another ten minutes of external chest compressions, Clark said: 'It's too late.' The Very Reverend Oscar Huber drew back a sheet that covered the President's face and anointed Kennedy's forehead with oil. He gave him conditional absolution – tendered when a priest has no way of knowing the victim's mind or whether the soul has yet left the body. Then he covered the President's face once more with the sheet and in English offered the Roman Catholic prayers for the Dying and for the Departed Soul. Jacqueline Kennedy stood next to the President's body, and in a clear voice prayed with the others: 'Our Father, Who art in Heaven . . .' and 'Hail, Mary, full of grace . . .'

Back at the scene of the assassination, a boy gave police a description of a man who had been seen leaving the building a few minutes earlier. At 12.36 p.m. an all-points bulletin went out over the radio to watch for a 'white male, about five foot, ten inches tall, weighing 160 to 165 pounds, about thirty years old'.

At East 10th Street, approximately four miles from the warehouse, Patrolman J.D. Tippit, thirty-eight years old, driving alone in a squad car, heard the call. Almost immediately he spotted a young man walking towards him: his height and weight matched the description. He had kinky brown hair, a prominent forehead, thick eyebrows, a crimped, tight mouth, and a defiant air. Something caught Tippit's attention. The suspect was sweating, yet he was wearing a jacket with the zip done up. (It was twenty degrees Celsius outside but Oswald was trying to conceal the .38 calibre revolver he had stuffed into his waistband.)

Tippit spoke to Oswald through the passenger window. He then got out of the car, his hand resting casually on the butt of his gun. Oswald pulled his own weapon and shot Tippit four times, hitting him in the head, chest and abdomen. Then he fled, leaving the officer to die on the pavement. A short while later, Tippit's wife found out she was a widow while watching the TV coverage of the assassination. It was 1.18 p.m.

A bystander jumped into Tippit's patrol car and managed to call police headquarters. 'Hello? Police Operator? We've had a shooting out here . . .'

Seven blocks and seven minutes away, the cashier at the Texas Movie Theater telephoned police to report that a suspicious-looking man had entered the movie house and was constantly changing seats. At 1.35 p.m. four cops entered the theatre, where the movie – *War Is Hell* – was just starting. The lights went up. Oswald rose and cried: 'This is it!' He aimed his revolver at one policeman and pulled the trigger – but the weapon failed to fire. The cops jumped him and there was a fierce but brief struggle. The assassin was carried off kicking and screaming. He kept kicking all the way to police headquarters.

Lyndon Johnson, guarded by contingents of agents, was hurried away from the hospital to the airport. He ordered that the announcement of Kennedy's death should be made only after he, Johnson, had left the hospital, in case his life was in danger from an international conspiracy. Preparations were already under way for him to be sworn in as the new President.

Malcolm Kilduff came out of the hospital at 1.36 p.m. His eyes red-rimmed, his voice barely controlled, he said: 'President John F. Kennedy died at approximately one p.m. Central Standard Time here in Dallas. He died of a gunshot wound in the brain. I have no other details of the assassination.'

Soon a white Cadillac hearse drew up in front of the entrance and a simple bronze casket was taken inside the hospital. Jackie removed the wedding band from her left hand and slipped it on the President's finger, and then the casket was closed. Mrs Kennedy wanted to return immediately to Washington. The casket, with Jackie walking alongside, her hand on its burnished surface, was carried outside. At

Dallas's Love Field, the presidential plane was waiting. As the plane flew, Johnson was sworn in as President of the United States: the oaths of office were administered by Federal Judge Sarah Hughes, who was in tears throughout the entire ceremony. Jackie Kennedy watched, still dressed in her bloodstained pink suit. She refused to change. 'Let them see what they've done,' she said.

The first TV announcement to the nation came at 1.38 p.m. from CBS newsreader Walter Cronkite who had interviewed Kennedy on several occasions. His newsroom was packed with almost everyone who worked at the station, from janitors to affiliates, as he broke the news to the country moments after it came in from the Associated Press in Dallas.

'From Dallas, Texas, the flash, apparently official: President Kennedy died at one p.m. Central Standard Time, two p.m. Eastern Standard Time, some thirty-eight minutes ago.' At this point Cronkite paused, obviously shocked, fighting for composure; he cleared his throat and continued. 'Vice-President Lyndon Johnson has left the hospital in Dallas, but we do not know to where he has proceeded. Presumably, he will be taking the oath of office shortly and will become the thirty-sixth President of the United States.'

At that moment, Jack Ruby, a fleshy, balding bachelor of fifty-two, was sitting at a desk in the display advertising department of the *Dallas Morning News*, working on an advertisement designed to promote the outstanding virtues of his droop-bosomed Carousel Club strippers. He stopped dead, incredulous upon hearing the news. He went into another office to watch television, then went back to his ad copy. Finally he returned to his strip club and wrote the word CLOSED across the front of his billboards outside.

Ruby spent the rest of the day in stupefied silence. He believed that the Communists had sent Oswald to kill Kennedy. His shock simmered into anger as he thought about how Jackie had suffered, and how the Kennedy children Caroline and John Jr had lost their father. At three a.m. the next morning, he woke his fifty-year-old bachelor room-mate George Senator, a former dirty-postcard salesman, to talk to him about the assassination. He then called his brothers in a distressed state, fingering the revolver he always carried, watching the TV.

The next day Ruby headed for police headquarters, where he organised sandwiches and coffee for the newsmen who were swarming about. In a way he had become a recognisable but unrecognised part of the interior decoration. One of eight children of Russian and Polish immigrants, Jack Rubenstein was born and raised in the 'Bloody 20th' ward of Chicago's West Side and never finished high school. He liked to think that he had connections with racketeers and he affected the sharp dress of the big-time mobsters – the white-on-white shirts and ties, pearl-grey hats, fake diamond pinkie ring. He loved name-dropping the city's most infamous hoodlums.

But the big-timers never even knew he existed. He was a 'novelty salesman', a man who would sell virtually anything, even if it was a little hot. He peddled cigars, janitorial supplies, calendars; he had a fondness for patriotic souvenirs such as little statues of General MacArthur.

Then, for a while, Jack turned organiser for the racketeer-infested Waste Material Handlers' Union. His union career was short-lived. He was admitted to the Army Air Force during the Second World War, served three inconspicuous years and returned to whatever buck-producing activity he could find. For a while he touted tickets for sporting events and boxed for a short time under the name 'Sparkling Ruby', earning the nickname 'Sparky'.

Like his three brothers, Jack legally changed his surname to Ruby. In 1949 he went to Dallas to help out a sister who was running a two-bit nightclub. He played bartender for a while and then took over management of the Carousel and spent much of his time begging newspapers for publicity. Ruby was picked up twice for carrying a concealed weapon, and occasionally for violation of state liquor laws and of the city dance-hall ordinances. But Ruby loved the company of cops and hung around police headquarters, becoming a familiar figure. He was also a health nut; he was particularly worried about hair loss and had sought the services of a Dallas trichologist.

On Sunday morning, 24 November, Jack Ruby got up early, took his regular morning swim in the pool at his apartment house (wearing a bathing cap in an attempt to prevent further baldness), then headed for police headquarters. Dallas Police Chief Jesse Curry, mostly bowing to the demands of television crewmen that they should be allowed to set up their cameras in time to see anything and everything that might happen to Oswald, announced that Oswald would be transferred at ten a.m. to the county jail. The publicised plan called for Oswald to be moved in an armoured car from the basement garage at headquarters. This was a subterfuge, for Curry really intended to use the armoured vehicle as a decoy, spiriting Oswald away in an unmarked police car. The police checked the garage area and the ante-room through which Oswald would be escorted. Parked cars were examined, and everybody was shooed out of the garage. Then police admitted dozens of newsmen, screening them carefully.

They were not careful enough. Because he had become such a familiar part of the scenery, Jack Ruby was deemed by reporters to be with the police and by the police to be with the reporters. At eleven a.m. a knot of detectives and uniformed cops took Oswald out of his carefully guarded security cell on the fifth floor. His hands were manacled, and for extra safety Homicide Detective James Leavelle cuffed himself to Oswald. 'If anybody shoots at you,' said Leavelle, 'I hope that they are as good a shot as you are.' Oswald sniggered: 'Nobody's going to shoot at me.'

Down in the elevator and into the garage came Oswald and his guards, heading for the armoured car. Somebody shouted, 'Here they come!' Newsreel cameras whirred. Live TV cameras watched the action and flashed the scene instantaneously across the nation's television sets. Precisely twelve seconds after Oswald appeared, Ruby ducked out from his position among the newsmen. A detective recognised him and spotted the gun. 'Jack!' he cried. 'You crazy son of a bitch!' As the cop spoke, Ruby pointed his .38 at Oswald and fired one shot, point-blank, through Oswald's abdomen. JFK's assassin died a hundred minutes later from internal haemorrhaging at Parkland General Hospital, forty-eight hours – less seven minutes – after the same doctors had tended to JFK.

The much-derided Warren Commission, set up in the immediate aftermath of the assassination (one of its members was Gerald Ford who, as President from 1974–76, was to find himself the target of two female assassins), concluded that Oswald was the assassin and had acted alone. The House Select Committee on Assassination, set up some time after the Warren Commission, did an incredibly thorough job and listened to and tested all the conspiracy theories of the time and also concluded that Oswald assassinated Kennedy, probably as the result of a conspiracy. However, the committee noted that it believed that the conspiracy did not include the governments of the Soviet Union or Cuba, nor the FBI, the CIA, or the Secret Service. It also stated it did not believe the conspiracy was orchestrated by any organised-crime group, nor any anti-Castro group, but that it could not rule out individual members of either of those groups acting together. But the conspiracy part of the HSCA's findings was based on acoustic evidence which was later found to be unreliable (more on this later).

So the end result of the official investigations is that Oswald fired the shots that killed Kennedy and injured Governor Connally. Not good enough, say innumerable conspiracists who have made countless conjectures about the assassination. That we now look for conspiracies in assassinations is of course thanks to Lee Harvey Oswald. Who could accept the idea that this short, scrawny young man with unkempt hair and cheap white T-shirt assassinated John F. Kennedy, one of the most popular, charismatic and gifted leaders in the world, without any help?

More than forty years on, there are a great many theories but still no concrete evidence that conclusively supports a conspiracy, or the conjecture that Oswald didn't fire the shots that killed JFK. Despite this, a poll carried out on the fortieth anniversary of the assassination in 2003 by ABC News found that only ten per cent of one thousand interviewees thought that Oswald was the shooter and there was no conspiracy. This was no doubt thanks to the legions of conspiracy theorists who have so far produced almost five hundred books, countless essays, websites and documentaries along with one Hollywood blockbuster. All of this has done a pretty good job of convincing us that the US government is hiding something, that there was a conspiracy orchestrated by either the Mafia, the CIA, Khrushchev or Castro, or a combination thereof, to take the President's life.

The question is, though, what evidence do conspiracy researchers put forward and how reliable is it?[10] First of all, dozens of amateur investigations, JFK books and perhaps most influentially, Oliver Stone's *JFK* tell us that there were many witnesses who heard shots coming from the Grassy Knoll in Dealey Plaza, the open piece of land opposite the school book depository. Conspiracists who argue that Oswald was a dumb patsy believe that a second shooter fired the shots that killed Kennedy from the Grassy Knoll. In Oliver Stone's *JFK* and in several conspiracy books, we are told that no less than fifty-one witnesses heard shots coming from the Grassy Knoll. Sounds like a convincing case for a shooter on the Knoll, doesn't it? But close examination of the data reveals that the conspiracy theorists have gone to some dubious and decidedly unscientific lengths to get people on that Grassy Knoll list.

Stewart Galanor, author of *Coverup*, claims fifty-two Knoll witnesses (the HSCA reckoned there were twenty), although he concedes there were forty-eight Depository witnesses. Galanor decided to classify every witness who thought they might have seen smoke in Dealy Plaza as a Knoll witness (whether cigarette smoke, vehicle exhaust or steam) but didn't exclude any of these witnesses

[10] The interested reader could do no better than go and consult John Adams's website: http://mcadams.posc.mu.edu/. This is arguably the finest and most thorough Kennedy assassination site in existence; it provided me with an invaluable jumping-off point into the chasm of Kennedy conspiracies.

who said they didn't hear any shots coming from the Knoll. Now, smoke seen on or near the Knoll might sound convincing as evidence for a second shooter but there is one significant flaw with this theory: modern guns don't produce smoke.

When directing JFK, Oliver Stone couldn't find a gun that gave off a half-decent cloud anywhere, so had someone pump smoke out of a pair of bellows. 'An appropriate metaphor for the entire film, say some researchers,' wrote JFK assassination aficionado John Adams.

To date, assassinologists have listed and proven more than one hundred significant factual inaccuracies in *JFK*, a film that has done much to increase the belief of people across the world that there was a conspiracy and that Oswald did not shoot the President. (It has also helped to boost sales of conspiracy-theory books.) The one positive thing to come from this movie was the passing of the 1992 JFK Assassination Records Collection Act, created after the public outrage that *JFK* caused. (Needless to remind you, *JFK* is a work of fiction, using invented dialogue and made-up characters, that takes bits from a variety of conspiracy theory books who all have their own entirely different ideas.) Thanks to the JFK Assassination Records Collection Act, millions more pages on the assassination have been made public and simply reinforce the idea that Oswald acted alone; none, so far, have shed any light on any conspiracy despite some people's claims.

Back to the eyewitness testimony for a moment. Unfortunately, as has been proven time and time again by experimental psychologists, lawyers, judges and policemen, eyewitness testimony can be very unreliable. Factors such as poor viewing conditions, brief exposure, stress, expectations, biases, and personally held stereotypes create erroneous reports. Memory can be radically altered by the way an eyewitness is questioned after the fact. New memories can be implanted and old ones unconsciously altered under interrogation. For example, in 2002 a team of psychologists led by the renowned memory expert Elizabeth Loftus got over a third of subjects who had been to Disneyland to say that they shook hands with Bugs Bunny while there (Bugs Bunny is not a Disney character). But, surely, to have been present at the JFK assassination would be considerably more dramatic than a trip to Disneyland? Wouldn't witnesses retain crystal-clear memories of that extreme event?

Well, sadly, no. Shock caused by witnessing a traumatic event causes amnesia; danger also increases heart rate and adrenalin release. Once this reaches a certain point, around 175 heartbeats per minute, there is an absolute breakdown of cognitive processing, the forebrain shuts down, and the mid-brain, the most primitive part of the brain – one that humans share with cats and dogs – takes over. This is why it is impossible to have a rational discussion with someone who's frightened – it's the same as talking to your dog. People in a state of fear, as many clearly were on 22 November 1963 as they instinctively ran for cover or dived on their children, make notoriously unreliable witnesses.

Memory can also be affected by information added after an event is observed. In the case of the Kennedy assassination and the subsequent Warren Commission and HSCA, eyewitnesses would have read and seen so much about the assassination that it is more than likely that some memories would have become distorted. And given the leading questions of conspiracy theorists and Warren Commission investigators, mixed with observers' desire to be helpful, eyewitnesses will often tell people what they want to hear. This is not to say that all testimony from such sources is worthless, simply that it might not be as reliable as conspiracy researchers assume.

For example, in a well-replicated experiment, subjects were divided into two groups. The first group was asked 'Do you get headaches frequently, and if so how often?' The second group was asked 'Do you get headaches occasionally, and if so how often?' The first group reported twenty-five per cent more headaches than the second – they were responding to inbuilt bias in the question. Now for the Kennedy data. Incredibly, seventy-eight per cent of those who were asked 'Did you hear gunshots come from the Grassy Knoll?' answered 'Yes' while seventy-two per cent of those who were asked 'Where did the gunshots come from?' answered that the shots came from the Depository.

Numerous witnesses who changed their testimony and leaped on the conspiracy bandwagon started remembering all sorts of things from Dealey Plaza. Someone saw Jack Ruby with a gun, a woman recalled a little dog in the limousine between JFK and his wife (she also described seeing a shooter standing on the Grassy Knoll), someone saw a man running away with an object that could have been a rifle, and another man saw two men, one firing a gun from behind a stockade, the other disassembling it. A witness who claimed to have been on the Grassy Knoll said he heard a shot whiz past his ear and then had his camera confiscated and another man claimed to have seen a Secret Service agent on the Grassy Knoll (this later turned out to be a simple case of mistaken identity). If all these witnesses were correct, then several shooters were in Dealey Plaza on 22 November.

As for the *physical* evidence of there being one or more shooters on the Grassy Knoll who fired at Kennedy, there is none. There is, however, overwhelming evidence that the shots were fired from behind the motorcade. Several witnesses saw a shooter – or at least a gun – in the sixth-floor sniper's nest window. The medical evidence is clear that both Kennedy and Connally were hit from behind (more of this later). It is hard to see how shots could also have come from the Grassy Knoll, in front of the motorcade, without more witnesses reporting shots from more than one direction. Only eight per cent of witnesses heard shots coming from *both* directions, which is very suggestive.

But how many shots *did* the witnesses hear? 76.7 per cent heard three, 8.7 per cent heard four or more and 10.5 per cent heard one or two. Most conspiracists need at least five shots to prove their theories. The bullet that gives them particular trouble is the one that hit JFK in the head, which was fired from behind (from the Depository), something which even those who favour conspiracy have been forced to concede. To support theories of a head-shot from the Grassy Knoll, Kennedy would have to have been hit in the head from the front as well as the back. As for the bullet which passed through Kennedy's back, out of his neck and hit Connally, some researchers have separated it into three separate bullets. They argue that the first hit Kennedy in the back and stopped there while a second bullet fired from the Grassy Knoll hit Kennedy in the throat and a third bullet fired from behind hit Connally in the back. These mysterious 'bullets' were never found, which only added fuel to the conspiracists' fire – all too often if something that would support their theories can't be found then it has been 'covered up'.

If there were other shooters apart from Oswald, then who were they? One of the more bizarre theories was that a man holding an open umbrella fired a flechette (poisoned dart) that hit the president in the throat, paralysing Kennedy to set him up for the head shot.

Now, this does seem a little suspicious at first glance; the 'Umbrella Man' can be seen as clear as anything on the Zapruder Film (more on this in a moment). November 22 was a warm, clear day with not a rain-cloud in sight. Unfortunately for the conspiracists, the Umbrella Man (real name Louis Witt) was tracked down by the HSCA who were amused to discover that he was simply exercising his right to political protest. The only problem was that it was so obscure that nobody got it. The umbrella was supposed to represent the Nazi appeasement policies of UK Prime Minister Neville Chamberlain (he always carried a brolly and he too was known as the 'Umbrella Man'), policies which JFK's father had supported. Although this is in itself an odd explanation, it is a much more likely one than a poison-dart-shooting umbrella (surely a smaller device or more inconspicuous device could have been used on a sunny day – one of Gottlieb's dart-firing pens perhaps?) which would require precision timing: it would have been madness to entrust such an incredible assassination to a man with an umbrella. If Kennedy had so much as turned his head, Jackie would have got the poisoned dart, not her husband.

Then there were the three hobos, the tramps who were close by at the time of the shooting and were brought in for questioning by an enthusiastic FBI agent. They have since been accused of carrying out the assassination and have been given all sorts of identities, from former President George Bush Senior to the hit-man Charles Voyde Harrelson (see page 220). But the men, who in the words of the HSCA looked as though they had 'been fired from a cannon through a Salvation Army thrift shop', really were tramps. They were tracked down by researchers in 2003 who matched their fingerprints to their 1963 charge sheets. The men had by then, forty years later, stopped being tramps and were leading very normal lives.

And what about the image of a man, supposedly Oswald, who was skulking in the doorway of the Book Depository at the same time the shots were fired in Dealey Plaza? Some conspiracy theorists still cling to this blurry picture as conclusive proof that Oswald didn't fire the shots; it can be found on dozens of websites. Professor James Fetzer, no less, wrote in his book *Murder in Dealey Plaza*: 'A man many people think strongly resembles Lee Harvey Oswald is pictured standing in the front entrance of the Book Depository Building. If it is, in fact, Oswald, he could not have been on the sixth floor of the building when the shots were fired . . . The identity of the man in the photo has never been clearly established.' Wrong. The man in the photo is Billy Nolan Lovelady, one of eight witnesses who testified to this effect to the HSCA. Three separate pieces of amateur film footage all clearly reveal that the man in the doorway is clearly not Oswald.

The Zapruder film. It's the most famous, important piece of home movie footage ever recorded. It was made even more famous in the film *JFK*, where lawyer Jim Garrison shows the film to an audience for the first time. To make his point that the bullets could not have come from behind the President he rewinds the film time and again to the point of impact: 'Back, and to the Left. Back, and to the Left. Back, and to the Left.'

It's supposed to prove that Kennedy was hit in the head by a shot fired from the front from the Grassy Knoll. Obviously the head wouldn't move backwards if it was hit from behind, it would move forwards, right? Wrong. An object hit by a bullet will sometimes react by moving in the direction from which the bullet was fired. And some of the US's foremost experts in forensics and wound ballistics do not agree that a bullet fired from the Grassy Knoll would have driven Kennedy's head 'back and to the left'. This was demonstrated by physicist Luis Alvarez and Dr John Lattimer, who fired the same ammo using the same rifle as Oswald at human skulls. These results have been replicated many times since, using everything from melons to goats.

Those who support the Grassy Knoll shot tend to change their testimony as it suits them from case to case. Forensic Pathologist Cyril Wecht stated that Kennedy's 'back and to the left' motion clearly demonstrated that a shot must have come from the Grassy Knoll. When he appeared as an expert witness in another trial, he insisted that it was bad science to use basic physics to try and tell how a body will react after being shot.

But what about the Magic Bullet, the supposedly 'pristine' bullet found on Connally's stretcher at Parkland Hospital? Most conspiracy books show only one photo of the bullet – side-on where it does indeed look in pretty good condition. What they don't show is the photo taken from above the tip, which is squashed flat. They also don't mention the ballistic tests that show that the non-fatal bullet wounds to Kennedy and Connally were caused by the same shell.

In one recent test, set up by the Discovery Channel, two mannequin figures made of ballistic anatomical substances (animal skin, gelatin, and interior bone-like casts) were set up in the exact position of JFK and Connally. A marksman, at a distance equal to that from the sixth floor of the Book Depository Building, fired the same rifle model found in the Book Depository, using a round from the same batch of the same Western Case Cartridge Company 6.5x52mm ammunition purchased with the surplus Carcano weapon in early 1963. (Three expended brass shell cases and one live round had been found with the Carcano in the Book Depository.) The path of their single bullet (followed by high-speed photography) and its impact duplicated, almost exactly, the profile of the wounds suffered by the victims that day, the only difference being that the bullet did not have quite enough energy to penetrate the 'thigh' substance in front of the Connally figure's torso, due to striking an extra bone in the 'rib' model (i.e. it fractured two ribs in the model as opposed to one rib in the real Connally). It was also slightly more deformed, possibly for the same reason.

Then there is the *cause célèbre* featured in every single JFK conspiracy book: Oswald could not have fired the shots in the allotted time. The popular conspiracy theory is that Oswald had less than six seconds to get three shots off (most lone-gunman theorists reckon Oswald had 8.5 seconds). Robert Frazier, an FBI weapons expert, got off three accurate rounds with Oswald's rifle in 4.5 seconds. Conspiracy author Josiah Thompson (author of *Six Seconds in Dallas*, published in 1967) was the first author to claim that Oswald could not have fired the shots in time. Thompson was filmed for a TV documentary in the 1990s where, using the same Carcano, he demonstrated to the camera crew his theory that cycling the mechanism cannot be completed in under 2.3 seconds. What he didn't realise was that he had actually just done it in 1.83 seconds! This is hard to believe, a conspiracy author debunking his own work, but video footage of Thompson shooting himself in the foot, so to speak, is on the internet for all to see (the video footage can be found at www.assassinology.org).

In 1994, researcher Bill Adams discovered FBI documents that related to a revolver being found in a Dallas street on the day of the assassination, but nothing to do with the location. He told this to journalist Anthony Summers who reported in *Vanity Fair* in December 1994 that the gun was found in the 'immediate vicinity' and before long researchers were saying it had been found on the Grassy Knoll, had been dropped by a blonde stripper that worked for Jack Ruby and, of course, that the weapon had been fired at Kennedy. Adams eventually got to the bottom of this story by getting hold of a police report about the revolver being handed in – it was found at the junction of Ross and Lamar Streets, several blocks away from Dealey Plaza, and was handed to a police officer by one Willie Flat.

Then there was the story of the mysterious .45-calibre slug that was supposedly found by a government agent lying on the grass next to the pavement on Elm Street. The agent apparently placed the bullet in his jacket pocket and this vital 'evidence' vanished; all this was recorded by someone who happened to be photographing the scene. A quick examination of the photos shows a blurry image of a man bending down as if to look at something on the ground but coming up empty-handed.

The only thing that the House Select Committee on Assassinations thought they had discovered which might have leant weight to a conspiracy was acoustic evidence of four shots. This was based on impulses recorded on a Dallas Police Dictabelt tape along with the persuasion of some expensive scientific specialists.

Supposedly, one 'impulse' demonstrated that a shot had indeed come from the Grassy Knoll. Enter Steve Barber an amateur but very astute researcher who uncovered something that the high-priced consultants had missed. After listening to the recording dozens of times, Barber picked up the voice of Sheriff Bill Decker saying 'Hold everything secure' at the exact moment when the impulses were recorded. Thanks to police records and Decker's own testimony it was widely known that he had said 'Hold everything secure' about a minute after the real shots had been fired in Dealey Plaza. Thus the 'impulses' discovered by the consultants could not actually be gunshots. Barber's findings were checked and approved by the National Academy of Sciences, who declared the HSCA consultants' acoustic analysis to be seriously flawed.

Conspiracy buffs have another ace up their sleeve to answer the question, 'Why have no credible witnesses come forward with the evidence necessary to blow open the cover-up?' Because an assassination squad is travelling across the USA, cleverly killing them off in 'accidents'. Jim Marrs, author of *Crossfire*, perhaps the most widely cited book of its kind, put together a list of 103 people connected to the assassination who died suspicious deaths.

The existence of an assassination clean-up squad is highly unlikely for a number of reasons. For a start, the assassins have to become part of the conspiracy and might themselves spill the beans at a later date (requiring a new team of assassins, who would have to be aware that they were hunting a well-trained assassin, far more dangerous than your average target).

The people on the list are an extraordinary cast of characters and feature the Mafia, the CIA, anti-Castro Cubans, policemen, other criminals and people with a history of alcohol, drug abuse, or mental illness. All these people were likely to die earlier than average because of the above-average risk in their day-to-day lives. For Marrs's theory to work, one has to make the assumption that all these groups were in on the conspiracy, which, based on the evidence there is, is extremely unlikely. Almost half of those on the list died of natural causes. Of course, Marrs has an answer for this – the CIA has methods which can make a suspicious death look natural. Well, then, why did they let any of the deaths appear to be suspicious?

The final nail in the assassination squad coffin comes from the London *Sunday Times* which revealed that 'the odds against these witnesses being dead by February 1967, were one hundred thousand trillion to one'. The HSCA asked the newspaper how they arrived at these figures. The red-faced editor sheepishly wrote back:

> 'Our piece about the odds against the deaths of the Kennedy witnesses was, I regret to say, based on a careless journalistic mistake and should not have been published. This was realized by the *Sunday Times*'s editorial staff after the first edition – the one which goes to the United States and which I believe you have – had gone out, and later editions were amended. There was no question of our actuary having got his answer wrong. It was simply that we asked him the wrong question. He was asked what were the odds against fifteen named people out of the population of the United States dying within a short period of time to which he replied – correctly – that they were very

high. However, if one asks what are the odds against fifteen of those included in the Warren Commission index dying within a given period, the answer is, of course, that they are much lower. Our mistake was to treat the reply to the former question as if it dealt with the latter – hence the fundamental error in our first edition report, for which we apologise.'

Oops.

As any experienced detective knows, no crime scene provides all the answers. There will always be loose ends that just simply won't tie up, that won't make sense. The Kennedy crime scene is so huge, the witnesses and the expert researchers so numerous, that every crack in every paving slab and every cloudy memory can be related to the assassination as proof of conspiracy. There are too many random variables that can scupper or suggest almost any theory. Presidential appearances at events attract oddballs and people with puzzling agendas like the umbrella man. Also, sadly, many JFK researchers have done assassinology a disservice by their own sad desire for attention and high sales figures.

Conspiracy buffs are keen to believe any story about extra shooters, extra bullets, or extra weapons around Dealey Plaza. But wait a minute: if all this evidence is valid, just how many assassins were blasting away at Kennedy from different directions using different weapons (don't forget the poison-dart-firing umbrella) and different ammunition types? Surely somebody would have noticed this – or were they all in on it: the entire crowd, the witnesses, the police, Kennedy's security?

Conspiracists have built a tower of conspiracy so enormous that it crumbles under its own weight. To misquote the world's most famous fictional detective with a slightly altered version of his most famous maxim: 'When you have eliminated all which is impossible, then whatever remains, however *probable*, must be the truth.'

If there was ever going to be an assassin then Oswald fitted the bill almost too perfectly with his communist leanings, a history of assassination and mental abnormality. As we shall see, Oswald serves as the perfect model for future and past lone assassins who shared an incredibly similar psychology, appearance, age and parental history.

Kennedy had announced his Civil Rights Bill in 1963, on the day of Medgar Evers's assassination. It had been blocked by the Republicans in Congress but after Kennedy's assassination President Lyndon B. Johnson made it his mission to get the bill through the Senate and urged politicians that it deserved to be passed as Kennedy's legacy.

It was by no means a simple battle and its enforcement in the southern states, particularly in Alabama, would take some years. But on 2 July 1964 LBJ signed the Civil Rights Bill into law. After he had signed the document, the President remarked: 'We have lost the South for a generation.' LBJ was elected in 1964 with a much improved majority for the Democrats, due at least in part to the passing of this Bill.

Eight

By Any Means Necessary

The year 1965 saw an important development in assassination prevention with the invention of Kevlar. The bulletproof vest came into being at the end of the nineteenth century when, in 1881, Dr George Emery Goodfellow of Arizona stumbled across a gun battle between two men. When Dr Goodfellow subsequently rushed to tend the chest wounds suffered by one of the combatants he was amazed that 'not a drop of blood' had come from the wound. The man had been shot through his breast pocket. The bullet had ripped through his clothes, but had failed to penetrate his folded silk handkerchief. By the end of the century, wealthy gangsters were wearing $800 silk vests (that's £5,000 in today's money). On 28 June 1914, Franz Ferdinand, Archduke of Austria and heir to the Austro-Hungarian throne, was wearing such a silk vest. But he died when Gavrilo Princip shot him in the neck.

Improvements continued to be made and by the 1930s criminals had started to wear less expensive but stronger vests made from cotton padding and cloth. The police's response was to develop the .357 Magnum cartridge (which was also used on non-bulletproof-vest-wearing criminals to devastating effect – fatalities in shootings by police increased by twenty per cent a year after it was introduced). But by 1965 a key development had been made by the DuPont Company. They created Kevlar, a light material five times stronger than steel, an invention which, from day one, would have saved the lives of many assassin-prone men and women, not least of whom was Malcolm X.[11]

Malcolm X always knew that he was likely to be assassinated. On 20 March 1964, *Life* magazine published the infamous photograph of the black nationalist firebrand holding an M1 carbine, an old but popular rifle, and pulling back the curtains to peer out of a window. The photo was taken in connection with Malcolm's declaration that he would defend himself 'by any means necessary' from the daily death threats that he and his family were receiving. 'This thing with me will be resolved by death and violence,' he told supporters in January 1965, by which time he feared assassination from the Ku Klux Klan, the Nation of Islam and the US government. (The FBI had planted moles among his supporters.)

Malcolm X was famous for spouting what he believed to be the truth without regard for the outrage it would cause. After the 1962 plane crash in France that killed 121 whites from Georgia, he rose before a Los Angeles audience and said: 'I would like to announce a very beautiful thing that has happened. I got a wire from God today. He really answered our prayers over in France. He dropped an airplane out of the sky with over 120 white people on it because the Muslims believe in an eye for an eye and a tooth for a tooth. We will continue to pray and we hope that every day another plane falls out of the sky.' He constantly ridiculed Dr Martin Luther King Jr, declaring that non-violence was the 'philosophy of the fool'. In response to King's famous 'I Have a Dream' speech, Malcolm X quipped, 'While King was having a dream, the rest of us Negroes are having a nightmare.'

On 12 February 1965, Malcolm X was in Birmingham – not Birmingham, Alabama, but Birmingham, England, or more specifically the small Midlands town of Smethwick. Having completed his tour of Africa and made his visit to Mecca, he had

[11] Bhutan's Premier Jigme P. Dorji, Iran's Premier Hassanali Mansur, Adib Shishekly, the former dictator of Syria, and Portugal's General Humberto Delgado all met their ends with bullets fired into their chests in 1965.

renounced violence and carried with him a spirit of peaceful global rebellion. As part of his visit to the UK he had given acclaimed talks to students at the London School of Economics and the Oxford Union where he outlined his vision for the black community, a 'global rebellion . . . of the exploited against the exploiter'.

But it was in the small town of Smethwick, not at one of the UK's finest academic institutions, that Malcolm X would make his final and greatest impact on British blacks. Smethwick had come to symbolise English racism (Oswald Mosley, who formed and led the British Fascist Party, was its MP in 1926). During the general election a few months earlier, some of the supporters of the successful Tory candidate Peter Griffiths used the slogan: 'If you want a nigger for a neighbour, vote Labour'.

On Smethwick's Marshall Street, white residents had gained council support to bar blacks from moving to the area. The Tory-run local council had agreed to buy any houses which came up for sale and sell them only to white families. It was Marshall Street that Malcolm X chose to visit with television cameras and reporters in tow. He told reporters: 'I have come here because I am disturbed by reports that coloured people in Smethwick are being badly treated. I have heard they are being treated as the Jews under Hitler. I would not wait for the fascist element in Smethwick to erect gas ovens.'

Malcolm was roundly condemned for his pronouncements. But his message – act now before it's too late – immediately energised black Britain and new organisations sprang up, such as the Racial Action Adjustment Society (RAAS), which by May was lending its support to the first important strike of black workers, at Courtauld's Red Scar Mill in Preston.

Upon his return to the USA, two days after his UK visit, Malcolm X was at home asleep with his wife Betty (who was pregnant with twins) and their four children when a petrol bomb was hurled through their window. The family was forced to flee the ensuing inferno in their nightclothes. Malcolm blamed the Nation of Islam: he had recently leaked stories about their leader Elijah Muhammad's infidelities (extra-marital affairs are against Muslim law) which Malcolm claimed had led to the birth of eight illegitimate children. This discovery had led Malcolm to split from the NOI and form his own Organisation of Afro-American Unity. He was soon joined by many NOI defectors, including two of Elijah's sons.

In response, Elijah Muhammad had said: 'Only those who wish to be led to hell, or to their doom, will follow Malcolm. The die is set, and Malcolm shall not escape.' The Nation of Islam accused Malcolm of planting the bombs in the house himself, partly for publicity purposes, partly because they had lent him the house in the first place and were now about to evict him. No one was hurt and no one was ever charged with the crime.

For a few days the Malcolm X family stayed with friends. On 20 February Malcolm checked into an $18-a-day room at the New York Hilton. Within a few hours, three men turned up in the lobby and began questioning a bellhop about his room number. They left when hotel detectives started taking note of their interest. Next day Malcolm left the hotel for a speaking engagement at the Audubon Ballroom, a nondescript two-storey building on Manhattan's upper Broadway.

It was a bright sunny Saturday afternoon. Entering the auditorium with his wife and four children Malcolm cried '*As-salaam alaikum!* [Peace be unto you].' The audience replied in unison: '*Wa-alaikum salaam* [And unto you be peace].' Suddenly a disturbance broke out several rows back. 'Get your hand off my pockets!' a man shouted. 'Don't be messing with my pockets!' Reacting to the distraction, Malcolm raised his hands. 'Now, brothers!' he shouted. 'Be cool, don't get excited . . .'

As he spoke, three men rushed down the aisle towards him. Eight feet away, they opened fire. One man with a double-barrelled sawn-off shotgun blasted Malcolm in the chest. He was so close that the shotgun pellets hit Malcolm's body within a seven-inch circle. Malcolm grabbed his chest and fell backwards, cracking his head on the stage, knocking himself unconscious. Men and women threw themselves to the floor as the gunmen seized the opportunity to run forward and blast Malcolm's still body into oblivion.

Another thirteen shotgun pellets tore into Malcolm's chest and heart; half a dozen slugs from .45- and .38-calibre pistols shattered first his ribcage and then the bones of his thighs and legs. Two audience members who were too slow to dodge the assassins also caught a few rounds. Betty pulled her four children under a bench and covered them with her pregnant body. A woman screamed: 'Why you got to kill each other?'

As the assassins tried to flee, the crowd started to react. One enraged audience member hit one of the gunmen so hard that the murderer flew backwards down a staircase. Gene Roberts, an undercover policeman posing as one of Malcolm X's protégés, grabbed a chair and brought it down with all his strength upon the shotgun assassin, who dropped his weapon. Dazed but still conscious, the assassin tried to scramble away.

Reuben Francis (Malcolm's head of security) drew his gun and blasted the killer in the leg. The man staggered, falling through the panicked crowd before reaching the stairs. He slid down the banister until he was caught by Malcolm X's furious followers, knocked down, kicked and stomped on. Police rescued him, took him to a hospital, and charged him with homicide. He was Thomas Hayer, alias Talmadge Hayer, a New Jersey thug with a police record. His two accomplices, waving and firing their guns in the air, managed to escape.

Gene Roberts tried to revive Malcolm by giving him CPR, as did a nurse who happened to be on the stage. Betty, also a registered nurse, saw that it was too late and fell to her knees beside her husband's body. Minutes after the shooting, Malcolm was lifted from the stage, placed on a rolling bed that had been wheeled over from the nearby Columbia Presbyterian Medical Center, and rushed to an emergency operating room. A team of doctors laid open his chest, tried to revive him via open-heart massage. But Malcolm X was dead.

'He will be avenged,' said his half-sister Mrs Ella Mae Collins. Malcolm X follower Leon 4X Ameer was more specific: 'We are going to repay them for what they did to Malcolm . . . I don't know if Elijah will live out the month.' In Harlem, less than thirty-six hours after the murder, a firebomb tossed from an adjacent rooftop through an upper window of the Black Muslims' Mosque Number Seven sent flames shooting thirty feet into the night sky. The building was gutted. Six firemen were hurt when a wall caved in, and 320 cops rushed to Harlem from three boroughs under a 'rapid mobilisation' order after hundreds of protesters took to the streets.

In Chicago, Elijah Muhammad professed unconcern, despite rumours that six pro-Malcolm triggermen were after him. 'We are innocent of Malcolm's death,' he said. 'Malcolm died of his own preaching. He preached violence, and violence took him away.'

Despite Elijah's protestations of Black Muslim innocence, New York police arrested and charged twenty-seven-year-old Norman 3X Butler with Malcolm X's murder. Butler was described as a Black Muslim enforcer. When arrested, Norman 3X was free on $10,000 bail for the non-fatal January shooting in New York of another Black Muslim defector. A third man, thirty-year-old Thomas 15X Johnson was arrested soon after.

Chicago police guarded Elijah Muhammad's nineteen-room red-brick mansion. When a delivery truck pulled up at Elijah's house with what the driver said was a grandfather clock, the police bomb squad rushed to the scene. They found that it was indeed a grandfather clock, a gift from Muslim women in Philadelphia. Elijah's promised assassination never materialised but he believed the threat was so great that he all but disappeared from public life.

Malcolm Little/Malcolm X/John Doe was buried as Al Hajj Malik Shabazz, the name he had earned in 1964 by making his pilgrimage to Mecca and being received as a true Muslim believer. He was dressed in the white robe that signified his faith. In the four days before his burial, more than twenty thousand people filed past his body as it lay on view in a glass-topped, wrought-copper casket. Following Muslim custom, when Malcolm was buried in suburban Westchester's Ferncliff Cemetery his head was to the east, towards Mecca. His wife gave birth to healthy twins, Malaak and Malikah, a few weeks later.

Butler, Johnson and Hayer were all successfully prosecuted for the murder of Malcolm X. Hayer claimed that Butler and Johnson, both Fruit of Islam members, were not part of the conspiracy and later named his co-assassins in an affidavit as Fruit of Islam members Leon David and Wilbur McKinley. Butler, a karate expert and Fruit of Islam lieutenant, and Johnson, a former bodyguard to boxer Muhammad Ali and a Nation of Islam enforcer, were both well-known New York Muslims and would have been immediately recognised by Malcolm's security staff had they appeared at the Audubon Ballroom that day.

In his affidavit, Hayer claimed that David and McKinley were both members of Newark's Nation of Islam Temple Twenty-five, which contained a small hard core of enforcers and zealots who would punish anyone defaming the Messenger of God. According to former NOI members, the extremists in Temple Twenty-five operated without direct orders and read between the lines for what should be done. A *Muhammad Speaks* cartoon (from Elijah Muhammad's NOI newspaper) that appeared in January 1965 showed the severed head of Malcolm X bumping down the road to a graveyard for traitors – not much room for misinterpretation there. David and McKinley were never investigated and no evidence was produced to link them to Malcolm X's death. Hayer, who was paroled in 1985, was appointed by the NOI to head a Harlem mosque. (Butler and Johnson were released on parole after serving twenty and twenty-two years in prison respectively.)

After Malcolm met his violent end, his decision to renounce violence was lost in the tumult among black nationalists. The publication of *The Autobiography of Malcolm X*, named by *Time* magazine as one of the ten most influential books of the twentieth century, influenced the founders of the Black Power movement and the Black Panther Party which advocated the use of violence to defend themselves.

Nine

The Monstrous Tapeworm

In 1966 a lone assassin came up with the ideal way to get close to his target. Cleaners, clerks, cooks, servants are all anonymous jobs that require basic skills that most people can learn pretty quickly. Taking on one of these jobs is the ideal way for an assassin to get close to their target. And as the UK's tabloid reporters who have found work waiting on the Queen have proved all too clearly, security checks are sometimes lacking. In this case, if his employers had checked this assassin's background they would have learned that he believed he had a six-foot tapeworm living in his stomach, a belief which would have probably excluded him from working in South Africa's parliament building.

6 September, 1966 was a fine spring day. Outside the South African House of Assembly men and women lounged on park benches marked 'Europeans Only' while the non-Europeans who lived in District Six of Cape Town, only a couple of miles distant, learnt they were being forcibly evicted from their homes. Their crime: too many non-Europeans were too close to the city centre.

Inside the building, no one noticed the anxious-looking parliamentary messenger who stood at the rear of the chamber. He flinched as the warning bell rang, summoning the Members of South Africa's Parliament to their seats.

Thoughtfully stroking a small scar on his jaw, Prime Minister

Hendrik Verwoerd marched down the aisle and took his green leather seat on the front bench. The scar was a reminder of the assassin's bullet that had nearly killed him in 1960.[12] Verwoerd had penned a rousing speech for this, the first major session of the season, and he was looking forward to delivering it to the packed house in what was his eighth year as Prime Minister.

Dimitrios Tsafendas had become a messenger but a month before. Of Mediterranean appearance, a big man in his late forties, Tsafendas had curly grey hair, an unblinking stare and sliver-capped teeth. Witnesses would later recall that he seemed agitated; he had hardly touched his canteen lunch and now, as the bell rang, he refused to run an errand for a journalist, telling him: 'I have something to do.' He strode quickly into the chamber and down the aisle towards the Prime Minister, a six-inch dagger and stiletto tucked in his belt.

Tsafendas had been born in 1918, the product of a brief 'affair' between his father, Michaelis Tsafendakis, a Greek seaman, and Amelia Williams, who had a white father and a Swazi mother. Tsafendas never got to know his mother; he was raised by his adoring paternal grandmother in her home, his only experience of love and security.

Suddenly, when he was sixteen, Tsafendas started complaining of severe pains in his stomach. A pharmacist diagnosed constipation and supplied him with a laxative that took effect almost immediately. While sitting on the toilet, Tsafendas looked down and was horrified to see a vision of a monstrous tapeworm in his faeces. He could not, however, see the 'monster's head'. To make sure that

[12] Verwoerd was shot twice in the face by a wealthy white farmer, 52-year-old David Pratt, two weeks after the Sharpeville massacre. From his hospital bed, Verwoerd told his wife: 'I have been spared to complete my life's work.' The Afrikaner *volk* regarded his recovery as proof that God had chosen Verwoerd as his divine instrument to forge the South African nation. And forge he did. He introduced the rigid apartheid laws, in the process stripping the non-whites of rights basic to all in most countries. David Pratt hanged himself at Bloeinfontein Mental Hospital on October 1, 1961.

it had not remained inside him he ran to his grandmother and begged that she should take the worm to his doctor for examination. Instead, much to his dismay, she flushed it away.

Shortly after this incident, Tsafendas ran away from home and, in a confused mental state, drifted in and out of employment as he travelled across Africa and Europe on an odyssey of poverty, arrest, mental breakdowns and deportation. In Hamburg, Germany, in 1954 his landlady heard him screaming repeatedly '*Bandwurm!*' in his bedroom. She became alarmed and called the police. When they arrived, Tsafendas became so violent that he had to be put in a strait-jacket, taken to the local lunatic asylum and confined in a padded cell. Doctors diagnosed him as schizophrenic but Tsafendas simply walked out of the hospital once the nurses removed the straitjacket.

Although he was refused resident status in South Africa where he was identified as a 'Communist' (he joined the party when he was eighteen), he returned in 1963 on a temporary visa after the death of his father. He was now a member of the religious sect the Followers of Christ and stayed at one of their missions near Cape Town. His fellow cultists were often puzzled, if not alarmed, by Tsafendas's eccentric behaviour, such as keeping his hat on while having a meal or spraying chickens with water to cool them down, and, of course, his obsession with the tapeworm. Before breakfast one morning, a fellow cult member was astonished to find Tsafendas in the kitchen devouring a huge meal of steak, eggs, onions and tomatoes without a knife and fork. Tsafendas explained that he had to feed the ravenous tapeworm. He left soon after this and arrived in Cape Town in 1966, where, despite his schizophrenia, he was able to find work as a parliamentary messenger.

In the press gallery above, Political Columnist Stanley Uys of the *Johannesburg Sunday Times* watched as the messenger elbowed his way through the crowds of Assemblymen towards Verwoerd. 'I thought he was going to pat Dr Verwoerd on the shoulder,' he later told his fellow reporters. 'I thought he was being excessively familiar. Then I saw the knife.'

Tsafendas approached the Prime Minister, who was smiling and chatting to MPs who were trying to find their seats. Verwoerd looked up expectantly as the messenger reached him. Without saying anything Tsafendas drew his dagger and, with all of his considerable weight behind it, he dived forward and plunged it into Verwoerd's chest. It wasn't fast; it slid in steadily, horribly, right up to the hilt. Verwoerd's upper body rose in a reflex response. Tsafendas withdrew the blade and, as stunned witnesses looked on, he quickly stabbed his victim another three times. Verwoerd tried to defend himself, raising an arm. But it was too late; with blood pouring out of his terrible wounds, his strength vanished and he toppled to the floor. Tsafendas was grabbed by several Assemblymen who wrestled him to the ground. Others, including three doctors, rushed to try to revive Verwoerd. But Tsafendas had made sure. The blade had literally cut straight through the heart of apartheid. Verwoerd had been assassinated just two days short of his 65th birthday.

The country went into shock. To many it was incomprehensible; for some it was overwhelming. When a bus driver in Johannesburg passed a newspaper stand and saw the headlines, he fainted at the wheel. Black and white snatched up copies of updated newspapers as they came in and read them in the street. Hundreds of thousands of whites flocked to their churches, praying for solace. Cape Town's Afrikaans-language *Die Burger* wailed 'May the God in whom we believe make clear to us in his own time what this horrible event is to signify to our country and her people. Now, we cannot fathom it.' Six years before, the white Afrikaners had taken Verwoerd's survival of an assassination attempt as a sign of his destiny, that God had chosen him to lead South Africa into a new era of apartheid. Now, they were in turmoil.

There was little mourning in Black Africa over Verwoerd's death. Prime Minister Jonathan barely managed, by a vote of twenty-nine to twenty-eight, to get a motion of condolence through Basutoland's Assembly. (Verwoerd had just returned from a visit to Basutoland as his guest.) Laughter broke out in the Zambian legislature when the assassination was announced. Ethiopia's Foreign Minister called Verwoerd's death 'the natural result of apartheid, which breeds blind hate and evil'. In England, the satirical fortnightly magazine, *Private Eye*, ran the headline 'Verwoerd: A Nation Mourns' with a picture of black African tribesmen jumping for joy.

Tsafendas's defence lawyer Wilfrid Cooper first met the assassin in his cell nearly three weeks after Verwoerd's murder. He later recalled: 'Before me on the floor an inert shape lay sprawled on a dirty blanket. As it rose slowly, it revealed the swarthy, heavily built, unkempt figure of a middle-aged man who, on the street, would have been taken for a down-and-out hobo.'

Tsafendas told Cooper that he did not know why 'the Lord' (a reference to the tapeworm) should have chosen an 'infirm' person such as he to carry out its will, to kill Verwoerd. When Cooper asked him 'What did you feel when you committed the murder?' Tsafendas replied 'Nothing. Just a blank.' The whole episode to him was like a dream.

Cooper spent many hours with Tsafendas and thought he was of above average intelligence. He also found him courteous, humourless and out of his mind. Tsafendas told Cooper that not long before the assassination he had fallen in love with a coloured woman, and had himself applied for reclassification as coloured under South Africa's apartheid laws. (Sexual relations between people of different races were illegal under apartheid.) He said that his application had been refused but efforts to find the woman failed to produce any leads.

At Tsafendas's trial the prosecution made a spirited if futile demand for the death penalty, arguing that the assassin was part of a conspiracy, but the judge was soon convinced of his insanity. Despite this, his sentence was incredibly cruel, some would say far worse than death. The judge said 'I can as little try a man who has not in the least the makings of a rational mind as I could try a dog or an inert implement. He is a meaningless creature.'

Tsafendas was put in a cell on death row in Pretoria Central

Prison next to the room in which men were hanged, sometimes seven at time. Tsafendas remained there for nearly thirty years, and died in Sterkfontein Mental Hospital in 1999, at the age of 81. Just before his death, Tsafendas, sobbing throughout, told a visiting journalist that he regretted what had happened and described it as 'a whole other time. I am not that kind of person. It was something that happened, it was not in my nature. Besides, I was sick.' He still believed that the 'dragon tapeworm' was inside him.

The government reaffirmed its faith in apartheid even before Verwoerd's blood had been cleaned off the floor of Parliament.[13] To most Afrikaners – and to many British South Africans as well – Verwoerd was much more than their Prime Minister. In a very real sense, he was the Great White Father of the nation and everything it believed in.

There were a number of possible candidates for Verwoerd's violently vacated position but the favourite was fifty-one-year-old Defence Minister Pieter Willem Botha who, although inexperienced, had become a leading theoretician of apartheid. But the man who ended up succeeding Verwoerd was fifty-year-old former Hitler-sympathiser Johannes Balthazar Vorster, the burly Justice Minister responsible for the police force that had massacred the sixty-nine women and children of Sharpeville. To the Afrikaners he represented the thing they wanted most: security. By 1968 Vorster had abolished the last four parliamentary seats that had been taken by white representatives of black voters: apartheid had never been stronger.

[13] While the blood is gone, the scuff marks left by the struggle can still be seen today.

Ten

Murder in Memphis

1968 was one of the most troubled years of the twentieth century. The Soviets invaded Czechoslovakia; genocide was revealed in Biafra; Israel clashed with Jordan; New Left strikes in France turned into massive civil and economic disobedience by ten million people; and there were large-scale riots in Mexico, Tokyo, Italy and Peru. In Vietnam, 14,600 young Americans lost their lives in escalated fighting; it was the year the North Koreans seized the electronic surveillance ship, the USS *Pueblo*; the year of the skyjackings to Cuba; and the year two US aides were killed by Guatemalan extremists.

It was also a defining year for violence in the United States. The government, under President Lyndon Johnson, was frightened and paranoid as the very foundations of America shook around them. It was a year of urban riots – especially in Baltimore, Chicago, Kansas City, Boston, Pittsburgh and Washington DC: hundreds were killed, thousands were wounded, tens of thousands were arrested. It was the year that students clashed with police at Columbia University, and at the Democratic National Convention in Chicago. Thousands of students took up Timothy Leary's mantra 'Tune In, Turn On and Drop Out' and the Black Nationalists of New Libya attempted a revolution. It was an astonishing sequence of events, a graphic year, an intense collage of television footage, scenes of where-I-was-when-I-heard the news. Pop Art exploded, rock'n'roll hardened and darkened as the Rolling Stones snarled about the 'Street Fighting Man' and Janis Joplin's public drug abuse took her to the edge of the abyss as she sang 'Freedom's just another word for nothing left to lose'. Uprisings, suppressions, the end of dreams, blood in the streets, and, just in time for Christmas, three men whizzing around the moon for the first time.

In the late 60s, the young created their own world, a 'counter culture,' fired by the Vietnam War which alienated the American young from their elders. In the autumn of 1967, 35,000 young demonstrators had marched on the Pentagon and had attempted, with mystic chants, to levitate the war machine. Draft-dodging had become a conspicuous form of youthful revolution. Lyndon Johnson had campaigned for the White House in 1964 by promising that 'we are not about to send American boys 10,000 miles away to do what Asian boys ought to be doing for themselves'. He pushed the positive war angle hard. The *New York Times*, influenced by Government briefings, reported that 'military indicators in Vietnam present the most dramatic and clear-cut evidence of progress in the war since the dark days of 1965.' Reality bit at dawn Vietnam time on 30 January 1968 when Viet Cong and North Vietnamese forces began a wave of attacks on thirty-six of the country's forty-four provincial capitals. They overran all but a corner of the historic former capital: Thich Quang-Duc's home town of Hué. Communists penetrated the heart of Saigon. They attacked the US embassy, the presidential palace, the government radio station. All this was the work of an enemy that the Johnson Administration had reported to be 'struggling to stave off military defeat'.

'What the hell is going on?' TV anchorman Walter Cronkite demanded when he heard about the offensive. 'I thought we were winning this war.' The Tet Offensive turned American opinion decisively against the war. Then, a camera's lightning-fast shutter caught the moment a bullet from a police chief's gun pounded into a fear-wrought Viet Cong's brain. A summary execution that, like the image of the burning Buddhist monk, swelled the already rising tide of the anti-war movement.

President Lyndon Johnson squandered the resources of his presidency and his country on Vietnam. Millions of his younger fellow countrymen wanted him gone. In Madison, Wisconsin, anti-war graffiti read 'Where is Lee Harvey Oswald now that we need him?' At the end of March, peering out at America through the scratchy black-and-white television screen, Johnson surprised the nation: 'Accordingly, I shall not seek, and I will not accept, the nomination of my party for another term as your President.' Youthful anti-war protesters and draft-dodgers danced with joy while older voters sat stunned. America barely had time to react to this bombshell when, five days later, an assassin plummeted the country into chaos.

On Thursday 4 April, at four p.m., the assassin bought a pair of Bushnell binoculars from Main Street's York Arms Company in Memphis, one of the businesses whose windows were smashed during race riots that had taken place a week earlier. He bought a selection of newspapers and checked his target's location. The Lorraine Motel, room 306. He climbed into his white Ford Mustang which he had driven from Atlanta to Memphis, arriving late the previous night, and drove slowly downtown through the wet streets to the Lorraine, a drab, two-storey motel on Mulberry Street.

Tornadoes had hit the state the previous day, ripping up roads and killing seven. In Memphis, squalls had turned into lightning storms the previous night and the clouds' dark bellies still weighed ominously over the Lorraine.

In that tempestuous year, Memphis was a coiled spring; a series of strikes by black rubbish collectors had turned violent and had been ruthlessly quelled by the National Guard. They had pulled out of the city just a few days earlier; as another march by the striking workers loomed, many believed the streets weren't safe. If the twisters didn't get you then the rioting would.

As the assassin studied the building, pedestrians hurried past, unaware that the man in the Mustang, looking back and forth, was calculating angles of fire and distances from the balcony of room

306 and assessing his chances of escape from a variety of possible exit points. None of the surrounding buildings were perfect. It was either the fire station or the flophouse. A straightforward decision really – the fire station was too risky, he had no business to be there. Giving the landlady the name John Willard, he rented a room for $8.50 per week in Bessie Brewer's flophouse. With the seven-power Bushnells, he was able to read room numbers on the Lorraine's doors. His Redfield rifle scope made the people in room 306 appear only ten metres away. The scope was mounted on a .30-06 Remington Gamemaster; its 150-grain slug would reach the motel balcony with just over 1000kg of knockdown power – enough to stop a charging rhinoceros dead in its tracks. It was Remington's fastest non-automatic big-game rifle; their brochure stated proudly: 'Accuracy is there: crisp trigger and precision rifling, helping you put that buck in the freezer.'

Although, by law, gun suppliers had to record the names of purchasers, they didn't require ID. The assassin, an escaped convict on the run for almost exactly a year, had used the name Harvey Lowmeyer. The Remington was almost identical to the model he had used in the army. Military records show that a modern army scores one enemy fatality for every fifteen thousand combat rounds fired by its infantry. For snipers, the result is twelve-and-a-half thousand times better – one enemy fatality for every 1.2 combat rounds.

It would be a difficult shot. Some time had passed since he had handled a rifle and the odd angle of the building next door meant the assassin could fire the long gun only by leaning out of his window. He checked the hallway and found that, from the communal bathroom, he would have a clear shot from a window above the bath. He couldn't hog the bathroom all day, so would have to wait until he sighted his target from the room, then run the thirteen steps with the rifle down the hallway to the bathroom, find it unoccupied, and hope the target stayed long enough on the balcony to get a clear shot. It wasn't ideal, but it was his best chance. He hoped the rain would hold off, otherwise the mark might never even emerge onto the balcony. Shooting through the motel window was too risky.

Whether the assassination succeeded or failed would be down to luck. But to the assassin, it was worth the risk.

In room 306, at about five o'clock, Andrew Young, one of Martin Luther King's principal lieutenants, arrived in his room. King, in a sudden fit of laddish behaviour, grabbed Young and wrestled him to the floor. Ralph Abernathy, King's deputy, A. D. King, King's brother, and two others joined in what became a wild free-for-all pillow fight. Breathless and laughing, the men were interrupted by a messenger who told them that they would be allowed to go ahead with the march as they had planned to on Monday. They would be allowed to follow a designated route, carry no weapons and would walk in narrow file so that the marshals would have plenty of room to keep spectators at a distance.

The relief felt in room 306 was tremendous and they all set about their task with renewed zeal. The pillow fight had released some of the tension that had built up recently before King's arrival in Memphis. King's popularity was on the wane; the moral style of the 39-year-old preacher had gradually become irrelevant to many and was regarded by younger blacks as out of touch with reality, with changing times of the late 60s. He was sometimes disparagingly referred to as 'de Lawd'. He was short of money, harassed by the FBI and his marriage was in trouble thanks to his affairs. He was in Memphis trying to regain traction as the pre-eminent American black leader before starting a campaign for another mass demonstration, a 'Poor People's March', similar to the 'I have a dream' march in Washington that took place in 1963, made him *Time* magazine's Man of the Year and won him the 1964 Nobel Peace Prize.

It was understandable that young blacks, frustrated by the slow progress of King's Ghandian non-violent resistance, became more radical. 'Integration is irrelevant,' cried twenty-four-year-old Stokely Carmichael, Chairman of the newly formed Student Non-violent Coordinating Committee. 'Political and economic power is what the black people have to have.' Despite the SNCC's title, most of its most prominent members refused to rule out violence. In 1966,

The Black Panthers, a new all-black political party in Alabama, was formed. They spurned whites altogether and armed themselves. Many young blacks declared that they should at least defend themselves, an understandable position after a lifetime of beatings – in a recent demonstration in Philadelphia, a pick-up truck had careened down the column while a white man in the passenger's seat flailed at the marchers with a club. When the demonstrators knelt to pray, they were sprayed with a hose while the police stood and watched.

In another protest 3,000 blacks were tear-gassed and beaten by more than 100 armed state Highway Patrolmen, county deputies and local cops. They were gathering on the grassy grounds of an all-black primary school. A *Time* journalist reported: 'At one point, an eerie silence enveloped the field, punctuated only by what sounded like men kicking footballs; it was the hollow clunk of cops kicking and clubbing fallen marchers. A white woman, her blue dress streaked with mud and grass stains, stumbled over to a platoon of blue-shirted city cops. "How could you be so cruel?" she sobbed. "Don't you know I'm a human being?" "Lady," snickered one of them, "I wouldn't be so sure."'

Two weeks earlier, King had been in Memphis, supporting the black sanitation workers' strike; on the night of 18 March he spoke to 14,000 supporters before what was supposed to be a peaceful demonstration. As King led the crowd, a few of the protesters got rowdy and smashed the windows of a storefront. The violence spread and soon countless others had taken up sticks and were breaking windows and looting stores. Police moved in to disperse the crowd. Some of the marchers threw stones at the police. The police responded with tear gas and nightsticks. At least one of the marchers was shot and killed. King was appalled at the violence that had erupted on his march and immediately scheduled another march in Memphis for April.

On 3 April, only 2,000 people came to hear King speak. Doubtless many were put off by the storms, but some would see this as the continued decline in support for King and the start of a new violent phase in the campaign for civil rights. Nonetheless, King arrived at the hall at 9.30 p.m. to a rapturous ovation. As his speech drew to a close he quietened for a moment as he referred to the numerous threats against his life: 'And some began to say the threats – or talk about the threats – that were out, what would happen to me from some of our sick white brothers. Well, I don't know what will happen now. We've got some difficult days ahead. But it doesn't matter with me now.'

His voice rose and shook as he continued as the crowd cheered and jumped to its feet: 'Because I've been to the mountaintop, and I don't mind. Like anybody I would like to live – long life – longevity has its place.' He paused and the crowd hushed and the sky rumbled and rain lashed the roof. 'But I'm not concerned about that now,' said King. 'I just want to do God's will. And he's allowed me to go up the mountain,' King cried, building intensity. 'And I've looked over. And I have s-e-e-e-e-e-n . . . the Promised Land.' His eyes watered as he looked directly into the crowd with a soft yet confident smile. 'And I may not get there with you,' he shouted, 'but I want you to know, tonight ["Yes!"] that we as a people will get to the promised land!' As King trembled, the preachers on the stage with him moved in close. 'So I'm happy tonight! I'm not worried about anything! I'm not fearing any man! Mine eyes have seen the glory of the coming of the Lord!' He stumbled, was caught by Abernathy, who, along with the preachers, helped him to a chair. Some of them were crying, while the euphoric crowd screamed King's name.

The speech had reignited media interest in King and was seen by his supporters as a masterful demonstration of his Nobel Prize-winning power. As a result, the mood at the Lorraine the next day was exuberant and his supporters were rejuvenated. Just below King's balcony, the Reverend Jesse Jackson rehearsed a singing group and bystanders crowded into the room to belt out extra hymns.

King biographer Taylor Branch later pieced together the moment-by-moment events in the hotel room that evening for *Canaan's Edge*, the final part of his magisterial trilogy. Reverend Billy Kyles left the rehearsal to hurry King along for a dinner which he was hosting. The room was full of laughter as Abernathy joked that King didn't much care for *nouvelle cuisine*, having instead a strong preference for more traditional fare. Kyles told him there would be more soul food than King would be able to cope with. 'Your wife can't cook, anyway,' King joked. 'She's too good-looking.' The civil rights leader launched into a humorous rant about how plain wives made better homemakers, arguing that beautiful ones were the troublemakers. Abernathy proved King's point by striding into the bathroom with a grin, calling out that he was going to put on his special cologne especially for Kyle's wife.

King then walked out through the balcony doors with Kyles just behind him. He placed his hand on the rail and stared down at the car park below where his supporters were busy preparing for the march.

The assassin put down his binoculars, checked the bathroom was clear, which it was, collected his rifle and jogged down the hall.

Jesse Jackson entered the car park from the hotel in the company of saxophonist Ben Branch. King spotted them and called out: 'Jesse, I want you to come to dinner with me.'

The assassin stood on the bath and steadied the Gamemaster.

Jackson called up to King: 'Doc, you remember Ben Branch?'

King leaned forward, raising a hand. 'Oh, yes, he's my man. How are you, Ben? Make sure you play "Precious Lord, Take My Hand" in the meeting tonight. Play it real pretty.'

'OK, Doc, I will.'

It was 6:01 p.m.

The assassin squeezed the trigger.

The crack of a gun caused everyone to duck instinctively. The heavy bullet hit King so hard that his tie was ripped free from his collar as it struck the right side of his jaw, ripped through his neck, and severed his spinal cord before bursting out of his back. King fell back onto the balcony; a pool of blood grew rapidly, the result of his torn jugular. Abernathy dropped to his knees and held King's head saying, 'Martin, it's all right. Don't worry. This is Ralph. This is Ralph.' Kyles stood in shock for a moment, horrified at the enormous wound in the side of King's face before running inside to call for an ambulance. Others stood pointing, their fingers stabbing the air, along the line the shot had taken, shouting for help in catching the killer. Marrell McCollough, a Memphis police officer, grabbed a towel and tried to stop the flow of blood.

Ten police cars with three or four men in each car were near the Lorraine Motel at this point; closest were Tac Unit 10, located at Fire Station No. 2, next door to Bessie's flophouse. The officers were drinking coffee when the shot jerked them into action. Two of them drove from the fire station to the hotel while the others jogged down the street towards the Lorraine.

The assassin threw the rifle on top of the bed along with the rest of his things; pulled up the bedspread into a bundle and left the hotel. He was seen skipping down the stairs by another resident. As the killer started towards the Mustang, he stopped. A police car turned the street corner. He panicked and dropped the bundle in the doorway of Canipe's Amusement Company. Then, as the running tac-unit officers passed him, he vanished into the Memphis dusk.

Martin Luther King, still alive, arrived at St. Joseph's hospital fifteen minutes after the shot had been fired. Police with riot guns took up positions at the building's doors. At 7.30 p.m., Paul Hess, the hospital's assistant administrator, issued a one-sentence statement to the large crowd that had gathered outside the hospital.

'At seven p.m., Dr Martin Luther King expired in the emergency room of a gunshot wound in the neck,' he said. Some of the crowd couldn't hear. A woman turned and shouted, 'They have killed Dr King!'

Later that evening, Robert Kennedy was campaigning for the Democratic leadership in Indianapolis. He stood on a flatbed truck in a parking lot and addressed an angry, grieving crowd of blacks. 'Those of you who are black can be filled with hatred, with bitterness and a desire for revenge,' he said. 'We can move toward further polarisation. Or we can make an effort, as Dr King did, to understand, to reconcile ourselves and to love.' Kennedy had his response within the next twenty-four hours.

It was as if all the violent feelings among American black people had been held in check by King and with his death it had been unleashed with all the unstoppable force of a Tsunami. America was swept with riots. Forty-six people died, all but five of them black. The Black Panthers took up arms and within two days were shooting it out with police in Oakland. Washington, the city where King had led his triumphant, non-violent march in the summer of 1963, was swamped by arson and looting. The rioting was almost as bad in Baltimore, Chicago and Kansas City. In all, there was violence in 125 cities. The authorities called out 20,000 regular Army troops and 34,000 National Guardsmen. On April 15, Chicago's Mayor Daley ordered his police to shoot to kill arsonists and to shoot to maim looters.

It didn't take the police long to find the bundle. The assassin had left two fingerprints on his rifle and more on the radio he had kept from his time in prison. It still had his prison number etched into it.

James Earl Ray, forty, was from a poor family and had left school at fifteen before eventually joining the army. He was sent to Germany after the end of World War II where he had his first taste of prison on a charge of being drunk and disorderly. He was eventually discharged for failing to adapt to army life and drifted into crime. Eight months for burglary in 1949. Two years for armed robbery in 1952. Three years for forgery in 1955. Twenty years for armed robbery in 1959. An escape attempt in 1961 was followed by a successful effort in 1967 when he hid in a bread truck.

At his own request, in 1966 Ray began psychological counselling. It backfired badly as the authorities who had watched him do his time quietly learned they had a neurotic, obsessive-compulsive paranoid on their hands. The examining doctor wrote: 'It is doubtful that he should be considered for parole.' The report also revealed that Ray was a racist: 'He was approved for our Honor Farm but was never actually transferred to the Farm due to the fact that he did not feel he could live in an Honor Farm dormitory because they are integrated . . .'

Meanwhile, Ray drove to Toronto, Canada, where he booked into a hotel. He took the name Ramon George Sneyd, a Toronto policeman, selected at random from the local phone directory, and acquired a passport in Sneyd's name.

Conspiracists have long argued that because Ray was able to get false passports he must have received some expert assistance (the US government topping the list of suspects) but, being an experienced criminal, Ray was aware of Ontario's lackadaisical procedure over the issue of birth certificates. He posted a $2 money order and received Sneyd's certificate by return. All he needed was the maiden names of Sneyd's mother and his date of birth – both of which could be found from old newspapers in the local library. Once he had the birth certificate, all that was left to do to get a *bona fide* passport was to fill out the form and to attest to being Canadian.

On 6 May he flew to London, and the next day on to Portugal where he hid out in a hotel. The FBI, meanwhile, had launched the biggest manhunt in its history, warning officials in Mexico and Canada, previous hideaways of Ray's, to be on the alert. Scotland Yard and Interpol joined the manhunt, and the FBI sent agents to Europe and Australia. For all the manpower and expense, Ray's trail grew steadily cooler. Then, on 1 June, came the first big break. At the US's request, the Royal Canadian Mounted Police had been checking passport photos for the slippery suspect. After assiduously studying 300,000 mugshots they spotted Ray.

By this time Ray had a strong feeling that the police were on to him. He altered his passport by changing the 'd' in Sneyd to 'a', telling the consul at the Canadian embassy that his name had been misspelled. On 16 May, shortly after he had been given a new passport, he flew to London. He should have stayed put. Under a sixty-year-old treaty with the US, Portugal (which abolished the death penalty in 1867) would not extradite any criminal sought on a capital charge. Ray could have safely stayed there for as long as he liked.

On 28 May he checked into the New Earl's Court Hotel. On 5 June he telephoned journalist Ian Colvin of the *Daily Telegraph* to enquire about mercenary forces in Africa. Colvin suggested that if he was interested in that sort of thing then he should head to Brussels. Two months after King's assassination, Ray tried to board a BAE flight to Brussels but was spotted by a sharp-eyed immigration official who took one look at his passport and asked the bespectacled Sneya to join him in a back room for some 'routine' questions. Sneya was found to be carrying a loaded pistol in his back pocket, plus his old Canadian passport. And when Scotland Yard detective Tommy Butler took over, the alert immigration official's original suspicions were confirmed: fingerprints proved that Sneya was, in fact, forty-year-old James Earl Ray. He was taken to a maximum-security cell in Wandsworth Prison.

Ray's first appearance in London's Bow Street Magistrate's Court caused a sensation; everyone who entered the building was searched for weapons. In the end the procedure lasted eighty-two seconds and Home Secretary James Callaghan immediately authorised his extradition. When he finally arrived in court in America, Ray pleaded guilty and was promptly sentenced to ninety-nine years.

Although Ray was the only person to have been convicted in relation to the assassination, speculation that the FBI might have played a part in the killing began in earnest in the 1970s. This was when the public became aware of COINTELPRO, the Bureau's counterintelligence programme that had King as one of its targets.

The all-powerful head of the FBI, J Edgar Hoover, was consumed with ruining King and did much to weaken King's authority. The FBI's surveillance touched every aspect of King's public and private life. Phones were tapped in at least fifteen of the hotels in which King stayed. Religious leaders and institutions were influenced by Hoover's sly anti-King propaganda machine, and leaks about King's private life, in particular his liaisons with a number of mistresses, found their way into many journalists' tape recorders and were even presented to the President. When it was announced that King was to have an audience with the Pope, Hoover sent the pontiff every little dirty secret he had on King (the meeting went ahead as planned).

Hoover did in a sense try to kill King; it started with character assassination and progressed to the stage where he tried to talk the civil rights leader into committing suicide. As the date for the presentation of King's Nobel Peace Prize in Stockholm neared, Hoover sent the hotel tapes to King's wife Coretta with an unsigned letter addressed to King which read: 'King – there is only one thing left for you to do. You know what it is. You have just thirty-four days in which to do it [before he was awarded the Nobel Prize]. It has definite practical significance. You are done. There is but one way out for you. You'd better take it before your filthy abnormal self is bared to the nation.'

The fact that King had been the subject of such a campaign of paranoid hatred has led many close to King, including his own family, to speculate as to whether Ray had some assistance from the government or whether he was a stooge framed to take the rap. 1968 had seen a sudden flurry of publications of investigations into the JFK assassination and large numbers of the public were starting to doubt the government. This distrust rose steadily in the 1970s when it was revealed that the CIA had tried to assassinate several foreign heads of state.

Conspiracists were given further hope by Ray who, after receiving his ninety-nine-year sentence, suddenly back-pedalled, claiming that his lawyer had talked him into pleading guilty and he had been set up to take the fall by a mysterious man called Raoul.

Ray claimed that he first met Raoul after his 1967 jailbreak and that he had convinced him to take part in a smuggling scheme in Canada and Mexico. In 1968 Raoul told Ray to buy a white Mustang and a Remington rifle (the one that fired the shot that killed King). Raoul then told Ray to go to Memphis where they would start gun-running. The following day Raoul vanished with the rifle to 'meet with underworld connections' and the next thing Ray knew he was under arrest for the assassination.

Besides Ray's startling claims, the prosecution case wasn't helped by the fact that despite 257 man-hours of study (which consisted of eighty-one comparisons of the bullet taken from Dr King's body with test-fired bullets, as well as exhaustive microscopic, visual, and chemical analyses) the bullet that hit King could not be identified or eliminated as having been fired from the rifle found near the murder scene. This in itself provided excellent ammunition for conspiracists who were not slow in suggesting that another gun was used to kill King.

But while the firearms panel could not say conclusively that the rifle found in front of Canipe's shop (which had Ray's fingerprints on the stock and scope) fired the fatal shot, it did conclude that it was quite probable that the shot was fired from that rifle, as the bullet that killed King did share general characteristics with the barrel of the gun. Expended bullets are not like fingerprints; they do not, as some conspiracists would have us believe, always produce unique patterns that match the interior of a gun barrel.

Thanks to the enormous volume of public interest and political pressure, the House Select Committee on Assassinations (HSCA) re-investigated King's assassination in the mid to late seventies. The final results were published in 1979. Investigators did in fact uncover a conspiracy to kill King – but it was not orchestrated by any government agency (the last thing the US government wanted was the intense rioting that followed the assassination; arguably the worst ever to take place on American soil in the twentieth century). Instead the HSCA found that King had been assassinated thanks to a pair of St Louis-based racist businessmen: John Sutherland and John Kauffmann (both of whom had since died of natural causes).

Sutherland, the wealthier of the two men, had put a $50,000 bounty on King's head. He knew Hugh Maxey, Missouri State Penitentiary's prison doctor, who, prison records show, had treated Ray before he escaped in 1967. Maxey was allegedly involved with John Kauffmann in the distribution of amphetamines in the prison and Ray sold the drugs on to his fellow inmates – Ray pushed a food cart in the prison hospital and so the two men had plenty of time to organise a drug-dealing business together.

Sutherland and Kauffmann were loyal supporters of George

Wallace, the Governor of Alabama and 1968 presidential candidate. Wallace (who would later face his own lone-wolf assassin, see page 155) campaigned on a racist platform. In 1963 he had stood barring a schoolhouse door to keep out black students and used the slogan 'Segregation now, segregation tomorrow, segregation forever!' In his 1958 attempt to become Governor, Wallace lost to a candidate who had taken a harder line in support of racial segregation. As a result he swore he'd never be 'out-niggered' again. John Sutherland helped finance Wallace, while Kauffmann was actively involved as a campaign worker (Sutherland paid his salary).

Kauffmann was often found in the company of other Wallace campaigners at the Grapevine Tavern in St Louis, a stone's throw from Wallace's campaign offices and the assembly house of the White Citizens' Council of St Louis where Sutherland would attend meetings. James Earl Ray's brother John owned the tavern, and the pair of them, despite being convicted felons and therefore denied the vote, campaigned actively on behalf of the American Independent Party's 'Wallace for President' campaign. The Grapevine was a distribution point for campaign literature. The $50,000 bounty was discussed in the tavern and John probably talked about it with his brothers Jerry and James.

When the HSCA's conclusions were combined with Ray's admissions, fingerprint evidence, and the testimony of other witnesses, there is ample evidence to conclude that Ray bought the .30-06 rifle, transported it to Memphis, shot King and dropped the murder weapon in front of Canipe's Amusement Company while fleeing from the scene of the crime. There was no indication that the mysterious Raoul, who Ray said organised the assassination, ever existed.

Donald Wood, the clerk at Aeromarine Supply, where the rifle purchase and exchange took place, told investigators that Ray was unaccompanied on his visits to the store. Wood recalled that Ray said he had been advised by his brother that the rifle he bought, a .243 calibre Remington, was not the one he wanted and exchanged it for the Remington 30.06 that was used in the assassination. Ray claimed he got his advice on the rifle purchase from Raoul.

Ray acknowledged in public hearings that he purchased a 1966 white Mustang in Birmingham in August 1967 and that he drove the Mustang to Bessie Brewer's roominghouse in Memphis on the day of the assassination, where he used the name John Willard to rent a room.

Brewer first showed Ray to room 8. This was near the front of the building and therefore did not provide the all-important view of the Lorraine Motel which could only be seen from the back. Ray told Brewer it was unsuitable, adding that he wanted a room, not an apartment. After something more satisfactory was found, he checked in under the watchful eye of fellow-lodger Charles Stephens who later gave an accurate description of him to the authorities.

The HSCA hired Vincent Scalice of Forensic Control Systems to appraise the fingerprint evidence. Latent prints taken from the rifle, the telescopic sight, the binoculars, a Schlitz beer can, a bottle of aftershave lotion and the front page of the *Memphis Commercial Appeal* were all Ray's. No other prints were on the rifle.

The HSCA also concluded that Ray had another motive to carry out the assassination apart from the $50,000 bounty. Ray was a committed racist who hated African Americans, something he didn't try to keep secret. He gave King the nickname 'Martin Lucifer King' and witnesses observed his extreme hatred of black prisoners while he was doing time at Missouri State. William Bradford Huie, author of *He Slew the Dreamer*, interviewed a female friend of Ray's who recalled Ray's openly racist views expressed over dinner in a Canadian restaurant in the summer of 1967: 'He said something like, "You got to live near niggers to know 'em." He meant that he had no patience with the racial views of people like me who don't "know niggers" and that all people who "know niggers" hate them.'

In the 26 January 1976 edition of *Time* magazine, George McMillan, the author of *Making of an Assassin*, published later the same year, wrote that Ray's childhood friend and fellow convict Walter Rife had said: 'Yeah, Jimmy was a little outraged about

Negroes. He didn't care for them at all. Once he said, "Well, we ought to kill them, kill them all..."' While on the run in Mexico, Ray tried to attack four African American sailors sitting at the same bar as him but he was physically restrained by bar staff before he could get his pistol from his car. Two similar incidents occurred in Los Angeles.

Ray was a lone assassin attracted by notoriety; he dreamed of escaping to a friendly foreign country, he made no secret of the fact that he had made enquiries about living in Rhodesia and South Africa (English speaking countries where there might be sympathy for the assassination), a place where his brothers could wire him the bounty and where he would wait for the day when white supremacists governed America and would welcome him home as a hero.

While waiting to be extradited from the UK, Ray constantly expressed a feeling of pride for his act to his captors. Scotland Yard's Detective Inspector Alec Eist recalled: 'He was continually asking me how he could hit the headlines in the newspapers, and he kept wanting news of publicity. In fact, he said to me, when I told him it hadn't really made too much of an impact in the British press, that is, as far as he was concerned, he was telling me, you haven't seen anything yet. I will be in the headlines one of these days. He was quite proud of the fact that he was going to make the headlines.'

A major question for those who wanted to believe Ray was part of a larger conspiracy was: how did he finance himself in the months after he escaped from prison? They argue that he must have received help from Raoul, right? Wrong. James Earl Ray was an experienced and fearless criminal, more than able to plan and execute criminal operations with some degree of sophistication – as his 1967 escape indicated. The HSCA found that Ray's 'unexplained income' came from a bank robbery.

In an interview with the St Louis Post-Dispatch the day following his brother's arrest, John Ray pointed out an obvious fact, one of which conspiracists should take note: 'If my brother did kill King he did it for a lot of money, he never did anything if it wasn't for money

– and those who paid him wouldn't want him sitting in a courtroom telling everything he knows.' If he was part of a conspiracy, then presumably his powerful co-conspirators would have too much to lose by letting him live. It was and remains notoriously simple for someone to meet their end while in jail awaiting trial and no attempt was made on Ray's life – until thirteen years after the assassination.

In 1981, James Earl Ray was stabbed twenty times by a group of his fellow prisoners. He contracted hepatitis during the subsequent blood transfusion and it was this that killed him almost thirty years after King's assassination in 1998.

Despite a ludicrous attempt to reawaken conspiracy theories by Ray's new lawyer, Dr William Pepper, in 1995 (a case that was dismissed as having absolutely no credible evidence by a team of Department of Justice Investigators) no evidence has ever lent firm support to a government conspiracy.

Although King may have been prepared to accept a violent death, he had a responsibility to his movement to try and prolong his life. There were some simple steps he could have taken to make his assassination more difficult that would not have hurt his image – obvious things such as avoiding balconies and staying away from the windows, wearing a bullet-proof vest. As it was, his death was a disaster for the civil rights movement. King would have been appalled at the violence his assassination caused. He would have hoped for a peaceful, respectful protest by the black community that would do something to help free the United States from racism. Instead, both blacks and whites, equally horrified and frightened by his violent end, became ever more polarised.

Eleven

The Route of Most Danger

The day after Martin Luther King died, Senator Robert F. Kennedy told the nation that 'no martyr's cause had ever been stilled by an assassin's bullet'. He was wrong. King's assassination had robbed the civil rights movement of its greatest orator and personality. Although Ralph Abernathy took over King's role, he failed to produce the necessary momentum and control and the Poor People's March on Washington, which began on 18 May 1968, turned into a disaster.

For a start, President Lyndon Johnson had made the march redundant before it began by signing into law the Civil Rights Act of 1968, exactly one week after the assassination of King. The law prohibited discrimination in renting and buying housing, which was the focus of the protest. Despite this, over seventy thousand people marched into the city centre and set up camp. While most protesters slept in cardboard huts, Abernathy chose to stay in a comfortable hotel, an action which evoked stern criticism from the more fiery civil rights leaders, most notably the Reverend Jesse Jackson. Even worse, in 'Resurrection City', as it became known, people were raped and robbed and as a result the protest was forcibly broken up by riot police.

While the civil rights movement was falling to pieces, things were looking good for the New York Senator Robert Kennedy who had just stepped onto the first rung of the presidential ladder. He had offered not to put his name forward for the presidency if President Johnson offered to 're-evaluate' America's role in Vietnam but Johnson declined, saying, 'We are going to win.' Kennedy joined the race as a latecomer, but for eighty days he campaigned relentlessly, and by the day of the California primary, a must-win state for Kennedy to seriously challenge his rival Hubert Humphrey, his health was waning. The night before, he had been too weary to finish a speech in San Diego, and by the time he reached Los Angeles in early June he appeared to be running on fumes.

On Tuesday, 4 June 1968, the day of the California primary, Kennedy took six of his ten children (his wife Ethel was pregnant with the eleventh) swimming in the surf off Malibu. He was dozing when he heard the cries of twelve-year-old David Kennedy as he lost his battle against a strong undertow which pulled him towards open water. Despite his exhaustion, Kennedy dived into the ocean and outswam the current to save his son.

By this time Sirhan Sirhan was already on his way to the Los Angeles Ambassador Hotel. In his pocket was a fully loaded snub-nosed Iver Johnson eight-shot revolver, model 55 SA. He had bought it from an eighteen-year-old who had no use for it. The gun had been given to the teenager by a female neighbour who had originally bought it for protection but had instead become more scared of having a gun in the house with her children. It was a cheap model that retailed for about $31.95 and twenty-four-year-old Sirhan could have picked up a much better model from any of the many hundreds of Los Angeles's licensed dealers. But, because he was a resident alien, he could not legally own a gun in California.

As he neared the Ambassador, Sirhan stopped at an advertisement announcing a march down Wilshire Boulevard the following day to commemorate the first anniversary of Israel's victory in the Six-Day War. The sign fanned the flames that had been burning within Sirhan for over a decade. The Jews were celebrating the fact that they had beaten the hell out of his people and now Robert Kennedy was helping them to rub his nose in it. On the day that Kennedy told the nation that the US had a firm commitment to Israel's security Sirhan had written in his diary: 'Kennedy must die before June 5.'

The Ambassador Hotel was on Wilshire Boulevard, a wide, four-lane street lined with modern skyscrapers. Sitting squat, White House-shaped, six storeys high, two hundred metres long with five hundred rooms, the hotel was a well-known LA landmark. It had hosted numerous Academy Awards ceremonies and seven presidents had spent the night there. The diminutive Sirhan had no trouble entering the building among the dozens of people coming and going via the lobby. He wandered through to the back of the hotel and into the Embassy ballroom. There was no trick getting in: no serious attempt was made at security screening of the ballroom by either the hotel or the Kennedy staff. Although a presidential candidate, Senator Kennedy was not entitled to Secret Service protection: he had to rely on his campaign team who employed Ace Security, a local private-security firm made up of ex-police officers and FBI agents.

Sirhan walked into the vast ballroom that would soon be tightly packed with almost two thousand Kennedy supporters, news cameras and hotel staff. Sirhan rightly guessed that when Kennedy left he would have to take a side exit. He checked the stage. Behind the speaker's platform was a gold curtain. Behind that there was an exit via a narrow corridor which held catering equipment. This could either take Kennedy out of the hotel or into a conference room that had the notice 'Press' stuck to the door.

As expectant crowds started to fill the ballroom, Sirhan asked a woman whether Senator Kennedy would come that way. She wasn't certain. Someone told him that Kennedy would pass through the corridor for his post-speech press briefing. Sirhan picked his spot, next to some stainless-steel warming counters, slipped the safety off his revolver and quietly waited while waiters, busboys, Kennedy campaigners and reporters dashed to and fro down the corridor.

Six floors above Sirhan, Robert Kennedy sat glued to the television in the Royal Suite as the ballot boxes, which had closed at sunset, were emptied and sorted. He was in good spirits; as the results had come in his vigour had returned. Kennedy had considered remaining out of the limelight for the evening and resting but now, by 11.30 p.m., it was clear that victory was imminent. Almost two thousand loyal supporters who had worked tirelessly for his victory were waiting for him in the ballroom (not to mention a phalanx of national TV stations). They deserved a victory speech. His campaign managers talked to the press and promised them that they would get a quiet chat with Kennedy in the nearby conference room. This would have to be followed by a large private celebration for Kennedy's closest friends and supporters at a fashionable nightspot, The Factory. It was going to be a long night.

As Kennedy emerged onto the stage close to midnight, the jubilant ribbon-wearing crowd, waving banners and balloons, applauded frantically. Flashbulbs popped as an orchestra played a victory march and the crowd chanted 'Bob-eee! Bob-eee!' Kennedy raised his hands above his head and quietened the crowd. He was clearly a symbol of the youth and toughness, the wealth and idealism of the nation that he sought to lead.

He greeted his supporters with a characteristic mixture of serious talk and jokes about his dog Freckles. As he wound up the speech, he referred to Martin Luther King's assassination, which had taken place exactly two months before, telling the crowd: 'I think we can end the divisions within the United States, the violence.' David Kennedy was sitting up late, alone in the Royal Suite, proudly watching his hero dad on TV as he gave the victory sign and the ballroom crowd cheered, stomped and chanted 'We want Bobby! We want Bobby!'

The next stop was to be the press room. For once, a tired Kennedy did not want to plunge through the crush and shake hundreds of hands to reach the room's main door. Bill Barry, the bodyguard from Ace Security, wanted to go that way despite the crowd: he did not like the idea of using a narrow back passageway. There was little chance that he would be able to provide a protective ring of security agents around the Senator. But RFK told him 'It's all right.' So they went directly behind the speaker's platform through the gold curtain towards the serving kitchen that led to the press room. The Senator walked amid a clutch of aides, hotel employees and newsmen, with Ethel a few yards behind. Barry lost Kennedy at this point as he stopped to help the pregnant Ethel off the stage.

Meanwhile, RFK was swept along the route without any bodyguard in front and he pushed through the swinging doors and into the hot, malodorous, corridor-like chamber. At his side was twenty-six-year-old security guard Thane Eugene Cesar who took his right elbow. There were another seventy-seven people in the room – it was like a train packed full of commuters at rush hour.

On Kennedy's left were the stainless-steel warming counters where Sirhan lurked, on his right a large ice-making machine. Taped on one wall was a handwritten sign: THE ONCE AND FUTURE KING.

The kitchen staff, most of them coloured, pressed in towards the Senator and Kennedy paused to shake their hands. He took the hand of a smiling dishwasher, turning slightly to his left as he did so. At the same time he was speaking to a local radio reporter who had just asked him a question about his rival, Hubert Humphrey. In the background, the ballroom crowd could be heard chanting 'Kennedy, Kennedy, ra, ra, ra!' Kennedy released the hand of dishwasher Jesus Perez and started to reply: 'I think . . .' At this moment, Sirhan propped his right elbow on the serving counter and, from behind two waiters, yelled 'Kennedy, you son of a bitch!' Snarling, he fired from a distance of four feet.

Kennedy raised his arms as he saw the gun. Sirhan's first bullet hit RFK in his right armpit, drilling through his shoulder and stopping at the base of his neck. Kennedy twisted to his left as Cesar went for his gun and Sirhan moved forward, arm straight out, pointing at Kennedy's head. At the same time a woman screamed: 'Somebody shot Robert! Oh my God!' Sirhan squeezed the trigger.

The second bullet hit Kennedy in the back of the head. He fell. Two hotel security men dived onto the assassin, but they could not reach his gun hand which was still pointing at Kennedy.

A man's voice shouted: 'Close the door! Close the door!' The doors to the ballroom were pushed shut, preventing anyone else entering the corridor, but this also meant that nobody could leave. There was nowhere to take cover as the assassin's gun waved wildly.

The shocked radio reporter who was standing right next to the Senator kept talking: 'Kennedy has been shot . . . He still has the gun! He's pointing it at me at the moment.'

Another bullet left the gun's barrel. It hit Paul Schrade, Kennedy's speech-writer, in the forehead. He dropped. The radio reporter continued his commentary: 'I hope they can get the gun out of his hands. Get the gun. Get his gun. Break his hand if you have to!'

Author George Plimpton and Kennedy aide Jack Gallivan joined the wrestling match. But the gun, waving wildly, kept pumping bullets. Seventeen-year-old Erwin Stroll buckled as he was hit in the left shin.

Rafer Johnson, an Olympic decathlete, joined the four men already struggling with Sirhan, but still the bullets came. Ira Goldstein, a nineteen-year-old part-time employee of the Continental News Service, was hit in the left hip and screamed.

'Get a hold of his thumb – break it if you have to!' somebody cried. William Weisel, an American Broadcasting Company associate director, cried out in agony as the assassin's next bullet ripped through his stomach, and it started to leak acid. Kennedy supporter Elizabeth Evans flew back against a table as a slug slammed into her forehead.

By now seven men were grappling with Sirhan and finally, as Roosevelt Grier, an eighteen-stone American football player, waded in, they got the gun. But by then its chambers were empty of bullets.

The attack had lasted forty seconds.

Grier lifted Sirhan and slammed him against the counter so that he was bent double with his hands behind him. 'I can explain! Let me explain!' Sirhan cried. Two men started pounding him with their bare hands; they were fended off by the hotel security. Someone shouted: 'Let's not have another Oswald!'

From both ends of the serving kitchen scores of people pressed in. The sounds of revelry churned into bewilderment, then horror and panic. Schrade writhed on the floor and then stopped moving – he was the one who appeared dead to onlookers but only Kennedy was critically wounded. 'Come on, Mr Kennedy, you can make it,' pleaded busboy Juan Romero who cradled the fallen Senator's head while camera bulbs popped. Kennedy answered, 'Is everybody all right?' and passed out. Somebody thrust a rosary into Kennedy's hands, which closed on it. A young policeman rushed in, carrying a shotgun. Someone yelled, 'We don't need guns! We need a doctor!' A priest materialised and started giving Kennedy the last rites.

Television crews and photographers fought for position. Assembly Speaker Jesse Unruh swung at one of them. Ethel, shoved back to safety by a hotel employee at the first sound of gunfire, appeared moments later. While trying to get to her husband, she heard a youth scream and asked what had happened. 'Lady,' he replied, 'I've been shot.' Ethel knelt to comfort Stroll and kissed his cheek.

Finally she got to Bobby. She knelt over him, whispering. His eyes opened and his lips moved. She rose and tried to wave back the crush. A photographer captured the moment: Ethel's face a picture of horror as she stretched out her arm as if to cover the lens. Someone blew a whistle. The crowd began to give way. Someone clamped an ice pack to Kennedy's bleeding head, and someone else made a pillow of a suit jacket. His blue and white striped tie was off, his shirt open, the rosary clutched to his hairy chest. An aide took off his shoes.

Time journalist Hays Gorey, who had been covering the event, wrote in his notebook an unpublished paragraph: 'The lips were slightly parted, the lower one curled downwards, as it often was. Bobby seemed aware. There was no questioning in his expression. He didn't ask, "What happened?" They seemed almost to say, "So this is it."'

The news that Kennedy was wounded spread back to the ballroom. Amid the screams and the weeping, Kennedy's brother-in-law Stephen Smith's controlled voice came through the loudspeaker system, asking that the room be cleared and appealing for a doctor. Three women fainted. Several people kneeled and started praying. Within a few minutes, physicians were elbowing their way towards Kennedy.

The first doctor on the scene was Stanley Abo who eased himself between Kennedy and Ethel. Searching for a wound, he found a small hole at the back of the head, below the right ear. He prodded it, trying to get it bleeding to relieve the pressure on Kennedy's brain. The Senator's breathing improved. 'You're doing good, sir,' the doctor said.

More policemen arrived; none had been in the hotel, but a police car had been outside on other business. Rafer Johnson and 'Rosy' Grier turned over to the cops their prisoner and the gun. The police hustled the man out, carrying him part of the way past threatening spectators. Jesse Unruh bellowed: 'I want him alive! I want him alive!'

Finally, twenty-three minutes after the shootings, the ambulances collected the stricken victims. With Ethel by his side, Kennedy was taken first to nearby Central Receiving Hospital where doctors could only keep him alive by cardiac massage and an injection of adrenalin and alert the better-equipped Good Samaritan Hospital to prepare for delicate brain surgery. A too-eager news photographer tried to barge in and was knocked to the floor. A guard attempted to keep both a priest and Ethel away from the emergency room and flashed a badge, which Ethel knocked from his hand The guard tried to restrain her but two Kennedy aides restrained the guard instead.

Meanwhile, a team of neurosurgeons was being assembled. It was known that Robert Kennedy had been hit twice. One of the .22-caliber 'long rifle' hollow-nosed slugs had entered the right armpit and worked its way up to the neck; it was relatively harmless. The other had penetrated his skull and passed into the brain, scattering fragments of lead and bone. It was these that the surgeons had to probe for in what turned out to be an operation that lasted three hours and forty minutes.

In the intensive-care unit after the operation, Kennedy was never left alone with the hospital staff. Ethel rested on a cot beside him, held his unfeeling hand, whispered into his now-deaf ear. His sisters hovered nearby. Ted Kennedy, his shirt-tail flapping, strode back and forth, inspecting medical charts and asking what they meant. The three eldest children – Kathleen, sixteen, Joseph, fifteen, and Robert, fourteen – were allowed to see their father.

In the confusion, no one came to check on rescued son David Kennedy for several hours. When two Kennedy supporters, astronaut John Glenn and author Theodore White, at last entered the hotel room, David was still sitting in front of the television set, unable to speak.

Outside, beneath the fifth-floor window, hundreds of well-wishers gathered for the vigil; some stayed for the rest of the week. The even rise and fall of the patient's chest offered some reassurance; the blackened eyes and the pallor of cheeks that had been healthy and tanned a few hours before were frightening.

As the doctors fought for one life, Police Chief Thomas Reddin worried about another. Dallas in 1963 might not have taught the nation how to preserve its leaders, but it had demonstrated the need to protect their assassins. The man seized at the Ambassador was taken to North Los Angeles Street police headquarters. His first court appearance would have to take place at the Hall of Justice, a few blocks away, and Reddin was determined to make it as private a proceeding as possible. A judge was recruited to preside at an unannounced 7.30 a.m. session, an hour before the court usually convened. With Public Defender Richard Buckley representing him, the prisoner was charged with six counts of assault with intent to kill.

Subsequently the suspect was transferred to a windowless maximum-security cell in the hospital area of the Central Jail for Men. A guard remained in the cell with him. Another watched through an aperture in the door. Altogether, the county sheriff's office assigned one hundred men to personal and area security around the cell and the jail. For the suspect's second court appearance, the judge came to him and presided at a hearing in the jail chapel.

The police had few clues as to the assassin's identity: he was tiny, five feet three inches tall and fifty-five kilos in weight; eyes, brown; hair, thick, black; accent, foreign, but not readily classifiable. He had a broken index finger and a sprained ankle as a result of the struggle in the pantry, but otherwise he seemed to be in good health. His fingerprints revealed no criminal record. Reddin thought he might be a Cuban or a West Indian. He carried no identifying papers, but had four $100 bills, a $5 bill, four singles and some change; a car key; a recent newspaper column noting that Kennedy, while a dove on Vietnam, was a strong defender of Israel.

Silent at first, the suspect later repeated over and over: 'I wish to remain incommunicado.' He did not seem particularly nervous. Reddin described him as 'very cool, very calm, very stable and quite lucid'. The assassin, named John Doe by the police, demanded the details of a Los Angeles murder case. 'I want to ask the questions now,' he remarked. 'Why don't you answer my questions?' He talked about the stock market, an article on Hawaii that he had read recently, his liking for gardening and his belief that criminal justice discriminates against the underdog. When he felt that the investigators were talking down to him, he snapped: 'I am not a mendicant.' About the only things that he would not discuss were his identity and the events at the Ambassador Hotel. After a few hours, the police fed him a pre-dawn breakfast of sausage and eggs and abandoned the interrogation.

At 2 a.m. on 6 June, the hospital crowd spotted Kennedy's press secretary Frank Mankiewicz leaving the hospital, looking grim, heading for the makeshift press room. The crowd hushed. 'Senator Robert Francis Kennedy . . . died at 1.44 a.m. today . . . He was forty-two years old.' Bobby Kennedy had died under the eyes of his wife, his brother, his sisters Pat and Jean and his sister-in-law Jackie. He had survived for twenty-five hours and twenty-seven minutes after being shot.

The United Nations lowered its flag to half-mast – an

unprecedented tribute to one of Kennedy's modest official rank. Pope Paul announced at a formal audience the shooting of the junior Senator from New York. Condolences came from Charles de Gaulle, Aleksei Kosygin, Queen Elizabeth, Marshal Tito and scores of other world leaders. Richard Cardinal Cushing, who had married John and Jackie Kennedy, concluded: 'All I can say is, good Lord, what is this all about? We could continue our prayers that it would never happen again, but we did that before.'

Of all the words written that week in the mind-numbingly saturated news coverage, some of the most poignant came from Mary Sirhan, who sent a telegram to the Kennedys. 'It hurts us very bad what has happened,' Mrs Sirhan said. 'And we express our feelings with them and especially with the children and with Mrs Kennedy and with the mother and the father and I want them to know that I am really crying for them all. And we pray that God will make peace, really peace, in the hearts of people.'

The 'mother and father' were the seventy-nine-year-old Joseph Kennedy, long partially paralysed by a stroke, and Rose, seventy-seven. Of their nine children, they had buried four by 1968: Joe Jr., who had died in the Second World War; Kathleen, who had perished in a 1948 plane crash; John; and now Robert. Ted, the only remaining son, had nearly died in a 1964 plane accident. While he was recovering Robert had cracked: 'I guess the only reason we've survived is that there are too many of us. There are more of us than there is trouble.' Ethel's parents died in one plane crash, her brother George in another. George's wife Joan later choked to death on food lodged in her throat. Kathleen's husband had been killed in the Second World War.

The Los Angeles medical examiner, Dr Thomas Noguchi, presided over a six-hour autopsy, attended not only by members of his own staff but also by three government doctors summoned from Washington – again a lesson from Dallas. Sirhan was indicted for murder by a grand jury. Meanwhile, once again, the nation watched the grim logistics of carrying the coffin of a Kennedy home in a presidential Boeing 707. This time the craft carried three widows:

Ethel, Jackie (who would marry Aristotle Onassis that October) and Coretta King, wife of Martin Luther King.

Hundreds and thousands watched the cortège first-hand. Millions more watched it on television. The party arrived in New York City at nine p.m. on Thursday, and already the crowd was beginning to form outside St Patrick's Cathedral on Fifth Avenue. The church was not to be open to the public until five-thirty a.m. but some waited on the pavements through the warm night. Then, thousands upon thousands, in line for as long as seven hours, they marched past the great bronze doors for a glimpse of the closed mahogany casket. The black, the young and the poor were heavily represented: Bobby Kennedy's special constituents.

'He loved life completely and lived it intensely,' Ted said, in a reading that was unusual for a Roman Catholic funeral. Frequently using Bobby's own words, Ted concluded with the lines adapted from George Bernard Shaw that Bobby used to end many of his own speeches: 'Some men see things as they are and say "Why?" I dream things that never were and say "Why not?"'

At his trial, Sirhan claimed that he could not remember a single detail about 'that night'. He did admit that he might have gone temporarily insane, angered to the point of rage over Kennedy's recent shows of support for Israel. The trial, which ended on 14 April, had lasted fifteen weeks and had involved testimonies from eighty-nine witnesses. On 17 April 1969, after three days of deliberation, the jury emerged from its huddle to present a verdict that wasn't unexpected – guilty of first-degree murder of Senator Robert F. Kennedy and guilty of five counts of assault with a deadly weapon. On 21 May Sirhan Sirhan was condemned to death in the gas chamber. Sirhan survived after the state abolished capital punishment in 1972 but will probably die in Corcoran State Prison in California (he has so far been refused parole twelve times).

Soon after the trial, conspiracy theories started to appear in the press. Reports claimed that more than eight shots had been fired. This suggested that Sirhan had not acted alone – that there had been a second gunman. Some witnesses said that Sirhan was never closer than two or three feet from Kennedy, yet there were powder burns around the bullet hole on Kennedy's neck, something that only occurs if bullets are fired from point-blank range.

Mistaken eyewitness testimony was blamed, as was the fact that some of the bullets ricocheted around the room, creating extra bullet holes in the ceiling and doors. No more than eight bullets were ever recovered and they all came from the same gun. It was also thought that Kennedy had been twisted around by the impact of the first shot and had been falling towards Sirhan's gun when the fatal shot was fired. This did nothing to deter conspiracy theorists, however, and some named the second gunman as Ace Security guard Thane Eugene Cesar who, according to witnesses, had drawn his gun and fired it. However, Cesar's service revolver was a .38 and only .22 bullets were recovered from the scene. The conspiracy theorists, now plucking at straws, suggested that he had pulled a .22 from his sock. Cesar was never charged.

One curious witness did emerge shortly after the shooting. During Kennedy's speech, twenty-one-year-old campaign worker Sandy Serrano stepped out onto the hotel balcony for a cigarette. Two men and a woman who was wearing a white polka-dot dress went past her into the building. A few moments after the shooting they ran out, nearly knocking Serrano over. Serrano claimed that she heard the woman shout 'We shot him!' Serrano asked whom they had shot and the woman supposedly replied 'We shot Kennedy!'

The police eventually found a woman named Cathy Fulmer who matched the description but Serrano failed to identify her as the woman in the dress. Serrano also failed a lie-detector test (although she was put under tremendous pressure by the aggressive interviewing technique of the officer in charge).

Sirhan's lawyer, Lawrence Teeter, suggested that the woman in the polka-dot dress was there to 'activate' Sirhan who was, in Teeter's words, 'a true Manchurian Candidate – he was programmed through hypnosis to fire shots in the presence of Senator Kennedy without knowing what he was doing and without being able to recall or explain his actions or the programming process.' But if the polka-dot woman really was a conspirator, it would be unlikely that she would run from the crime scene shouting 'We killed Kennedy!' A more likely explanation was that she was simply an innocent bystander who cried out '*He* killed Kennedy!' as she ran for safety.

Nonetheless, Teeter still claimed: 'Operatives connected with the CIA's MK-ULTRA programme and Operation Artichoke could well have accomplished this remarkable instance of life imitating film.' The CIA had been experimenting with hypnosis since Pearl Harbor. Dr George Estabrooks, chairman of the Department of Psychology at Colgate University, famously told the CIA 'I can hypnotise a man – *without his knowledge or consent* – into committing treason against the United States.' But research before and since, performed extensively by the CIA as well as independent investigators, has shown that this is simply not possible: hypnotised subjects have a habit of answering any question truthfully, which would make them of little use in a conspiracy.

It is often suggested that the Mafia were behind the murder. They certainly had the motive. As Attorney-General under John F. Kennedy, Robert Kennedy had fought hard against the mob. The Mafia could expect more of the same if he became President. However, despite considerable effort, linking Sirhan to organised-crime figures has so far proved more difficult than in the case of Oswald and Ruby.

One name put forward was that of the gangster Mickey Cohen. The leading RFK and JFK conspiracist John H Davis stitched together a convincing argument for this in his book *Mafia Kingfish*. Cohen had been hunted down by RFK while JFK's younger brother had been Attorney-General in the early 1960s but the gangster had escaped jail. If RFK ever became President, then it was likely that he would resume his pursuit of Cohen. And Cohen owned the racetrack where Sirhan Sirhan worked.

Sadly, Davis left out the facts that Cohen had been in jail for most of the twelve years that Sirhan had been in America and that the gangster had been hit over the head with a lead pipe by another convict in 1963. This had left him partially paralysed and in addition he was far too busy fighting off the homosexual advances of a prison guard to worry about Robert Kennedy. By 1968, still in prison, Cohen was just getting to grips with a Zimmer frame. Besides, it was widely known that he was Jewish and Sirhan would never have had anything to do with him for this reason alone.

Conspiracists have also claimed that Sirhan had no motive to kill Kennedy but in fact he had more than most: as we shall see in Chapter Thirty, he fits the psychological profile of a lone-wolf assassin very well. Besides this, as described by James W. Clarke in his 2006 book *Defining Danger: American Assassins and the New Domestic Terrorists*, Sirhan carried his motive in his top pocket – a clipping from a 26 May edition of the Pasadena Independent Star-News. It was a column by political commentator David Lawrence entitled 'Paradoxical Bob' in which Lawrence criticised Kennedy for opposing the war in Vietnam while advocating military aid for Israel. Kennedy had made a speech supporting the sale of fifty jet bombers to Israel that same day and Sirhan had listened to it on the radio. RFK was clearly on the side of the Jewish people; as a young man he celebrated the new nation's independence in Israel in 1948; he wore a yarmulke when he addressed audiences in synagogues and had several rich, powerful and famous Jewish friends.

During Sirhan's trial, both the prosecution and defence made it very clear that the young assassin despised Jews. His diary was full of anti-Jewish statements ('Sirhan is an Arab', 'Long live Nasser'), born from his time of suffering as a Palestinian refugee. As Sirhan told author Robert Kaiser, 'June 5 stood out for me, sir, more than my own birth date. I felt RFK was coinciding his own appeal for votes with the anniversary of the Six-Day War'.

Numerous witnesses supported this, including members of the Organisation of Arab Students as well as his college drinking buddy and local radical, Walter Crowe. Earlier that year, while they drank cocktails and ogled topless dancers, the two friends had discussed Palestine, the Six-Day War and Arab terrorism, during which time Sirhan made his hatred of Jews crystal clear.

As Sirhan saw it, if RFK became President, the Jewish people would have the world's most powerful ally and the Arabs would suffer dearly for it. Sirhan thought that the assassination of RFK would lead to greater publicity for the Arab cause, which it did, and assure him hero status, which it did not (although several Arabic newspapers sought to justify and understand his actions in terms of the USA's pro-Israel stance).

In Sirhan's mind, the assassination meant that he had fulfilled his destiny; he had long believed that he was bound for some kind of immortality. He was furious when his lawyers tried to force him to plea that he was under 'diminished responsibility', and spoke at length and with some coherence on exactly why he had to kill Kennedy, proudly telling the court: 'They can gas me, but I am famous; I have achieved in one day what it took Robert Kennedy all his life to do.'

In 1984, sixteen years after the assassination of RFK, Sirhan Sirhan indirectly claimed another life. Twenty-eight-year-old David Anthony Kennedy, Bobby and Ethel's fourth child, died alone in a hotel room from a drugs overdose. Being a Kennedy had become for him an unbearable burden and in 1973, while at college, he had turned to heroin, a drug that sweeps traumatised minds blank, if only for a few precious hours at a time. He had never recovered from that most momentous day in his life – his own life saved, his father's lost as the twelve-year-old boy watched the event on a grainy black-and-white TV.

Twelve

Something Bold and Dramatic

Once again, an American politician would discover the costs of ignoring advice from their security team. The assassin this time was similar to Sirhan Sirhan in that he wanted to achieve a kind of celebrity through murder, but his fame paled in comparison with that of the legendary fictional character he inspired, the unforgettable Travis Bickle, the non-political would-be assassin from *Taxi Driver*, played by Robert De Niro. Bickle's real-life inspiration was incredibly similar to Sirhan and Oswald: he was slight, short, socially incompetent and psychologically imbalanced. He was also remarkable because he kept a diary, a document of a young man's frustration with the society of which he utterly failed to become part.

At times unintentionally hilarious, often tragic, with a wild use of grammar, the diary of Arthur Bremer remains the only chronicle of its kind in the world, giving a unique insight into the mind of an assassin. He remains quite simply the most incompetent lone-wolf assassin there has ever been. There were numerous occasions when Bremer should have been detained, but incompetence and sheer luck allowed to him to achieve what should, especially in the wake of JFK and RFK, have been impossible.

'Now I start my diary of my personal plot to kill by pistol either Richard Nixon or George Wallace,' twenty-one-year-old Arthur Bremer wrote on his diary's first page. This slightly built, short and blond young man wasn't interested in politics. He wanted 'to do SOMETHING BOLD AND DRAMATIC, FORCEFULL AND DYNAMIC, A STATEMENT of my manhood for the world to see'.

Arthur Bremer was born in Milwaukee on 21 August 1950, one of four sons of Sylvia and William Bremer, an abusive, alcoholic couple. He escaped his ugly reality by pretending that he 'was living with a television family and there was no yelling at home and no one hit me'. At school he was academically unremarkable and had no friends to speak of thanks to his odd, socially inept behaviour.

Bremer found school intolerable. 'No English or History test was ever as hard, no math final exam ever as difficult as waiting in a school lunch line alone, waiting to eat alone . . . while hundreds huddled and gossiped and roared, and laughed and stared at me.'

By the time Bremer was twenty-one, in October 1971, he had found work as a busboy at the Milwaukee Athletic Club. But because he constantly talked to himself and only walked in time with the music, customers complained and Bremer was demoted to dishwasher. He filed a discrimination complaint but the investigator assigned to his case described him 'as bordering on paranoia' and offered to put him in touch with a psychiatrist. Instead of taking his advice, Bremer bought a gun and joined a local shooting range. Guns, along with pornography and suicide, became his main interests.

A turning point for Bremer came in the autumn of 1971 when he met fifteen-year-old Joan Pemrich. Bremer became fixated on the girl: she was the first person to respond positively, albeit tentatively, to him. She broke off their relationship after only three dates because he acted, in her words, 'goofy' and 'weird'. His inappropriate behaviour escalated after the break-up – at one point he shaved his head 'to show her that inside I felt as empty as my shaved head' – and on 13 January 1972, the same day that George Wallace announced his candidacy for the 1972 Presidential election, Pemrich's mother told Bremer to leave her daughter alone.

Bremer's thoughts turned to assassination and he soon came up with the idea of shooting President Richard Nixon. Nixon, who had lost to John F. Kennedy in 1960, and was losing to Robert F. Kennedy in the polls before RFK's assassination, won the 1968 election by a narrow margin. By 1971 he had dragged Cambodia into the Vietnam War but he improved relations with China in 1972 by paying a visit to Chairman Mao Tse-Tung in February. He was the first American President to set foot on Chinese soil. The visit was a success – especially important because Nixon was seeking re-election. The two superpowers, in their closing statement on Nixon's visit, dwelled on the need for friendship without getting down to many specifics.

There was one secret footnote that had stunned President Nixon and Henry Kissinger, his National Security Adviser who had accompanied him. Behind closed doors, during the fifteen hours of talks, Mao suddenly made a reference to the mysterious disappearance of his appointed heir, Lin Pao, who had suddenly fallen out of favour.

Kissinger later recalled the conversation: 'Mao used the context of a generally teasing conversation about Nixon's political prospects to mention his own political opposition. There was a "reactionary group which was opposed to our contact with you", he said. "The result was they got on an airplane and flew abroad." The plane crashed in Outer Mongolia, Mao explained, in case we had missed the reference to Lin Pao.' Mao was clearly suggesting, in a 'light-hearted' manner, that Nixon might improve his chances of re-election by terminating his opponents with extreme prejudice.

Nixon was the ideal target for Bremer. By assassinating him in the run-up to the election he could be assured of changing history and, most importantly, becoming famous. By now, Bremer's diary filled a school exercise book. Expecting it to be found and read worldwide after his death, Bremer wrapped the book in aluminium foil and masking tape, placed it in a briefcase and buried it in a local landfill. This was on 3 April 1972, the day before he flew to New York to put his plot against Nixon into action. He took a new exercise book with him and used it to record his 'awesome incompetence', as he described it. He tried to lose his virginity to a young prostitute called Alba but his libido failed him and she soon grew bored when he tried wooing her with what he thought was his witty and sensitive conversation. In New York, he learned that Nixon was heading for Canada and decided that he would catch up with him there.

In a motel room, about to cross the border, he played with his gun, practising poses, not unlike the famous 'You talkin' to me?' mirror scene from Taxi Driver. But instead of looking tough, Bremer accidentally fired his Browning into his trousers as he put it in his belt – the bullet missed but Bremer spent an anxious few minutes cowering as he awaited arrest. Luckily for him, he had switched on the TV and a war film was showing; the climactic battle scene was in full flow and nobody came to check out the gunshot. As he travelled across the border from Wisconsin, customs officers took one look at Bremer and waved the frustrated would-be assassin through, no questions asked. Bremer had cleverly hidden his gun in the boot of his car but when he tried to retrieve it he discovered he had wedged it so far into the bodywork that he couldn't get it out again.

Once he was in Ottawa, Bremer got lost trying to locate the President. Eventually, several hours later, he asked a local garage for directions and promptly got lost again. Bremer was about to abandon the assassination attempt altogether when he spotted a limousine parked outside the US embassy. Thinking it was the President's he dashed back to his hotel room to wash and smarten up. He was extremely concerned about looking his best at the moment the world's eyes were upon him: 'If I killed him wearing a sweatty tee-shirt some of the fun and Glamore would definently be worn off.' But when he returned, the limo was gone. Angry with himself for missing a good opportunity, he scrawled in his diary: 'Does the world remember if Sirhan's tie was on straight? SHIT, I was stupid.'

For Bremer, image was everything; as important as killing the President and as important as his own death (he expected to be killed by the Secret Service after the assassination): 'Got to think up something cute to shout out after I kill him [Nixon], like Booth did.' Still in Canada, Bremer booked himself into a hotel. As he reached his room he noticed that about three dozen Secret Service agents were staying on the same floor. Undeterred, he attended most of the rallies where Nixon was speaking, where he became furious with the protesters, who he felt conspired against him, attracting attention that was rightfully his. 'Those noise makers were all on news film! He should of photographed the quiet ones. He never pointed his camera at me.' As his frustration mounted, his diary entries became more explosive. 'I want something to happen,' he wrote on 24 April, shortly after his failed trip to Ottawa. 'I was supposed to be Dead a week and a day ago. Or at least infamous.'

He thought about incinerating his diary: 'Burn all these papers . . . and no one would ever know half of it. But I want 'em all to know. I want a big shot and not a little fat noise . . . tired of writing about . . . about what I failed to do again and again.' He couldn't do it however – he needed the world to know; it was the belief that it would be published after his death that kept him going.

Bremer returned to New York by plane. After disembarking, he went to the men's room where he was surprised to hear his name called over the airport tannoy. He returned to the arrivals gate where the captain of the plane was waiting. He smiled as he returned Bremer his guns, which he had left on the seat next to him.

By the time Bremer followed the President back to Washington he had run out of money. It was only after he arrived back in Milwaukee that he read that Nixon had spent an hour shaking hands with tourists just as Bremer had left the city. Bremer wrote, 'I could have killed him for doing that alone.'

Bremer's general uselessness had saved Nixon. The incompetent assassin gave up on the President and decided to pick on an easier target nearer Milwaukee. He considered Democratic presidential hopeful, Senator George McGovern, but decided that, as the rank outsider, he wasn't worth the bullets. He turned his attention to another Democratic presidential candidate, the Governor of Alabama, George Wallace. Wallace had just won the Democratic primaries in Florida with a massive forty-two per cent of the vote, defeating nine other candidates, including George McGovern. Wallace was more accessible and was due to make speeches a short distance from Milwaukee, and although Bremer knew that his assassination would have nowhere near as much impact, he decided he would have to do. 'I won't even rate a TV enteroption in Russia or Europe when the news breaks,' he wrote, 'he won't get more than three minutes on network TV news.' Nonetheless, Bremer assiduously set about following Wallace and attending political rallies.

Three days before the attempt, on Saturday 13 May, Bremer wrote his last diary entry: 'Is there anything else to say? My cry upon firing will be "A penny for your thoughts".' Bremer drove to Michigan and again got lost looking for the rally. Eventually he found it and the young assassin shouted to get Wallace's attention, one hand waving in readiness to shake the governor's hand, the other round the butt of the gun in his pocket.

Governor George Wallace stood behind a three-sided 350-kilo bullet-resistant podium every time he delivered a speech. He knew that he was a prime target. 'Somebody's going to get me one of these days,' he told the *Detroit News*. 'I can just see a little guy out there that nobody's paying any attention to. He reaches into his pocket and out comes the little gun, like that Sirhan guy that got Kennedy.'

Wallace had been born in 1919, in a rural-crop county of south-eastern Alabama. His father was a farmer and county commissioner, his mother a county health worker. The short, dark-eyed farm boy became a keen boxer, earned his law degree from the University of Alabama and served in the Second World War as a flight engineer on B-29 bombing missions over the Pacific. After the war, he became an assistant state Attorney-General; then he ran successfully for the Alabama House of Representatives in 1946. Although popular and with a long and successful political career, there were plenty who hated him. As Governor of Alabama in 1963 he had stood barring a schoolhouse door to keep out black students and had campaigned on a racist platform which included denying coloured people the vote. He once threatened to run over coloured demonstrators who blocked the path of his limousine.

Wallace was worried as he approached the stage in Maryland on the final day of campaigning. The Secret Service had advised the widely hated candidate against appearing at such an open venue where protection would be limited. 'Somebody's going to get killed before this primary is over,' he told a friend, 'and I hope it's not me.'

Rioting had erupted during one recent speech in Hagerstown and as Wallace had left a rally a week later in Frederick, a brick had hit him in the chest. That same day, University of Maryland students threw ice lollies at him. At noon, at a shopping plaza north of Washington, tomatoes and eggs arced out of the crowd as Wallace spoke at a rally.

As his entourage rolled into another shopping centre at 3.15 p.m. Wallace knew that he was in unfriendly country. Three marksmen were stationed on the shopping-centre rooftop, scanning the area for potential assassins. He was surrounded by a ring of policemen as he made his way through the car park and through the 2,000-strong audience while country-and-western singer Billy Grammer and his band warmed up the crowd with sprightly Dixie numbers.

Wallace's guards sighed with relief as the Governor climbed onto the specially erected stage and got behind his bullet-resistant podium that was draped in red, white and blue. Wallace, smiling, began with his customary 'Hi, folks!' It was an odd collision of Southern neighbourliness and danger – police gazes raking the crowd and Wallace all but lost behind his armour-plating.

Wallace was not at his best that day. His voice cracked several times as he worked his way through his standard phrases such as 'those pointy-headed intellectuals who can't park their bicycles straight' and time and again he referred to 'Princess George County' when he was in Prince Georges County. From the rear, laughing college students heckled: 'Go back to Alabama. You don't even know where you are.' Wallace plunged on, railing against 'social schemers' and 'ultra-false liberals'. After fifty minutes, he advised the folks to vote 'to shake the eye-teeth of the Democratic Party. Let's give 'em the St Vitus dance. And tell 'em a vote for George Wallace is a vote for the average citizen.'

The applause was thunderous. Wallace stepped back from the

lectern and blew a kiss to the crowd, then gave a snappy salute, smiling broadly. The sun broke out from behind a cloud. As Billy Grammer and his men plunged into a Dixie version of 'For He's a Jolly Good Fellow', Wallace walked down the steps from the stage and decided to shake a few hands.

CBS cameraman Laurens Pierce, who had been following Wallace's campaign for some weeks, made a sweep of the crowd and stopped as he came across a short young man in a blue suit, a red-white-and-blue shirt and sunglasses. He had short pale blond hair. Pierce recognised Bremer from another rally and remembered him as a fanatic fan of the Governor, so he zoomed in for a close-up shot. (Pierce had in fact caught the strange little man on film twice before.)

A middle-aged woman nearby, in Wallace blouse and Wallace hat, shouted groupie-fashion: 'Over here, George, over here!' Wallace took off his jacket and handed it to an aide. Then, flanked by security men, he moved to his left to work down a line of supporters behind a cordon on the right side of the platform. 'Nice to see ya,' he said. 'Nice to see ya.'

Bremer was on the left side and began shouting frantically 'Over here, over here!' In response, the Governor's aides guided Wallace across to Bremer where about forty people pressed forward in an effort to shake his hand. Twenty-seven-year-old Jack Ingram was standing right next to Bremer and was trying to get his hand past the assassin but Bremer kept yelling, 'Hey, George! Hey, George!' and leaned across his path.

Wallace was only a few feet away at this point. Bremer withdrew his hand, elbowing Ingram as he reached into his pocket for the snub-nosed .38 revolver. Ross Spiegle, a forty-six-year-old crane operator, had just grabbed Wallace's hand when Bremer dived forward and thrust his gun towards Wallace's stomach, firing rapidly. The security men close to Wallace reacted at lightning speed and threw themselves at Bremer, blocking his view of Wallace as the Governor fell back onto the ground.

Secret Service Agent Nicholas Zarvos scrabbled for the gun and knocked it as Bremer continued to fire. The next bullet hit Zarvos in the throat causing him to stagger back, clutching his neck, blood pumping through his fingers from a large wound. Bremer lost his balance as the nearest police officer ran into him and the assassin flailed the gun through the air, still pumping out bullets as the panicking crowd screamed and stampeded away, tipping over and smashing a table laden with Wallace campaign materials while the Dixie music crashed to a halt. State trooper Captain E.C. Dothard had placed himself in front of the Governor and caught a slug in the stomach.

As Wallace was pulled back in an effort to get him on the ground, a round caught Dora Thompson, a local Wallace campaign worker, in the right leg. She screamed, then slumped to the ground. A swarm of policemen finally caught up with Bremer and beat him to the floor with their boots and nightsticks while isolated cries of 'Kill him! Kill him!' came from the crowd. Instead, the policemen disarmed the still-wriggling Bremer and carted him into the nearest police car.

Wallace, clutching his stomach, lay on the asphalt, conscious but stunned. Blood streamed from his right arm and oozed from the lower right ribs. He was gasping for breath as seventy-six-year-old Bryan Warren, a local doctor, ran to his side and pulled up his shirt. There was a bullet hole in his lower right chest and the doctor guessed that it had pierced the lower part of the lung and liver.

Dothard, the wounded Alabama trooper, waved away attempts to assist him. 'Take care of the governor, take care of the governor first!' he shouted. Policemen and aides rushed Wallace to a nearby staff car but as they did so the ambulance arrived, which then slowed down as it tried to drive through the fleeing crowds. George Magnum, the campaign's national coordinator, grabbed the microphone and pleaded for order: 'If you're for him, please let us get through!'

The Governor told Dr Warren, 'I'm having trouble breathing.' But there was nothing the doctor could do. The ambulance left on an agonising twenty-five-minute race to the hospital. Meanwhile, the loudspeaker urged the crowd to disperse quietly. 'Governor Wallace will live,' his sound truck promised the shocked crowd. 'Just vote for Wallace on 16 May.' Though ashen from shock and loss of blood, Wallace never lost consciousness. He spent much of the time consoling his terrified wife Cornelia.

At the hospital, four emergency doctors worked over the Governor who received a transfusion of at least one pint of blood. Police and reporters scuffled at the hospital entrance while a crowd of curious onlookers gathered. By nightfall a team of surgeons were at work on Wallace. Two bullets had passed through his right arm and shoulder, while another had glanced off his left shoulder blade. A fourth had torn through his abdomen, perforating his stomach and nicking his large intestine. This one was successfully removed.

But the real problems came from a slug that had entered the fluid-filled spinal canal and come to rest head downward opposite the first lumbar vertebra, just at the waist. The doctors knew immediately that it must have severed all or part of the bundle of nerves that carries impulses from the lower body to the brain. They let it be – any attempt to move the bullet could cause paralysis. The impact alone had bruised the delicate nerve tissue severely, causing grave injury. Wallace told doctors that he had no feeling in his legs and neither his bladder nor his bowels were functioning normally. He would never walk again.

News of the shooting flashed across the nation. From previous experience in such affairs, many Americans automatically assumed that Wallace would not survive. His adversary, Hubert Humphrey, instantly suspended campaigning and went to the hospital to console Mrs Wallace. 'I don't know,' he told her disconsolately. 'We didn't seem to learn anything four years ago.' President Nixon sent presidential physician William Lukash and ordered immediate Secret Service protection for Ted Kennedy, just in case another lone nut was suddenly inspired.

Some reacted to the news with satisfaction, or even with bitter glee. A black worker in Baltimore said after the shooting: 'I'm celebrating tonight. As far as I'm concerned, that little cracker bastard was shot fifty-two years too late. If you live by disrespecting the law, you will die by it.' Roy Innis, head of the Congress of Racial Equality, said: 'You might say this was the chicken come home to roost. But that would be unkind.' Most other blacks, however, remembering the assassinations of Malcolm X and Martin Luther King Junior, simply deplored more violence. Reverend Jesse Jackson told reporters in a grave voice that 'killing can no longer be justified, whether it is in Vietnam or Maryland or Memphis'.

Mark Felt of the FBI took charge of the case. Felt would later become the famous 'Deep Throat', the source for the *Washington Post* journalists Bob Woodward and Carl Bernstein of the Watergate-scandal information which would cost Nixon the presidency in 1974. Felt told his trusted contact in the White House, Charles Colson, about the Wallace incident.

Less than ninety minutes after the shooting, a remarkable conversation was recorded between President Richard Nixon and two of his top aides. The tapes, which were made available in 2002, reveal just how low Nixon could stoop in efforts to assassinate the character of his political adversaries. On the tape, the President told Bob Haldeman and Charles Colson (both later implicated in the Watergate scandal), 'Look, can we play the game a little smart for a change?' He told them to plant a false news story linking Arthur Bremer to Senator Edward Kennedy and Senator George McGovern, possible opponents in the approaching elections. 'Screw the record,' Nixon growled, 'just say he was a supporter of that nut [no one knows to which senator he was referring]. And put it out. Just say we have an authenticated report.'

Reports later came out that Colson ordered Everett Howard Hunt to break into Bremer's apartment and plant incriminating literature – and remove anything that might incriminate Nixon. The President told Colson that he was concerned that Bremer 'might have ties to the Republican Party or, even worse, the President's re-election committee' (the body that was implicated in the Watergate scandal).

Felt gave Colson Bremer's address; Colson then called Everett Howard Hunt and asked him to break in to Bremer's apartment and to search for any documents which linked him to Nixon or McGovern. Hunt claimed that Colson called off the operation a few hours later. Then James Rowley, who was head of the Secret Service, sent an agent to break into Bremer's apartment.

When the FBI arrived at the apartment and found a Secret Service agent inside they were furious; by this point the agent had already removed several documents. Nobody knows why Rowley did this or whether they planted any incriminating evidence in Bremer's home – which seemed to be about as busy as Times Square or Piccadilly Circus on that day. No one thought to seal off the apartment; several reporters were able to pick their way through it, during which time they helped themselves to a variety of his possessions.

Colson had called journalists from the *Detroit News* and *Washington Post*, telling them that Bremer was a left-winger connected to the McGovern campaign and that he was a 'dues-paying member of the Young Democrats of Milwaukee'. The *Washington Post*'s Bob Woodward wrote up the story the following day. Bernstein and Woodward later searched for a conspiracy in the Bremer shooting but could find none.

The FBI discovered Bremer's 137-page diary in his blue Rambler car the day after the attempt. Any suspicion that Nixon was behind the assassination vanished with its discovery, as the very first sentence read: 'Now I start my diary of my personal plot to kill by pistol either Richard Nixon or George Wallace.'

That same day President Nixon, in an effort to show that Bremer had done nothing to alter the business of being a people's President, was being followed by a gaggle of journalists when he joined a group of tourists on a package trip around the White House. One man said: 'It is good of you to come out in public, Mr President.' A second tourist stood beside Nixon and asked a friend to take their picture.

Nixon smiled and replied: 'Go ahead and shoot'.

Meanwhile, that same day, voters hit the primary polls and gave Wallace one of the most impressive victories of his career. In

Maryland, he took thirty-nine per cent of the vote, trailed by opponents Hubert Humphrey (twenty-seven per cent) and McGovern (twenty-two per cent). In Michigan, the two major candidates had all but conceded the primary to Wallace. But the surprise was the extraordinary breadth of Wallace's victory. He came in with fifty-one per cent of the vote, compared with twenty-seven per cent for McGovern and a humiliating sixteen per cent for Humphrey.

Wallace gradually developed the view that one of Nixon's aides had ordered the assassination attempt. His hospitalisation meant that he was unable to continue his race to become the Democratic candidate for President (the position which was taken by George McGovern) but later that year he announced he would become a third-party candidate: this would deprive Nixon of many of his voters and would possibly cost him the election. But Wallace's recovery from his injuries took longer than he hoped and he was soon forced to cancel his campaign, a factor which undoubtedly helped to hand Nixon his second term.

A week before the Presidential election, voters were asked how they would have voted if Wallace had been the third-party candidate. The results were: Nixon forty-four per cent; McGovern forty-one per cent; Wallace fifteen per cent. It would have been a much tighter election had Wallace run. In the end, Nixon secured one of the biggest election victories in American history against the anti-Vietnam War candidate George McGovern, winning sixty per cent of the popular vote.

After the shooting of Wallace, Secret Service protection was made mandatory for Presidential candidates and Wallace quickly accepted by telegram, remembering that he had ignored the Secret Service's advice not to enter the shopping mall where he had been shot. 'I will make one commitment to the future,' he said. 'I will do my best to follow their advice.' He also said that he bore no bitterness towards Bremer. 'Justice was done, although when he gets out he will be a free man and I'll still be sentenced to a wheelchair for the rest of my life. But I have no ill feelings about that . . . All these years I had been thinking maybe that everything I did was because I was strong, but I suddenly realised it wasn't that at all. I suddenly realised how fragile life is and how uncertain it is and how one ought to always be prepared to go.'

Wallace ran his final Presidential race in 1976, losing to Jimmy Carter. By then he had changed his segregationist position and was elected Governor of Alabama again, thanks to the support of black voters. His final term as Governor saw a record number of black Alabamans appointed to government positions. He died in Montgomery, Alabama, in 1998, aged seventy-nine. He had fought a long battle against Parkinson's disease, a struggle made more difficult by the lingering effects of his wounds. He died of a heart attack with his son, George Wallace Jr, and one of his daughters, Peggy Wallace Kennedy, by his side.

Bremer's trial lasted only five days. His attorney Benjamin Lipsitz argued that Bremer was a 'schizophrenic' who could not be held responsible for his actions. Eight psychiatrists and two psychologists testified but they were divided on the issue of his sanity. Before sentencing, the judge asked Bremer if he had anything he would like to say. 'Looking back on my life,' Bremer replied, 'I would have liked it if society had protected me.' Bremer was convicted of attempted murder and sentenced to sixty-three years in prison. In August 1972, three appeal judges reduced Bremer's sentence to fifty-three years. For most of his sentence Bremer has remained at the Maryland Correctional Institute.

Speaking from his cell in 1996, it was clear that Bremer was obviously still wallowing in his own failure: 'Everyone is mean nowadays . . . [We've] got teenagers running around with drugs and machine guns, they never heard of me . . . They never heard of the public figure in my case, and they couldn't care less. I was in prison when they were born. The country kind of went to hell.'

Bremer started to have parole hearings as far back as 1996. He failed his first psychological evaluation. Bremer explained this failure thus: 'If you ask a Nazi psychologist what he thinks, you'll get a Nazi's opinion. If you ask a Jewish psychologist what he thinks, you'll get a Jewish opinion.' In 1997 he wrote that he should be freed because 'segregationist dinosaurs . . . are extinct, not endangered, by an act of God'.

Finally, after a dozen or so hearings, Bremer convinced the prison board that he could be trusted and, after thirty-five years, the fifty-seven-year-old was freed just before daybreak on 9 November, 2007. Bremer became the first American assassin (albeit failed) to be fully freed from prison. His release caused outrage in Alabama, particularly amongst Wallace's family.

When he left jail, Bremer refused to speak to reporters. According to state Parole Commission Chairman David R. Blumberg, Bremer 'kept a decidedly low profile. He's turned down all requests for notoriety and interviews, including some that had money attached to them.' As to where Bremer is now and what he plans to do with the remainder of his life, only his parole officer knows. Hopefully, we won't be hearing from him anytime soon.

Thirteen

Spain's First Astronaut

As Arthur Bremer proved, assassins do not have to be the sharpest tool in the box to achieve their goal. The following attack was later regarded as one of the most important in modern history and shows what can be achieved with enthusiasm, determination and, most importantly, dumb luck.

The four young men began digging the tunnel from 104 Claudio Coello Street in Madrid on 7 December 1973. They were members of *Euskadi Ta Askatasunai* (ETA, Basque Nation and Freedom), a small revolutionary organisation, who had for a year searched for the best way to assassinate seventy-year-old Prime Minister Admiral Luis Carrero Blanco, eighty-one-year-old dictator Francisco Franco's designated heir. ETA's chief aim was to regain for two million Basques their ancient, almost tribal, traditions of self-government over their four rich provinces. They had been enemies of the State since they had fought against Franco in the Spanish Civil War of 1936 – when for a few months an autonomous Basque Republic had existed. In addition to many arson and bombing attacks, the small band of fanatical Basque separatists had since 1969 committed six assassinations, three kidnappings and forty bank raids, collecting close to ten million pounds. The assassination was supposed to be an act of revenge – their military leader, Eustaqui Mendizabel, had been killed in a shoot-out with police the previous April.

Most Spaniards were certain that Blanco represented the past, present and future of the Franco regime and that he would continue the repressive government exactly as it was, despite recent growing opposition from the Church, the workers, students and, of course, the Basques. Blanco had only two answers for the opposition: either to ignore it altogether or crush it by force. 'Politics for me consists of total loyalty to *El Caudillo* [The Leader],' he proclaimed proudly. 'My loyalty to his person and to his work is total, without a shadow of any personal conditions or a trace of mental reservation.' When he took over the reins of day-to-day government Blanco quickly replaced those officials he thought were liberal, or even slightly forward-looking, with ironclad conservatives.

'Operation Ogre' was originally intended to involve the kidnapping of Blanco, the 'Ogre', but the four men, led by José Miguel Bañaran Ordeñana, known as 'Argala', had reluctantly decided that Franco's security was potentially strong enough to resist a direct assault. Instead, they decided to find a way of assassinating the PM.

Blanco was a man of precise habits and it was this that would be his undoing – he had followed an almost unvarying schedule long before his inauguration the previous June. Every morning at about nine a.m. his Dodge Dart would park in front of Madrid's San Francisco de Borja church, only a hundred metres from his home, and Blanco would attend Mass. Approximately forty-five minutes later he would leave for his office in the Paseo de la Castellana.

This was the moment when the four men intended to end his life. They had decided to tunnel out into the street and dig a chamber that would be filled with explosives. When Blanco's car passed overhead, slowed down by a double-parked car, the explosives would be detonated from a distance by using an electric switch. The men were inexperienced in such operations but went about their difficult task with much enthusiasm and determination.

To explain the fact that they were always covered with dust and carried a variety of digging tools they told their landlord that they were student sculptors. Although he accepted their story, things soon started to go wrong. Their first problem was that they brought pickaxes that were too large for the small tunnel they were digging, so swinging them with any force became impossible. One of the diggers then discovered that he suffered from claustrophobia. As they dug they were rained on by a sewerage overflow and afflicted by strange noxious gases that turned their skin a greasy ashy-green; they couldn't leave the flat in case their queer appearance drew too many enquiries. Another effect of the gas was to intoxicate the assassins so that they became prone to giggling fits, dizziness and wild fantasies.

Meanwhile, their flat was filled to overflowing with sacks of stinking earth and they could think of no way to secretly remove it. In the tunnel there were innumerable roof falls; the conspirators each carried a pistol in their pocket in case the tunnel collapsed, thus giving them a quick alternative to a slow, stinking death by suffocation. Then one of the assassins had the bright idea of borrowing a book from the library on tunnel construction and they realised that they should have been using tunnel props.

Eventually it was done. On 15 December they met with other ETA members from the Basque country who brought eighty kilos of stolen explosives, two hundred metres of electric cord and two detonators. The explosives were placed in the seven-metre chamber, linked by the cord that led back to the apartment, and then, forming an electric cable, the cord was stretched the length of Claudio Coello Street alongside the telephone wires. At the appropriate time, the split cable would be attached to an electric trigger-box hidden in a briefcase. A man carrying the briefcase could then flick the switch which would detonate the bomb. The date of the assassination was set for 20 December. The newly released film *The Day of the Jackal* was playing in Madrid at the time and the four men went to see it.

20 December was a cloudy raw winter's day. Blanco left as usual at nine for Mass. Within a few minutes he was in the church. He was due to leave at 9.30 a.m. Argala was in position, lounging on a street corner with the briefcase which concealed the switch. Two others,

dressed as mechanics, walked up and down on the other side of the road. At 9.25 a.m. a young boy asked Argala for a match and, after some nervous fumbling, the assassin produced one. A minute or so later the boy returned, asking for another. The ETA man, desperate to get rid of him, threw the child the box.

At precisely 9.30 a.m. Blanco left the church with Police Inspector Don Juan Antonio Bueno Fernandez and his driver Don José Luis Perez Mojeda. The Dodge pulled away from the church and moved down Serrana, a one-way street, and slowed as it came alongside the double-parked ETA vehicle. It was 9.36 a.m. The switch was thrown.

A deep *whump* was followed by a very brief swelling of the road surface before it exploded in a vast mushroom cloud of dust and debris. The ETA members fled, shouting to stunned witnesses that there had been a gas explosion. They left a scene of utter devastation and confusion behind them. A twenty-five-metre hole gaped in the middle of the street; it was rapidly filling with water and stinking sewage from ruptured conduits and drains. The prime minister's escort car was a ruin, its three occupants all injured. Several parked cars had been blasted onto their sides. Police radio communications recorded in the immediate aftermath document the arrival of the first police car.

> 'H-20 [police headquarters] wants to find out what happened – what caused the explosion?'
>
> 'It was a gas explosion on Claudio Coello!'
>
> 'Good, H-20 has the message. Can you tell us if the premier's car that went by there suffered any damage?'
>
> 'No, nothing happened to the premier. There are five or six cars that have been damaged, two badly. It appears the wounded have been taken to Montesa Hospital . . . water is spilling over.'
>
> 'Has anything happened to the premier of the government? Yes or no? His car must have been in the vicinity . . . They are trying to locate the president's car to make sure everything is

normal. Over. Please see if you can inform us whether anything has happened to the premier's car.'

'No, got it, no, I thought one car . . . but the escort car . . . not his . . . One of the traffic policemen told me his car had passed by already.'

'Can you find out if anything has happened to the premier's car?'

'We have no information. We will check on the wounded at Montesa.'

'Go over, go over to the premier's house in Hermonas Becquer and find out if the president's car is in front of the door. Over 16.'

'We will check it out.'

'Yes, check it out. To see if anything has happened to the premier.'

At first, because they couldn't find the prime minister's car, it was assumed that he had somehow escaped and been driven to safety. But the assassin had timed his explosion well: Blanco's car had been directly over the bomb. It took off like a missile, rising an incredible five storeys as it gradually arced backwards, clipping the church spire before landing on its rooftop terrace. Incredibly, Blanco was still alive on the rooftop when the first fireman reached the car – but he didn't last for long. The policeman on the ground was on the radio to headquarters as the information came in.

'According to what they tell us, one car got directly hit and is on the roof of the church. The firemen are just coming down. Car and three occupants. Over K-20 . . . It seems that the car rose, that the explosion sent to the roof is the premier of the government's car! I can't yet confirm – it appears he is dead. The car on the roof is the president's car! It appears that he is dead.'

Blanco was the first head of government in Western Europe to be assassinated since 1934, when Austria's Engelbert Dollfuss had been shot in Vienna. While secret jokes about Blanco becoming Spain's first astronaut circulated through bars and cafés, and Basque musicians played a new dance, the 'Waltz of Carrero', Generalissimo Francisco Franco immediately called his Cabinet into emergency session to consider counter-measures and appoint an interim prime minister. Although the country remained calm, the police clamped down hard on ETA, arresting fourteen suspects.

Even as police searched for the assassins and the country braced itself for a counter-attack from militant rightists, it was clear that the ageing Franco had only two choices – to liberalise his regime or face the threat of having his country racked by more violence. The death of his protégé seemed to age Franco still further: his flesh hung loosely on his old frame and his mouth started to sag. Observers recalled that his palsied right hand sometimes shook so badly that he had to grip it in his left. His voice, always shrill, became strained and thin. 'I will continue as long as God grants me life and health,' he promised. When the newspaper *Madrid* suggested that he emulate France's Charles de Gaulle and retire, its presses were silenced by government decree for six months and the paper eventually went out of business. Nonetheless, Franco had already booked his tomb in the 'Valley of the Fallen', the grandiose memorial mausoleum carved by Republican prisoners of war in and around a granite mountain thirty miles from Madrid to hold Civil War dead.

Since Blanco could have become the most powerful figure in Spain upon Franco's passing, his death was instrumental in the transition of the nation towards a democratic government. It facilitated the decidedly non-revolutionary reform of the regime in the years which followed. ETA had changed the course of Spanish history before the eyes of the world, leading historian Raymond Carr to describe it as 'one of the most brilliantly planned assassinations in the history of terrorism'. This was not exactly true – the four assassins made the murder unnecessarily complex and put themselves at considerable risk time and again. They were inexperienced in the means they chose to murder Blanco and their hard work would have been instantly voided if Blanco had changed churches, his route or moved house during the year they were planning *Operacion Ogro*. If the double-parked car needed to force Blanco's Dodge over the tunnel bomb had been a car bomb then they need not have gone to the trouble of digging the tunnel and using the considerable quantity of explosives which were necessary to blow the road apart, thus putting many more innocent people in jeopardy. But, somehow, all the random variables worked out in favour of the assassins, and while it was perhaps not the best planned of killings it had the greatest possible effect. In his first speech on 12 February 1974, Blanco's successor, prime minister Carlos Arias Navarro, promised liberalising reforms, including the right to form political associations. Though he was denounced by hardliners within the regime, the transition had begun.

One postscript to the story is that although Blanco was widely despised, he did nonetheless have a small, fanatical following. On the morning of 21 December 1978, just after the fifth anniversary of Blanco's assassination, Argala the assassin stepped out of his cottage in the small French town of Anglet and walked to his car. He turned the key in the ignition, pressed down on the accelerator – and was promptly blown to pieces by an enormous bomb.

Fourteen

Operation Pandora's Box

Shortly after 9/11, US Secretary of State for Defence Donald Rumsfeld announced at a press conference that until that fateful day no one had ever imagined an airplane being flown into the White House. Rumsfeld, who was serving as the United States Ambassador to NATO in February 1974, could be forgiven for having missed the events surrounding this attempt on the life of President Richard Nixon, which until the Hollywood interpretation of proceedings (*The Assassination of Richard Nixon*, 2004) were lost to obscurity (but the essentials of which were outlined on page 537 of the 9/11 Commission report).

On 16 October 1972, Secret Service agents had questioned Samuel Joseph Byck, an unemployed tyre salesman, after he had made a plane trip during which he loudly contended that 'someone ought to kill President Nixon'. Byck was described by the agents as quite intelligent and well read and he struck them as an innocuous type. They tracked down his psychiatrist who said that Byck was a 'big talker who makes verbal threats and never acts on them'. He had been treated in a mental hospital that year for depression and the agents shrugged him off as a harmless crank.

If they'd dug a little further, however, they would have discovered that Byck had been arrested twice for protesting in front of the White House without a permit, and that he had also dressed in a

Santa suit for another anti-Nixon protest and had, bizarrely, tried to join the Black Panthers, a militant Black Power sect with whom he sympathised (Byck was white).

Byck was a neurotic personality, who, after a lifetime of failure and rejection, decided to assassinate Richard Nixon as a way of winning public adulation. He felt betrayed by his wife who had divorced him and taken away his children and by his mother who had left the house where she was living with him. On 20 February Byck wrote his last will and testament: 'I will to each of my children . . . the sum of one dollar each. They have each other and they deserve each other.'

In a series of rambling tape recordings and letters, Byck outlined his plan, which he dubbed 'Operation Pandora's Box'. He posted the letters to newspaper columnist Jack Anderson, inventor of the polio vaccine Jonas Salk, composer Leonard Bernstein, Senator Abraham Ribicoss and Senator Jacob Javits. His tapes revealed that he held the government's corruption as a prime cause of his personal woes. At the time, the Watergate scandal (President Nixon had authorised the bugging of the campaign offices of his political opposition) that eventually forced Nixon to resign was reaching a crescendo.

At seven a.m. on 22 February 1974 a burly middle-aged man ambled up to the front of the line at Gate C at Baltimore-Washington international airport. Aviation Administration Police Officer George Neal Ramsburg stood with his back to the line. The man pumped two shots into his back with a stolen .22 revolver – Ramsburg was dead before his body thudded to the floor. As passengers screamed, the killer, carrying a briefcase containing a home-made bomb made from two-gallon containers of gasoline and a lighter, jumped over the security chain, raced down the boarding ramp and burst into the jet's unlocked cockpit. Levelling the .22 at the pilot and co-pilot, Reese Lofton and Fred Jones, he fired a shot inside the cabin and said 'Fly this plane outta here!'

Lofton replied that until the wheel-blocks were removed the plane wouldn't take off. Byck didn't believe him and so shot the co-pilot in the stomach and shouted: 'The next one will be in the head!' He then grabbed a female passenger and pushed her towards the controls, shouting 'Help this man fly this plane!'

Suddenly, two shots sounded from outside the plane. Charles Troyer, a local off-duty cop, had taken the .357 pistol from Ramsburg's body. Byck wheeled round and shot the co-pilot again, this time just above the left eye; firing once more, he hit the pilot in the shoulder. As Byck reloaded, the pilot made a desperate last call to warn the control tower.

> Pilot: 'Ah, ground control, this is . . . ah . . . Delta at the ramp C8 . . . do you read?'
> GC: 'Delta C, go ahead.'
> Pilot: 'Do you read?'
> GC: 'I cut Delta out. Go ahead, Delta.'
> Pilot: 'Emergency, emergency, we're all shot . . . ah . . . can you get another pilot here to the airplane . . . ah . . . this fellow shot us both. Ground . . . I need ground . . . ah, this is a state of emergency. Get a hold of our ramp and ask the people to unhook the tug [the blocks].'

The pilot then passed out as Byck finished reloading. Byck grabbed another woman passenger by the hair, yanked her into the cockpit, and pumped another shot into each of the pilots. The co-pilot was already dead. Police snipers fired into the cabin while the woman screamed for Byck to let her go. Two shots hit Byck in the stomach and chest. He fell to the floor, pressed the barrel of his gun to his right temple and squeezed the trigger.

When the police entered the cockpit, Byck was still conscious and said 'Please help me' as he died. The plane never left the gate, and Nixon's schedule was not affected by the assassination attempt. The captain pulled through and resumed his job five years later.

Byck's assassination attempt faded into obscurity. While the news media reported on his actions, the Secret Service did not disclose why he had attempted to hijack the plane, fearing that it would lead to copycat crimes. In 1987 a Federal Airlines Authority report entitled 'Troubled Passage: The Federal Aviation Administration During the Nixon–Ford Term 1973–1977' referred to Byck's failed hijacking: 'Although Byck lacked the skill and self-control to reach his target, he had provided a chilling reminder of the potential of violence against civil aviation. Under a more relaxed security system, his suicidal rampage might have begun when the airliner was aloft.'

Fifteen

The Bite of the Cobra

Assassinations take the world by surprise, often causing leaders across the globe to gasp in horror as they hear the news. This next case was dramatically different in that prime ministers, presidents and dictators sighed in relief when the reign of the most powerful man on the planet was suddenly curtailed in 1975. This ranks as one of the most significant assassinations in the history of the world but the full extraordinary story has remained untold. Until now. Where else but in an assassination story would you find characters like a drug-dealing Saudi prince, an American B-movie actress and German Stasi agents?

As soon as twenty-seven-year-old Prince Faisal Ibu Musaed stepped off the royal jet at Saudi Arabia's Riyadh Airport, his passport was confiscated. The wild-eyed, long-haired youth, fashionably dressed in Western jeans and oversize tinted Ray-Bans, received disapproving looks from his uncle's welcoming committee. He was taken by bullet-proof limousine to the palace where his uncle and guardian, King Faisal ibn al Saud, the sixty-nine-year-old absolute ruler of Saudi Arabia, told him that he had become an embarrassment to his country and would never be allowed to leave Saudi Arabia again. The young prince listened calmly to his uncle's admonishments and as soon as the ticking-off was over he bowed gracefully and left the palace without saying a word.

Prince Faisal was one black sheep among the three thousand princes of the House of Saud. He was the son of Prince Musad, a Muslim fundamentalist and exiled half-brother of King Faisal. Musad had rejected what he saw as the king's moderate Western-friendly rule and had fled Riyadh to lead a nomadic life. He had lived quietly until 1965, when the king decided to install a television station; under Musad's strict interpretation of the Koran, broadcasts of the human image were blasphemous. With a band of like-minded brigands, Musad's eldest son Khaled led a violent protest against the TV station. In the ensuing clash with the King's soldiers the protesters were fired upon with machine guns and Khaled was one of the first to be blasted to the ground, dead.

Musad's other son, Prince Faisal, who was seventeen at the time of his brother's death, showed no intention of following his family's hard-line example. In fact he went to the other extreme. He left the care of his family, embraced Western values and in 1970 persuaded his uncle the king that he should be allowed to travel to America to study.

But instead of reading for his business degree, first at the University of California, then at the University of Colorado, the young prince spent all his time chasing women and taking LSD and marijuana. He joined student political groups who were overjoyed to learn that the nephew of the king of Saudi Arabia was among them. They impressed upon him the idea that King Faisal and the royal institutions were standing in the way of a progressive Saudi Arabia and that he had a responsibility to do something about it. These intense, drug-fuelled discussions were to have a long-lasting impact on Prince Faisal.

While at university he met and fell in love with a startlingly beautiful blonde model, an ambitious actress called Christine Surma. After using all his princely charm (which consisted of most of his allowance) to woo her, they moved into an apartment together. While the prince attended 'political meetings' (essentially an excuse to take drugs), where young activists urged him to liberalise Saudi Arabia, Christine disappeared each day to work on her latest project, a B-movie called *Bite of the Cobra*. The prince, who before taking LSD had been a quiet, almost unnoticeable character, had since developed into a wild-child college drop-out with his fashionably long hair, jeans and tight leather jacket. The prince was only too aware that once his family discovered he wasn't taking his studies seriously, his allowance would be stopped, so he decided to start dealing drugs so that he could maintain his lavish lifestyle with Christine.

Disaster struck almost immediately. Prince Faisal was arrested in Boulder, Colorado. The police officers found their young prisoner to be exceptionally paranoid, and sometimes it seemed as if he didn't hear their questions, that his mind was elsewhere. A psychiatrist concluded that he was suffering from the effects of 'marijuana addiction' and should be institutionalised.

Prince Faisal was acquitted of the drugs charges (thanks in part to diplomatic immunity) but was sentenced to twenty-eight days in the Brooke-Hall Mental Hospital in Westport, Connecticut. Christine waited for him and after his release he applied to study political science at Berkeley. This didn't last long before he decided to leave the USA for Beirut to have a crack at the international drugs trade. At the end of 1974, as the opening salvoes were fired in what would become the savage Lebanese civil war (during which Muslims were publicly executed by having their throats slit) Faisal travelled to Communist-run East Germany – an odd choice perhaps, given his Western leanings.

But East Germany was a safe European base for the terrorist group known as the Palestine Liberation Organisation, who received most of their funding from King Faisal. They welcomed his young nephew with the deep wallet who was eager to fund a drug-dealing operation. The PLO had spent years considering raising more money by investing in the drugs trade.[14] Unfortunately for the prince, the PLO regarded him as too much of an unstable hothead and sent him

[14] The British National Criminal Intelligence Service reported that by the late 1990s the PLO had worldwide assets approaching $10 billion and an additional annual income of about $2 billion, much of it generated from drug trafficking.

on his way. From this moment on the prince's movements before he turned up in Saudi Arabia two months later were unknown.

Until now, that is. Buried deep in the vaults of the East German Secret Police building in Berlin, hidden among the thirty million pages that fill five million manila folders kept by the Stasi, probably the most meticulous bureaucrats in the world, lies a remarkable file entitled 'Prince Faisal Ibu Musaed'. It's not surprising that the Stasi had a file on the prince: with its 90,000 employees and 300,000 informants, it seemed as though the Stasi had a file on nearly everyone in the country. A Middle Eastern prince was hardly going to go unnoticed.

According to his file, Prince Faisal arrived in East Berlin in late 1974, just as the East Germans were starting to feel the effects of the 1973 oil crisis. The sudden drastic changes in oil prices had an inevitable, though somewhat delayed, impact on East Germany, which relied on the Soviet Union for its oil. After the 1973 crisis, the Soviets enforced a new pricing system where calculations were made every year based on average world market prices for the previous five years. At the start of 1975, East Germany suddenly felt the pinch and entered a terrible economic recession. Even if you had the money and wanted to buy a new TV, telephone or Trabant, you were placed on a ten-year waiting list. A shortage of towels and scissors meant that those who wanted a haircut had to bring their own implements when they visited their hairdresser. East Germany's state food manufacturer struggled to produce German sausages. They simply could not afford to import or manufacture goods (you needed a lot of oil to do either), a disastrous position for a nation determined to show the rest of the world that its communist regime was superior to that of any capitalist state. The man directly responsible for the oil crisis and East Germany's predicament was Prince Faisal's uncle, the king of Saudi Arabia.

Both in his own right and as a symbol of the other newly powerful potentates of oil, King Faisal, the dour, ascetic and shrewd undisputed ruler of Saudi Arabia, was, in the early 1970s, the most powerful man on the planet. His bleak and sparsely populated country was by far the world's greatest seller and reservoir of oil and Faisal was the principal proponent behind the increasing of oil prices: he held more power than any other leader to lower them or raise them. United in history's most efficient cartel, OPEC[15] exploited modern civilisation's dependence on oil.

Again and again in 1972 and 1973, the cartel raised the price of oil until it reached unprecedented heights, leading to the greatest and swiftest transfer of wealth in all history. The thirteen OPEC countries earned one hundred and twelve billion dollars from the rest of the world in 1973. Because they could not begin to spend it all, they ran up a surplus of sixty billion dollars. This sudden shift of money shook the whole fragile structure of the international financial system, severely weakened the already troubled economies of the oil-importing nations and gave a great new political strength to the exporters.

In 1974, Faisal's Saudi Arabia earned 28.9 billion dollars by selling nearly one-fifth of all the oil consumed by non-Communist countries. The king channelled part of these funds into a massive development programme aimed at building factories, refineries, harbours, hospitals and schools for his 5.7 million people. Faisal also spent about two billion dollars on modern weapons for his small but growing armed forces. He was the primary outside bankroller of the Egyptians, Syrians, Jordanians and the PLO. He also made 1.2 billion dollars in multilateral loans and grants and pledged to give some two hundred million dollars to poor countries outside the Arab world.

But all the king's spending and all the king's plans could not come close to using up Saudi Arabia's wealth. The new financial giant of the world, Saudi Arabia in 1974 stood to accumulate a surplus of about twenty-three billion dollars – at that time a potentially unsettling force in the field of global finance. King Faisal

[15] The Organisation of Petroleum Exporting Countries in 1973 comprised Saudi Arabia, Iran, Venezuela, Nigeria, Libya, Kuwait, Iraq, United Arab Emirates, Algeria, Indonesia, Qatar, Ecuador and Gabon.

was not merely the richest of the OPEC leaders. He was also a spiritual leader of the world's six hundred million Muslims because his kingdom encompassed Islam's two holiest cities, Mecca and Medina. The King, who was sixty-nine, wanted to pray within his lifetime in Islam's third most holy city, in Jerusalem at the Dome of the Rock, and to walk there without setting foot on Israeli-held territory. Unless and until he got his wish, peace was unlikely to have much future in the Middle East.

Faisal hated Zionism with a cold passion. For many months in 1973, the king warned the US that unless it forced Israel to withdraw from the occupied Arab territories and settle the Palestinians' grievances, he would slow down oil production. The State Department thought that the threat was hollow; President Nixon warned on television that the Arabs risked losing their oil markets if they tried to act too tough.

The Arab–Israeli war of October 1973 moved the Arabs to impose a reduction in oil output – and to do much more. Within ten days after the Egyptians and Syrians had attacked Israeli-occupied territory, the Arabs and Iranians in OPEC, long derided in the West for their disunity, agreed to raise prices from $1.99 to $3.44 per barrel. A few days after that, King Faisal spearheaded an even more robust move. Angered by the US's military resupplying of Israel, the Saudis and the other Arabs embargoed all oil shipments to the US and started cutting production. Very quickly their output dropped twenty-eight per cent. When the West made no response, OPEC realised its own strength and kept right on raising prices through 1974.

This huge success gave new pride and political power to all the Arabs and brought King Faisal widespread respect in the Arab world, many of whose leaders had earlier scorned him as an unregenerate conservative. The Middle East became a magnet for Western bankers, each with his own creative plan for dispensing the Arabs' cash. Western governments vied with the Soviets over which side could sell the Arabs more fighter jets, tanks and missiles. So much foreign money washed into Arab oil-producing countries that ordinary statistics no longer made sense. Some planners worried about keeping a work ethic going. Said a Saudi government minister: 'We will have to be very careful not to spoil our citizens.'

As the price of oil increased, it kicked up the prices of countless oil-based products, including fertilisers, petrochemicals and synthetic textiles. To battle inflation, all Western nations clamped down with restrictive budget and credit policies, causing their economies to slow down simultaneously for the first time since the 1930s. The danger of a global recession grew because, as people spent more for oil, they had less money to spend on other things. The overall decline in demand reduced production and jobs. Because non-OPEC nations had to pay out so much for foreign oil, they moderated their buying of other imports; that slowed the growth of world trade, a major source of international cooperation since the Second World War. For most of the year, Western European nations and Japan refused to follow the US's call for a united front against the oil producers, essentially because European leaders considered the consumers' bargaining power to be too feeble.

The Europeans and the Japanese were dependent on the Middle East for respectively seventy and eighty per cent of their oil. The US had to import more than one-third of its supply. The nation's bill for foreign oil rose from 3.9 billion dollars in 1972 to twenty-four billion dollars in 1973. The oil rise, which Yale Economist Richard Cooper called 'King Faisal's tax', reduced Americans' purchasing power and consumption of goods by as much as a ten per cent increase in personal income taxes would have done. Japan's eighteen-billion-dollar bill for oil imports was the biggest single factor in lifting its inflation rate to a punishing twenty-four per cent, causing the first real post-war decline in economic growth. Inflation rates doubled in many Western European nations: to sixteen per cent in France and Belgium, eighteen per cent in Britain, twenty-five per cent in Italy. To meet its trade deficit, Italy borrowed more than thirteen billion dollars, incurring interest payments of nearly one billion dollars a year. Prime Minister Harold Wilson said that the fivefold increase in oil prices had caused Britain's worst economic crisis since the 1930s and was severely testing the country's social and political fabric. For Europeans, life became a little darker, slower and colder. Heating-oil prices virtually doubled and thermostats were turned down.

The poorest countries of Africa, Asia and Latin America were the worst hurt victims of the oil squeeze as the extra costs for oil in 1973 totalled ten billion dollars, wiping out most of their foreign aid income of 11.4 billion dollars from the industrialised world. India suffered too. Its oil import costs hit 1.6 billion dollars, up fivefold in two years, leaving it little money to import food and fertiliser, machines and medicine. Pakistan's plight was almost as critical: its imports of oil and fertiliser topped 355 million dollars. Sri Lanka's rice farmers had to pay nearly four times more for fertiliser; they reduced their buying so much that the rice harvest fell almost forty per cent below expectations. The embargo against the USA ended in 1974 but prices remained high and by 1975 King Faisal still maintained his position as the most powerful man in the world, a man with a stranglehold on the world's economy, who could change the economic fate of nations – even the mighty USA – with a few words.

Needless to say, the Stasi were very interested in talking to the young Saudi Arabian prince. They arranged it through a student group essentially made up of Stasi informers who were no doubt delighted to discover that American students had already been encouraging the prince to rebel against his uncle. (Incidentally, King Faisal was an enemy of the Eastern Bloc because he was vehemently anti-communist.) While the prince took LSD and smoked marijuana the Stasi agents did their utmost to convince him to end the rule of his uncle for the good of the world.

Prince Faisal returned to Riyadh two months later, where his passport was confiscated and he was confined to his palace rooms. All seemed to be going well as he settled down: he even started teaching at Riyadh University while maintaining a long-distance relationship with Christine Surma by telephone.

Early on the morning of 25 March 1975 King Faisal was receiving a Kuwati delegation as part of the celebrations to mark the 1,405th birthday of the Prophet Muhammad. Among them, his long hair and Western clothing hidden underneath a traditional flowing headdress and white robe, was Prince Faisal. He gripped his pistol tightly.

The king first welcomed the Kuwaiti Oil Minister before turning to greet his nephew. He lowered his head so that the prince, following custom, could kiss the tip of his nose. Instead the prince drew his revolver and shot the king in the face, blowing his chin almost clean away. As the Oil Minister, Sheikh Yamani, shouted at the young prince to stop, Ibu Musaed fired again, this time into the king's ear. As he fired a third time one of the king's security guards struck the prince to the floor with his still-sheathed golden sword. The prince threw away his gun and shouted 'Now my brother is avenged!' The king was rushed to a nearby hospital; shortly after noon an announcer on Radio Riyadh, his voice breaking with emotion, said that Faisal was dead. The royal family chose Crown Prince Khalid ibn Abdul Aziz to succeed his brother and Interior Minister Prince Fahd was named the next Crown Prince.

Across the Middle East, radio stations broke into their regular programmes to replay the emotion-choked voice of the Riyadh announcer. Panic and hysteria swept through the dusty streets of the Saudi Arabian capital as the news spread. Fierce Bedouin tribesmen wept openly; army and police units moved into strategic positions throughout the city. Within hours, every Arab government had proclaimed extended periods of mourning. Egypt's President Anwar Sadat, who had received extensive aid and political support from the Saudi King, called Faisal 'a tireless fighter for the Arab cause'.

Even US officials who despised King Faisal for his oil-based control of the world's economy appeared shocked by the news of his death. King Faisal had at least been vehemently anti-Communist. In Washington, President Gerald Ford described him as 'a close friend of the United States' whose 'wisdom and stature earned the respect of the entire world'. Ford dispatched Vice-President Nelson Rockefeller to Riyadh to convey his condolences to the royal family.

Secretary of State Henry Kissinger, who had conferred with Faisal only six days earlier in Riyadh, spoke of the King's 'extraordinary personality' and of his unique influence on 'both the moderates and the radical elements in the Arab world'.

At first, investigators assumed that the assassin was insane. But Saudi religious figures said that Prince Faisal had suffered the evil of too much travel (to place this somewhat odd statement in perspective: his exodus to the US had come only two years after Saudi Arabia outlawed slavery) and too much foreign influence. Radio Riyadh later said that the prince had confessed to the assassination, explaining it as an effort to rid Saudi Arabia of the rule of Islam because it stood 'in the way of the development of the country'. It also emerged that Prince Faisal had another motive – revenge for his brother's death.

Prince Faisal's American friends described him to journalists as a likeable, notably unstudious young man. Christine Surma said in a TV interview that the prince had never shown any hostility towards his uncle and was a 'perfect gentleman', adding, 'If he's crazy, he's become so since he left the US.' But Surma failed to mention Faisal's stay in the mental hospital and his arrest for dealing in LSD. The twenty-six-year-old actress vanished shortly after the interview – and as for the B-movie *Bite of the Cobra*, no film with that name exists. Some investigators speculated that she had been working in some capacity to encourage Prince Faisal to assassinate his uncle, but there is no evidence to support this.

The rest of the world breathed a sigh of relief when King Faisal was replaced by the moderate King Khalid, who eventually increased oil production and released so much oil that prices actually fell back to below pre-1973 levels.

As for the assassin, Saudi Arabian justice was swift, sure and deadly. Loudspeaker vans rumbled through the streets of Riyadh announcing that a *sharia* (religious) court had found the twenty-seven-year-old prince guilty and he would be executed immediately. Within minutes, an estimated six thousand Saudis had streamed into the city's Court of Justice Square facing the Riyadh Mosque. At the appointed hour, the young prince was led, blindfolded, to the square. As he knelt with his hands tied behind his back, one of the sharia judges read him the court's verdict which was, in keeping with the words of the Prophet Muhammad, 'a soul for a soul'.

First a security guard prodded the condemned man in the side with a sharpened stick. Then, as the prince straightened his body in an automatic reflex, the executioner's enormous gold-handled sword flashed, and with a single stroke Prince Faisal's head rolled from his shoulders. The crowd, silent until that moment, broke into shouts of '*Allahu akhbar* [God is great]!' For fifteen minutes the prince's head was displayed on the tip of a spike for the crowd's inspection; eventually an ambulance collected it and the body for burial in an unmarked grave.

A few days later, in the Stasi's headquarters in Lichtenberg, one of the thousands of anonymous bureaucrats retrieved Prince Faisal's file from the labyrinthine shelves and stamped *Subject Deceased* on its cover.

Sixteen

Terror in Rome

In the 1970s Europe was in the grip of home-grown terrorists. In London in 1975 the IRA tried to bomb a Tory MP but instead almost blew up Caroline Kennedy, daughter of JFK. Fortunately, a telephone call recalled her to her house as the bomb detonated. Instead, it claimed the life of a passing doctor. Founder of the *Guinness Book of World Records* and political activist Alan Ross McWhirter offered a reward of fifty thousand pounds for the capture of those involved. Sadly, McWhirter jumped straight to the top of the IRA's hit list and they shot him dead on his own doorstep.

In Germany, the Red Army Faction (RAF) terrorists were doing their level best to create anarchy. The RAF was a leftist guerrilla group with no discernible aims other than creating fear and chaos in the futile hope that the German government would eventually collapse. In the autumn of 1977 they kidnapped West Germany's leading industrialist and head of the West German Industries Federation Hanns Martin Schleyer, demanding the release of imprisoned comrades for his safe return. The German government refused and Schleyer's body turned up a few days later in the boot of a car with seven bullets in his body.

Even more spectacular was the extraordinary 1978 case of the Italian Premier, Aldo Moro. This terrible tale is all the more unusual because it now seems as though some elements within the Italian government ended up colluding with the terrorist group known as the Red Brigade in an effort to speed Moro's demise.

On the damp morning of 16 March 1978 Roman florist Antonio Spiriticchio was distraught. Vandals had slashed all four tyres of his van; his stock would wilt and die unsold. But for the Red Brigade, this was a vital part of their plan. Disabling Spiriticchio's van meant one less key eyewitness as well as the removal of a significant obstruction at the junctions of Via Stresa and Via Fani.

At 8.55 a.m. that same morning, Aldo Moro, five times premier of Italy and the popular leader of the ruling Christian Democratic Party, emerged from his grand mansion in the green Monte Mario district that sat on a hill overlooking Rome. Moro had recently achieved the impossible by bringing together the Communists and the Christian Democrats, Italy's two largest parties, stabilising the normally fractious Italian government. He kissed his wife of thirty-three years, Eleonora, goodbye and walked to his car. Like all important political leaders, Moro, who was expected to become the country's next president, was well guarded. But unlike the then-current president Giovanni Leone's limousine, Moro's Fiat 130 was not bulletproof.

With Moro was forty-two-year-old Oreste Leonardi, tall, dark, discreet, an expert marksman who had shot more than his fair share of Italian bank robbers before becoming Moro's faithful bodyguard fifteen years earlier. Domenico Ricci, thirty-four, was the driver of Moro's Fiat. His silent temperament, his ice-cold nerves and his remarkable driving ability had been the reason for his requisition from the *Caribinieri*, Italy's gendarmerie. He would be followed by a specially modified Alfa-Romeo Alfetta saloon (its engine had been upgraded to a powerful racing-standard 2.4 litres) containing three agents.

The two cars moved off down Via del Forte Trionfale and then into the narrow Via Licino Calvo. As they drove down the narrow street, four men dressed in Alitalia pilot uniforms, waiting outside a closed bar, turned and watched.

The two-car convoy was forced to a slow crawl by a Fiat 128, a tiny family car, with diplomatic plates. Ricci and Leonardi realised straight away that something wasn't right. Ricci edged to the side, changed down a gear and, pushing down the clutch slightly, gently squeezed the accelerator, looking for a chance to burst through any gap, to slam the Fiat aside. But it suddenly twisted and stopped dead. Ricci responded quickly and managed to avoid hitting the Fiat but the escort car, caught by surprise, slammed into him, pushing Moro's car into the rear right offside corner of the Fiat. They were trapped.

Leonardi reached for his holster as the rear doors of the 128 flew open and a man with long fashionable hair and moustache and a woman with long straight blonde hair, both carrying sub-machine guns, leaped out, took careful aim and shot Ricci dead through the windscreen. Leonardi yelled at Moro to hit the deck as he came up with his .357 pistol, kicking the car door open just as the man with the moustache appeared and blasted him in the chest. Leonardi fell back, mortally wounded.

As the men in the Alfetta started to respond to the attack, the four 'pilots' marched towards the car, firing handguns. The driver, moustachioed thirty-year-old Francisco Rizzi, who was about to go on leave so that he could get married, was killed first. His companion tried to fire back through the windscreen but wasn't quick enough – a terrorist slug blew his brains out. The third, final and youngest guard, Giulio Rivera – he was twenty-four – managed to dive out of the rear offside door and, using the car door as cover, fired wildly at the four men as they ducked round the other side of the Fiat.

As the four 'pilots' kept Rivera pinned down, firing dozens of rounds of ammunition while he frantically tried to reload, the blonde woman walked calmly round Moro's car so that she was behind him. She took careful aim and as Rivera turned to face her she squeezed off a single shot. Rivera fell, a bullet hole precisely at the centre of his forehead. Moro, who had been hit in one of his buttocks by a ricocheting bullet, was pulled from the car by the 'pilots' and was shoved into a waiting blue Fiat 132 that had been strategically parked so that it blocked traffic at a nearby junction, keeping the road ahead clear. As it pulled away, two other cars picked up the hit squad and they drove off in different directions. It was 9.06 a.m.

Within the hour, three thousand policemen had been instructed to drop every other investigation and to turn Rome inside out in a ceaseless search for Moro. At the scene, police found more than sixty spent bullet casings from a mix of Italian, Czech and Soviet weapons. At key road junctions outside the city concentric rings of roadblocks were manned by police and thousands of soldiers were called in from around the country. Some ten miles further out, another ring of roadblocks was set up. Police stopped cars and levelled their guns at drivers, while soldiers stood at the ready in the background, sometimes behind sandbags. Tens of thousands of vehicles were checked.

That day and the next, they found the cars but that was all. Two hundred twelve-man squads performed three thousand home and ten thousand car searches in twenty-four hours; soon fifteen thousand men were on the case. But the kidnappers had vanished. There should have been clues – cars had to be stolen, used and exchanged, weapons had to be obtained, the scene had to be staked out, Moro must have been watched for days, if not weeks, safe houses must have existed – but the police could find nothing. Foreign help arrived in the form of a team of specialists from the West German Federal Criminal Bureau and two agents from Britain's Special Air Service. Still nothing was turned up – until the kidnappers sent a message to the police via a newspaper. The police checked an automatic photo booth in the city centre. On its roof was a photograph showing Moro in captivity, along with a message informing them that Moro would be 'tried' in a court with his kidnappers as judges.

By the morning of the next day, Spiriticchio the florist, with new tyres on his van, was doing brisk business as people flocked to lay floral tributes to the murdered bodyguards at the corner of Via Stresa and Via Fani. TV cameras recorded a flock of teenage schoolgirls solemnly disembarking from their bus to lay wreaths. The Italian press named the day *Strage di Giovedì Nero* – the Massacre of Black Thursday.

Aside from the intensive manhunt, the uneasy country was all too aware of the duel of nerves being played out between the state and the terrorists in two vastly different trials. The first was the legal trial, in a fortified barracks in Turin, of fifteen Red Brigade members charged with previous counts of kidnapping, assassination and armed insurrection. Though this trial was repeatedly postponed as a result of Red Brigade intimidation, the authorities were more determined than ever that it had to go on. The defendants made the most of the kidnapping, shouting to the courtroom 'Moro is in the hands of the proletariat, and he will be tried. Long live the Red Brigade!'

The Red Brigade was an urban-guerrilla group that had grown from the failure of left-wing political groups to take hold in Italy. It had terrorist contacts throughout Europe and the Middle East. Since its formation in 1974, its members had specialised in the kidnapping and murdering of Italian judges, politicians and businessmen. The young Marxist terrorists who operated under the vague revolutionary motto *Vogliamo tutto e subito!* ('We want everything now!') numbered about five hundred hard-core members organised into small cells, or 'columns'. They were led by a husband-and-wife team, Renato Curcio and Margherita Cagol (who was killed in a shooting in 1975). When Curcio was arrested in January 1976, the Red Brigade tried to force the Italian government to release him by mounting a campaign of murder and intimidation. But, after a lengthy and highly publicised trial in 1978, Curcio was sentenced to life in prison.

The other trial, being conducted in a middle-class apartment in a nondescript area of Rome, was the 'People's Tribunal' trying Moro. This was the terrorists' way of dealing with the man whom they accused of 'criminal counter-revolution'. Other public officials who'd been similarly kidnapped in the past had also been subjected to these 'trials', which consisted largely of forcing the victims to endure endless Marxist diatribes before they were released. As it was, Moro was being tried by one man, thirty-two-year-old Red Brigade chieftain Mario Moretti, who was amazed that the kidnap had gone as well as it had. He was also impressed by his captive who had told him that there would be no rescue, no negotiation; that Moretti would have to kill him. The reason: certain members of his government had much to gain by his death. Moretti had performed a service for Moro's enemies. Moretti refused to believe him.

The following Saturday, Moro's captors issued 'Communiqué Number Two' almost simultaneously in Rome, Milan, Turin and Genoa. The 1,700-word message, a rambling revolutionary harangue about the 'menace of imperialist terrorism', made no demand for an exchange of prisoners. It did claim that Moro was being 'interrogated' and warned that he would be given 'proletarian justice'.

Six days later, Moretti handed Moro pen and paper. 'We will test your theory. Write to your colleagues, ask them for their help; to negotiate.' Moro wrote to Interior Minister Cosiga asking the government to negotiate his release and naming the Vatican as a possible negotiator.

The government made no response. Moro's deputy, now the caretaker prime minister Giulio Andreotti, made it clear as soon as he read the letter that any correspondence from Moro would be treated as extorted and 'not morally imputable' to him.

On 4 April there was still another communiqué and another letter from Moro: 'I am a political prisoner and your brisk refusal to enter into any kind of discussion about the fate of other, similarly detained persons gives rise to an untenable situation. Time passes fast. Any moment might be too late.' Moro's family was outraged by the government's failure to turn up any clues or even attempt negotiation as a means to gathering more information, let alone for Moro's safe return.

In all, Moro wrote twenty letters during his kidnapping to the principal leaders of his party and to Pope Paul VI. Some were very critical of Andreotti (and were at the time held back from the public). Moro argued, understandably, against the government's policy of non-negotiation and advocated that the state's primary objective should be to save people's lives, and that the government should strive to comply with his kidnappers' requests. He was ignored. Government-hired experts told Moro's family that judging by the letters he was being tortured and was writing under the influence of mind-altering drugs. Meanwhile, Moro told Moretti that he thought his party had been neutralised 'by someone or something'.

On 18 April a message arrived saying that Moro had been executed after the people's court passed a death sentence. His body could be found five thousand feet up the Abruzzi Mountains, seventy-five miles north-east of Rome. There was however, no body. On 24 April, after an appeal by Pope Paul VI who said that he was 'begging on his knees' for Moro's safe return, a communiqué arrived that said unless the imprisoned Red Brigade members who were on trial in Turin were released, Moro's sentence would be carried out. Moro's enclosed letter said: 'We are almost at zero hour, seconds rather than minutes from the end.' Eleven days of silence followed.

In reality, the kidnappers were at a bit of a loss. According to Moretti, several of them wanted to let Moro go while others insisted on his execution. Moretti, the leader of the operation, was the only one to speak to Moro throughout the entire ordeal and had the final say. He asked Moro to write another letter – he could write about anything he liked. He wrote to Andreotti, ordering that no one from his party should attend his funeral. He wrote 'My blood will be upon you, upon the party, upon the Nation.'

Not one of Moro's colleagues, not one of his friends who had known him for years, lifted a finger to try and save him. The order had been given, however cryptically, that the Mafia didn't want Moro to live because he knew too much about their ability to influence the government. Many of Moretti's comrades argued that they should let him go for this very reason. Moretti disagreed: they should only be concerned with the release of their comrades, the other politics didn't concern them. He put it to a vote.

On or around 6 May Moro was told by Moretti to write a last letter to his family. 'Dear Nora,' Moro wrote to Eleonora, 'soon they will kill me. My friends could have saved me but did not. I kiss you for the last time. Kiss the children for me.' In a series of late-night phone calls to party leaders, Eleonora pleaded once more for a change in the party's stand against negotiations, but the government refused.

On the morning of 9 May, Moretti told Moro to get himself ready. They were moving him to a new safe house and the prime minister was escorted by four members of the Red Brigade to a dusty garage where he was forced into the boot of a burgundy-red Renault. As soon as one of the kidnappers threw a blanket on top of the premier, Moretti executed Moro with eleven shots fired from a Czech-made Skorpion 7.65mm pistol. Eight shots were centred around his heart.

Shortly before one p.m. the same day (the fifty-fourth since the abduction), Moretti telephoned the Christian Democratic headquarters. 'Go to Via Caetani,' he said. 'A red Renault. You will find another message.' Police quickly spotted the Renault and its grim contents. An autopsy showed that Moro had been shot earlier that morning, dressed in the same navy suit coat that he'd been wearing when he'd been kidnapped. The Renault had been dumped a hundred metres from Communist headquarters and seventy-five metres from those of the Christian Democrats – the two parties Moro had spent much of his political career bringing together.

President Giovanni Leone announced the assassination on television: 'Aldo Moro has been pitilessly and horrifyingly slain . . . Yet while this death appals and disturbs, it will never succeed in defeating us . . . a tragic error has been committed by these wretched heirs of the most barbarous assassins that mankind has known.'

A spontaneous outpouring of sorrow suddenly supplanted the cynicism with which many Italians had come to regard the kidnapping. Flags flew at half-mast. Both chambers of parliament closed to hold memorial sessions. Crowds poured into the piazzas of the cities to vent their anguish and their frustration.

The next day Moro was buried, following a private funeral attended only by his family and friends, in a cemetery at the village of Torrita Tiberina, thirty miles north of Rome, where the Moros had a country home. On Saturday the government held a televised state funeral in Rome's Cathedral of St John Lateran. While hundreds of Italian politicians, including Communist Party boss Enrico Berlinguer, and representatives of more than a hundred countries stood in hushed silence, Pope Paul VI devoted a special prayer to his friend. The Pontiff asked 'that our heart may be able to forgive the unjust and moral outrage inflicted on this dearest man'.

The kidnappers, meanwhile, remained at large. Not only had they avoided capture and hidden Moro for fifty-four days while maintaining communications with the authorities in three cities, but they had also continued their operations: they had wounded a former mayor of Turin and shot a Christian Democratic politician, two Fiat officials in Turin and industrialists in Genoa and Milan. The Turin trial continued regardless and long sentences were eventually handed down. The end finally came in 1983 when thirty-two Red Brigade terrorists were jailed for life for their part in the Moro assassination. Among them was the executioner, Moretti, captured in a shoot-out, and nine women. They were betrayed by several Brigade members who informed on their 'comrades' for lighter sentences.

After hailing the execution of Moro as an act of 'revolutionary justice' thirty-six-year-old Renato Curcio, on trial in Turin for armed insurrection, shouted to those assembled in the crowded courtroom: 'Perhaps you have not understood what has happened in these days or what will happen in the coming months for Italy!' In fact, everyone understood only too well. In murdering a man dedicated to the principle that people who differ could find common cause Moro's assassins had neither divided nor conquered but had united the nation in a new determination to preserve that vision. Moro's assassination might have prompted a political crisis in Italy (in the immediate aftermath, Interior Minister Cossiga resigned) but the 8 July elections saw the eighty-one-year-old Socialist Sandro Martini into power and he immediately pledged to maintain continued cooperation between Italy's Communists and Roman Catholic Christian Democrats, who each held about one third of the vote.

Moro's assassination alienated from the rest of the country the Red Brigade which until then had received a surprising amount of popular support. As this support melted away and members left to pursue other careers, both criminal and legal, the Brigade fell apart. As Moretti later recalled: 'The execution was done with the awareness that from that moment forward our struggle would be one of desperation. I had a sense of doom. Moro knew it was over. I didn't deceive him. All I told him was to get himself ready because we had to go out. You can't imagine what you feel. I told myself over and over that it was a political choice, that it was unavoidable. That it was taken collectively, that we're not the ones to blame for the failure to negotiate. But the time for reasoning had run out. Now it was the time to pick up a gun and fire.'

A few months after Moretti's capture, a document smuggled out of the prison where most of the Red Brigade members were confined reached the newspaper *La Repubblica.* Headlined 'The Armed Struggle is Over', it read: 'The phase of revolutionary struggle which started in the early 1970s . . . is substantially finished.' It also advised their comrades to 'seek new means of revolution'. The war, which had claimed the lives of fifty innocent people in nine years, was over.

One question remains, however. Why, alone among all the terrorist kidnappings in Italy, was no effort made to obtain Moro's release by force or negotiation? What some members of the Cabinet feared was that Moro had carried out a threat, implied in his first letter, to tell his captors secrets that would compromise his colleagues. Because of these letters, which were especially critical of Giulio Andreotti, journalist Mino Pecorelli, managing editor of the magazine *Osservatorio Politico*, investigated and, in 1979, prepared to publish a book which detailed Andreotti's Mafia connections and activities.

In a career spanning nearly half a century, Andreotti had occupied nearly all the ministerial posts, and had been prime minister seven times, foreign minister six times; he had held the confidence of five Popes and had met every president and prime minister several times. The one post that he had not held and that he dearly coveted was that of president.

Pecorelli's book would have ended this. Then, on 20 March 1979, the journalist was shot four times as he sat in his car. He died at the scene.

In 2002, Giulio Andreotti was convicted and sentenced to twenty-four years' imprisonment for ordering the hit but he was cleared on appeal the following year. Also in 2003, a court in Palermo acquitted him of ties to the Mafia, but only because the statute of limitations meant that any alleged crimes took place too long ago to warrant a prosecution. However, thanks mainly to the evidence of Mafia informant Tommaso Buscetta, the court stated that Andreotti had had ties to the Mafia until 1980, and that these ties were so strong that he could be considered to have been part of the Mafia itself. Moro knew this; and, as his letters make clear, he was certain that it was this knowledge that had sealed his fate.

Seventeen

The Umbrella of Death

Until the poisoning by radiation of Alexander Litvinenko in 2006, the 'Umbrella of Death' hit was probably the most well-known assassination ever to have taken place in London. It was made infamous by its unusual method (appropriated from the CIA's very own Black Sorcerer, Sydney Gottlieb) and was orchestrated by the Bulgarian secret service (with a little help from the KGB). It was a part of a short and effective campaign of assassination, the memory of which has lingered as an enduring mystery, as the full story has never been revealed – until now.

On 5 September 1978, Vladimir Kostov, a well-connected Bulgarian journalist, emerged from the Etoile Metro station into the freezing Paris autumn. As he pulled his thick coat around him, he checked the exit suspiciously. He knew that he was a likely target for assassination. His high-profile defection a few months earlier meant a substantial loss of prestige and sensitive political information for the Bulgarian government. As a senior political commentator and correspondent for the state radio and television media, Kostov had been privy to a few important state secrets, such as the Communist leader Todor Zhivkov's scheme to have Bulgaria incorporated as the sixteenth republic of the Soviet Union.

Bulgaria had been under the Soviet jackboot since the end of the Second World War and Zhivkov became the longest-serving leader of any of the Eastern Bloc nations by doing everything that Moscow told him to do. In Sofia, the Soviet ambassador Nikita Tolubeyev served as a kind of proconsul, channelling Moscow's instructions to Bulgarian officials. 'The Soviets run everything in the country, from the subway system to the secret service,' said Stefan Sverdlev, previously a colonel in the Bulgarian security service, after his defection in 1971. Former CIA Director Richard Helms agreed: 'It is well known in intelligence circles that, point one, the Bulgarian service is closest to the KGB of any satellite and, point two, that it has the reputation of being the most obedient.'

As Kostov skipped up the last few steps to street level, he felt a sudden sting in his back. Turning, he saw a man with an umbrella running down into the Metro system. The stinging soon passed; Kostov continued his journey and forgot about the incident. The next day he developed a fever and fell ill.

Two days later, in London, Georgi Markov, prizewinning Bulgarian author and BBC broadcaster, was walking past a crowded bus stop near Waterloo Bridge. For nine years he had lived in danger, and for nine months he had known for certain that his enemies planned to kill him. Until 1969 he had been one of Bulgaria's top novelists and playwrights: his work was known throughout the Eastern Bloc and he was acquainted with President Zhivkov.

Born in 1929, the son of an army officer, Markov had seen the Communists take over Bulgaria in 1944. As a student he was imprisoned for his political beliefs and this left a profound impression on him. He decided then that he would become as successful as he possibly could within the Communist system and would then try to change it. After surviving both meningitis and tuberculosis, Markov qualified as a chemical engineer, and ran a metallurgy factory while writing in his spare time. Gradually, writing took over his life and at the age of thirty-three, he was suddenly one of the country's top authors. He got to know everyone of influence in Bulgaria and along the way witnessed the corruption brought about by absolute power. Once he felt that he was suitably well established he started objectively criticising the Zhivkov regime through his writing. As a result, his play *The Assassins*, which featured a plot to kill a general in a police state, was singled out for censure in a newspaper article signed by Zhivkov.

In 1969, after just one performance of a new play, *The Man Who Was Me*, forty-year-old Markov defected. He described driving out of Sofia for the last time as like 'going to a funeral'. Within ten days a newspaper article appeared in the Bulgarian press criticising his works, describing them as 'alien to socialist society'. Within two months all his plays had been taken off the stage. Within a year he was described as a traitor. Three and a half years later, a special court sentenced him in absentia to six and a half years in prison and his property was confiscated. The court sent a message to Markov: 'We hope that in the West they know how to bury dogs.'

In 1975, in a series of weekly talks broadcast by the Munich-based station Radio Free Europe (RFE), Markov began to share his memories of the land he had left behind. He joined the Bulgarian section of the BBC's external services and wrote for the German station *Deutsche Welle*. His play *The Archangel Michael* won a prize at the Edinburgh festival in 1974 and he began a literary collaboration with an English friend, David Phillips, that resulted in the first of what was supposed to be a series of novels. He was overjoyed that his radio broadcasts on RFE were being listened to by five million Bulgarians, half the population. The situation was such in Bulgaria that if anyone dared to criticise the regime they would face – at best – a lengthy prison term. By broadcasting from outside the system, by using his inside knowledge of the Bulgarian leadership, Markov was able to satirise President Zhivkov and his family. (Zhivkov's son was a playboy alcoholic, his daughter an eccentric Culture Minister obsessed with the Far East who constantly tried to inject an oriental influence into Bulgarian art and design – with disastrous results.) This was something that no one else had been able to do for twenty-five years.

Markov also helped expose illegal arms dealing in Bulgaria. The Bulgarians sent arms to Angola, Vietnam, Algeria, Mozambique,

South Africa, Lebanon, Yemen, Chile and Tanzania. Many deals were handled by government-sanctioned foreign-trade companies, notably a Sofia-based firm called Kintex. About a hundred Bulgarian 'advisers' worked for the Sandinista regime in Nicaragua and more than a thousand Palestinian guerrillas received military training in Bulgaria. Sofia sold millions of pounds' worth of weapons to Turkish smugglers, who supplied both right-wing and left-wing terrorists in their native land. In return for running the guns, Bulgaria permitted Turkish dealers to transport European-bound heroin across its borders, no questions asked.

The power and influence of Markov's broadcasts was unquestionable. The desperate attempts by the Bulgarian government to launch a propaganda campaign against him backfired – it simply raised public interest in Markov who laughed when he heard that the party leaders were regularly tuning in to hear all about themselves. In January 1978, he received a call that if he continued the broadcasts he would be killed. The man who made the call then visited Markov personally and told him that the decision had been taken by the Politburo and the means by which the murder would be committed had already been transported to the West.

Early in 1978, General Dimitar Stoyanov, the Bulgarian Interior Minister, appealed to his colleagues in Russia for help with liquidating Markov. The request was considered at a meeting chaired by the Head of the KGB, Yuri Andropov, and attended by Deputy Chairman Vladimir Kryuchkov and Oleg Kalugin, Head of Counter-Intelligence. Though reluctant to take risks, Andropov accepted that to refuse would be too unkind a rejection for the loyal Stoyanov. 'But,' he insisted, 'there is to be no direct participation on our part. Give the Bulgarians whatever they need, show them how to use it and send someone to Sofia to train their people. But that's all.'

The KGB centre made available its top-secret poisons lab. Sergei Mikhailovich Golubev, a poisons specialist, was put in charge. A tiny canister filled with high-pressure gas, attached to a pellet of the deadly bio-toxin ricin – seventy times more poisonous than cyanide

– was placed inside the tip of an umbrella. The canister was connected at one end to a spring-lock system triggered by tapping a button located near the umbrella's handle. At the opposite end of the umbrella the tip was bored, creating a barrel through which the lethal pellet would be propelled. The Bulgarians ran a trial test with a condemned prisoner – he survived. But after modifications and another test, this time successful, the weapon was considered reliable enough for use in the field.

The assassin was a man called Francesco Giullino, code-named 'Agent Piccadilly' for the operation, a Dane of Italian origin who travelled Europe in a caravan, pretending to be an antiques salesman. Giullino, who was born in Bari in 1946, was originally recruited by the Bulgarian Secret Service (*Durzhavna Sigurnost* or DS) in 1970. Caught smuggling drugs and currency on the Bulgarian border, he was 'turned' by the agency, which used him to spy on foreigners in Bulgaria before deploying him abroad – first in Denmark, and later in Belgium, Italy and Turkey. He used a variety of covers, from owner of a picture-framing business to itinerant antiques salesman, complete with an Austrian-registered caravan. His instructions to murder Markov came from General Stoyan Savov, the Deputy Interior Minister with special responsibility for state security. Markov was given the codename *skitnik* (tramp).

After he received the warning, Markov naturally assumed that poison would be administered orally and he took appropriate precautions. When on holiday in Italy with his wife and two-year-old daughter, he received an anonymous phone call telling him that the attempt would be made there and then. He thought they were just trying to upset him and he told his wife: 'They're playing with me.' In fact, two attempts – a poisoned drink and poisoned gel smeared on a door handle – had been cancelled at the last minute.

On the morning of 7 September 1978 (Zhivkov's birthday), in front of a crowded London bus stop, Markov suddenly felt a sharp pain in his right thigh and turned to see a heavy-set man carrying an umbrella. 'I am sorry,' Agent Piccadilly muttered in a thick accent before hopping into a taxi. Markov noticed that the driver seemed to struggle to understand where he was being directed but eventually the taxi left.

That evening, Markov developed a fever. He'd thought the earlier incident so trivial that he hadn't mentioned it to his wife when he'd returned home, even when he'd noticed a swollen red pimple on his leg and started to run a high temperature. In the early hours of the next morning, Markov awoke feeling much worse and told his wife: 'I have a horrible feeling that this may be connected with something which happened yesterday.' He then collapsed and was rushed to hospital where he was only temporarily saved through the efforts of doctors and his own great will to live.

Markov survived for two more days, believing that he would be able to talk with Special Branch officers. But the poison in his system was impossible to resist. He died on 11 September. After his death, doctors at Porton Down, a government facility for military biochemical research, found a small platinum pellet, some 1.5mm across, embedded in his leg. Further examination found that it had two small holes drilled in it, which contained traces of the super-toxin ricin.

When the discovery of the pellet was made public, Vladimir Kostov reported the Paris incident and on 25 September doctors found a pellet, identical to the one in Markov's thigh, buried in Kostov's back. Because of his thick coat and jumper, the pellet had failed to get deep enough under his skin for the wax seals to melt and it had only released a tiny amount of the poison.

Then, in early October, thirty-year-old Vladimir Simeonov, a Bulgarian defector working in London for the BBC failed to show up for work. Concerned, a colleague went to his east London terraced house to investigate. He found Simeonov dead, clad in a bathrobe and pyjama bottoms, face down at the bottom of his stairs. Police found no tell-tale injuries on his body, and a post-mortem indicated death by asphyxiation: the victim had suffocated in his own blood after breaking his nose.

During 1977, President Zhivkov had been attempting to improve relations with the West. He claimed that Markov and Simeonov were liquidated by Western intelligence services trying to ruin the country's image. Zhivkov offered to help British authorities deal with the case. His offer was refused. British Special Branch officers were convinced that the murders had been carried out by the Bulgarian secret service. Unfortunately, they were unable to produce any proof.

Markov was murdered for telling the truth – he went on telling the truth after his death. His memoirs were published in Bulgaria in 1982 while Zhivkov was still in power. He was described as Bulgaria's Solzhenitsyn (the exiled Russian author had suffered poisoning at the hands of the KGB in 1971, but had survived) and his tombstone epitaph read that he died 'in the cause of freedom'. Vladimir Kostov was subsequently hired by RFE as a broadcaster specialising in Bulgarian foreign policy and security affairs.

After Markov's assassination, Zhivkov, despite becoming increasingly corrupt, autocratic and erratic, was able to hang on to power until 10 November 1989 (by which time he had been president for forty-five years). He resigned while the Berlin wall was being torn down and while his own people were rioting, demanding *glasnost*. Zhivkov was eventually arrested for crimes against the state and placed under house arrest. He died in 1998.

Eighteen

The Serial Assassin

In the late 1970s some of the world's most infamous serial killers were plaguing America. David Richard Berkowitz a.k.a. the 'Son of Sam' murdered his victims with a .44-calibre handgun; William Bonin, the 'Freeway Killer', killed more than twenty young men and boys; Ted Bundy butchered between thirty and a hundred young women, and Jeffrey Dahmer began his cannibalistic career in 1979. The following tale documents the story of a forgotten serial killer from this period, the story of the first serial killer to become a serial assassin. His reasons for his murderous activities were as extraordinary as the crimes themselves as he worked his way towards his ultimate target: the President of the United States.

Larry Flynt, the outspoken multimillionaire pornographer, had come a long way since having sex with a chicken at the tender age of fifteen. (Older boys had told him that the experience was similar in sensation to having sex with a woman.) He killed the unfortunate bird afterwards to prevent any suspicion falling on him.

Flynt was born in the town of Salyersville (population: 1604) in 1942. His mother divorced his alcoholic father when he was ten. Flynt left home five years later and lasted barely a year in the army before eventually opening a successful strip club in 1964. Several others followed before he decided to publish *Hustler*, a magazine which pushed the boundaries of pornography by showing explicit close-up views of its models. It was soon outselling the tamer *Playboy* and, at its peak, sold three million copies every month. By 1978 he was a multimillionaire and at the height of his notoriety. America was watching him take on court after court in obscenity cases and win, using the First Amendment to push the boundaries of mass-market pornography.

On 6 March 1978, Flynt was fighting one of his many legal battles in Gwinnett County, Georgia. About 130 feet from the courthouse, lying in the long grass behind some bushes, was James Clayton Vaughn Jr. He was positioned next to a telegraph pole. Vaughn had hammered two ten-inch nails into the pole, rested the end of the forestock of his Remington 700 sniper rifle on them, and sawed it back and forth, leaving little scratches in its underside, until he felt comfortable. He had then squirmed down so that he was lying prone, the best sniping position there is. A bicycle was propped up behind him, ready for a quick getaway. From this position he had a clear view of the front steps of the courthouse where Flynt was fighting his legal battle.

Born in Mobile, Alabama, Vaughn had been abused by his alcoholic father who regularly disappeared from the family home, returning months or sometimes years later only to beat his son again. Vaughn developed an eating disorder and became extremely religious; he was fascinated by cults. At high school he was doing well until a bicycle accident caused him to lose the vision in his right eye and left him partially sighted in the other. This spared him a trip to Vietnam but it also cost him his education. He dropped out of high school and married in 1968.

Soon after the wedding, Vaughn's bride noted a change in his personality 'like night and day'. He began to beat her, emulating the father he hated, and on other occasions his wife would find him weeping for no reason. Around the same time, their all-white neighbourhood became racially integrated and, after his mother's death in 1972, Vaughn veered hard right, straight into the arms of the Ku Klux Klan and the American Nazi Party. In 1976, he changed his name to Joseph Paul Franklin after Paul Joseph Goebbels, the Nazis'

Propaganda Minister, and the groundbreaking US politician Benjamin Franklin. He became an outlaw; he drifted, robbed banks in a number of disguises (he would dress up as a cowboy, Hell's Angel, businessman or mechanic) and eventually decided to start a full-on war against the Jewish and coloured people of America.

His war started spontaneously after a car blocked his getaway from a bank robbery. Franklin shot dead the mixed-race couple inside, Alphonse Manning and Toni Schwenn, both twenty-three years old. After this, there was no going back. He had spent years practising with his one half-decent eye and reckoned that he was a better shot than many army snipers. So he began a horrifying series of carefully planned sniper attacks which started two months after the double murder. From a distance of a hundred and thirty yards he shot three young men, Gerald Gordon, Steven Goldman and William Ash, as they left a synagogue. While Gordon died, the other two men survived their injuries.

Franklin admired Larry Flynt and was a regular reader of *Hustler*. But this all changed in February 1978 when, in support of President Jimmy Carter's policy of appointing a record number of women, blacks, and Hispanics to government and judiciary jobs, the pornographer, who loved to dabble in politics, published a mixed-race edition of the magazine. Franklin flipped and decided to kill Flynt.

As the front door of the Gwinnett County courthouse opened, Franklin squinted through his one half-decent eye down the sight. His finger tightened on the trigger as he watched Larry Flynt emerge with his local lawyer, Gene Reeves Jr, who had been struggling to contain the outspoken bipolar pornographer's outbursts in front of the judge. As they strolled towards his position and prepared to answer reporters' questions, Franklin positioned the Remington's sight over the chest of Reeves, who was on Flynt's left, and waited until he was about a hundred feet away. He pulled the trigger. The gunshot was loud and there was a *crack* as a puff of pink mist blew out from Reeves's back. He dropped like a puppet with its strings cut.

Flynt stood dumbfounded for a moment until Franklin pulled his trigger a second time and the .44 bullet tore through Flynt's body, smashing his spine. As people screamed and ducked for cover, Franklin squirmed back into some bushes, placed his rifle in a guitar case, pedalled back to his car and vanished.

While Reeves would make a full recovery, doctors told Flynt that he would never walk again. The millionaire's life started to disintegrate as a result of his injury. He became addicted to his pain medication, renounced his new-found Christianity and turned into a recluse. With no witnesses, no motive and no clues to go on, the police were at a loss.

Franklin waited four months after his attempted assassination of Larry Flynt before striking again, on 29 July 1978. He hid in the long grass around a Pizza Hut in Chattanooga, jumping out to shoot Bryant Tatum dead with a twelve-gauge shotgun before blasting his white girlfriend Nancy Hilton (who survived). The following year, on 12 July 1979, twenty-seven-year-old black Taco Bell manager Harold McIver was shot dead by a bullet fired from a distance of a hundred and fifty yards through his office window in Doraville, Georgia. On 18 August 1979 Franklin used his sniper rifle to kill a black man seated in a Burger King in Falls Church. On 21 October 1979 he killed a mixed-race couple in Oklahoma City, firing five shots at a distance of one hundred yards, hitting Jesse Taylor, who was black, three times and Marian Bresette, who was white, once.

On 5 December 1979 the assassin killed fifteen-year-old white prostitute Mercedes Lynn Masters with a shotgun. In January 1980, in a long-distance sniper attack in Indianapolis, he murdered a nineteen-year-old black man who'd been standing with his father outside a fried-chicken restaurant. A few days later he shot a black man with the same rifle from a hundred and fifty yards in Indianapolis. On 2 May 1980, he shot white hitch-hiker Rebecca Bergstrom with a handgun in Monroe County, Wisconsin. One thing linked all these latter crimes. The people he killed were in mixed-race relationships. Bergstrom was white but told Franklin that she would date a black man if she thought he was cute, as did Masters the prostitute.

Throughout 1980 Franklin plagued the Secret Service with letters threatening the American president's life. President Carter had won a narrow surprise victory over Gerald Ford back in 1976. Carter hadn't been expected to run for president but this soon changed after Governor George Wallace, still recovering from his bullet wounds, proved to be a spent force. Carter's presidency had been a difficult one and four years later, embarrassed by his failure to deal with several crises at home and abroad, it looked as if the 1980 election was going to swing towards the sixty-nine-year-old former Hollywood star, Ronald Reagan. In addition, Carter's policy of appointing as many coloured people as possible into government positions had angered many people, especially Joseph Paul Franklin.

The threats, which arrived weekly at the White House, were deemed so worrying that a pair of Secret Service field agents were assigned to try and track Franklin down. But because of Franklin's itinerant life the letters were postmarked from towns and cities all across the US and so tracing him seemed impossible. Franklin continued to commit armed robbery, changing his car and weapons as he travelled from town to town and waiting for an opportunity to kill Carter. His chance came in April 1980.

Plains, Georgia, is a tiny hamlet whose inhabitants mostly farm peanuts. It is also home to Jimmy Carter and an annual peanut festival.[16] In April 1980 Carter took his holidays at the family farm in Plains; it was considered a wise choice – the electorate would appreciate a president who holidayed at home with his family.

There was nothing that Jimmy Carter liked more than to fish. Although his Secret Service agents accompanied him as far as the river banks, there was only enough room in the tiny rowing boat for

[16] With a population of 650 and one thirteen-foot smiling peanut, the town motto is *Plains: Peanuts and a President*.

one man. So the agents waited in the woods while the President of the United States rowed his way merrily downstream and cast his line. It was at this point that a berserk swamp rabbit decided to attack.[17] The rabbit, gnashing its teeth, jumped into the river and made directly for the President's boat. Carter grabbed hold of a paddle and, while the boat wobbled precariously, he brought the rabbit to its senses with a few determined thwacks. The entire incident was caught on film by a White House photographer who had been wandering through the woods. Needless to say, it made headlines. The *Washington Post* ran the story on its front page with the immortal, once-in-a-lifetime headline: PRESIDENT ATTACKED BY RABBIT.

What didn't make front-page news was the fact that while President Carter was fending off questions about his treatment of the swamp rabbit, serial sniper Joseph Paul Franklin had sneaked through the woods and settled down in a sniper's nest a short distance from the Presidential fishing-hole where he was waiting for Carter to return. But thanks to the swamp rabbit, the President decided to cancel any further fishing that holiday and Franklin, low on cash, packed up his newly acquired 30.06 Remington sniper rifle and headed out of the state of Georgia. For a while he stalked civil-rights leader Jesse Jackson but Jackson seemed to be permanently surrounded by security, preventing any chance of a clear shot. Franklin decided on a less well-protected target.

At two a.m. on 29 April 1980, Vernon Jordan, forty-four-year-old president of the National Urban League and one of America's foremost black leaders, was driving his companion's fire-red Pontiac Grand Prix back to the Marriot Inn in Fort Wayne. Beside him sat thirty-six-year-old Martha Coleman, an attractive blonde, four times divorced and long-time civil-rights activist. As they drove they were buzzed by a car full of white youths who drew alongside to yell racist abuse before turning off.

Five hours earlier, Jordan had delivered a speech on the racism

[17] A not-so-cuddly version of the domesticated kind, the swamp rabbit has enormous paws and can swim across rivers.

that was still plaguing the US as it entered a new decade. (Riots had broken out in Miami after four cops accused of racist brutality were acquitted.) He described Carter's presidency as 'an administration of promises made and promises unkept'. After the meeting the pair had driven in Coleman's car to her large two-storey white frame house in a racially mixed neighbourhood where they drank coffee and chatted.

Waiting for Vernon in the muggy darkness outside the hotel was Joseph Paul Franklin. He was in his favourite position, lying prone on a patch of grass surrounded by scrub in the darkness, the Remington now propped on a sniper's tripod. He had been practising getting his sights zeroed in as people had parked their cars and made their way into the hotel. By two a.m. the well-lit car park had been quiet for some time and Franklin could hear the sound of the Pontiac approaching from a distance.

Jordan stepped from the car and started to bid Coleman goodnight when a shot shattered the night stillness. The bullet tore a fist-sized hole in the lower left side of his back, sliced through his intestines and burst out through his chest. Jordan slumped against the boot of the car as the second bullet left Franklin's gun. The killer's aim was slightly off, possibly from a combination of adjusting to compensate for Jordan's fall and his own poor eyesight. The bullet broke into two pieces as it glanced off a chain-link fence a few yards short of Jordan, ricocheting at lethal speed into his right thigh and upper left chest.

Jordan collapsed on the pavement, his head resting near the left indicator light. 'Help me, I've been shot!' he cried. When Coleman saw him wounded and bleeding, she dashed inside the motel and asked the desk clerk to summon police and an ambulance. Then she called her lawyer.

Within minutes, paramedics were wheeling the unconscious Jordan into the emergency room of Parkview Memorial Hospital, where surgeons operated on him for four and a half hours. He was going to make it, though Surgeon Jeff Towles, who had extensive experience with gunshot wounds, told reporters it had been damn close: 'There was an explosive effect like nothing I've ever seen before.'

Jordan was lucky in that he would have been killed outright if the angle of the first shot had been a degree different from its actual path.[18] President Carter called the hospital three times during the next day to check on Jordan's condition. Jordan was soon joined at the hospital by his wife Shirley, who suffered from multiple sclerosis, and their twenty-year-old daughter Vickee.

Fort Wayne, an industrial city of 200,000 (twelve per cent of whom were black), had suffered no serious racial incidents since the 1960s. At first, law-enforcement authorities suspected that the shooting was what Police Public Relations Director Daniel Gibson delicately called a 'domestic-type thing', but this soon changed to a possible lone-wolf assassination theory. Even with twenty FBI agents and all thirty Fort Wayne police detectives assigned to the case, no arrest had been made by the end of the week. Thankfully, after a plea for calm from Jordan and others, the nation's ghettos did not erupt in anger and in grief as they had after the assassination of Martin Luther King.

Franklin meanwhile resumed his serial killing and stepped up the pace. On 8 June 1980, he killed teenage cousins Darrel Lane and Donte Evans Brown in Cincinnati. On 15 June he shot and killed an interracial couple, Arthur Smothers and teenager Kathleen Mikula, in a woodland area in Johnstown, Pennsylvania. Ten days later he used a .44 Ruger pistol to kill two young hitch-hikers, Nancy Santomero and Vicki Durian, in West Virginia. On 20 August 1980, he killed two black men from forty yards with a Marlin Firearms lever-action rifle as they jogged with white women in Salt Lake City. The white women got a good look at Franklin as he fled, and one of them even spotted the tattoo of an American bald eagle on his arm.

In early September, as President Carter cajoled Egypt's President

[18] Jordan went on to become a Washington power broker and was a close adviser to President Bill Clinton during the Monica Lewinsky scandal.

Anwar Sadat and Israel's Prime Minister Menachem Begin towards peace in Aspen, Colorado, Franklin was picked up by the police during a routine check in Florence, Kentucky. He was driving a Chevrolet Camaro, with two unlicensed rifles and two handguns (including the Marlin and Ruger) concealed. The policemen escorted him as far as the police station but by then Franklin had convinced them that he wasn't a felon, just a gun enthusiast. So they left him unguarded and he slipped out the back.

Franklin was now in trouble. The police were looking for him, he had no getaway car, no cash and no guns with which to rob. He needed some money urgently. Seeing a sign offering money for blood donations he marched quickly into the clinic and asked how much it was possible to give. The nurse rolled up his sleeve, recognised the tattoo from a television broadcast and called the police.

A recalcitrant and unrepentant prisoner, Franklin claimed that his only regret was that killing Jews was not legal. He said that he hoped his crimes would inspire others to take up arms against ethnic minorities and he told his lawyers to drop their idea of an insanity defence, calling it 'hogwash'. He also threatened to rape a Jewish psychologist who came to interview him and diagnosed him as paranoid schizophrenic, and he tried to escape custody during a jury adjournment.

Franklin was tried in several different states for the murders of twenty people as well as for sixteen bank robberies and two bombings. He made several confessions in the late 1990s on the condition that he confessed to 'an attractive white female investigator'.

Investigators who interviewed Franklin eventually discovered the pattern behind his killings. When he was talking about the two white female hitch-hikers he had killed he told officers that he had decided to kill them after one of them admitted to having a black boyfriend. He said, 'They told me they were into race-mixing, I just decided to waste 'em.' In 1996 he confessed to the shooting of Flynt and his solicitor. Shortly after this, he made the acquaintance of a black prisoner who asked him, 'Did you shoot Vernon Jordan?' Franklin said 'Yes.' A couple of nights later, he was cornered by five black prisoners with knives made from tin cans, and they stabbed him thirty-eight times. Remarkably, he survived and recovered in time for his sentencing in 1997: death by lethal injection.[19]

Larry Flynt eventually recovered from his drug addiction as doctors managed to stop the pain caused by Franklin's bullet with a series of operations. He has since run for public office a number of times, has married five times and has five children. In 2001, his net worth was around four hundred million dollars. In 1996, a Hollywood film of Flynt's life was released to largely good reviews. His character was played by the famous Hollywood actor Woody Harrelson, whose own surprising connection to an assassination 'first' in the year after the attempt on Flynt's life is told in full for the first time below.

Even in El Paso, a rough Texas border town with a history of renegades and easy money, the Chagra family stood out. Lee, the eldest son, was a flamboyant lawyer with a taste for cocaine who specialised in defending drug dealers. He carried thousands of dollars in his cowboy boots and handed out gold bracelets engraved with his motto, FREEDOM. When he bought a limousine equipped with a bar and television, he also ordered a special nook for the gun he always carried. In December 1978, the night after he picked up the car from the dealer, he was shot dead during a robbery in his fortress-like office. He was forty-one.

Lee's brother Jamiel a.k.a. 'Jimmy' was a professional gambler who'd been known to win or lose a million dollars in a single night in Las Vegas. But his gambling was financed by a more deadly game. In 1979, Jimmy, described by federal prosecutors as the kingpin of a narcotics empire in the Southwest, was charged with drug smuggling. He was rightly fearful of sixty-three-year-old

[19] As of 2007, Franklin is still on death row.

United States District Judge John Herbert Wood, Jr. Wood was known as 'Maximum John' because he liked to hand out full-term prison sentences to drug dealers. In ninety cases involving heroin traffic he gave out maximum sentences in sixty-five of them and never granted probation. Jimmy fully expected to get the maximum sentence of thirty years.

In a desperate gambit, Jimmy Chagra's lawyer requested that Wood excuse himself from the case, claiming that his record with drug dealers biased him against his client. But Wood refused. As a result, Jimmy's younger brother Joseph, thirty-five, along with Jimmy's wife, Elizabeth, twenty-six, decided to have the judge assassinated, and in the spring of 1979 Elizabeth delivered a quarter of a million dollars to Charles Voyd Harrelson (father of Hollywood actor Woody Harrelson, of whom he was the spitting image) in Las Vegas for the job.

Harrelson's first conviction had been for robbing an eighty-four-year-old doctor at gunpoint. He had later been convicted for the 1968 contract killing in Texas of a grain dealer called Sam Degalia. The investigation into Degalia's death was headed by a famed Texas ranger, Captain Jack Dean, who eventually secured a confession from Harrelson's co-conspirator, a man named Jerry Watkins who told all in return for a reduced sentence.

'Degalia met Harrelson at a motel restaurant,' Watkins said in his statement. 'They had a cup of coffee and departed. I drove, with Harrelson beside me in front and Degalia alone in the back seat. They talked grain deals until I entered the road to the abandoned shack. That's when Harrelson pointed a gun. "My God!" Degalia shouted, "What's the matter?" Harrelson told him "Get on the floor." Degalia tried but he was six foot two and pretty big. He couldn't get his shoulders below the seat level. Harrelson told me to move the seat forward and Degalia got down, his face against the floor. Still pointing the gun, Harrelson used his free hand to bring a short length of rope from his pocket and tied Degalia's wrists. Degalia kept asking "What's wrong?" Harrelson said: "I'll have to teach you to keep out of other people's business."'

Harrelson had been hired by Degalia's partner, Pete Scamardo, to kill him. The motive: sole ownership of their business and a twenty-five-thousand-dollar insurance policy. Harrelson's fee was two thousand dollars – about a third of the price of the car he was driving. Watkins parked the car. Harrelson helped Degalia out of the back seat. Gripping his gun in one hand and holding the end of the rope binding Degalia's wrists in his other hand, he walked his captive through the high weeds towards the remote shack. Watkins, still in the car, was lighting a cigarette when he heard the first shot. He was picking the cigarette up when he heard the second. Forty-five minutes later, Harrelson and Watkins were flying back to Houston. A pretty stewardess would remember the tall blond killer. She told Dean: 'He made a pass at me and tried to kiss me on the cheek two or three times.'

After Dean tracked Harrelson down and arrested him, the assassin hired famed Houston criminal lawyer Percy Foreman (who had also been counsel for James Earl Ray that same year). Just when it looked liked Harrelson was to be convicted, Foreman sprung a surprise witness. A female nightclub singer with a questionable background claimed that she had been with Harrelson at the time of the murder. The trial ended in a hung jury: eleven for conviction, one for acquittal.

Harrelson was retried in 1974. Dean was in the courtroom waiting for the nightclub singer to appear, this time with an arrest warrant for perjury in his pocket. However, the singer was tipped off and she quickly fled. Without the help of the singer's testimony, there was no hung jury. Harrelson was found guilty, sentenced to fifteen years in prison but, with time off for good behaviour, he was free by 1979. Scamardo, convicted of hiring Harrelson to commit the murder, was sentenced to seven years' probation.

Harrelson was also linked to the murder of Alan Berg, a carpet executive whose decomposed corpse had been found in a thick clump of cedars along a Texan beach. For that killing Harrelson was charged, tried and acquitted.

*

On a sunny May morning in 1979, 'Maximum John' Wood waved goodbye to his wife and climbed into the front seat of his car. Mrs Wood was in her own car about to leave from the north side of their home when she heard the gunshot. She rushed to her husband, who had fallen from his car onto the pavement, his shirt soaked in blood. The bullet, a high-velocity .243-calibre one fired from a powerful hunting rifle, had shattered his chest. Although an ambulance was on the scene quickly and the paramedics worked furiously to save his life, Maximum John died within the hour. He was the first federal judge in American history to be assassinated. The killing triggered one of the most extensive and expensive (five million dollars) federal investigations and prosecutions in US history.

President Jimmy Carter called the crime 'an assault on our very system of justice'. United States Attorney Fred Rodriguez made it clear from the start that everything was going to be done to bring the killers of Wood to justice. 'Every rock is a possible rock that will be turned over. Manpower is not going to be spared,' he told reporters.

But the FBI soon realised that they were working on a near-impossible case. They had a list of three thousand people who might have wanted Maximum John dead and had the wherewithal to organise it. But, even with three thousand suspects, there had to be one name at the top of the list. Three weeks after Wood's death, the trial of El Paso-based mobster Jimmy Chagra, accused of smuggling several tons of marijuana and hundreds of kilos of cocaine, was supposed to start.

FBI agents managed to find out, thanks to the recently passed Gun Control Act that made gunshop owners keep records of purchasers, that just days before the crime, forty-two-year-old Jo Ann Harrelson, wife of Voyd, had purchased a rifle exactly like the one ballistics experts had tagged as the murder weapon. But the FBI couldn't make an arrest because witnesses who could have clinched the case saw certain disadvantages in testifying against a man who murdered for money. They wouldn't talk as long as Harrelson remained free. If they were going to get anywhere, the FBI would have to bring him in.

The FBI persisted with seventy agents, court-authorised bugs and wire-taps, jailhouse snitches and 214,000 investigative entries into their computer. Seven months passed without any sign of Harrelson. It was 1 February 1980 when Special Agent Mike Taylor got a tip that Harrelson was in Houston to hold up a high-stakes poker game.

Taylor combed Harrelson's likely hang-outs and finally found him in a nightclub. He quickly enlisted the aid of two city detectives to keep the hired killer under surveillance. They followed him to an apartment in the south-west of the city. After an interminable fifteen hours of observation with no sign of any movement inside, Taylor decided to make himself obvious by driving his car within sight of Harrelson's windows.

Suddenly, five men bailed out of the apartment. Four scattered throughout the neighbourhood. Harrelson, bag in hand, leaped down the steps, bounded down the path and dumped five guns into his sleek new black Lincoln. He fired up the engine, screeched out of the driveway and barrelled down the street. But Taylor was ready for him, and took some delight in denting the assassin's gleaming Lincoln with his old detective's Chevy as he rammed the hit man and brought him to a halt. Taylor grabbed a twelve-gauge shotgun that was ready on the seat next to him and opened the car door.

Harrelson dived to the floor of his car and came up holding a Colt Diamondback .357 Magnum revolver. A police cruiser pulled up beside Taylor. Another skidded to a halt behind the Lincoln. Harrelson scowled through his windshield, gun in hand, contemplating the twelve-gauge shotgun that Taylor was aiming at his face. He surrendered. Aside from the weapons, the officers found a pair of loaded dice and some cocaine in the Lincoln.

At his trial, Harrelson claimed that it was impossible for him to have killed Judge John Wood because on the morning in question he, Harrelson, had been in Dallas, running some extraordinary errands: returning a golf putter that he had borrowed to determine how much cocaine he could hide in its shaft for a drug-smuggling scheme, buying a cashier's cheque to pay for a car he had bought under an assumed name, and collecting some gambling debts. To demonstrate his prowess as a professional card-sharp, Harrelson offered the court an impromptu exhibition. 'No, thanks,' said the unamused US District Judge William Sessions.

Harrelson was convicted largely due to the testimony of the youngest Chagra brother, Joseph, an El Paso lawyer who agreed to plead guilty to the murder-conspiracy charge and testify against Harrelson in return for a ten-year sentence. Harrelson ended up with three life sentences. Assistant US Attorney Ray Jahn, the chief prosecutor, said: 'When Judge Wood died, justice did not die.' Unfortunately, Jahn had spoken prematurely. Although he had been convicted for the drugs offences and sentenced to thirty years for them Jimmy Chagra had yet to be prosecuted for his part in the assassination.

At Jimmy's trial, Jahn introduced tape recordings made secretly by the FBI when Joseph had visited Jimmy in 1980 in prison. But perhaps the most dramatic piece of evidence came from Jimmy's twenty-eight-year-old wife, Elizabeth, who was charged with covering up the crime. Kathryn Wood, the judge's widow, read to the court a five-page handwritten letter that she had received the previous September from Elizabeth Chagra. In the letter, Elizabeth apologised for her involvement in the murder. 'One day in March three years ago, I was in the kitchen cooking fried chicken when my husband came home and said, "I'm going to kill Judge Wood," ' she wrote, adding that she did not take the threat seriously. That summer, she went on, her husband had asked her to deliver some money to Las Vegas. 'He said that this was for the pay-off for your husband's murder.'

Unfortunately the prosecution wasn't prepared for the brilliant defence of Jimmy Chagra by lawyer Oscar Goodman who claimed that it would not have been worth the risk for Chagra to order the assassination. More importantly, he added that Chagra often boasted to his wife and fellow prisoners that he had 'offed' people when he hadn't. He cited the case of Mark Finney during his short cross-examination of the prosecution's star witness Joseph Chagra, Jimmy's brother.

'Describe how Mr Chagra told you he killed Mark Finney,' Goodman asked Joseph.

'I think he said he shot him.'

'Are you sure of that?'

'I'm sure he told me he offed him,' James said.

'You're as sure of that as you are that Mr Chagra told you he murdered Judge Wood?'

'That's right,' James said.

'No more questions,' Goodman said.

The prosecution appeared momentarily perplexed. Then Goodman added, 'Call Mark Finney.' The supposedly dead man strolled into court and raised his right hand.

The prosecution evidence rested entirely on the fact that Jimmy Chagra had boasted about the death of the judge to his wife, brother and fellow prisoners. Goodman was able to demonstrate that Chagra always lied about having people killed to show that he was a 'tough guy'. Jimmy Chagra was acquitted for the assassination. In 1984 he pleaded guilty to conspiring to murder Assistant US Attorney James Kerr (Kerr survived unscathed after dodging a hail of machine-gun fire in a roadside ambush). Jimmy had confessed as part of a deal to try and get his wife released early. Elizabeth was dying from ovarian cancer. The appeal court judges rejected the deal however, and Elizabeth died in prison in 1997. In 2003, police officials reported that Jimmy Chagra had been released from jail (seven years before he was eligible for parole) and entered the witness protection programme after assisting prosecutors in other cases.

In 1995, Harrelson found a special way to celebrate the Fourth of July by attempting a prison breakout with a home-made ladder. He and his colleagues gave up when a guard fired a warning shot and Harrelson was then transferred to the dreaded Federal ADX Supermax prison in Colorado. In 1998 Harrelson's son, Woody, by now a famous actor, sent in some high-powered attorneys to get his father's conviction overturned and secure a new trial, but it was to no avail. Four years earlier Woody had played a mass murderer in the film *Natural Born Killers*. The director was Oliver Stone of *JFK* fame.

Nineteen

You Talkin' to Me?

As the new decade – the 1980s – began assassinations across the world continued apace. In San Salvador, America had welcomed a *coup d'état* in October 1979 and the establishment of what appeared to be a moderate combined military- and civilian-run junta. It soon turned out, however, that the civilian government was powerless and the military embarked on the mass murder of their opponents, a policy that led to all-out civil war against guerrilla forces.

The outspoken Archbishop Oscar Romero, nominated for the Nobel Peace Prize in 1979, in a nationwide broadcast pleaded with the peasant soldiers to disobey their leaders: 'Brothers, you are from the same people; you kill your fellow peasant . . . No soldier is obliged to obey an order that is contrary to the will of God . . . In the name of God, then, in the name of this suffering people I ask you, I beg you, I command you in the name of God: stop the repression.' The next day, seconds after finishing a sermon in his cathedral, he was shot dead by an army sniper. Romero's murder was a savage warning. Even some who attended his funeral were shot down in front of the cathedral by army sharpshooters positioned on nearby rooftops.

In 1980, amid the rising violence, Romero had written to President Jimmy Carter pleading with him to cease sending military aid to the government because 'it is being used to repress my people'. The US sent one and a half million dollars in aid every day for twelve years, pausing only briefly after the murder of four American churchwomen. When Ronald Reagan stepped into the White House, he increased military aid from $35.5 million in 1981 to $196.6 million in 1984. As far as Reagan was concerned, it was better to have a right-wing junta terrorising the country than a guerrilla-run republic. In the civil war over 75,000 Salvadoreans were killed and one million would flee the country with another million left homeless, constantly on the run from the army; this in a country of only five and a half million.

In the Paraguayan capital of Asunción, an era ended on 17 September 1980. Shortly after ten a.m. Anastasio Somoza Debayle, fifty-four, the exiled former dictator of Nicaragua, climbed into his white Mercedes-Benz 280 limousine along with his chauffeur and a business associate, and drove away from his luxurious suburban villa.

The limousine, followed by a back-up car carrying three bodyguards, had travelled a mere half-mile when a truck full of gunmen pulled up alongside. An expert sniper shot Somoza's chauffeur dead through the driver's window. Then the gunmen unleashed a hail of automatic rifle fire. As Somoza's bodyguards shot back, a bazooka rocket, launched from the porch of a nearby house, hit the limousine square on, tearing away the roof. The dictator, along with his companions, was killed instantly. The hit team made a clean getaway.

When news of Somoza's death reached Managua, Nicaraguans went wild with joy. Thousands of people poured into the streets, singing and dancing and setting off fireworks. Said a journalist in Managua: 'Somoza finally brought happiness to his countrymen.' The leaders of the ruling Sandinista junta denied any direct role in the assassination. In a brief communiqué, they called it *ajusticiamiento* – justifiable execution – reminding their followers that the dictator had been responsible for the deaths of a hundred thousand Nicaraguans.

The assassination came a few days after the Nicaraguan junta revealed that it had thwarted a plot by former National Guard officers to free thousands of jailed former soldiers and put together teams to kill the Sandinista leadership. They identified Somoza's eldest son, twenty-nine-year-old Anastasio 'Tachito' Somoza Portocarrero, as the 'principal leader' of the plot.

As with the military junta of San Salvador, America had seen the Somozas of Nicaragua as a bulwark against communism in South America. But the atrocities committed by the Somozas received wide media attention in the United States and the Carter administration withdrew military aid and support not long after an earthquake devastated the capital Managua.

Somoza hung on for a few more years until the Sandinistas, named after their founder Augusto Cesar Sandino, forced them to flee in July 1979. The Sandinistas clung on to power for almost twelve years, despite facing both political and violent opposition from the counter-revolutionary Contras who received support from the United States.

The 1980s were to become the most violent decade in America's history – on average one American was murdered every thirty minutes. Between 1980 and 1989 more than 275,000 Americans were murdered in the US, five times the number of soldiers killed in Vietnam. The first year ended as the decade meant to go on with the slaying by gun of one of the twentieth century's greatest popular icons: John Lennon was shot in the back four times by a deranged young man while his wife Yoko Ono looked on. Lennon staggered up six steps towards his building, said 'I'm shot,' and then fell face down.

The assassin, twenty-five-year-old Mark David Chapman, a mentally imbalanced born-again Christian and unemployed security guard, told police: 'He walked past me, and then a voice in my head said "Do it, do it, do it," over and over again, saying "Do it, do it, do it, do it," like that. I pulled the gun out of my pocket, I handed over to my left hand, I don't remember aiming, I must have done it, but I don't remember drawing the bead or whatever you call it. And I just pulled the trigger steady five times.'

Lennon had just come back from a series of radio interviews, part of the publicity surrounding the release of his new album *Double Fantasy.* He told a DJ from San Francisco: 'My life revolves around Sean [Lennon and Ono's son, then five years old]. Now I have more reason to stay healthy and bright . . . And I want to be with my best friend. My best friend's me wife. If I couldn't have worked with her, I wouldn't have bothered . . . I consider that my work won't be finished until I'm dead and buried, and I hope that's a long, long time.'

For more people than anyone could ever begin to number, the killing of John Lennon was like a death in the family. A teenage girl in Florida and a man of thirty in Utah killed themselves, leaving notes that spoke of depression over Lennon's death.

The outpouring of grief, stunned disbelief and shared devastation that followed Lennon's murder had the same breadth and intensity as the reaction to the killing of a world figure: a popular politician like John or Robert Kennedy, or a spiritual leader like Martin Luther King Jr. Sorrow was expressed, sympathies extended by everyone from presidents, prime ministers, governors and mayors to the hundreds of fans who gathered at the arched entryway to the Lennons' Manhattan apartment building, the Dakota, crying and praying, singing and decorating the tall iron gates with wreaths and single flowers and memorial banners. CHRISTMAS IN HEAVEN, read one.

Ringo Starr flew to New York to see Yoko. George Harrison, 'shattered and stunned', went into retreat at his Oxfordshire home. Paul McCartney, whom Lennon plainly loved and just as plainly hated like the brother he never had, said, 'I can't tell you how much it hurts to lose him. His death is a bitter, cruel blow – I really loved the guy.' Yoko Ono said, 'This is not the end of an era. The 1980s are still going to be a beautiful time, and John believed in it.' The day after Lennon's death, Bruce Springsteen told his Philadelphia audience: 'If it wasn't for John Lennon, a lot of us would be some place much different tonight. It's a hard world that asks you to live with a lot of things that are unliveable. And it's hard to come out here and play tonight, but there's nothing else to do.'

At his first parole hearing Chapman said that he had committed the murder to gain attention, 'to steal John Lennon's fame'. He said, 'In some ways I'm a bigger nobody than I was before because, you know, people hate me,' adding 'and now I – I've come to grips with the fact that John Lennon was a person. This has nothing to do with being a Beatle or a celebrity or famous. He was breathing, and I knocked him right off his feet, and I don't feel because of that I have any right to be standing on my feet here, you know, asking for anything. I don't have a leg to stand on because I took his right out from under him, and he bled to death. And I'm sorry that ever occurred.'

Chapman's parole hearings will continue until he is freed or dies in jail. It is definitely safer for him inside. In a petition made by Lennon fans demanding that Chapman stay in jail for the rest of his life are comments such as: 'If he is set free, something will happen to him. This is New York. "Accidents" happen.' 'If Mark David Chapman is let out of jail, he wouldn't last a day. There are too many people who want him dead.' A man identifying himself as 'Kelsey' wrote, 'I'll kill him myself if he doesn't stay in jail.'

In the week after Lennon's death, another confused, suicidal young man was among those at the tribute in New York. Three weeks later, he confided his thoughts to a tape recorder. 'I just want to say goodbye to the old year, which was nothing, total misery, total death,' he said. 'John Lennon is dead, the world is over, forget it . . . Anything I might do in 1981 would be solely for Jodie Foster's sake. Just tell the world in some way that I worship and idolise her.' The young man's name was John Hinckley.

Hinckley, a chubby young man with unkempt blond hair, sat down at the small desk in room 312 in the Park Central Hotel, two blocks from the White House and directly opposite the Secret Service's headquarters. The weather had until then been unusually pleasant but that morning the sky turned lead grey and the drizzle steadily wetted the city streets.

After a few minutes' thought twenty-year-old Hinckley started writing.

Dear Jodie,
There is a definite possibility that I will be killed in my attempt to get Reagan. It is for this very reason that I am writing you this letter now.

As you well know by now I love you very much. Over the past seven months I've left you dozens of poems, letters and love messages in the faint hope that you could develop an interest in me. Although we talked on the phone a couple of times I never had the nerve to simply approach you and introduce myself. Besides my shyness, I honestly did not wish to bother you with my constant presence. I know the many messages left at your door and in your mailbox were a nuisance, but I felt that it was the most painless way for me to express my love for you.

I feel very good about the fact that you at least know my name and know how I feel about you. And by hanging around your dormitory, I've come to realize that I'm the topic of more than a little conversation, however full of ridicule it may be. At least you know that I'll always love you.

Jodie, I would abandon this idea of getting Reagan in a second if I could only win your heart and live out the rest of my life with you, whether it be in total obscurity or whatever.

I will admit to you that the reason I'm going ahead with this attempt now is because I just cannot wait any longer to impress you. I've got to do something now to make you understand, in no uncertain terms, that I am doing all of this for your sake! By sacrificing my freedom and possibly my life, I hope to change your mind about me.

This letter is being written only an hour before I leave for the Hilton Hotel. Jodie, I'm asking you to please look into your heart and at least give me the chance, with this historical deed, to gain your respect and love.

I love you forever,
John Hinckley

Hinckley sealed the letter and addressed it to the eighteen-year-old actress Jodie Foster, who was in her first year at Yale University. He did not mail it and instead placed it in his suitcase, confident that it would find its way to her soon enough.

Hinckley, who had followed Lennon's life since childhood and collected every scrap of information he could about the slain pop genius, had spent a week in vigil outside his New York home after his murder the previous year. While John Lennon was Hinckley's hero, Foster was his obsession. He became fascinated with her after watching the movie *Taxi Driver* which starred Robert De Niro as an obsessed gunman who plans to assassinate a Presidential candidate, a role inspired by real-life would-be assassin Arthur Bremer, who had shot Governor George Wallace in 1972. His literary tastes also ran to those who had lived by the gun: true-crime books about serial killers, spree-killers, hijackers and assassins – especially those who had achieved world infamy through their crimes.

As well as writing to Jodie Foster, Hinckley had phoned her three times but had been politely refused when he got through to her Yale dormitory. Hinckley had travelled to New Haven repeatedly over the previous nine months, yet he never spoke to Foster and although the other students spotted him; they regarded him as a harmless oddball.

Hinckley wasn't surprised to find that Foster wasn't interested in him; after all there were plenty of better-looking, wealthier (Hinckley came from an oil-rich family but his father didn't willingly hand over any cash to his son) and more intelligent guys at Yale (Hinckley had graduated from high school but after six years at Texas Tech University he had failed to achieve any certificates of higher learning).

On the bed a copy of the *Washington Star* newspaper lay open at the page that listed the President's schedule. Hinckley was almost out of cash – the latest instalment he had managed to extract from his father – and after months of contemplation he was trying to make a decision. In New Haven he could become a spree killer, shooting randomly at Yale's students before turning his gun on himself, or in Washington he could either kill senator Edward Kennedy (whose biography he had just finished reading) and charge the senate firing his gun as he went, or assassinate President Ronald Reagan.

Rechecking rooms at 1.15 p.m. to replace some used towels, the maid found Hinckley still in the room, wearing a light-coloured jacket, sports shirt and casual trousers. He stood by the bathroom door and watched without expression or comment as she hung the towels.

After the maid left, Hinckley removed a .22 calibre pistol from his jacket pocket and extracted a box of bullets from his suitcase. Among the forty-three bullets, Hinckley carefully picked out the six deadly 'devastator' bullets (which explode inside the victim) and slotted them into the chamber of his .22 'Saturday Night Special'. He stuffed a handful of ordinary slugs into his jacket pocket and exited the room, leaving his suitcase behind.

He hailed a cab. As they drove, Hinckley was suddenly overcome by a call of nature and he got the cab to stop at the Holiday Inn (which was close to the Hilton). He quickly paid the fare before dashing into the toilet. When he came out he spotted a group of journalists and TV cameras by the entrance of the Hilton Hotel and walked over to join them.

President Ronald Reagan had received a standing ovation as he entered the Hilton's International Ballroom to address 3,500 union representatives. It was the largest audience he had faced in person since his Inauguration seventy days earlier. Reagan was sixty-nine when he defeated Jimmy Carter in 1980 and became the oldest President the US has ever seen. He won all but six states and, in the Senate, for the first time in almost thirty years, the Republicans had total control, giving Reagan the power to secure whatever legislation he put forward. In foreign policy Reagan immediately talked tough and reprimanded the Russians for their ever-expanding weapons programme. Eventually the two leaders agreed to 'discussions about negotiations'. Reagan and the ruler of the Soviet Union, Leonid Brezhnev, were poised to decide the fate of the world. This US President was a worthy target.

Reagan was having on off day. His delivery was flat, he drew weak applause, and the crowd failed to laugh at his punchlines. But one sentence in the eighteen-minute speech would always be remembered: 'Violent crime has surged ten per cent, making neighbourhood streets unsafe and families fearful in their homes.'

Outside the Hilton, on an adjacent sidewalk, Hinckley was pacing nervously.

On the seventh floor of a nearby building, John M. Dodson, a Pinkerton's detective and computer specialist, trained to spot the odd man out, had already picked Hinckley. 'He looked fidgety, agitated, a little strange,' Dodson recalled later.

Dodson was right on the money; sadly no one else who had encountered Hinckley ever seemed to be. On 2 October the previous year, he had stood in the crowd watching President Jimmy Carter giving a speech, 'just close enough to shoot'. A week later, he was arrested on 9 October at Nashville airport with three handguns in his luggage. He was released after a few hours and amazingly, despite his arrest, was able to buy another gun almost immediately – the same model that Chapman used to kill Lennon. This was also while he was in the middle of therapy (his therapist had noted that Hinckley was unstable but not dangerous and would not carry out any threat).

Until this incident, Hinckley had kept a diary. He decided to destroy it; if the police officers who had arrested him had read it they would have treated him differently, full as it was with references to the assassination of the President. He had decided to keep a diary after reading Arthur Bremer's, which had been published a few years previously.

Hinckley decided to give up on Carter when it looked as if he was going to lose the election by a long way – he was not going to 'do a Bremer', who disappeared into relative obscurity after he gave up on assassinating President Richard Nixon and instead shot Wallace. Reagan, on the other hand, who held the fate of the world in his hands, was the perfect target to guarantee him infamous immortality.

The unmarked entrance, consisting of steel double doors under a concrete canopy, was designed precisely to provide security for presidents and other celebrities who attended affairs at the Hilton. The doors opened onto a wide pavement that ran along a curving driveway at the base of a high stone wall. On this day the Secret Service had roped off an area along this curving wall about ten metres from the doors. Hinckley watched from behind a group of TV and still photographers who were there to carry out what they called 'the bodywatch', to capture any Presidential calamity, from a trip-up to a heart attack (Reagan referred to this as the 'awful-awful').

Amazingly, Hinckley wasn't sure if he was going to go through with it even at that late stage. Standing close to the wall, he complained about the press, who had been griping about onlookers getting in the way. Radio reporter Walter Rodgers was pushing his way along the wall, extending his fishpole microphone, when he heard Hinckley: 'They ought to get here on time. They think they can do anything they want. Don't let them do that.'

The press jostled as Reagan emerged from the hotel and waved at the crowd. Hinckley waved back.

As always, curious onlookers pressed in for a glimpse of the President. They included some union members who had either arrived late for the lunch or left it early to get a closer view of Reagan. There were ordinary citizens armed with cameras, mothers with their children, and even a passing mayor from Iowa.

Hinckley battled with cameramen and reporters who were elbowing spectators and one another for a clear view of the President. As a reporter tried to shove Hinckley out of the way, waving his press card, Hinckley pushed back. 'No way, we were here first,' he said.

'Mr President, Mr President!' came a familiar shout from behind the rope. Associated Press Reporter Michael Putzel was trying to ask Reagan a question. Presidential Press Secretary Jim Brady stepped ahead to help field any press queries. Still smiling, Reagan looked at the milling group behind the rope.

It was 2.25 p.m.

Hinckley crouched low; gripping the pistol in a professional two-handed position he took good aim and methodically fired left to right as the Secret Service agents pushed Reagan towards the black bullet-proof Lincoln. His first bullet hit Brady in the head. The press officer fell face-down, flattened against the pavement, his arms twitching at his sides. At the sound of the first shot, Reagan's grin vanished and he stopped dead at the door to his limousine. Secret Service agent Tim McCarthy started to dive across to cover the President, pushing him towards the car as Hinckley kept firing. Police officer Tom Delehanty was the next to fall, hit in the neck; a gaping hole was left by the bullet and, remaining conscious, he writhed in agony next to Brady, who tried to push himself up but failed as his blood trickled into a drain from a pea-sized bullet-hole over his left eye. The third shot narrowly missed the head of Presidential aide Michael Eaver and sent plaster dust and concrete flying from the building behind him. By now McCarthy, still diving, arms outspread, had become a human shield. Suddenly he froze as a devastator bullet blasted into his stomach and he dropped, leaving Reagan exposed and Hinckley with two bullets left.

Agent Jerry Parr, who was at Reagan's side, instinctively pushed the President's head down and shoved him hard through the open armoured car door. Reagan's head struck the roof of the door as they piled in, milliseconds before Hinckley's fifth bullet smashed into its bullet-resistant window with a terrific crack. Without the window the bullet would have struck the left side of the President's head. Parr and Reagan landed on the floor, half-in and half-out of the car, just ahead of the rear seat, Parr on top of the President. 'Take off!' Parr shouted to the driver. 'Just take off!'

One bullet left. Reagan was still half-in and half-out of the car, Parr was frantically working to shove him inside. Hinckley, his aim steady, fired as Parr lifted and then dived on top of the President. The bullet took an almost impossible path towards its target. It hit the rear fender, ricocheted off, passed through a crack in the still-open door and blasted Reagan in the left armpit where it tore through his chest and into his lung – a mortal wound unless it was treated immediately. Reagan groaned as the door slammed shut. 'You son of a bitch, you broke my rib,' Reagan said as the Lincoln's tyres spun on the wet street.

Hinckley had fired six shots in 1.8 seconds. Four people were in critical condition. Secret Service agents had pushed through the crowd to pounce on the assassin, who had already been grabbed by a union member and a policeman. He struggled furiously for at least twenty seconds before the gun was snatched away from him. One agent brandished his Uzi submachine gun to fend off any threat from the screaming crowd; for all he knew, there might have been a team of gunmen.

Another agent, jammed against the wall in the melee, waved his pistol and yelled, 'Get a police car! Get a car!' Handcuffing Hinckley and throwing a jacket over his head, the officers shoved him towards one police car, but found the rear door locked. They pushed him into a second and sped off to Washington police headquarters.

Tim McCarthy lay doubled up on the pavement, hands clutching the bullet wound in his stomach. Delehanty was conscious but struggling to breathe through his neck wound. Most disturbingly of all, Brady had stopped moving as his blood pooled across the pavement.

Meanwhile, in the limo, Parr and the President himself were both still unaware that he had been hit. The driver, Drew Unrue, was following normal procedure in such emergencies which was to return directly to the White House, the most secure area in the city. Had the procedure been followed in this instance, Reagan would have died.

'Jerry, get off me. You're hurting my ribs,' Reagan protested. 'You really came down hard on top of me.' The agent helped Reagan sit upright on the rear seat and checked for wounds but couldn't see anything. Reagan repeated that his ribs hurt, 'I can't breathe so well,' he complained. Parr noticed he had turned ashen and then the President coughed; blood reddened his lips. Parr thought that one of his ribs had been broken and had punctured a lung. Reagan agreed.

Parr ordered the driver to turn right and race to George Washington University Hospital, two miles from the Hilton. By radio Parr advised the Secret Service command post at the White House: 'Rawhide is heading for George Washington.' Rawhide was Reagan's Secret Service code name (in keeping with the cowboy theme, his car was called 'Stagecoach').

Unrue changed routes, taking the support cars, still struggling to catch up, by surprise and losing them in the process. Parr radioed ahead to alert the emergency-room staff. Not knowing that Hinckley was the lone assassin, he was worried that there might be a second assassin waiting at or en-route to the hospital. For now, it was just him and the driver guarding the seriously wounded President.

As they pulled up at the hospital, Parr was surprised to see no one waiting for them. He thought about the possibility of a second shooter. Now would be the perfect time as they stumbled together towards the hospital doors. 'I can't breathe,' said Reagan, and fear flashed into his eyes as the last of his strength left him. It was only after the agents had lifted Reagan onto the table in the trauma unit and scissored off his coat and shirt that anyone realised that the President had been shot.

Fortunately for Reagan, the ER doctors were well used to dealing with gunshot wounds: Washington was at that time the number one city in America for gangland shootings. Doctors found the entry wound, a small jagged hole under his left arm, but no exit wound. The devastator bullet was still inside. Reagan's blood pressure plummeted as he coughed blood and his breathing faltered.

Dr Jospeh M Giardani, chief of the trauma team, immediately suspected that the President had suffered a collapsed lung, plus damage to the heart and major blood vessels. A chest tube was inserted and a blood transfusion was started in an effort to replace the pint the President had already lost.

His wife, Nancy, was at the White House when she learned of the shooting. She reached the hospital only minutes after Reagan and dashed to his side. 'Honey,' he whispered as she bent over him, 'I forgot to duck.'

Despite his dire and worsening condition, the President somehow remained in good spirits. Still conscious but fading fast, he noticed the masked faces, backed by the bright surgical lights, as they leaned over him in the operating room. He whispered, 'Please tell me you're Republicans' and passed out.

It was a complex three-and-a-half hour operation. The bullet, according to Dr Benjamin Aaron, was 'flattened almost as thin as a dime'. It had bounced off Reagan's seventh rib, past the heart and into his lung. Amazingly, it had not exploded because it had hit the door of the limousine first. The merest deviation in the bullet's path and the wound would have been fatal.

While Reagan was undergoing surgery all hell was breaking loose at the White House. Vice-President George H. W. Bush was in transit and Secretary of State Alexander Meigs Haig, Jr, a military hawk who, like Bush, did not support negotiations with Russia over nuclear disarmament, somehow thought that he should assume ultimate control in the meantime and called a press conference. Defence Secretary Caspar Weinberger's memoir of that afternoon records a remarkable coincidence: 'There had been a FEMA [Federal Emergency Management Administration] exercise scheduled for the next day on the procedures of Presidential succession, with the general title "Nine Lives". By an immediate consensus, it was agreed that the exercise should be cancelled.'

Haig, however, could have done with a crash course in Presidential succession. He mistakenly assumed that while Reagan was in surgery and while Bush was in transit to the White House, he should assume control of the Oval Office. He called what became a career-ending press conference. To begin with, the Secretary of State was not the most eloquent of speakers. Before the phenomenon of the Bushism there was the Haigism. Haig won notoriety in the press earlier in the year for confusing Russian translators while involved in aggressive talks with the Soviet Union, coming out with phrases such as 'careful caution', 'careless caution', 'longstanding in time' and 'That's not a lie. It is a terminological inexactitude.'

At the press conference about the assassination attempt Haig stunned reporters by claiming that 'I'm in control here', which was widely reported as nothing less than the worst coup attempt in history. This statement cost Haig his job. But, for the time being, Haig set up a crisis control centre in a White House situation room and tried to maintain order. Besieged by political infighting, erroneous press reports, faulty equipment and incompetent personnel, he struggled to make sense of the crisis at hand. Fortunately, Bush soon took over; he spent most of his eight hours as President playing tennis and let everyone get on with their jobs.

First reports about the President's condition were intended to disguise the serious nature of Reagan's injury. A hospital spokesperson assured the media that the President was A-OK, having 'sailed through surgery', and would be able 'to make decisions by tomorrow, certainly'. Those who saw him knew differently. But for the actions of Secret Service agents Jerry Parr and Tim McCarthy, an excellent trauma team and two exceptionally skilled surgeons, Reagan would have become the fifth US President to have been assassinated. The fate of the world would have been changed once more by a young misfit.

Jerry Parr and Tim McCarthy are to be commended for their action. With no time to prevent the attack, there was no chance of drawing weapons and firing back, only time to risk taking a bullet to save the target. Several other bodyguards spent the 1.8 seconds that Hinckley was firing trying to draw their guns, find the target and fire back – an impossible task. If Parr and McCarthy had reacted in the same way, Reagan would probably have been assassinated.

The President was in a bad way for several weeks; he often needed an inhalator for extra oxygen and could concentrate for only a few minutes at a time. His supposedly quick recovery was just a carefully staged performance to make it clear to the world that the captain was still in charge of his ship. As soon as he was well enough, Reagan was told about the fate of the others who had been injured. McCarthy and Delehanty would eventually make a full recovery, but Jim Brady was not so lucky. He survived but was left brain-damaged and would be confined to a wheelchair.

Reagan wept after hearing about Jim Brady's dreadful injuries. Brady did make a better recovery than was expected, however, and became an advocate for gun control, successfully campaigning for a bill (popularly known as the Brady Bill) which enforced stricter background checks on the purchasers of guns.

The day after the assassination attempt, just when it seemed that things were under control, the *Houston Post* published a startling story under the headline: BUSH'S SON WAS TO DINE WITH SUSPECT'S BROTHER. Reporters had discovered that Scott Hinckley, John's older brother, was to have been a dinner guest that very night at the home of Neil Bush, son of the Vice-President. Neil Bush admitted that he was personally acquainted with Scott Hinckley, having met with him on one occasion in the recent past, and that he also knew the Hinckley family. He was asked if he also knew John Hinckley Jr. 'I have no idea,' said Neil Bush. 'I don't recognise any pictures of him. I just wish I could see a better picture of him.'

Elder son and future President George W. Bush was asked the same question: 'It's certainly conceivable that I met him or might have been introduced to him. I don't recognise his face from the brief, kind of distorted thing they had on TV, and the name doesn't ring any bells. I know he wasn't on our staff.'

Sadly for the conspiracists, there was absolutely zero evidence of any larger plot behind Hinckley's attack.

Thrust innocently into a national spotlight she had not sought, the actress Jodie Foster held a news conference at Yale to confirm that she had received many 'unsolicited' love notes from Hinckley. None had mentioned the President, she said, and none had contained any hints of violence.

The detailed FBI files of the subsequent investigation and

interviewing of Hinckley are extraordinarily detailed and include some moments of real comedy as the interviewing detectives tried to get the would-be assassin to open up.

At first he denied everything: 'I don't know anything about the shooting.'

The detective came back with a line that Reagan would have been proud of: 'Come on, now, John. You must be a democrat.'

When a doctor came in to check Hinckley's physical condition an agent asked for a sample of pubic hair.

'Pubic hair?' the detective replied. 'For chrissakes. He didn't *fuck* Reagan; he *shot* him.'

As this bantering continued, Hinckley relaxed and spent much of the time worrying about whether the attempt had been filmed and whether it would be shown before the Academy Awards ceremony that night. Like Sirhan and Bremer, he was hoping for notorious immortality.

Hinckley was incarcerated in a secure mental hospital, St Elizabeth's in Washington, where he was diagnosed with a collection of classic symptoms. The eighteen-page report concluded that Hinckley 'suffers from a complex and serious mental disorder' that 'makes him an unpredictably dangerous person.' When psychiatrists asked Hinckley whether he regarded himself as dangerous to Foster he replied: 'Not now. If released I would go the other way but in one or two years if things go on the same, no response from her, then I'll kill her.' Unsurprisingly, the report concluded that: 'Hinckley is presently a danger to himself, Jodie Foster and any other third party whom he would consider incidental in his ultimate aims.'

At the trial in 1982, charged with thirteen offences, Hinckley was found not guilty by reason of insanity on 21 June. The defence psychiatric reports found him to be insane while the prosecution reports declared him legally sane. The not-guilty-by-reason-of-insanity verdict led to widespread dismay; as a result, the US Congress and a number of states rewrote the law regarding the insanity defence. Three states have since abolished the defence altogether. In the United States, prior to the Hinckley case, the insanity defence was used in less than two per cent of capital cases and was unsuccessful in almost eighty per cent of the trials in which it was used.

Hinckley responded well to antidepressant and anti-psychotic medication. His violent fantasies involving Jodie Foster receded. Despite a setback in 1983 when he attempted suicide, Hinckley's mental health continued to improve and on 28 December 1986, accompanied by members of the Secret Service, he was allowed out on a family visit. According to some news reports, in 1987 Hinckley fell in love with a fellow patient, a woman who had shot her seven-year-old daughter dead before attempting to take her own life by blowing off her arm with the same weapon.

Hinckley made a bid for more supervised visits with his family. And it looked as if he was going to get them until his Attorney, Vincent Fuller, found out that he had written to a famous serial killer. This revelation, along with several others, found its way into the *Washington Post* on 26 August 1988. Hinckley's embarrassed psychiatrists were forced to tell the judge: 'He has written recently a letter to – I think his name is Bundy, a convicted mass murderer in Florida – expressing his sorrow as I understand it, his feelings, the awful position that Bundy must be in.'

It also emerged that Hinckley had corresponded with President Gerald Ford's would-be assassin, Lynette 'Squeaky' Fromme, and had asked for Charles Manson's address. When the Judge ordered a search of Hinckley's room, hospital staff found twenty photographs of Jodie Foster. His obsession continued: the following summer he tried to order a drawing of a naked Foster through a mail-order catalogue.

In 2005, District Judge Paul L. Friedman agreed that Hinckley, by then in his fifties, should be allowed seven visits to his parents' home within a wealthy gated community in Kingsmill. On 2 February 2006, Hinckley travelled to the family home with only his parents to guard him. The Hinckleys ate lunch in Kingsmill's tennis, golf and conference centre where, on the same day, 125 Democratic members of the House of Representatives, including former Vice-President Al Gore (who had hinted he would run for President at the next election) were gathered to discuss homeland security.

Jodie Foster refuses to speak about Hinckley today, although she did refer to the incident briefly when being interviewed by *USA Today* in 2007 about a new film she was starring in. 'I totally believe in *Taxi Driver*,' she said. 'It's a classic, beautiful film. It's a beautiful marker for our time. That movie spoke to generations of people – who didn't shoot anyone.' Later in the same interview she also said: 'I don't think picking up a gun is brave. I don't think shooting someone is brave. Knowing who you are, living your life the way you want to live it. That's brave.'

Twenty

The Pope Must Die

An assassination that was to become one of the twentieth century's greatest mysteries dominated 1981: did the assassin who shot Pope John Paul II act alone or was he obeying orders? Thanks to a team of Italian investigators who in 2006 revealed their reports of the official investigation, the (almost) complete story can now be told for the first time.

As unrivalled head of a worldwide flock of one billion Roman Catholics, the Pope can exercise moral, political and spiritual influence across the globe. As Joseph Stalin once famously quipped, the Pope commands no military divisions but, in 1981, the sixty-one-year-old Polish Pope John Paul II had maximised his arsenal, which included constant charismatic globe-trotting (twenty-one countries on five continents in two years) and a deft diplomatic touch.

Coming to Rome from behind the Iron Curtain, John Paul II knew just what notes to hit in both public and private to inspire his fellow Poles and others in order to undermine the Communist regimes. In Poland, he challenged Soviet communism's collectivist ideology – and a year later, the workers of Poland launched the Solidarity Movement under the leadership of Lech Walesa. It was for this reason that, unlike Joseph Stalin who sneered at the Pope and his imaginary divisions, the long-serving KGB chief Yuri Andropov saw this anti-communist pope as a mortal danger to Soviet control over Eastern Europe. Unfortunately for Andropov, the Pope, who had played professional rugby as a young man, was fighting fit and extremely popular – the only way his influence might be halted was if he met with an accident . . . Meanwhile, Andropov's opposite number and keen rival (whose identity cannot yet be revealed) at the top-secret GRU (Russia's Chief Intelligence Directorate, responsible for all military intelligence) had already decided that just such an 'accident' could be arranged. The rough equivalent of Britain's MI6, the GRU operated with no morals and little accountability. It willingly operated alongside some of the world's most infamous terrorists, including Abu Nidal (see page 267).

Many thousands of people regularly swarmed to St Peter's Square every Wednesday afternoon; clergy, Roman Catholics, non-believers, pilgrims and ordinary tourists from every nation. All of them were there to catch a sight of the Pope, something that John Paul II had made far easier for them. Previously, Papal general audiences were held indoors, in St Peter's Basilica, and the Pontiff, an aloof figure out of reach of the crowds, was carried into the vast church on a portable throne called the *sedia gestatoria*. But John Paul II changed all that. Whenever the weather permitted, audiences were held outdoors in the square. This was despite the occasional threats to the Pope's life. (In February 1981 a grenade exploded in a stadium in Karachi, Pakistan, twenty minutes before John Paul II entered; the incident was hastily covered up at the time.)

On 13 May 1981, a glorious early summer's day, a crowd of about fifteen thousand people had turned out. It was a typical multinational, multiracial gathering which included a group of waterworks officials attending a convention in Rome; Poles from a parish in Cracow; cycling clubs from northern Italy with their bicycles; US schoolchildren shepherded by nuns; gaggles of camera-toting Japanese tourists, and so on.

Twenty-three-year-old Mehmet Ali Agca had joined the crowds

after having walked for fifteen minutes from his room at the Pensione Isa, a cheap hotel. The young Turkish man had checked in three days earlier after travelling to Rome under the name of Faruk Ozgun. That morning he wrote a letter which he left on his bed to be found after he had assassinated the Pope with the Browning 9mm he now carried in his pocket.

Agca, a convicted murderer, had a colourful past. He had left his home to study literature at the University of Ankara, then economics at Istanbul University. There he became a devotee of terrorist politics and joined the Grey Wolves, the militant wing of the ultra-right National Action Party. On 25 June 1979, when police swept into an Istanbul café notorious as a hang-out for right-wing extremists, Agca was among those rounded up. Police had received a tip-off that he was behind the assassination of Abdi Ipekci, editor of Istanbul's respected left-of-centre daily *Milliyet*. Agca confessed and went on trial in October 1979.

On the night of 23 November, while the case was still being heard, he was secretly whisked out of his cell in an Istanbul maximum-security prison by fourteen sympathetic military men (who later received lengthy sentences for their trouble). Three days after the escape, *Milliyet* received a letter from Agca demanding the cancellation of an imminent visit to Turkey by Pope John Paul II.

In the letter Agca wrote that the Pope was coming as part of a Western imperialist plan to erode the unity of the 'brotherly Islamic countries'. It also contained the line: 'I will shoot the Pope if his untimely visit is not cancelled.' The shooting never materialised and the Pope's visit went ahead as planned. Agca might have been busy elsewhere at the time. A month after his escape, the Grey Wolf informant believed to have fingered Agca for the Ipecki murder was tortured and killed in Istanbul.

During 1980, Agca travelled from Turkey to Iran, back through Turkey, on to Bulgaria for a few months, then to Yugoslavia. On his travels, he met Ilich Ramirez Sanchez, a.k.a. international terrorist Carlos the Jackal, in Sofia. The Jackal recommended Agca as a good man with a gun to his Bulgarian contact, an employee of the

Durzhavna Sigurnost (the Bulgarian Committee for State Security, essentially an extension of Russia's secret services).

In the autumn Agca travelled to West Germany on a reliability test for the DS, where he became a suspect in the contract-style political murder of a fellow Turk. He then received new orders and travelled to Rome where he met Ivan Dontchev, a fifty-six-year-old Bulgarian Embassy official who had no idea what Agca's mission was. His orders were simply to oversee Agca's stay in Italy and provide him with finances – including enough cash for a place on a two-week package tour to Palma de Mallorca. (His tour operator remembered that he dutifully took all the sightseeing excursions.)

At exactly five p.m. on 13 May, Pope John Paul II made his entrance via the Arch of Bells, standing in his open-top jeep-like *campagnola*, dubbed the 'Popemobile'. He appeared relaxed as he circled the square through a narrow lane formed by low wooden barricades. The crowd cheered and waved white-and-gold papal flags.

In the speech that was meant to follow, the Pope had intended to revert to one of his consistent themes: the duty of the rich to help the poor. He swept babies into his large hands and kissed them, touched outstretched fingers, extended his arms in blessing.

At 5.19 p.m. the Popemobile had nearly completed its second and final circuit. John Paul picked up and held high a little girl and tousled her blonde hair as he hugged her. After he put her down, the Pope leaned out of his car and held his hand out to a little girl dressed in white. Behind the girl, some people were being harangued by a nervous-looking man who was also arguing with a group of pilgrims lining the low wooden barricades along the Popemobile's lane; he was gruffly telling them that they were blocking him from getting close to the Pontiff.

Giving up on the argument with the pilgrims, Agca suddenly plunged headlong into the crowd. An Irish woman spotted the gun waving between a pair of heads and recognised it as a Browning 9mm. (She had seen and heard the same type of weapon many times before in her home country.) There was a crack as the first shot was fired from only a few yards from the Pope. It shattered the two joints of the Pope's ring finger of his left hand, ricocheted and grazed his right arm. The second followed immediately and blasted into his abdomen, passing completely through his body, ripping up the Pope's intestines but narrowly missing his pancreas, abdominal aorta and spine.

The Pope stood immobile for an instant. Then he collapsed backward into the arms of his personal secretary as another pair of bullets whizzed past. The first struck Rose Hall, a twenty-one-year-old American woman married to a Protestant missionary posted to West Germany. It broke her left arm. Ann Odre, fifty-eight, a widow from Buffalo and a devout Roman Catholic who had just realised her lifetime's ambition of seeing the Pope, was hit in her abdomen. At week's end she was in a serious condition after a long operation to remove her spleen, but she would survive.

The Pope looked at his hands, one of which was bloodied. Bright red blood began to spurt from his abdomen onto his gleaming white cassock. Francesco Passanisi, inspector general of the Vatican police, who had been following close behind the *campagnola*, leaped aboard and ordered the driver to move back and forth, presenting a blurred target for any further shots. The Pope said 'Thank you, thank you' and 'Don't worry.'

Immediately after the shots, Agca edged out of the crowd; his expression was tense, and he still held the gun at the end of his outstretched arm. He almost backed into a first-aid trailer. Then he turned around and ran towards the columns and the streets of Rome.

Vatican plain-clothes security guards and numerous members of the crowd had spotted him; the quickest off the mark was Sister Letizia, a large, robust and athletic young nun. She sprinted after the gunman as he darted behind an ambulance and slipped on the cobblestones. Letizia pounced upon him and screamed 'Why did you do it?' She was dragged away as the police arrived to rescue the small, thin-faced, dark-haired man from the ferocious crowd.

Agca was marched off in a tight headlock by a tall, blond plain-clothes man and surrounded by five or six others who hustled him through the hostile throng, who were ready to commit some truly unholy acts of revenge.

Meanwhile, after a few seconds of to-ing and fro-ing in evasive-action manoeuvres, when it became clear that there would be no more shots, the Popemobile whirred off as rapidly as its small engine could drive it, at the painfully slow rate of twelve miles an hour, through the Arch of Bells to an ambulance always parked near papal appearances. On the twenty-minute drive to Gemelli Hospital, John Paul II, bleeding profusely, murmured 'Madonna, Madonna' over and over in Polish.

As the ambulance pulled up to the emergency entrance, an attendant jumped out and shouted to stunned doctors and nurses: 'It's the Pope! It's the Pope!' John Paul II was wheeled swiftly to the intensive-care unit, given a blood transfusion and taken to the ninth-floor surgical clinic. As he was being moved into surgery, the Pope asked a male nurse: 'Why did they do it?' Then he passed out. The machines that monitored his vital signs rang their alarms as his blood pressure fell and his pulse all but disappeared.

For almost five and a half hours rumours flew around the world and hospital patients in bathrobes mingled with Italian dignitaries and journalists to exchange shocked speculations. Eventually Giancarlo Castiglioni, the chief of surgery, who had leaped on a plane from Milan to join the surgical team halfway through the operation, emerged from the theatre to brief reporters. He was still wearing his green gown; his eyes were red-rimmed with exhaustion. In a barely audible voice, he announced: 'The prognosis is reserved, but there is hope that the Pope will recover and stay with us.'

In reality, the battle for the Pope's life was a close contest fought between the devastator bullet and the experienced surgeons. Thankfully, in an almost exact duplication of the Reagan shooting, the bullet had not shattered on impact as it was supposed to and had missed the aorta by millimetres. Despite this, the Pope lost sixty per cent of his blood due to massive internal haemorrhaging and two feet of his intestines ended up in the surgical waste-bin. He was also at risk of developing an infection. But he was a tough guy and he pulled through.

After a brief stop at the Vatican police station, Agca was quickly bundled into an armoured car and driven to central police headquarters in downtown Rome. During twelve hours of almost uninterrupted interrogation conducted at a small table in a bare-walled chamber, the gunman's identity emerged. In the words of Alfredo Lazzarini, head of the Rome police anti-terrorist squad, Agca was 'a terrorist with a capital T'. He was considered so dangerous that Turkish police had been given orders to shoot him on sight.

Agca told them to look in room 31 of his hotel and there they found his student card, his false passport, an extra cartridge clip for the Browning and a letter in Turkish boasting of the Pope's death. In the familiar tones of his 1979 letter, it denounced 'Russian and American imperialism' and made John Paul the scapegoat for both.

The outpouring of anger, outrage and sympathy for the fallen Pontiff was all but universal – far more extensive than it had been for Ronald Reagan six weeks before. Shooting presidents was politics, after all; for many this was like taking a shot at God. Reagan, still recovering from his own bullet wounds, promised 'I'll pray for him,' while Yuri Andropov and the head of the GRU hoped for bad news. Soviet President Leonid Brezhnev sent a telegram: 'I am profoundly indignant at the criminal attempt on your life.' Indian Prime Minister Indira Gandhi told reporters: 'I am too shocked for words. What more can I say?'

Agca started talking the next day and identified a man he called Sergei Antonov from a series of photographs of St Peter's Square, taken at the time of the assassination. Agca convinced detectives that Antonov was his accomplice who was there to help him escape and that his job was to set off a small bomb to create a distraction.

Sergei Antonov, then head of the Balkan Air office in Rome, was an odd character who wore large glasses, collected miniature liquor bottles, loved flowers and pop music and smoked Havana cigars. After his arrest he denied ever having met Agca.

On 8 July, as Agca was being moved from police headquarters, he said offhandedly within earshot of reporters that 'in the attack on the Pope, even the KGB took part'. Andropov vigorously denied the accusation to the Politburo while the chief of the GRU kept quiet.

In June 1985 the Italian government put Antonov and six suspected accomplices (two Bulgarians and four Turks) on trial, charging them with conspiracy to assassinate the Pope. But prosecutors were stunned when Agca, their only star witness, took the stand and said: 'I am Jesus Christ. In the name of the omnipotent God, I announce the end of the world. No one, neither the Americans nor the Soviets, will be saved. There will be destruction.'

Agca added that there were more conspirators in the assassination attempt: members of a secret Italian Masonic lodge and the Italian Secret Service. The trial collapsed because Agca was now widely accepted to be insane. He was convicted of attempted murder but was pardoned in 2000 before being returned to Turkey where he began serving out his sentence for the murder of Abdi Ipekci, the newspaper editor. Antonov was freed, returned to Bulgaria and denied any involvement in the plot to kill the Pope, despite the findings of an Italian investigation into the assassination, the results of which were published in 2006. According to Paolo Guzzanti, the commission's president, the key evidence was a photograph taken on the day of the assassination in St Peter's Square which showed Agca and, not far from him, a man wearing a moustache and large spectacles. After analyses of the picture using the latest computer technology, Guzzanti became a hundred per cent convinced that the man with the moustache was Sergei Antonov, something Antonov continues to deny. Whatever the case may be, Antonov is safe. Under Italian law he cannot be tried a second time.

Meanwhile, the Pope made a full recovery and, along with Reagan and Soviet President Mikhail Gorbachev, who won the Nobel Peace

Prize for his efforts, became one of the decisive players in the end of the Cold War. Without his support combined with one crucial religious assassination (see page 271), Communist Poland would never have fallen when it did.

Twenty-one

Z-Squad Incorporated

In the 1980s, a secret South African death squad was responsible for maintaining apartheid by carrying out a series of assassinations of political opponents. The murders were then made to look like accidents or suicides. On the record, at least fifty opponents of the apartheid regime were killed by this death squad. Yet, in November 1981, one particular assassination would backfire badly, and inspire a woman who was to become an influential and outspoken figure. And when she became the next target, the death squad unwittingly plunged South Africa into a state of civil war, hastening the end of apartheid.

Griffiths Mxenge awoke to the sound of his children screaming in terror. He leaped out of bed, calling their names as he ran downstairs and into his front garden. As a prominent human-rights lawyer, political activist and former Robben Island prisoner, Mxenge was used to having his phone tapped and receiving threats but what he found in his garden was something else.

On the lawn were his two bull terriers. One was dead; the other was writhing in silent agony, foam bubbling out of its mouth. He gathered his screaming children in his arms and took them inside to his wife Victoria. Griffiths rushed the terrier to the local vet where it died on the examination table. His dogs had been poisoned with strychnine.

Although shaken, Mxenge still went to work as normal. Griffiths Mxenge had got his law degree from the University of Fort Hare, the same institution that African National Congress leaders Nelson Mandela and Oliver Tambo had graduated from twenty years earlier.

Mxenge initially made his name by successfully proving in court that the word *kaffir* was offensive. Then he took on the impossible task of prosecuting the police over the deaths of two young men, Mduli and Mohapi, both of whom had died in police custody.

Griffiths joined Mandela and Tambo on Robben Island prison in 1967 after he was sentenced to two years for helping the ANC (at that time an outlawed organisation). He was a member of the Release Mandela Committee, Lawyers for Human Rights and a founding member of the South African Democratic Lawyers Association. He had campaigned tirelessly against apartheid and defended hundreds of victims charged under the Suppression of Communism Act, the Group Areas Act, the Terrorism Act, the Influx Control Act, the Police Act and the Pass Laws Act. Mxenge was popularly known as 'the ANC lawyer'. To say that he was a threat to the apartheid regime was an understatement. He was the worst kind of enemy: he fought the system from within. He was educated, intelligent, a persuasive orator and a brilliant lawyer.

Mxenge took the poisoning of his dogs to be a warning – but this incident was just a precursor for something much, much worse.

'Make a plan with Griffiths Mxenge,' said Brigadier Jan van der Hoven, chief of the police security branch in Natal. Those words had a particular meaning for Captain Dirk Johannes Coetzee: they were orders for an assassination.

Van der Hoven continued briefing his captain: 'He is a former Robben Island convict and an attorney who gives us a lot of trouble. Mxenge defends the accused in terrorist trials and more than one hundred thousand rand from the ANC recently passed through his account. We tried to bring a case against him but failed. We just do not have enough evidence to charge him.'

Coetzee asked his boss 'What do you want us to do with him?'

'Don't shoot or abduct him. It must look like a robbery.'

Dirk Coetzee, handsome, tanned, clean-shaven and blond, the best student of his year's police college intake, had enthusiastically climbed his way up the police ranks to become the commander of the secret South African Police death squad (also known as 'Z-Squad Incorporated'). It was based at the Vlakplaas (the Farm on the Plain), an idyllic location that could have passed for a holiday retreat; it nestled beside a gravel road in a crescent of hills on the banks of the Hennops River, just thirty kilometres outside the administrative capital of Pretoria.

Coetzee was directly responsible for six assassinations committed between January 1977 and December 1981 and had been party to dozens more. He had never heard of Griffiths Mxenge until he was instructed to 'make a plan' but a few days of investigation were all he needed. He chose his four-man assassination team from the sixteen *askaris* (former ANC and Pan-African Congress guerrillas who had been captured, turned and drafted into the security police) who worked for his unit. He picked Brian Ngqulunga, a loyal friend; David Tshikalanga, whom Coetzee had known since he had recruited him into the police force eight years previously; Almond Nofemela, a sober guy who, Coetzee said, 'had the guts of a tiger', and Joe Mamasela, an experienced killer.

They spent two days on surveillance. Coetzee told the *askaris* to wear old clothes and shoes which could be thrown away, and to keep nothing in their pockets. He gave them a big hunting knife and a pair of foot-long okapi knives. The *askaris* thought they might assassinate Mxenge at home and make it look like a burglary, but they were worried about Mxenge's dogs making a noise and attacking them.

Coetzee got some meat from the police mess and poisoned it. Nofemela threw it over Mxenge's wall. In the end, Mxenge's dogs died for nothing as the assassins decided to attack Griffiths on a lonely road as he drove home from work. Coetzee provided them with one of Z-Squad's vehicles, a grey pick-up truck, and arranged to pick them up at a Durban bar just after the hit.

At eight p.m. on 19 November 1981 Griffiths Mxenge bade his colleagues goodnight and left his Victoria Street law firm. A thick blanket of mist and rain threatened to slow his journey home to Umlazi. He had just bought a new car, a white Audi, and so drove carefully.

After a few minutes he saw a grey pick-up van with its bonnet open blocking his way. A man stepped out from behind the vehicle and waved his hands. Mxenge stopped and wound down the window. The man asked if he had any jump leads. As Mxenge got out of the car, two other men appeared. The man nearest to him drew a pistol and said: 'Do as I say – get into the back of the car.'

Mxenge thought he was being robbed and pleaded with the men: 'Where are we going? Please don't kill me. You can take everything I have. You don't have to shoot me.'

They stopped next to the new cycling stadium in Umlazi. Mxenge was pushed out of the pick-up. The driver got out with an okapi knife in his hand. Behind him the other men pulled out knives while the driver stepped forward and plunged his blade into Mxenge's chest. Mxenge fell to the ground, and the three men stabbed him about a dozen times.

As the assassins stood back, breathing hard, they watched in amazement as the lawyer struggled to his feet. David Tshikalanga stepped forward and drove his okapi knife straight into Mxenge's chest. Somehow, Mxenge pushed Tshikalanga away, reached down, gripped the knife handle and withdrew the blade from his body. Okapi knife in his hand, he staggered towards the man who only a few minutes earlier had asked him for help.

Almond Nofemela raised a tyre-spanner with a sharpened end high in the air. He knocked the knife out of Mxenge's hand and hammered him over the head. Mxenge went down for the final time and the four men stabbed and kicked him into an unrecognisable mess. They removed his jacket, wallet and watch and drove off into the dark with their victim's brand-new car.

Coetzee walked into the bar at ten p.m. and found the members of his team were already there. Mamasela was wearing Mxenge's jacket and watch. The sleeves of Mxenge's jacket were too short for Mamasela. Coetzee beckoned them outside and the four men gave him a brief account in the street. They had already changed and put their clothes and shoes, the knives, and Mxenge's belongings in the boot of the car. They gave Coetzee the keys to Mxenge's car and told him they had parked it right next to the entrance of CR Swart Police Station (the office of Coetzee's boss – Brigadier Jan van der Hoven) in an open parking lot. The *askari* were paid a thousand rand each.

Coetzee went through the car and removed the stereo which ended up in the state-subsidised Mercedes of a senior police officer. Coetzee then made arrangements for the white Audi to be driven out to the desert and torched.

Thirty-nine-year-old Nonyamezelo Victoria Mxenge started out as a nurse before getting her law degree in 1974, after which she started working with her husband in 1975, and became a fully-fledged attorney in February 1981. On the night of 19 November she had left the law practice shortly before her husband and was expecting him home a few minutes after her. As the minutes became hours, she drove around looking for him, returning every now and then to their house, hoping that it was just the new car playing up.

At dawn Victoria drove to the King Edward VII Hospital, then to St Adrian's Hospital and the CR Swart Police Station where van der Hoven, the man who had ordered the killing, reassured her that he had not detained her husband. At eight a.m. she phoned the security branch in Natal. They had a body.

A by now distraught Victoria drove to the government mortuary in Durban where she was shown the covered corpse of an unknown black male that had been brought in earlier that morning in the back of a police van. The cloth was slowly pulled back. Victoria saw the bloody face of a man she struggled to recognise as her husband. His throat was slashed and his ears were almost severed from his head. Then, as her gaze moved down his body, she gasped as she saw the stab wounds in his chest and his stomach, which had been ripped open by dozens of savage knife-thrusts.

Grief-stricken and furious, Victoria immediately contacted the ANC and together they released a statement: 'My husband died in great pain . . . I don't believe this was the work of ordinary thugs, it was done by someone who was opposed to what he stood for . . . when people have declared war on you, you cannot afford to be crying. You have to fight back. As long as I live, I will never rest until I see to it that justice is done, until Griffiths Mxenge's killers are brought to book.' ANC leader Oliver Tambo commented: 'Agents of the Pretoria regime have brutally assassinated Griffiths Mxenge. Farewell, dear brother and comrade. Your sacrifice is not in vain.'

Griffiths Mxenge was buried a week later. Fifteen thousand people joined the procession. Speaker after speaker stood up to say that Mxenge's death must not be in vain. Nobel Laureate Desmond Tutu, the black Anglican Bishop of Johannesburg, told the crowd: 'Our liberation is going to be costly. Many more will be detained. Many more will be banned. But we shall be free.'

As Mxenge's coffin was lowered into the ground, a Transkei security policeman was found covertly tape-recording the proceedings. Tutu and another priest tried in vain to shield DC Albert Gungqwama Tafile from a frenzied mob who tore him apart with their hands, screaming 'Kill, kill the *impimpi* (sell-out)!'

'Have you come to bury Griffiths or kill one another?' shouted the bishop, his white robes splattered with blood, as the savaged policeman lay dying behind the makeshift VIP platform.

Two days later Victoria was back at work and she told reporters that she was awaiting with interest the result of the police investigation. Brigadier Jan van der Hoven appeared to agree that it was no ordinary murder but he pointed the finger at the ANC itself. It was known, he claimed, that the ANC was unhappy about the way

Griffiths Mxenge had been handling secret donations from overseas supporters.

He left the investigation in the incapable hands of the young, inexperienced and frightened Christopher Shange, who later admitted that the book he had been using to make notes on the case had disappeared from his filing cabinet in the police station. The final verdict: 'Griffiths Mxenge's death was caused by some unknown person or persons.' Victoria was not at all surprised and vowed to continue the fight to bring her husband's killers to justice: 'I'll continue even if it means I must also die.'

On 20 July 1985 five thousand people packed the Lingelihle Stadium near Cradock to pay their last respects to four community leaders who had been brutally murdered by a death squad three weeks before. Matthew Goniwe, Fort Calata, Sparrow Mkontho and Secio Mhlawuli had gone missing after attending an ANC meeting. Their bodies were later found dumped in the wild. Victoria Mxenge spoke at the service, calling the murders a 'dastardly act of cowardice' and adding: 'We are prepared to die for Africa.'

Since her husband's assassination, Victoria had emerged from the shadows to become one of South Africa's leading attorneys. She had come to represent the youth of South Africa after successfully defending students against the confiscation of their examination results by the Department of Education and Training. She was about to start a trial in which she would defend sixteen United Democratic Front and Natal Indian Congress members who were accused of treason. The treason case was said to be the country's biggest political trial since that of Nelson Mandela, who had been imprisoned for life in 1964. Victoria had high hopes: she had spent many months collecting evidence and carefully picking holes in the prosecution's case.

Twelve days after the service for the four murdered young activists, Victoria arrived home with an old friend, the Reverend Mcebisi Xundu, chairperson of the UDF in Natal. As Xundu prepared to drive away, he saw four men rush towards her. One of them was death squad member Almond Nofemela. Victoria spotted the men as she neared her front door and she ran back down the drive, still with bags of evidence for the forthcoming trial in her hands. She was screaming for help but they cut her off from the car.

The elderly Xundu realised correctly that he didn't have a hope in hell of stopping the men, so he drove at breakneck speed to the police station. Victoria's nineteen-year-old son Mbasa came running out to see what the screaming was about, much like his father had done four years before. One of the men pointed a gun at his head and said: 'Am I going to have to shoot you as well?' Mbasa shook his head and ran across the road and around the corner, away from the gunmen.

Moments later he heard two shots and returned to see his mother lying face down in a pool of blood. She was still alive when she reached the hospital but she died later that night.

The country erupted immediately after Victoria's killing. Thousands of students took to the streets in protest and riots tore across the country. The worst violence, which claimed fifty-four lives, occurred in townships surrounding the port city of Durban. In Umlazi, police used tear gas and rubber bullets against mobs of rampaging youths who burned shops and schools: nineteen people died. In KwaMashu, a gang attacked the home of a black policeman and set it ablaze. By Friday, some three hundred people had been admitted to hospitals with gunshot or assault wounds. The outlawed African National Congress increased its sporadic guerrilla attacks on the well-trained, superbly equipped South African Army (which had a one-billion-pound budget).

Ten thousand people attended Victoria's funeral (this was despite a government ban on mass funerals) where she was buried next to her husband, as a message from the still-imprisoned Nelson Mandela was read out. President Ronald Reagan condemned the killing: 'Mrs Mxenge was well known in South Africa and to many American diplomats who had served there as a dedicated, humane person. Her killing is a heinous and horrible crime. We call on the South African Government to bring to book the perpetrators.'

The celebrated South African newspaper editor Percy Qoboza captured the mood perfectly in his editorial the following day. 'Victoria Mxenge was a special person. So special that even my young kids, who have never met her personally but only know her through newspaper columns, wept hysterically. In a strange way, they identified with her emotionally. What appals me most is the deafening silence on the part of the Government over this latest incident. No message of condolence to the children of this tragedy, nothing, just silence. I am not suggesting that the government offer its condolences at the drop of a hat but Victoria was not just anybody. Or should I assume, like Steve Biko, they did not know who she was. I doubt it.'

On the day of Victoria Mxenge's funeral, President P.W. Botha declared a state of emergency. Urged by British Prime Minister Margaret Thatcher (among many other world leaders), Botha announced that he would make a speech which would resolve his country's most desperate crisis, a speech that would placate South Africa's blacks, who outnumbered the country's whites by 23.9 million to 4.9 million. The country breathed a sigh of relief: black leaders hoped that finally the end of apartheid was in sight, that Nelson Mandela would be freed, that the murders of innocents would stop.

Speaking in the port city of Durban before the Natal provincial congress of his ruling National Party, Botha began: 'I believe that we are today crossing the Rubicon in South Africa. There is no turning back.' Botha described his remarks as a 'manifesto for the future of our country' but his speech was an international and domestic disappointment. The outside world had expected the President to unveil a package of far-reaching reforms aimed at gradually dismantling apartheid. Instead, Botha held out a vague and tentative suggestion of negotiations and unspecified future constitutional discussions. He appeared more interested in broadcasting defiance than in stressing the changes that his government would countenance. 'I am not prepared to lead white South Africans and other minority groups on a road to abdication and suicide,' he declared. He issued a blunt warning to foreign governments pressing Pretoria to change: 'Don't push us too far.'

The disappointment was intense. Desmond Tutu said he was 'devastated' by the speech. He said bleakly, 'I think the chances of peaceful change are virtually nil.' Chief Gatsha Buthelezi, the moderate head of the six-million-member Zulu nation, declared that 'we are back to square one'. The white leader of South Africa's parliamentary opposition, Frederik Van Zyl Slabbert, concurred. 'The speech did not measure up even to any of the moderate expectation that had been generated.' In Johannesburg the country's largest daily, the *Star*, editorialised that 'each of us . . . prayed for a message that would tip the balance towards peace and better understanding. The weight went the other way, tipping us closer to disaster'. An ANC spokesman responded to Botha's speech with four chilling words: 'The armed struggle continues.'

And continue it did – the most violent years in the African struggle against apartheid took place between 1985 and 1989. In the days after Botha's speech twenty-eight people, most of them black, were killed in violent confrontations, mainly by police. In one particularly gruesome incident, Bill Mentoor, a black soldier, became the first person to be 'necklaced' (a car tyre was filled with petrol, placed over his neck and set alight). The home of Winnie Mandela, Nelson Mandela's wife, was firebombed. About nineteen hundred people were arrested without charge. The investigation into Victoria Mxenge's assassination followed the same pattern as her husband's and a few weeks later the verdict came in: 'Died of head injuries and was killed by person or persons unknown.'

Meanwhile, Almond Butana Nofemela, the man with 'the guts of a tiger' who had murdered both Griffiths and Victoria Mxenge, branched out into the well-paid world of freelance murder. He made the mistake of killing Jan Hendrik Lourens, a farmer. He had expected to get away with it as with all the officially sanctioned murders that he had committed.

But Lourens was white. The police investigation was swift and thorough and caught Nofemela by surprise. He was tried and was sentenced to hang; his death-squad commanders visited him in prison, reproached him for killing a white man and told him to 'take the pain', privately commenting among themselves that 'justice should take its course' because 'Nofemela knows too much'.

Nofemela was convinced, however, that he would be reprieved at the last moment, before he would have to walk that cold corridor in Pretoria prison along with up to six other victims – past Dimitrios Tsafendas, up the forty steps to the chamber where they would be dropped, their lolling tongues and bulging eyes covered by a white cloth bag.

As the hour of his death neared and Nofemela realised that there would be no reprieve, he desperately tried to get word to the authorities about the existence of the death squads and his involvement in Mxenge's death. He was reprieved the night before his scheduled execution.

When Nofemela's confession hit the news-stands in October 1989, it inspired something in Dirk Coetzee – who had been sacked from the police for insubordination not long after Griffith Mxenge's assassination. Fearing that he knew too much, Coetzee had fled to a secret location abroad.

Coetzee stunned the world when he confessed his crimes to investigative journalist Jacques Pauw in 1989. The story broke in *Vrye Weekblad* on 1 November: 'Bloody Trail of the SAP. Meet Captain Dirk Johannes Coetzee, commander of a police death squad. He exclusively reveals the full sordid tale of political assassinations, poison drinks, letter bombs and attacks in neighbouring states.'

In the article, Coetzee was asked to explain his attitude towards what he did. 'Extreme mixed emotions of anger, deep-seated anger for allowing me to get involved with this nonsense. Humiliation, embarrassment and the helplessness of a pathetic: I'm sorry for what I've done. What else can I offer them? A pathetic nothing. So, in all honesty, I don't expect the Mxenge family to forgive me because I don't know how I ever in my life would be able to forgive a man like Dirk Coetzee, if he'd done to me what I've done to them.'

Coetzee implicated former Commissioner of Police General Johan Coetzee (no relation), the police's forensic expert; the force's third-highest-ranking officer, General Lothar Neethling; and various security brigadiers and colonels in the assassination of Mxenge. By confessing, Coetzee betrayed the fundamental principle professed by the foot soldiers of the apartheid state: absolute loyalty.

In an essentially racist environment, the racism of apartheid's paid killers was often paternalistic, tempered by an ingrained ideological conviction that they were part of a nobler cause, dedicated to the betterment of all humanity. They saw themselves as hard men doing a tough but necessary job. Coetzee became a white *askari* for the enemy – he had gone from leading the assassination squad to being its number one target.

Booby-trapped headphones and a Walkman tape-player were sent to Coetzee's post office box address in Zambia. To allay suspicion, the sender's name was given as Bheki Mlangeni, an ANC lawyer with whom Coetzee had been in contact. The return address was Mlangeni's home in the Soweto township, west of Johannesburg. By the time the parcel arrived in Zambia, Coetzee had just moved. Uncollected, the lethal package was returned to Mlangeni's home in February 1991 where it was opened by the lawyer. He put on the headphones, which were packed full of explosives, and pressed *play* on the cassette. The blast blew his head off his shoulders.

By the time Coetzee's revelations had become public in November 1989, change was already sweeping through the South African government, sped up by the downfall of President Botha, who had suffered a stroke in February 1989. Although he recovered within a few weeks, he was forced to cave in to Cabinet infighting as well as to increased external pressure from the US and Britain. Botha was forced to resign.

The more moderate Frederik W. de Klerk, fifty-two, became President in September 1989 and in December he announced that the Ministry of Law and Order and the Ministry of Justice would conduct a fresh investigation into the assassination of the Mxenges and seventy-nine other victims of the assassination squad. A few weeks after this de Klerk announced the legalisation of the ANC and other anti-apartheid groups, the release of Nelson Mandela, the dismantling of the apartheid system and the negotiations that would eventually lead to South Africa's first racially all-inclusive democratic elections on 27 April 1994.

In October 1996, fifteen years after the assassination of Griffiths Mxenge, Dirk Coetzee, Almond Nofemela and David Tshikalanga appeared before the South African Truth and Reconciliation Amnesty Committee in Durban. (The TRC was a court-like body assembled after the end of apartheid where perpetrators of violence could give testimony and request amnesty from prosecution.) Another of the assassins, Brian Ngqulunga, had been murdered, allegedly for appearing as a witness against the state in another trial.

Dirk Coetzee told the committee: 'I don't think I will ever be able to put it behind me because I'll have to drag those corpses with me till the day I die. I will have to live with that, whether it's in jail, whether it's out of jail, I will have to live with that. That's a problem for me and that I will have to face, but you've got to reap what you've sowed.'

On 4 August 1997, Dirk Coetzee, Almond Nofemela, Joe Mamasela and David Tshikalanga were granted amnesty. Today, the whereabouts of all four men is a closely guarded secret.

Twenty-two

Death at the Dorchester

Not since the slaying of the Archduke Ferdinand in Sarajevo in 1914 has a hit team made war such a likely outcome. On 3 June 1982 Shlomo Argov, Israel's fifty-two-year-old ambassador to Britain, had accepted an invitation to a reception of ambassadors being given that evening at the Dorchester Hotel on Park Lane. As he left his residence near Kensington Palace, three London-based members of the Fatah Revolutionary Council (FRC), also known as the Abu Nidal Organisation, after its founder, set off for the Dorchester too, intent on Argov's assassination.

Abu Nidal[20] was, in 1982, the deadliest man alive. He was also incredibly hard to find, bragging that 'not even my eight-year-old son Bissam knows exactly who I am'. In 1981 alone, his group was responsible for thirty-three terrifying assaults, ranging from the 16 September bombing of Rome's Café de Paris (forty injured) to the 23 November hijacking of an Egypt Air jetliner (fifty-nine dead) to the slaughter of innocent travellers at airports in Rome and Vienna (nineteen dead, one hundred and twelve injured).

Initially a committed senior member of the Palestine Liberation Organisation (PLO), Abu Nidal split from Yasser Arafat's group in 1971 and by 1974 he was running his own terror operations from

[20] Real name Sabry Khalil Bana – Abu Nidal stands for 'Father of Struggle'.

bases in Iraq, Libya and Syria. Abu Nidal accused Arafat of cowardice for not using terror against their many enemies, in particular Israel and Jordan. His gunmen tried and failed to assassinate Arafat. In reply, the PLO sentenced Abu Nidal to death.

Shlomo Argov's assassination had been ordered by Abu Nidal to provoke an Israeli assault on Arafat's bases in Lebanon, creating a war that would weaken his two worst enemies. Naif Rosan, the FRC's man in London who had been with Abu Nidal since 1973, decided to eliminate Argov as he left the Dorchester. Two FRC 'sleepers' – Marwan al-Banna (a second cousin of Abu Nidal) and twenty-three-year-old Ghassan Said, who were in London as students – were 'activated' two hours before the assassination: an effective practice which gives young terrorists no time to dwell on what they are about to do. Al-Banna, who stored weapons for the FRC in his flat, brought with him a Polish-made sub-machine gun. Ghassan Said was to be the gunman. Rosan didn't tell him who his target was, only that he would point him out and that Said should shoot him before he made it to his car.

Shortly after eleven p.m. Argov left the dinner. Just behind him was the publishing magnate Robert Maxwell. As the ambassador, followed by his bodyguard, approached their car, Said quickly took the automatic out of a sports bag, rushed up, shot Argov twice in the face and then ran off down the busy street. The bodyguard, Constable Colin Simpson from Scotland Yard's Diplomatic Protection Squad, drew his weapon, took precise aim and shot the assassin in the neck.

After hearing the gunfire, al-Banna ran back to his car. A security guard named Trevor Willis who worked for the Hilton Hotel, next door to the Dorchester, saw him running and wrote down the car's licence-plate number. The conspirators were soon captured and both the ambassador and the assassin survived their bullet wounds – although Argov woke up from a three-month coma to find that he was permanently paralysed.

Israel ignored the fact that the assassination attempt had not been committed by the PLO and also ignored the fact that the next name on the FRC's death list, discovered by Scotland Yard detectives, was Nabil Ramlawi, the PLO representative in London. At last, the then Israeli defence minister Ariel Sharon had a pretext for his long-planned campaign to eliminate the PLO and its headquarters in the Lebanese capital, Beirut. In his memoirs, Sharon wrote that the Dorchester ambush was 'the spark that lit the fuse'. The Israeli Prime Minister Menachen Begin gave Sharon the go-ahead for what became 'Operation Peace for Galilee'.

Israel slammed PLO strongholds in southern Lebanon by air, land and sea. After two days, Lebanese officials reported that more than a hundred people had been killed and more than three hundred others had been wounded. Most were civilians. The first waves of Israeli jets concentrated on PLO targets in Beirut and its outskirts. Though the bombs were aimed mostly at guerrilla bases and other PLO installations, attacks were also made on non-military areas including Family Beach, a popular stretch of sand and surf just south of the capital. Israel's planes hammered hard at Beirut's Sports City, a former stadium converted into a storage depot for food and supplies for the PLO. Two floors of the structure collapsed under the attack, burying guerrillas and their families in a shattered mass of reinforced concrete.

The PLO, in a retaliatory strike of its own, fired scores of Soviet-made Katyusha rockets and long-range artillery shells at towns and settlements in northern Israel. Israeli gunners responded in border duels that continued throughout the night. At least sixty thousand Israeli troops, led by more than five hundred tanks, swept across the sixty-three-mile-long Lebanese border, then snaked steadily north on tortuous dirt roads.

The attack, undertaken despite the strong opposition of the Reagan administration, revealed how little influence the US had over its ally, Israel. The Israelis were also determined to end Syria's assistance of the PLO and attacked Syrian positions. In one of the biggest air battles ever in the Middle East, more than one hundred and fifty Israeli and Syrian jet fighters clashed in the skies over Lebanon's Bekaa Valley.

In a rare moment of lucidity during two decades as a bed-bound invalid, Argov lambasted the invasion. 'Israel cannot get entangled in experiments or hopeless military adventures,' he said in July 1983. 'If those who initiated this war in Lebanon had envisioned the scope of this adventure, it could have saved the lives of hundreds of our best young people.'

The war lasted for eleven months and Israeli forces did not begin to withdraw from Lebanon until June 1985. By the end, more than six thousand PLO troops and Palestinian civilians had been killed by the Israelis. Syria lost six hundred troops and 468 Lebanese civilians were killed, while Israel lost 368 soldiers.

On 19 September 1985 Israel began to withdraw from Beirut, eventually falling back to a four-mile-deep zone of occupation in southern Lebanon which they didn't leave for another eighteen years. In this zone, constant battles were fought between Israeli troops and the Hizbollah (Party of God) which was formed explicitly to drive Israel from Lebanon. Hundreds were killed on both sides.

The three assassins were convicted of the attempted murder of the envoy and in March 1983 were sentenced to life in prison. Argov died in 2003, a consequence of the injuries that he had sustained in the assassination attempt.

Twenty-three

Three Weeks in October

1984 was an especially chaotic year of violence. In September, a truck bomb came hurtling at the US embassy annexe in East Beirut, but a well-aimed shot by a bodyguard caused it to blow up short of its main target, saving many lives. Gun-toting Hizbollah members hijacked Kuwait Airways Flight 221 and executed two American citizens before they were overpowered. The awards ceremony for Nobel Peace Prize-winner Bishop Desmond Tutu was disrupted by a bomb threat. At Libya's embassy in a leafy London square, machine-gun fire killed Yvonne Fletcher, a young British policewoman. Colonel Gaddafi embarrassed himself when Egyptian authorities faked the death of a former Libyan Prime Minister marked for execution by Tripoli. Gaddafi took responsibility for the assassination that never was. But, as far as political violence is concerned, 1984 will be remembered as the year when three major assassination attacks took place within three weeks of each other.

In October 1984 the first crack appeared in the façade of the Communist Bloc. In Poland, Father Jerzy Popieluszko, a frail, anaemic man, spoke out against the repressive Communist regime from his pulpit and pledged his support for Solidarity, the banned trade union federation led by Lech Walesa. More than thirty thousand people flocked to hear the priest speak every week (political gatherings were banned, so sermons provided the only opportunity for people to gather legally in large groups).

On the night of 19 October Father Popieluszko was kidnapped, bound, gagged and imprisoned in a car boot. His repeated attempts to break free eventually infuriated his captors to the point where he was mercilessly beaten with a wooden stave by Captain Grzegorz Piotrowski of the Polish secret police before being thrown, trussed, with a noose around his neck and possibly still alive, into the icy Vistula River. His body was found eleven days later.

Solidarity leader Lech Walesa said: 'They wanted to kill, and they killed not only a man, not only a Pole, not only a priest. They wanted to kill the hope that it is possible in Poland to avoid violence in political life.' Over four hundred thousand mourners gathered for an open-air funeral Mass in front of Father Popieluszko's St Stanislaw Kostka Church. For the first time since the military crackdown Walesa was able to address the enormous crowd.

The Communist authorities believed that by removing the troublesome priest they had ended mass gatherings but instead their actions dramatically swelled the ranks of Solidarity. The murder of a priest was seen by most Poles as unforgivable, a crime against God. (The coffin was left open so that people could see for themselves the torture that the priest had suffered.) About ninety-seven per cent of Poles belong to the Catholic Church. People who were not perhaps all that politically motivated before became so in the wake of Father Popieluszko's death. It would take another five years but Solidarity won through in 1989 when the Communists finally caved in and allowed all-party elections.

Popieluszko's murder also focused the world's attention and intensified international diplomatic pressure on the ruling Communists. British Prime Minister Margaret Thatcher made a point of visiting the priest's grave in 1988 – a visit given extra significance when one bears in mind the dangers she herself had faced only a week before Popieluszko's assassination.

On 14 September 1984 a smartly dressed man walked into the lobby of Brighton's five-star Grand Hotel, greeted the concierge in impeccable public-school English, signed his registration card (giving the false name of 'Roy Walsh') for room 629 and took the lift up to his room. He placed a *Do Not Disturb* sign on the door handle and stepped inside. The man, who had recently spent time in a Libyan terrorist training camp, opened his suitcases, removed his tools and began to work. He checked out three days later, leaving sixty kilos of explosives hidden behind room 629's wall, set to explode in twenty-four days' time.

On 12 October the Grand Hotel was hosting the 1984 Conservative Party Conference. Staying in room 629 were the Chairman of the Scottish Conservative Party Sir Donald McLean and his wife, Muriel. At 2.30 a.m. they were fast asleep. Next door, in room 628, was John Shattock, the chairman of the Western Counties Conservative Association and his fifty-two-year-old wife Jean.

Norman Tebbit, President of the Board of Trade, had just finished working with a team of speech-writers on Prime Minister Margaret Thatcher's keynote address, to be given the next morning, the final day of the conference. Thatcher, meanwhile, famous for only needing four hours' sleep each night, worked her way through day-to-day government business. At 2.50 a.m., as she returned from the bathroom, an aide asked her to look at one last official paper. Tebbit had returned to his room, where his wife was already asleep.

At 2.53 a.m. Jean Shattock got up and went to the toilet. The bomb was directly behind her when it exploded at 2.54 a.m. She was blasted through several toppling walls, across the corridor and into room 638, where she died.

Margaret Thatcher, who had just sat down in an armchair with her back to the window was shaken by a loud *whump*. Everything seemed to lift for a moment – and then came the terrible sound of collapsing masonry as the hotel started to disintegrate.

Outside, a piercing flash lit up the seafront: masonry was flung into the night, knocking the heads off parking meters, shattering promenade shelters and denting dozens of parked cars. The blast took out the supports for the huge brickwork chimney stack at the top of the hotel and it crashed through ceilings and floors, picking up speed as it dragged eight levels with it. Sleeping guests were plunged into the foyer and basement. Dozens were trapped in the mangled mountain of wreckage, while the walking wounded staggered into the street where government papers and Cabinet documents fluttered around them.

John Shattock was buried under falling masonry. Sir Anthony George Berry, MP, the uncle of Princess Diana and father of six, was asleep in a room directly below the blast. He was killed as his room disintegrated in the bomb's maelstrom. Below him, the Tories' North-West Area Chairman, Eric Taylor, was swept away to his death among falling debris as the floors collapsed, leaving a gaping tear in the middle of the hotel. Norman Tebbit plunged two storeys and was buried by rubble. Muriel McLean was killed instantly; somehow, despite being first blown against a wall before falling several storeys, her husband Sir Donald was still alive when the fire crews arrived.

One of the first on the scene was fireman Fred Bishop who assumed that a drunken late-night reveller had set off the fire alarm. Instead, his team were stunned to find a thick fog of dust enveloping the seafront and an enormous gaping hole in the middle of Brighton's most famous hotel.

Almost immediately, two bodies were spotted dangling from joists. Firemen had to pick their way downwards, taking off the joists one by one to reach them. After a two-hour search, Norman Tebbit's foot was spotted poking through some beams. After another two hours, Tebbit was pulled from the rubble. His wife Mary was also rescued but her severe injuries meant that her life hung by a thread.

Next it was the turn of John Wakeham, the Tory Chief Whip, who was trapped in darkness, his legs crushed under tons of rubble. 'Keep talking to me,' he pleaded with firemen. 'Keep me alive.' Two hours later, unconscious and in a critical condition, he was freed. By then his wife Roberta was already dead.

Conference organiser Harvey Thomas fell two floors and was

buried under tons of rubble, fighting for breath as thousands of gallons of water poured over him from smashed storage tanks. He told his rescuers that his wife, who was not staying at the hotel, was expecting to give birth to their first child that morning. Firemen desperately worked to free him as the rubble shifted and pressed down on his chest, making it more difficult to breathe. He was eventually yanked free, suffering from hypothermia but with minor injuries.

Not since Guy Fawkes and the Gunpowder Plot of 1605 had such an audacious crime been attempted in the name of politics. In total, five people lost their lives to the explosion and over thirty were left injured. Later that morning, as crowds gathered under the perfectly clear autumn sky to gaze at the devastated hotel, police officers confessed their amazement that so many had escaped death. (This was largely thanks to the strength of the solidly constructed Regency building.)

Thatcher studied the ruins silently as she was driven past to the conference hall. As she approached the stage, the ovation that she received was colossal. The Prime Minister recalled: 'All of us were relieved to be alive, saddened by the tragedy and determined to show the terrorists that they could not break our spirit.'

The first debate of the day was on Northern Ireland. By the time Thatcher rose to give her hastily rewritten conference-closing speech, the packed hall was on tenterhooks as the world's press prepared to scrutinise the response of the Iron Lady. 'The bomb attack,' the Prime Minister said, 'was an attempt not only to disrupt and terminate our conference. It was an attempt to cripple Her Majesty's democratically elected Government. That is the scale of the outrage in which we have all shared. And the fact that we are gathered here now, shocked but composed and determined, is a sign not only that this attack has failed, but that all attempts to destroy democracy by terrorism will fail.' The ovation continued for twenty minutes.

Thatcher then left to visit the injured at the Royal Sussex County Hospital where she saw Muriel McLean on a drip feed; Mrs McLean would die later. Surgeons were struggling to save John Wakeham's legs (they were eventually successful). She also talked to Margaret Tebbit who told the PM that she had no feeling below the neck. As a former nurse, Mrs Tebbit knew well enough what that meant.

The IRA claimed responsibility and issued a statement, addressed to Mrs Thatcher, the next day. It read: 'Today we were unlucky, but remember we only have to be lucky once. You will have to be lucky always. Give Ireland peace and there will be no war.'

The following month six hundred delegates gathered in Dublin's eighteenth-century Mansion House for the annual conference of Sinn Fein, the political wing of the Irish Republican Army. (Although the IRA is banned in Northern Ireland and the Irish Republic, Sinn Fein is not.) They were exuberant. 'Far from being a blow *against* democracy,' thundered Sinn Fein President Gerry Adams from a platform flanked by huge posters of the devastated hotel, 'it was a blow *for* democracy.' Adams termed the bombing 'an inevitable result of the British presence' in Northern Ireland, which he called 'unwanted, illegal and immoral'.

The police investigation moved quickly. After sifting through tons of rubble from the bombing, experts were able to identify exactly the type of bomb and the timing device. They could also pinpoint the date on which the deadly package had been primed. Sussex police traced and eliminated eight hundred people from fifty countries who had stayed at the hotel in the month before the attack. Only 'Roy Walsh' could not be accounted for. David Tadd, a fingerprint expert with eighteen years' experience, managed to retrieve a partial palm and fingerprint from room 629's registration card. The prints matched those found at the Rubens Hotel in London, where a bomb had been discovered and successfully defused. But most incredibly, two months after the bomb, it was found that these prints matched those of a man called Patrick Magee, taken when he had been pulled over for a driving offence almost twenty years previously.

Magee had been born in Belfast but had moved with his family to Norwich when he was two. As a teenager he was nicknamed

'Chancer' because of his spur-of-the-moment car thefts. In 1969, eighteen-year-old Magee returned to Northern Ireland and, attracted by the conflict, joined the IRA. Bombing became his speciality and, by the mid-1970s, he was the IRA's Chief Explosives Officer.

Detectives did not want to issue a public alert for Magee, a move which would have sent him deep underground, so they waited, hoping that he would eventually make an appearance. In June 1985 police trailing another IRA suspect, Peter Sherry, arrested Magee at an IRA safe house in Glasgow where, along with four others, he was planning a series of attacks on British seaside hotels at the height of summer. Police also found a stockpile of weapons, bombs and timers.

In 1986 Magee was tried and convicted of the Brighton bombing at the Old Bailey and he received eight life sentences. Justice Boreham sentenced him to a minimum of thirty-five years behind bars, labelling him a man of exceptional cruelty and inhumanity. In response, Magee simply lifted his clenched fist and shouted in Gaelic the Irish Republican slogan '*Tiochfaidh ar La!*' – 'Our day will come!' He was released from prison in 1999 under the terms of the Good Friday Agreement, having served only fourteen years in prison.

While Margaret Thatcher grappled with the IRA, Indian Prime Minister Indira Gandhi, sixty-six, continued her own parallel struggle with the extremist Sikh population of India. For two years, the Sikhs had been threatening a rebellion in Punjab, their homeland on the Pakistani border. Their aim was to establish an independent Sikh nation, believing that they had been persecuted for long enough by India's Hindu majority. (The country's fifteen million Sikhs represented about two per cent of India's population.)

Gandhi gave the go-ahead for Operation Bluestar, one of the bloodiest, most controversial military operations ever carried out on Indian soil. At the centre of the operation was the virtual destruction of the Golden Temple in Amritsar, a seventy-two-acre complex and the holiest shrine of the Sikh religion which was harbouring the Sikh extremist leaders. By ordering the assault on the temple Gandhi successfully crushed the rebellion – but the surviving extremists plotted their revenge.

Almost five months later, on 31 October 1984, Indira Gandhi was in fine health and ebullient spirits as she prepared to seek a fifth term as Prime Minister of the world's largest democracy. She was in a buoyant mood as she opened the door of her private bungalow, came down the steps and walked onto the winding gravel path that led towards the larger building. Following discreetly were five security men. The Prime Minister was on her way to meet British actor-director Peter Ustinov, who was waiting with a television crew to conduct an hour-long interview. He had been with Indira Gandhi for two days on the campaign trail and she had come to enjoy the actor's sharp wit.

Standing at attention more than halfway along the path were two khaki-uniformed security men wearing the traditional beards and turbans that identified them as Sikhs. One of them, Beant Singh, had worked with Gandhi for ten years. Only two months previously, when Gandhi was asked if she could trust Sikh guards in the wake of Operation Bluestar she replied: 'When I have Sikhs like this around me, then I don't believe I have anything to fear.' When the director of the country's central intelligence organisation suggested to Gandhi in July that Sikhs should be removed from her security staff, she had refused. She also refused his most sensible suggestion that she should wear a bulletproof vest.

Indira Gandhi had already been physically attacked several times: a man had poked a loaded gun at her, someone had thrown a knife and the throwing of stones, bricks and bottles was all too common. But Gandhi was made of strong stuff. When she had been speaking to a crowd in Orissa in 1967, a stone had smashed her in the face, breaking her nose and cutting her lip. She had pulled her sari over her face to cover the blood, but had refused to leave the podium. 'I am frequently attacked,' she said. 'But I'm not afraid.'

Just next to Beant Singh stood twenty-one-year-old Satwant Singh, who had been assigned to Gandhi's detail five months before.

The two men were no more than seven feet away as she said: '*Namaste*' ('Greetings to you'), a traditional Indian salutation, accompanied by a crossing of hands in front of the face. It was 9.08 a.m. Beant Singh drew a .38 revolver and fired three shots into the prime minister's abdomen. As she fell to the ground, Satwant Singh emptied all thirty rounds from his Sten gun into her body. The two Sikhs then calmly dropped their guns.

As other security guards seized them, Beant Singh said, 'I've done what I had to do. You do what you want to do.' They were then taken to a guardhouse, where Beant Singh suddenly lunged for a guard's gun as Satwant Singh pulled a dagger from his turban. The guards shot them both. Beant Singh died almost instantly; Satwant Singh was critically wounded.[21]

When she first heard the shots in the garden below, Indira Gandhi's daughter-in-law Sonia rushed frantically down a flight of stairs, screaming 'Mummy! Oh, my God, Mummy!' Guards had already picked up Gandhi's body, her orange sari soaked in blood. Led by her long-time personal assistant, R.K. Dhawan, they carried her to her white, Indian-made Ambassador car. Sonia cradled Gandhi's head in her lap as they sped off to the All-India Institute of Medical Sciences hospital, a short distance away.

Ustinov and his crew, who had not been close enough to witness the shooting but had captured the sound of gunfire on their tape recorder, rushed to the Prime Minister's bungalow. 'It was a scene of confusion,' Ustinov said. 'The security men were still running around, shaken and unbelieving. One minute there was gunfire, and afterward the birds in the trees were singing. The security men kept us there for five hours, polite all the time, but they wanted to be sure we didn't have something on film that they could use as evidence. Sadly, we did not.'

At the hospital a team of twelve doctors desperately tried to perform a miracle. After putting Gandhi on an artificial lung and a

[21] He recovered from his bullet wounds only to be executed by hanging in January 1989.

heart machine, they removed seven bullets; in the process, they gave her eighty-eight bottles of blood. Cabinet ministers waited in the hospital conference room, some stunned and speechless, some weeping. 'They could not believe she was dead,' a young doctor said later. 'They would not accept that she was gone.' At 1.45 p.m. an Indian news service sent the bulletin: GANDHI IS DEAD.

British Prime Minister Margaret Thatcher, who spoke with Gandhi regularly by telephone, probably used the words that Indira would have if the IRA had succeeded in blowing her up only nineteen days earlier: 'India has been robbed of a leader of incomparable courage, vision and humanity. For my part, I shall feel greatly the loss of a wise colleague and a personal friend.'

For two days after her death, Indira's body lay in state. Then it was carried seven miles in a gun carriage to the banks of the Yamuna River, an area where Mahatma Gandhi (who had not been related to her) as well as her father and her younger son Sanjay (he had died when he had crashed his stunt plane the previous year) had also been cremated.

A million people lined the streets to watch the procession; millions more watched on television as Indira Gandhi's body was placed on a flower-covered pyre of sandalwood and brick, and set afire by her other son, Rajiv – who automatically became India's seventh Prime Minister. He was the third member of the House of Nehru – which had then run India for thirty-three of its thirty-seven years of independence – to hold that office.

But he was ill-prepared for the role. Until his death, it was Sanjay who had been earmarked to take over from their mother but his premature death thrust Rajiv – who had spent the last fourteen years as a commercial pilot flying Boeing 737s – into the hot seat. A team of extremist assassins would come for him seven years later (see page 317). But before that, in 1986, Rajiv Gandhi became embroiled in a surprising scandal involving a Swedish arms company – a scandal that might have led to an extraordinary conspiracy in Stockholm.

Twenty-four

The Stockholm Takedown

Probably the least-protected prime minister in history, it had always been a matter of pride for Olof Palme that he could, if he chose to do so, wander Sweden's streets without bodyguards – unheard of for a nation's leading politician in any other European country. It is hard to imagine, for example, any recent British prime minister walking the streets unprotected; Tony Blair, John Major and Margaret Thatcher would almost certainly have been assaulted by members of the public who held extreme political views. Ultimately, though, because Palme *was* so unprotected it made it clear to an enemy who might want to assassinate him that he would have an easy job. Palme considered he was lucky because he had few enemies – but he failed to realise that it would only take one.

On 28 February 1986 Olof Palme's day got off to a good start. He won a tough game of tennis against an old friend. He then returned a newly bought suit he had purchased the day before (his wife Lisbet objected to it) before travelling to his offices in the Rosenbad, a government building in central Stockholm. Once inside, the slight, hawk-nosed politician dismissed his bodyguards with a smile, telling them that they should start their weekend early.

Just before lunch he met with the Iraqi ambassador, Muhammad Saeed al-Sahhaf, to discuss the ongoing war between Iran and

Iraq.[22] Palme was the UN's official arbitrator. The war was still raging (an Iranian offensive to capture a large part of an Iraqi peninsula had been repulsed by the Iraqis just three days earlier) but after the loss of a million lives at a cost of over a hundred billion pounds, even Saddam Hussein was, albeit very tentatively, ready to accept that a diplomatic compromise would be necessary to end the conflict.

Palme was outraged by America's involvement in the Iran–Iraq War; the United States had supplied weapons to both sides. The Swedish prime minister was well known for generally disagreeing with American foreign policy. In 1968, when he'd been Sweden's Education Minister, he had teamed up with North Vietnam's ambassador to Moscow and marched alongside him at a rally to protest at the American role in the Vietnam War. As Sweden's prime minister in 1972, he had compared the US bombing of Hanoi to the Nazi bombing of Guernica. In response, President Richard Nixon expelled the Swedish ambassador from Washington In 1985, Palme told journalists: 'I know that the Thatchers and the Reagans will be out in a few years. We have to survive till then.'

During the Iran–Iraq war, tens of thousands of Iranians had been killed with Iraqi chemical weapons supplied by European and American companies. Donald Rumsfeld, then American Special Envoy to the Middle East, was responsible for providing American support for the Iraqis. He visited Saddam Hussein in Baghdad on 24 March 1984, the same day that the United Nations issued a report containing the first evidence that Iraq had used mustard gas. The Americans had also supplied weapons to the Iranians, using the proceeds to finance the Contras, a right-wing Nicaraguan guerrilla group, the opponents of the Sandinistas who had overthrown the US-favoured dictatorship led by Anastasio Somoza in 1979. Palme, not surprisingly, was firmly on the side of the Sandinistas.

During the meeting, Palme was surprised when al-Sahhaf

[22] Al-Sahhaf later became known as 'Baghdad Bob' and 'Comical Ali' for his outrageously fabricated declarations of Iraqi victory during the 2003 American-led invasion of Iraq.

suddenly mentioned the Swedish arms company Bofors. Al-Sahhaf told Palme that between 1983 and 1985 Bofors had sold several hundred Robot-70 portable ground-to-air missiles to Iran. Under Swedish law, neither the government nor any Swedish company was allowed to sell arms to countries at war. Bofors was also involved in an intricate and extremely lucrative deal to sell arms to India (Prime Minister Rajiv Gandhi was preparing for a 'preventative war' against Pakistan throughout 1986 and 1987, and ordered $1.2 billion-worth of howitzers). Al-Sahhaf told Palme that the Indian contract had been won by bribing influential Indian businessmen and senior politicians. Palme was furious.

After the meeting the prime minister spent some time alone in his office, making calls. He was twenty minutes late for lunch; his fellow diners noticed his bad mood but Palme refused to tell them why he was upset. By late afternoon, he had regained his composure in time for an interview with a local journalist. When a photographer asked Palme to pose in front of the window, the prime minister suddenly became serious and told the puzzled reporters: 'You never know what might be waiting for me out there.'

Despite this strange reference to a possible attack, Palme left his office and walked the short distance to his official residence without his security guards. At 6.30 p.m. he called his son Marten who suggested that they go and see a new film, *The Brothers Mozart*. Palme and Lisbet had planned to see the play *My Life as a Dog* but they eventually decided to join Marten.

They left for the cinema at 8.35 p.m. – again, without any protection officers. Lisbet was nervous about this. A plain-looking private woman, Lisbet was a child psychologist from an ordinary middle-class family; she disliked state events and the fame that came with her husband's job. She preferred to keep people away but this was impossible: Palme was instantly identifiable to anyone in Sweden; his face had been part of everyday life in newspapers and television for almost twenty years.

As they started their walk, they were immediately recognised by a surprised young couple. Once at the train station, a drunk shouted:

'Hey there, Palme, are you taking the subway today?' Both Olof and Lisbet felt nervous on the train which was packed full of commuters and Friday-night pleasure-seekers. After the film finished at eleven p.m. Marten suggested tea but his father declined and told him that they would walk the mile and a half home, despite the cold (it was minus seven degrees Celsius and the streets were covered with a thin layer of snow). As they left, a trade union leader who recognised Palme commented to his wife what a marvellous country Sweden was, that the prime minister can walk through the capital unguarded.

Music teacher Inge Morelius was sitting in his car waiting for his friends to withdraw some money from a cash machine. He spotted a tall dark-haired man wearing a blue ski jacket who was looking anxiously up and down the street as if he were waiting for someone. Morelius felt there was something sinister about him; perhaps he was planning a robbery or a drug deal. The music teacher watched as an elderly couple approached and the dark-haired man started to march towards them. Shocked, Morelius said out loud: 'Hell, he's going to snatch the old lady's handbag!' He watched as the dark-haired man walked briskly up to the couple, pulled out a handgun and fired two shots into the prime minister's back at close range. Palme crumpled onto the snow-covered pavement. The assassin calmly checked that his target was dead before holstering his gun and sprinting down the road, past a building site.

Lars Jeppsson heard the shots and saw Palme collapse. The assassin ran straight past him and dashed up a flight of eighty-nine steps, two or three at a time. At the top he turned to check that he wasn't being followed and then disappeared round a corner. Jeppsson, a short, thin bureaucrat in his mid-twenties, decided, with some trepidation, to give chase. He caught sight of the gunman some distance ahead, slipping on the ice as he dodged round into a side street. Jeppsson was unable to keep up.

Leif Ljungqvist, a building contractor, had turned his van around to see what the noise was. As soon as he saw the man lying in the street, he called the police. Oddly, the phone rang for ninety seconds without being answered. Ljungqvist hung up. At that moment, there was a patrol van with five young policemen in it parked near to where Jeppsson lost sight of the assassin.

While Ljungqvist redialled, teenager Anna Hage gave Palme heart massage despite Lisbet's screams for her to stop – blood poured out of Palme's mouth with each compression. A passing nurse, Gosta Soderstrom, tried to blow air into Palme's lungs but her breaths escaped through his chest with a terrible hissing sound. Finally the van full of young policemen arrived. Lisbet shouted at them: 'Don't you recognise me? My Olof has been shot.' Then she told them to give chase.

One officer complained that they had no bulletproof vests but at Lisbet's insistence they pursued the assassin on foot. After a short distance, one of the policemen stopped to be sick – he had drunk a can of Coke a few minutes before. They split up into two groups to try and cut off the assassin's probable escape route but only succeeded in running into each other a few minutes later.

Finally, the ambulance arrived. At first the paramedic displayed some confusion over what was going on. Lisbet screamed at him: 'Are you crazy? Don't you recognise me? I am Lisbet Palme, damn it, and there lies my husband Olof!' Once in the ambulance Lisbet, in shock, kept repeating the phrase: 'Palme . . . has . . . fallen.' On the way to the hospital, the ambulance driver, disconcerted by the hysterical Lisbet, took a wrong turning.

Once they arrived at the casualty department Lisbet complained of back pain – doctors then discovered that one of the bullets had grazed her spine. Olof Palme, meanwhile, was officially declared dead at 12.06 a.m. He was the first Swedish leader to be assassinated since King Gustav III was shot to death at a masked ball at Stockholm's opera house in 1792.

Police sealed off all exits to the city, called a national alert, and stepped up patrols at border crossings. It was the largest manhunt in Sweden's history, but, a few days later, with no new leads and no arrests, the police were facing accusations of incompetence. The roadblocks had not been set up until ninety minutes after the murder. The only physical evidence of the shooting, two bullet casings, had been found by passers-by – after the police had searched the area. The police were then ridiculed after they publicly announced their puzzlement at the origin and uniqueness of the copper-tipped .357 Magnum bullets. Newspapers were quick to point out that these bullets could have been purchased in a sporting-goods shop that was literally around the corner from the prime minister's office.

Stockholm Police Commissioner Hans Holmer called a news conference where he stated that his officers had followed up on four thousand leads and interviewed six hundred people. He also announced that the 120-officer team investigating the case was being expanded to three hundred and that the police were offering an unprecedented fifty-thousand-pound reward for information leading to the assassin's conviction. Said Holmer: 'This is a murder that cannot be compared to any other.'

Palme's assassination sent a wave of shock across Sweden, which for decades had advertised itself as a model society largely free of violence. Stunned Swedes tossed red roses on the murder site; some placed candles on the pavement. The following morning, lines of mourners wound around the block. A panoply of world leaders, including UN Secretary-General Javier Perez de Cuellar and Indian Prime Minister Rajiv Gandhi, attended Palme's funeral.[23] One of the speakers at Palme's funeral was an up-and-coming Social Democrat politician, Anna Lindh. 'A person can be killed, but ideas cannot. Your ideas will live on through us,' she said in her oration.

Police finally arrested and charged forty-one-year-old Christer Pettersson, an underworld debt collector and drug addict with dozens of convictions including manslaughter (he had previously stabbed a man to death with a bayonet not far from where Palme was murdered) and a record of mental illness. Pettersson's room-mate undermined his alibi – that he was on his way home at the time of the shooting. Shop records showed that he possessed a large-calibre gun and limped just as the assassin had been seen to do while fleeing

[23] Rajiv Gandhi was implicated in the Bofors arms-to-India bribery scandal which would eventually force him out of office. He was later exonerated.

the scene of the murder. Despite this, the police's case was shaky. The motive remained unknown and the evidence was circumstantial. But there was one key witness who could secure his conviction: Lisbet Palme.

Lisbet came face to face with her husband's alleged killer in the courtroom three years after the assassination. The tension fairly crackled as she was asked whether the man she had seen just after the shooting of her husband was present. 'Yes,' she answered. 'Are you sure?' asked the prosecutor. After looking briefly at Pettersson, Mrs Palme answered with a second 'Yes.'

The prosecutors were by now relying completely on her testimony. Four key witnesses recanted their pre-trial statements and two of them admitted they had initially been swayed by hopes of sharing in the cash reward offered by the government. Although the prosecutors were unable to come up with a murder weapon or a motive, Lisbet Palme's testimony secured Pettersson's conviction and he was sentenced to life.

But his lawyers immediately filed an appeal. There were doubts as to the ability of Lisbet Palme to identify reliably her husband's killer, someone she had glimpsed for a few seconds in the dark in extraordinarily stressful circumstances three years before. The seven appeal court members were unanimous in their decision. Pettersson was freed on appeal the following year. He was given fifty thousand pounds in compensation and the police were forced to reopen the case. In 2001, Pettersson gave an interview with Swedish writer Gert Fylking. He told the reporter: 'Sure as hell it was me who shot (him), but they can never nail me for it. The weapon is gone.'

In early September 2004, Pettersson contacted the son of Olof Palme, Marten, explaining that he had some information. Marten Palme said he was willing to meet Pettersson if he was ready to confess to the murder. Two weeks later Pettersson was found unconscious at the bottom of a flight of stairs. He was taken to hospital where he underwent emergency surgery for a cerebral haemorrhage but never regained consciousness; he died a few days later. It was never established how Pettersson came to fall – although it was well known he was a chronic drug and alcohol abuser.

Almost ten years after the Olof Palme assassination, a series of startling confessions turned the case on its head. Towards the end of September 1996 Colonel Eugene de Kock, a former South African police officer, gave evidence to the Supreme Court in Pretoria alleging that Palme had been shot and killed with the help of the South African police in 1986 because he 'strongly opposed the apartheid regime and Sweden made substantial contributions to the ANC'.

Swedish donations made up more than fifty per cent of the ANC's civilian budget in the 1980s and Sweden's most influential fund-raiser was Olof Palme, who ran fund-raising operations from his private office. Some of these donations were used to finance the work of the human rights lawyer and ANC activist Griffiths Mxenge, who was himself assassinated by a South African death squad in 1981.

Palme worked harder than any other head of state to end apartheid. He ensured that Sweden was the first country to impose sanctions against the South African government. One week before he was assassinated, on 21 February, Palme made the keynote address to the Swedish People's Parliament Against Apartheid held in Stockholm, attended by hundreds of sympathisers as well as leaders and officials from the ANC and the Anti-Apartheid Movement, including Oliver Tambo. As he began his address, an emotional Palme threw away his prepared speech and said: 'Apartheid cannot be reformed, it has to be eliminated.'

In October 1996, Swedish police investigators visited South Africa but, perhaps unsurprisingly after so much time, they were unable to uncover any evidence to substantiate de Kock's claims. It is well-known that South Africa's Secret Police were involved in several secret anti-ANC operations abroad, including the bombing of the ANC's offices in London on 14 March 1982 (Oliver Tambo, who was to have attended a meeting there at the time of the bombing, was their intended target) and the assassination of Ruth First, who was the wife of Joe Slovo and a close friend of Palme's. Stockholm's ANC office was bombed on 9 September 1986.

Several Swedish policemen (who can't be named for legal reasons) were members of the International Police Association (IPA) who, throughout the 1980s and 1990s, had made several trips to South Africa where they met with representatives of the security police. Swedish investigators discovered that some of these Swedish officers had formed a private right-wing club and had a secret office in Wallingatan 32, a short distance from the assassination scene. Members carried guns while off duty and forged close ties with South African police. Many former Swedish policemen from this group ran private security companies (they were essentially mercenaries) and became involved in the arms trade.

Palme's discovery of the Bofors arms-to-Iran scandal might have led him to threaten to terminate the lucrative deal with India and demand an investigation into Bofors. With their cut of the deal in jeopardy, middlemen and conspirators behind the arms deal, possibly Swedish IPA ex-policemen, would, along with the South Africans (who saw Palme as their number one enemy), have had all the motivation they needed to assassinate Palme.

The investigation into Palme's assassination has itself been the subject of three government-appointed commissions. The third of these published a 916-page report on 29 June 1999. The highly critical document stated that various leads were never followed up, or were even just ignored, in particular the suggestion that a network of Swedish and South African policemen with far-right political beliefs was linked to his death. Veteran diplomat Jan Eliasson, then the second-highest official at the Swedish Foreign Ministry, said that tips sent to the police disappeared into a 'black hole' and that the police showed no interest and little desire for cooperation. The report also criticised the Swedish police for mistakenly concentrating their efforts on linking the murder to the PKK.

These disputes over the Palme investigation only fuelled a widespread feeling among the Swedish public that no matter whether or not South African and/or Swedish police and security circles were actually involved in the murder of Olof Palme, neither the authorities in charge of the investigation nor the political establishment were interested in establishing a truth that could prove too hard to bear for a country that tends to regard itself as the world's most perfect democracy. As Carl Lidbom, Sweden's former ambassador in Paris and influential senior Social Democrat once put it: 'It would be best for all parties if the murder of Olof Palme was never solved.'

After Palme's assassination, the Swedish government continued to work against apartheid but with a less committed leadership – both donations and political pressure fell. Without a UN mediator, the Iraq–Iran War raged on; at the start of 1987, a six-week Iraqi offensive left fifty thousand Iranian dead.

Bofors, meanwhile, continued to operate and in February 2006 it announced that the United States Army had purchased its GPS-guided artillery shells (called Excalibur) for use in Iraq.

Twenty-five

A Very Modern Conspiracy

At the end of the 1980s, a team of assassins sealed the fate of East Germany in the wake of the Berlin Wall's collapse. At first glance, these outrages appeared to be straightforward terrorist strikes, but after some digging the incredible, unpalatable truth soon emerged. If there was ever any doubt that powerful conspiracies made up of big-business organisations and government agencies who are prepared to murder for their cause exist, then the following stories should eliminate it.

In the late 1980s the people of Poland, Hungary, Czechoslavakia and Romania overthrew their Communist dictatorships. In Russia, President Mikhail Gorbachev was winning his fight to push through his *Glasnost* (openness) and *Perestroika* (restructuring) reforms and on 15 October 1989 he was awarded the Nobel Peace Prize.

But nothing symbolised the fall of the old guard more than the collapse of the Berlin wall which came three weeks later. Originally approved by Soviet leader Nikita Khrushchev, the wall was a twenty-eight-mile barrier between West Berlin and East Germany that had stood for twenty-eight years. It had been built to stop the drain of labour and economic output caused by the huge numbers of professionals and skilled East Germans who worked in the West, as well as to halt the numerous defections. In addition to the wall, the whole of the border between East and West Germany was lined with chain fences, walls and minefields. The Wall became a key symbol of what Western powers regarded as Communist tyranny, particularly when East German marksmen went beyond mere symbolism and shot dead would-be defectors attempting to make the dash across no man's land to the West.

With the fall of Communist Hungary, the new Hungarian government dismantled its 218-mile security fence and East Germans were allowed to cross their borders for the first time in twenty-eight years. Overjoyed East Germans were then able to enter West Germany via Austria. The long-time leader of East Germany, Erich Honecker, resigned on 18 October 1989 and the new government decided to allow East Berliners to apply for visas to travel to West Germany.

Gunter Schabowski, the East German Minister of Propaganda, who had just returned from a vacation, was given the task of making the public announcement but was poorly briefed. Just before he was to appear at a press conference on 9 November, he was passed a note that said that East Berliners would be allowed to cross the border as long as they had proper permission. There were no further details and Schabowski read the note out at the end of the conference. When asked when the regulations would come into effect, he had no idea that the government wanted a few more days to prepare the border for the expected mass exodus and he replied: 'As far as I know, effective immediately, right now.'

Tens of thousands of East Berliners heard Schabowski's statement live on GDR television and flooded the checkpoints in the Wall demanding entry into West Berlin. The surprised and overwhelmed border guards were forced to open the gates, allowing people through with few or no identity checks. The ecstatic East Berliners were soon greeted by West Berliners on the other side in a celebratory atmosphere, and bars near the Wall gave out free beer.

Just over two weeks later, on 28 November, Alfred Herrhausen, the progressive, charismatic and outspoken Chief Executive of Deutsche Bank (Germany's largest, with assets of £122 billion) strode into what would be the most important business meeting of his life. Fifty-nine-year-old Herrhausen, who was also a personal economic adviser to Chancellor Helmut Kohl, was undoubtedly West Germany's most influential, powerful and progressive captain of finance who aggressively sought to change his bank from an insular institution to a global financial power. *Der Spiegel* had christened him 'the Lord of Money' only a few days earlier after Herrhausen, a mountain-climbing enthusiast who had once played field hockey for the West German national team, made a successful one-billion-pound takeover bid for the blue-blooded British merchant bank Morgan Grenfell.

Herrhausen took the lift to the twentieth floor of the Deutsche Bank tower in Frankfurt, stared at his colleagues and began one of the most extraordinary speeches ever given to a board of directors. He told them that as long ago as 1987, at the funeral of his fellow board member Werner Blessing, he had come to the conclusion that the debt crisis of the Third World could no longer be met with silence. For decades international banks had lent billions of pounds to semi- and under-developed countries before cutting off their credit lines with an explosive harshness, forcing developing nations into indebtedness. Unable to pay off the interest, they were then exploited mercilessly by foreign companies.

Herrhausen told his colleagues that a system in which a few financiers make a very high profit from the economy, at the expense of millions of people, could not endure. 'Economy and morality should go hand in hand. The debt crisis in the Third World cannot be solved without a partial waiver of claims by the Western creditor banks.' This was obvious to all banks but none were prepared to say so publicly – to do so would cost billions. Nonetheless, Herrhausen had prepared a detailed proposal which would form the basis for a speech he was due to deliver in New York on 4 December.

To say that this speech had had an effect was an understatement. The bank's board of directors flatly and uniformly rejected their Chief Executive's radical ideas without debate and Herrhausen left the meeting severely depressed.

The next day, at 8.32 a.m. on the morning of 30 November 1989, Herrhausen left his heavily guarded home in Bad Homburg and set out for Frankfurt's financial district in his armour-plated chauffeur-driven Mercedes-Benz 500SE, escorted by two other cars with four bodyguards. No efforts were ever made to vary the route and the assassin standing in the children's playground in a nearby park watched the convoy turn as usual along a tree-lined suburban street only five hundred metres from Herrhausen's house.

In his hands the man held a small wooden box, from which a cable ran down to the ground, through the park and then under the asphalt of the road through which a narrow channel had been chiselled out and then relaid overnight. The bomber flicked a switch that sent a thin beam of infra-red light across the road, and then he flicked another, activating the bomb.

It was an incredibly sophisticated device that required precision timing. The twenty-kilo device was hidden in the satchel of a carefully positioned boy's bicycle and would be activated as soon as the lead car broke the beam of light. Inside the satchel a copper plate had been placed between the explosive and the target. As the car broke the beam the device's fuse lasted just long enough for the first car to pass before exploding.

The heat instantly melted the copper plate, blasting it out across the street at two thousand metres per second. The molten copper, travelling ahead of the main force of the explosion, ripped through the air in the shape of a carrot, point first, sliced through the left passenger door and into Herrhausen, tearing him in two a moment before the car was spun violently by the force of the explosives, blowing out all the doors and both bonnet and boot.

The shock wave destroyed all the windows on one side of the street and the blast, compared later to the sound of a sonic boom, was heard three miles away.

The assassin took out a piece of folded paper, placed it on the ground and placed the box on top of it. He jogged across the park (he was wearing a tracksuit) and climbed into a white Lancia in which a driver was waiting. He'd kept the engine running.

Police poured into the area and soon found the small wooden box. Underneath was a piece of paper with a star-shaped symbol superimposed on a drawing of a Kalashnikov rifle: the trademark symbol of the ultra-left urban guerrillas, the Red Army Faction, who had terrorised Germany in the 1970s but had remained largely dormant since 1979. The federal prosecutor named as possible suspects thirty-one-year-old Christoph Seidler and thirty-year-old Horst Meyer, both RAF 'commandos'.

But most puzzling to the police was why, with most of its hardcore members dead or serving long prison terms and its extreme left-wing ideology on the wane, the group had chosen this moment to strike. The authorities concluded that the prospect of a united Germany in the wake of the collapse of the Eastern Bloc had fuelled the attack.

At a press conference in East Berlin, Interior Minister Peter-Michael Diestel confirmed that well-known terrorists from the RAF as well as the notorious Carlos the Jackal and Abu Daoud, a leader of the Palestinian terrorist group Black September, had been frequent visitors to East Germany when that country had been under the rule of Honecker. The suggestion was that ex-Stasi agents had joined forces with the RAF to fight German reunification.

Until recently, this view was accepted. No one was ever charged with the assassination and the investigation was eventually dropped. But Herrhausen was not a typical capitalist enemy; he did not fit the RAF's usual target profile. Parts of his speech were printed in the *New York Times* after his death. For some reason, the newspaper dramatically altered the text. The entire, unedited speech was published in German on the same day in *Die Zeit*. The original title in *Die Zeit* was 'New Horizons in Europe'. The *Times* excerpt was entitled 'Towards a Unified Germany', which was grossly misrepresentative.

In the speech, Herrhausen argued that he was not necessarily for unification and suggested that if East Germany wanted it, it could perhaps be achieved in about ten years but 'at this point' the question was still very much an open one. This section was omitted by the

Times as was the following quote, that such an endeavour 'would be a difficult and certainly a long process in view of the large economic and social differences that exist today'. Most importantly, the *Times* excerpt completely omitted Herrhausen's discussion of his proposals for debt cancellation and in-country development banks. These proposals, coming from a man in his position, were by far the most newsworthy items in the speech, yet the *Times* edited them out.

The method of Herrhausen's assassination was unusual in that it relied upon a sophisticated device unlike anything that the Red Army Faction had ever used before. The RAF, although lethal and fanatical, had a reputation for being one of the most chaotic terrorist groups in the world and was infamous for accidentally detonating explosives and misfiring rocket launchers. Finally, when they had attacked senior business leaders in the past they had chosen carefully, selecting only those with strong right-wing connections or with a Nazi past. Herrhausen had neither.

The RAF would not have killed the president of a bank without a special reason. The last time they had kidnapped an economic leader had been in 1977: their aim then had been to try and free imprisoned comrades. Somebody wanted, for a certain reason, the leading spokesman of the Deutsche Bank, on this day and in this manner, eliminated. Meanwhile the 'RAF' vanished and the attack was more or less forgotten until eighteen months later.

On 1 April 1991 at 11.30 p.m., Detlev Karsten Rohwedder, the manager of the *Treuhandanstalt* (the Trust Institution, the body responsible for the privatisation of the state-owned companies of East Germany, set up after Germany was unified only one year after the Berlin Wall fell) was going through papers at his mansion in Düsseldorf. It was the Easter weekend, the perfect time for the economist to try and catch up with his enormous workload. With him was his wife Hergard, a judge, who was also working in their study.

Rohwedder was trying to orchestrate the most massive denationalisation programme in the world. (The East German state owned eight thousand companies, together worth an estimated two hundred billion pounds.) Much to the disappointment of the new government and many economists, Rohwedder had so far sold just one thousand of the eight thousand firms. The reason for his slow progress was that Rohwedder, a committed Social Democrat, was trying to prevent mass redundancies. The East German state-owned companies were overstaffed and so private owners, with their money on the line, were likely to impose lay-offs and reduce wages and benefits. Rohwedder, born in East Germany but raised in the West, was demanding that any investors should keep redundancies to a minimum and was trying – in order to prevent mass unemployment – to come up with a worker-based solution to the problem.

In 1991, he came to the conclusion that reckless privatisation would have unacceptable social consequences. Therefore he resolved, in the first months of the year, to change the concept of the *Treuhand* into 'first restoration, then privatisation'. For this stance, Rohwedder came under pressure not only as a result of opposition from other members of the *Treuhand* board, but through various international consulting firms as well as from American and British investment bankers, who accused him of stopping foreign investment. Criticism also came from Germany's largest political party, the Christian Democratic Union, who claimed that he was failing Germany.

Rohwedder had an armoured car in Berlin and his house in a plush Düsseldorf neighbourhood was electronically protected. But there were weaknesses in his security; most importantly he refused round-the-clock surveillance by bodyguards.

It was a difficult shot, probably the most difficult of any sniper's career. Although Rohwedder was clearly visible through his window in his well-lit study, which overlooked the Rhine, his back was facing the window and he was hunched over, his head moving. The shooter was standing just over sixty metres away from the target, positioned next to a bench in some allotment gardens. It was dark, although the sniper's rifle had a powerful night-vision scope. The shot required perfect stillness and composure.

It was some time before the assassin took his first shot. The bullet hit Rohwedder in his right shoulder and he slammed down on the desk. The assassin re-aimed, a little to the left. The second round went through Rohwedder's back.

Hergard reached out to her husband and was caught by the third bullet in her left shoulder before the fourth bullet barrelled through her husband's heart. The assassin, satisfied, then took a folded piece of paper from his pocket, laid it on the bench and placed his binoculars on top. He then swept the empty bullet casings into a little pile next to the bench and left.

The communiqué was soon found by the police; again, it was apparently from the Red Army Faction. No arrests were ever made. On the surface, Rohwedder was a logical assassination choice for the RAF: he was, after all, responsible for the selling of the Communist state's assets. But his beliefs were closer to the RAF's political beliefs than were those of any other German economist: he put the workers first and was about to turn the *Treuhand* on its head after realising that rapid privatisation would be disastrous for both East and West Germany. On his death his post was taken by Birgit Breuel, the daughter of a banker from Hamburg, who let investors have a free rein. Financiers from all over the world flooded into East Germany, leading one senior American economist to comment: 'It's the Klondike [gold rush] on the Danube.'

These two assassinations removed the most influential Western opposition to what became the utterly catastrophic absorption of Communist East Germany into the Western capitalist fold. Herrhausen's slow-but-sure approach to East Germany's reform had a large following in East Germany. On 4 November 1989 – nearly four weeks before his death and five days before the Wall fell – one million people had marched through East Berlin, most of them chanting slogans calling for 'revolutionary renewal', not reunification. Millions of East Germans chose not to flee to the West and many worked to create a dynamic civic movement as part of a broader struggle for socialist renewal. This gave rise to a number of new political organisations, including the United Left, New Forum, Democracy Now, Democratic Awakening, the Social Democratic Party and the Green Party. They all shared an opposition both to capitalism and to reunification with West Germany.

Chancellor Helmut Kohl disagreed with Herrhausen on reunification. Two days after the economist's death, with his new personal economic adviser Horst Kohler, the state secretary in the German Finance Ministry, at his side (Kohler became President of Germany in 2004) Kohl announced his ten-point plan for East Germany's absorption into the West. Both the East German government and its civic opposition rejected this appeal for reunification. The newly elected prime minister, Hans Modrow, did, however, express his willingness to explore 'cooperative coexistence' or 'a treaty community between two independent states'. Over two hundred thousand East Germans signed a petition supporting this view.

Undaunted, Kohl pressed ahead with reunification, essentially a plan for East Germany to surrender to West Germany. Kohl offered East Germans a simple electoral choice: vote for parties favoured by the West and receive Deutschmarks, followed by a rapid reunification, or vote against the West in the forthcoming elections and receive no financial assistance.

West German political parties took steps to influence directly the outcome of the election. Each adopted and directed their opposite number in the East, providing them with speakers, consultants, money, and equipment. Even West German media were used to broadcast election propaganda back to the East.

Kohl himself travelled to the East many times to campaign for the Christian Democratic Union (CDU)-led alliance of conservative parties that he had helped form. His hard work paid off: the CDU and its allies won the election, receiving approximately forty-eight per cent of the vote. Kohl would now be negotiating reunification with his opposite number Lothar de Maiziere who clearly understood the words of Kohl: 'This is the accession of the East to the West and not the reverse . . . this is not the reunification of two equal states.'

This brief history of the German reunification process runs counter to the more widely held view that the collapse of the East left the West with no alternative but to pursue a rapid reunification. Quite the opposite was true. Kohl had many opportunities to pursue a gradual union of the two Germanys.

The West eliminated state subsidies for basic goods and services. Without the subsidies, prices doubled. The West also required East Germans to pay new income taxes and contribute to insurance and retirement funds. Nearly half the value of personal savings was lost in the conversion of East German currency into Western Marks. Perhaps not surprisingly, most East Germans used their new DMs to purchase West German goods, causing a noticeable increase in West German production and East German unemployment.

An even more significant blow to the East German economy was the West German insistence on the immediate privatisation of East German firms. After Rohwedder was replaced, a system was organised that benefited West German investors at East German expense. A process of closed bidding allowed West German firms to purchase the best East German firms at attractive prices. Many of these firms were later shut down, having been bought only to ensure that they would not become competitors.

Those working in the civil service were dealt with harshly. In all, approximately half a million East German civil servants were fired. In many cases, West Germans, often commuting daily or weekly, were hired to fill administrative positions in East Germany. The West German state justified these actions by cleverly modifying its traditional anti-communist propaganda. In the past, East Germans had been portrayed in West Germany as helpless victims of Communism. After reunification, the German state and media quickly transformed these same victims into active supporters of the past Communist system.

From 1989 to 1993, the birth rate per thousand people in East Germany fell by sixty per cent. In 1992 the number of marriages per thousand people was less than half what it had been in 1989. Death rates for men and women aged thirty-five to forty-four rose twenty to thirty per cent between 1989 and 1991. As *Business Week* noted in reporting on these statistics: 'Such changes are unprecedented for an industrial country at peace. The drops in births and marriages even eclipsed those that occurred in Germany in the final years of the Second World War.'

Since unification, Germany has spent a staggering one trillion pounds on the former East, much of it squandered. The money helped build railways, highways, schools and communications networks but it did little to create permanent jobs: in 2004, unemployment was above eighteen per cent, more than double the rate in West Germany. Economists predicted that it could take another twenty to thirty years for living standards in eastern Germany to reach the level of those in western Germany.

The assassinations of Rohwedder and Herrhausen were particularly spectacular cold-blooded murders committed against two of the highest-ranking and best-protected personalities in the country. The murders were carried out by professionals who appeared to have detailed inside knowledge not only of the localities and the victims' habits but also of security loopholes. The assassins struck right under the noses of some of Europe's best-equipped and most highly trained anti-terrorist forces. They deliberately left clues – letters of confession with the RAF's insignia, binoculars, neatly stacked cartridge cases and detonators – but these traces yielded no information about a perpetrator, nor did the police ever establish the authenticity of the messages of confession.

None of the known members of the RAF could be linked to the crimes. Normally, the RAF proudly and ideologically justified their deeds and left no doubt concerning their responsibility on their letters of confession, e.g. by applying inky fingerprints to their communiqués. This new generation was made up of phantoms. There were no traces of any of the logistical structures and preparations normally necessary for carrying out such hits: no apartments serving as hideouts, no weapon or ammunition stocks, no bank robberies to raise finances . . . nothing.

This 'RAF' was totally different. From its very beginning, the 'first-generation' RAF was completely anarchic and thoroughly infiltrated by undercover agents, its members permanently observed, hunted and tracked. The self-taught guerrilla fighters had no chance against much better trained and equipped police. Most of them were captured or killed by 1978 and the 'second generation', largely made up of escapees from a mental institution who called themselves the Socialist Patients' Kollective was totally chaotic and ineffective. By the time their leader Christian Klar was captured in 1982 the group numbered seven members.

Herrhausen was murdered as he prepared to start his crusade against Third World debt; a machine-gun attack against the American embassy in Bonn was carried out at the height of non-violent mass protests in Germany against the USA's role in the First Gulf War; Rohwedder, the chief of the *Treuhand*, was shot dead – with one of the guns used in the embassy shooting – only weeks before a planned mass rally of union members in Berlin against the brutal dismantling of the East German economy by the West. In all cases the effect was the same: the 'acts of solidarity' of the 'RAF' were in marked contrast to the ideals they claimed to support; the attacks deprived them of credibility. They eliminated the only two men who could have slowed the frenzied dismantling of the East German economy.

Herrhausen and Rohwedder were not typical symbolic figures of the 'fascist capital structure' as the 'RAF' described it. Both men were in fact in a position to take Germany down a very different path from that which it actually took. Herrhausen and Rohwedder were eliminated by professional assassins employed by people bent on ensuring the total collapse of socialist East Germany for both political and economic reasons. As to who the assassins were, there is no satisfactory answer.

Twenty-six

Dr Strangelove's Supergun

There are three kinds of target that seem to just cry out to be assassinated. They carry on regardless, as if possessing a death wish, failing to heed loosely coded warnings, so that when their time comes the only one surprised is them.

The first type are those who doggedly investigate the corrupt and the criminal. A good example was Robert Ouko, the Kenyan Foreign Minister who disappeared in February 1990 after preparing a report about corrupt businesses in his constituency. He was found mutilated by machetes and partially burned, with a can of diesel, some matches and a gun lying on the ground nearby. At first the Kenyan police rather optimistically tried to pass his death off as suicide. A subsequent investigation failed to turn up any clues.

The second kind are the ruthless dictators who take on the mantle of their predecessors with an even greater bloody determination. William Talbot was no angel but Samuel Doe, who wrested control of Liberia from him in a bloody coup in 1980, took the approach of a psychotic butcher to leadership. Despite this, he was a friend of President Reagan who nicknamed him 'Chairman Moe'. Doe once challenged some European diplomats to a fist fight when they criticised the US in his presence and he tried to impersonate Reagan when making his own speeches.

Sadly for Doe, things took a turn for the worse when the US, clearly winning the Cold War, decided that they no longer needed his help in Africa (Doe was a thug responsible for the deaths of thousands of people, after all) and decided to cut off vital aid (including weapons, thereby forcing Doe to turn to gun-runners). At the same time, Charles Taylor escaped from a US-run African jail and, sensing Doe's weakness, started a guerrilla war which ended up with Doe being tortured to death while faction leader Prince Johnson watched, sipping on a Budweiser while being fanned by his soldiers. The entire grisly scene, which included Doe's ears being sliced off, was videotaped: bootleg copies are still available in Monrovian markets.

The third type of self-doomed target is the obsessed: those who know that the dangers exist but are too driven to stop. One such man was Gerald Bull. All he wanted to do was make guns. His problem was that he didn't care who he worked for. Samuel Doe or Charles Taylor, it wouldn't make any difference – but not because Bull was especially greedy. A ruddy-complexioned, short and overweight Canadian scientist, Bull was one of the most dangerous of boffins: he was obsessed with producing the most powerful gun that the world had ever seen and he was crazy enough to work with anyone who shared his vision.

Known as 'Dr Strangelove' by his colleagues, Gerald Bull antagonised and alienated almost everyone he met or worked with. He had, for over thirty years, designed and built guns that had killed tens of thousands of people. Despite this, Bull could not stand the sight of blood. He revolutionised artillery by designing guns that fired further and with greater accuracy and killing power than anything in the NATO or Soviet arsenals. In the 1960s he built the biggest gun in the world and fired a shell one hundred and eighty kilometres into the sky, double the height achieved by his nearest rival.

But Bull's company, Space Research Corporation, did not always follow the rules. Representatives of the South African army had approached the CIA's station chief in Pretoria and asked for help in obtaining a long-range 155mm artillery system after their own army's artillery had been outdistanced by Cuban troops using Soviet artillery during the Angolan Civil War fought between 1974 and 1975. It was forbidden for the US and Canada to sell weapons to South Africa, which was, because of its apartheid regime, at that time under an international arms embargo.

Nevertheless, after the station chief hooked up Bull and the South Africans, Bull agreed to help and the parts for the guns were machined at his eight-thousand-acre Space Research Corporation compound at Highwater, Quebec. They were then exported from Canada to America on Space Corp's own private road before being shipped illegally to South Africa via Antigua and Spain, using false export declarations with US Customs.

Once in South Africa, Bull's guns halted the Communist advances made in southern Angola, where they also went on to save the forces of American-backed Jonas Savimbi from annihilation by Soviet-backed troops in the early 1980s. Savimbi went on to wage a bloody twenty-year civil war, refusing to accept peace on any terms. In 1992 he sold eight hundred million dollars' worth of blood diamonds to keep Bull's still-working guns supplied with shells. (Savimbi met both Ronald Reagan and George H.W. Bush during this period.) After his death in a gunfight in 2002, the country struggled through another four years of conflict until democratic elections were arranged for 2006.

It was thanks to Bull that Savimbi kept going for as long as he did – without those guns, the Soviet-backed forces of Agostinho Neto, a Marxist poet, would have retained control of the country.

In 1980, after a lengthy Canadian-led investigation, Bull pleaded guilty to smuggling two 155-millimetre gun barrels, thirty thousand 155mm long-range missiles and one radar tracking system consisting of two radar vans to South Africa. He spent six months in a US jail.

After his release he moved to Brussels, the centre of the world's arms trade, where he soon secured contracts with China and Iraq: he sold the Iraqis 155mm and 210mm guns, made and paid for via Austria. These guns decimated wave upon wave of Iranian suicide bombers who charged into Iraq in 1987, while China used Bull's guns to guard their border with the Soviet Union.

In 1988 Bull started work on his dream project, an idea that had obsessed him for most of his working life: Project Babylon.

Project Babylon was a gun with a 156-metre-long barrel and one-metre bore capable of firing a satellite into orbit. Including the breech and recoil mechanism the 'Supergun' would be two hundred metres long. It was not intended for 'normal' artillery purposes – but Bull had plans to build even bigger guns that would fire rocket-assisted shells across continents: accurate enough to hit an office building at a distance of 3,200 kilometres. Bull took his proposal for Babylon to NATO and to the US high command. Cautiously interested, they suggested that he should come back when he had some test results before they made a decision.

Ever impatient and deliberately ignorant of political sensitivities, Bull approached the Iraqi dictator Saddam Hussein who Bull knew wanted to become, in Saddam's own words, the 'sword of the Arabs'; his ambition was to turn Iraq into a superpower that controlled most of the world's oil supplies. Hussein was also desperate for nuclear power and had already invested billions in modern weapons and training his enormous army, the fourth-largest in the world.

The Iraqi president had even created the world's most successful illiteracy-eradication programme so that everyone in Iraq would be able to use modern weapons technology and fighting methods. As Saddam put it: 'The pen and the gun have one barrel.' When he learned that the Supergun could be used to launch satellites, to fire chemical, biological, conventional and nuclear weapons for distances over one thousand kilometres and could fire rocket-assisted warheads over 3,200 kilometres he eagerly invited Bull to Baghdad.

A smaller forty-five metres long, 350mm-calibre gun was soon completed for testing purposes: the results were even better than Bull had predicted. At this point the Iraqis told Bull that they would only go ahead with the project if he would also help with the development of their Scud missile project. Bull agreed immediately – anything to get his precious Supergun built. Construction of the individual sections of the new gun started in England, also in Spain, the Netherlands and Switzerland. Meanwhile Bull worked on the Scud, designing a new nose-cone for higher re-entry speeds.

It was at this point that someone started 'warning' him to stop working on the missiles; over a period of a few months his apartment was broken into several times. One day Bull returned home to find his furniture rearranged and a set of drinking glasses replaced by a different make. Nothing had been stolen. His luggage was 'lost' at airports so often that eventually he was forced to carry extra underwear and toiletry items in his hand luggage.

Bull took the warnings seriously but his obsession drove him on and he relied on sleeping pills to calm his nerves. He kept an untidy diary made up of a variety of notebooks and papers and noted in March 1990 that the strain was getting to him: 'My body aches . . . I'm so tired I don't know if I can make it through the day.'

That same month, David James, a ruthless British businessman who acted as a 'company doctor', was touring a steel manufacturer's factory in Halesowen in the West Midlands when he noticed three huge steel tubes, 'the thinnest of which had a thumping great muzzle, like something from a strip-cartoon siege gun'. He glanced at the waybill and saw that the tubes were bound for the 'Republic of Iraq Ministry for Industries and Petrochemical Project, Baghdad, Iraq'. Immediately suspicious, James got in touch with a contact at MI6, known as 'Mr Q', on 15 March. Mr Q asked James to use his banking contacts to track down the rest of the weapon before it left Teesport docks. Part of this cloak-and-dagger operation involved James getting nine hundred documents from the offices of Walter Somers (the owners of the factory), which were then photographed secretly through the night with MI6 equipment set up in a room at a Halesowen hotel.

The country that considered itself the most likely to suffer from the effects of the Supergun was Israel. Iraq and Israel were bitter enemies. Israel certainly had both the form and the motive for the type of assassination that was being prepared for Bull. Mossad

(Israel's Intelligence and Special Ops, known as 'the Institute') played a big part in the bombing of the Osiris nuclear reactor outside Baghdad on 8 June 1981, claiming that it was going to be used to produce atomic weapons.

Israel had also halted General Nasser of Egypt's ambitious programme to develop 'home-grown' ballistic missiles in the late 1950s and early 1960s. Many of the foreign scientists recruited by Nasser were ex-Nazis who had worked on Himmler's SS missile experiments during the Second World War. When anonymous threats did not deter these men, a series of letter bombs and mysterious accidents did. Survivors were informed by unsigned letters left on their beds in tightly guarded Egyptian compounds that they and their families were next. The project collapsed.

Bull was going too far and, despite regular warnings, he was still pushing forward with the Supergun and the Scuds. Mossad assembled a *kidon* team, essentially an assassination squad, and sent them to Brussels where they were welcomed by an activated sleeper unit. The *kidon* were expert killers and had access to a small poison laboratory, long- and short-blade knives, piano wire, explosives no bigger than a throat lozenge (capable of blowing off a person's head) and an arsenal of short-barrel pistols and sniper rifles. After a few weeks of surveillance, they had a simple and effective plan in place.

On 22 March 1990, sixty-one-year-old Gerald Bull grinned as he weaved his way erratically through the Brussels streets. He was a terrible driver. He ignored red lights, changed lanes randomly and often left his car with the engine running in the middle of the airport drop-off point, blocking traffic as he frantically dashed to make his flight to Baghdad. The expert driver, who was struggling to follow him discreetly, radioed ahead to the team waiting for Bull at his apartment block and told them to be ready.

With Bull was his secretary Monique Jamine who told him a story of how a newly employed secretary had tried to seduce her into having a lesbian affair. Bull laughed heartily and told Monique as she dropped him off outside his apartment building: 'Just wait until we get to the office tomorrow.' He loved any chance to have fun at someone else's expense and was still chuckling as he travelled in the lift to the sixth floor. For the first time in several weeks he was in a good mood. Only days before, his Supergun prototype had been successfully test-fired in Iraq. He was about to travel to Spain, and then to his family home in Montreal. His pockets were stuffed full with twenty thousand dollars in cash (for the Spanish trip and to pay for repairs to his Montreal driveway). He always paid in cash, believing that it led to better service.

Bull's assassin was waiting for him as he emerged from the lift. As the Supergun's creator fumbled for his door key, the gunman, who had been waiting on the emergency staircase, walked softly up behind him and shot Bull five times in the head, neck and back with a silenced automatic. He escaped down the stairs and was driven by an accomplice to Brussels South railway station where he took the first train to Germany.

Bull was found minutes later with the cash still in his pockets, and his large black canvas bag containing his precious papers was left by his side for the authorities to find.

In his last conversation with officials from Iraq, Stephen Bull, Gerry Bull's son, was told that their intelligence said that his father had been shot by agents of Israel's Mossad. They also believed that Israel's political leaders would not have sanctioned that action without consulting American political leaders as Bull was an American citizen. (Although he'd been born in Canada, Bull had a US passport.)

Thanks to the work of David James and MI6 other parts of the Supergun were seized in Greece and Turkey. Iraq's Foreign Minister Tariq Aziz said: 'Even if we buy a box of chocolates from Britain, they'll say Iraq will use it to produce an atomic bomb.' He also told reporters that Iraq would appeal against the confiscation of the parts, which he claimed were for a petrochemical plant. The appeal was never made and Iraqi scientists were unable to develop the prototype into a working weapon of mass destruction.

However, at least five hundred of Bull's advanced 155-millimetre howitzers were used against Allied troops in the First Gulf War, which began after Iraq invaded Kuwait on 2 August 1990. (The USA had decided not to purchase the howitzers, which had a longer range than their best artillery.) Thankfully, Bull had not finished his work on the Scud missiles so when Saddam Hussein finally decided to use them against Israel on 18 January 1991 they became infamous for their wild inaccuracy. They damaged a few buildings but caused no deaths. All the subsequent Scud launches were successfully intercepted by American Patriot missiles.

In April 1990 two men, a scientist and a director of the Walter Somers company, were charged in connection with the Supergun. However, charges against them were withdrawn suddenly and without explanation in November the same year and no company was ever prosecuted for assisting Iraq in their programme of weapons acquisition. Without Gerald Bull at the helm, his Space Research Corporation folded in the immediate aftermath of his death. The secrets of the Supergun died with Bull.

Twenty-seven

The Karate Death Chop

The beginning of the 1990s was as traumatic a time as any in the late twentieth century. There was the Gulf War, which saw a multi-national force drive Iraq out of Kuwait; a failed coup attempt against Soviet President Mikhail Gorbachev after he recognised three Baltic states who had declared their independence; violent protests as Germany struggled with reunification; the ongoing civil war raging in Yugoslavia.

There were three major signs of peace that gave cause for cautious optimism, however. Unusually, one came from the Middle East as peace talks finally brought Israelis and Arabs to the negotiating table. The other came with the end of the Cold War, as further nuclear arms cuts were announced by Gorbachev and President George H.W. Bush, while South Africa moved to dismantle apartheid and regain its international standing.

The year 1991 was dominated by the First Gulf War which began a few months after Saddam Hussein had ordered his army to take control of Kuwait, a small but oil-rich state which had been annexed by the British during the First World War. Saddam said that he wanted his territory back and claimed that the Kuwaitis were 'slant drilling' into Iraqi oilfields. Meanwhile, Iraq's neighbour Iran was quietly going about the business of assassinating its exiled opposition foes throughout Europe. One of the principal assassins has since turned out to be a possible Saddam of the future.

*

On the sweltering afternoon of 7 August 1991 three dark-haired men approached an ivy-covered villa in the Paris suburb of Suresnes. It was the home of seventy-six-year-old Shahpour Bakhtiar, exiled former Prime Minister of Iran and a leader of the anti-Khomeini opposition. Since fleeing Tehran in 1979, Bakhtiar had been one of the most closely guarded men in France, watched over by paramilitary police twenty-four hours a day. The arrival of the three men raised no alarm, since one was thirty-eight-year-old Farydoun Boyerahmadi, a Bakhtiar aide and confidant. He was bringing two friends, Ali Vakili Rad, thirty-two, and Mohammed Azadi, thirty-one, to meet the famous exile. The guards at the door collected the visitors' passports, frisked the men and waved them inside.

Bakhtiar and his personal secretary, Fouroush Katibeh, greeted the guests in a ground-floor salon. As soon as Katibeh went to the kitchen to make tea, one of the visitors leaped at Bakhtiar and, with a vicious, well-practised knife-hand karate chop, struck his throat, smashing his windpipe. It was a mortal blow. The secretary was similarly dispatched.

With two knives that they grabbed from the kitchen, the assailants completed their grim task by hacking at their dying victims' throats, chests and arms so savagely that one knife blade snapped in two. Then, less than an hour after arriving, Boyerahmadi calmly collected the trio's passports and the men drove off in an orange BMW. The guards failed to notice that Vakili's and Azadi's shirts were drenched in blood.

This vicious attack touched off one of the most intensive murder investigations in French history. Conducted by fifty-year-old Judge Jean-Louis Bruguiere, a dogged investigator of terrorist activities (he survived a grenade attack in 1987 and carried out his investigations with a .357 Magnum tucked under his jacket), the probe followed a winding trail that led through Switzerland and Turkey to the highest levels of the Tehran government. The secret 177-page prosecutor's report stated that: 'Iranian intelligence services effectively took part in carrying out this criminal conspiracy.'

The head of the intelligence and security ministry, Ali Fallahian, was believed to be in charge of Tehran's worldwide assassination networks. In an August 1992 interview on Iranian TV, Fallahian openly boasted of his organisation's success in stalking Tehran's opponents. 'We track them abroad, too,' he said. 'Last year we succeeded in striking fundamental blows to their top members.' Investigators also uncovered links to Iran's foreign ministry, telecommunications ministry, Islamic orientation ministry and state television network, IRIB.

Between 1979 and 1994, more than sixty Iranian dissidents were assassinated abroad. On 24 April 1990 Professor Kazem Rajavi, fifty-six, a renowned human-rights advocate and elder brother of Iranian opposition leader Massoud Rajavi, was heading for his home in the Geneva suburb of Coppet. Shortly before noon, a Volkswagen Golf swerved in front of his car and someone inside it sprayed the windshield of Rajavi's car with bullets. Two gunmen jumped out of a second car and methodically pumped five bullets into Rajavi's head. One of the killers leaned over and tucked a navy blue baseball cap into the car-door pocket. It was the third time police had found a blue baseball cap at the scene of an Iranian assassination.

One of those directly responsible for these assassination squads was Mahmoud Ahmadinejad who became a senior officer in the Special Brigade of the Revolutionary Guards in 1986. He had won notoriety and praise in the early 1980s when he had worked in the Internal Security department as an interrogator and torturer. He had also worked as an executioner in the notorious Evin Prison, where thousands of political prisoners were murdered in the bloody purges of the 1980s. His alleged job was to put torture victims out of their misery with a single shot to the head – he became known as 'One Thousand Bullets' because he shot so many people.

After he was transferred to the Revolutionary Guards, Ahmadinejad was stationed in Ramazan Garrison near Kermanshah in western Iran, the headquarters of 'extra-territorial operations', a euphemism for assassinations committed beyond Iran's borders. Ahmadinejad led many of these operations and took orders directly from Fallahian, who ensured that the foreign ministry provided diplomatic cover, material support and logistical assistance.

Ahmadinejad masterminded a series of attacks in the Middle East and Europe. He also planned to assassinate British author Salman Rushdie.[24] The ultra-conservative Ahmadinejad was elected mayor of Tehran in 2003 and decided to stand at the next presidential elections, which he won in August 2005. (There have since been two attempts to assassinate him.)

In April 2006, a Swiss judge issued an international arrest warrant for Ali Fallahian for his part in the assassination of Professor Rajavi. The warrant issued by Swiss Investigative Magistrate Jacques Antenen called on law enforcement agencies to arrest 'Ali Fallahian, former Minister of Intelligence and Security of the Islamic Republic of Iran, and transfer him to the Canton Vaud Prison in Lausanne, Switzerland'. Judge Antenen further announced: 'Minister Fallahian was responsible for assassinations and issuing the orders for all such missions.'

At this point, Fallahian was a security adviser in Ahmadinejad's government. Ahmadinejad, who identified the Jews as Iran's number one enemy, called the Holocaust a 'myth' and is at the time of writing attempting to turn Iran into a nuclear power while maintaining his top spot in America's so-called Axis of Evil, is not going to hand his friend Fallahian over any time soon.

[24] Although this plan never materialised, Hitoshi Igarashi, one of Japan's leading Islamic scholars who translated *The Satanic Verses* into Iranian, was stabbed to death on 11 July 1991. The killer was never caught.

Twenty-eight

One-Eyed Jack

Years before the world heard of Osama bin Laden or al-Qaeda, the Tamil Tigers of Sri Lanka were pioneering a new method of guerrilla warfare: the suicide bomber. The first blew himself up in the middle of a Sri Lankan army unit in 1987. While the Tigers lost one man, the army lost twenty soldiers – some died, some lost limbs.

Those odds stacked up pretty well in favour of the Tamils as far as the Tiger leaders were concerned. Hundreds more followed. The Black Tigers, as the Tamil suicide squads became known, adapted explosives so that they could be used on land, sea and air. (At one point they purchased a small squadron of microlight aircraft.) Bombs were disguised to fit around, and even inside, the body.

This next case was their most extraordinary and high-profile foreign operation and, remarkably, the assassin they chose for it was a seventeen-year-old-girl. But she had good reason to die for the Tamil cause, as did thousands of other young Tigers.

The bad blood between the Tamils and the Sri Lankan government goes back at least a thousand years to a time when a powerful Tamil dynasty in India invaded the island of Sri Lanka and pushed the Sinhalese natives deep into the south. Today the minority Tamil population wants independence from the Sinhalese-dominated government in the capital, Colombo. Tamils and Sinhalese speak a different language, and they look to different gods: the Tamils to the Hindu pantheon and the Sinhalese to Buddha.

The conflict between the two groups has ebbed and flowed ever since the original invasion but by 1991 it was raging more violently than ever – only by now the weapons were artillery and automatic rifles rather than swords and spears. Between 1989 and 1991 the Tigers assassinated eight senior politicians, including Defence Minister Ranjan Wijeratne who had taken a hard line against the Tigers. He was decapitated by a remote-controlled roadside bomb on 2 March 1991. In the previous eight years, around eighteen thousand people had died in the conflict.

The Tigers were supported by the government of India in the early 1980s, until Prime Minister Rajiv Gandhi's first term in power when he changed policy and attempted to make peace. He sent an Indian peacekeeping force of seventy thousand to the Tamil areas in 1987, only to wind up warring with the Tigers. The confrontation ended in a humiliating withdrawal of the Indians in 1990 after more than a thousand of their soldiers died.

Gandhi had lost the general election of 1989 to V.P. Singh, a former ally who turned against the prime minister after his investigations into the Bofors bribery scandal implicated the highest levels of the Indian government. Singh was elected as Prime Minister in Gandhi's place but after only eighteen months his government was in disarray and he had been forced to call a new election. Gandhi, who had done everything in the meantime to regain his 'Mr Clean' image, was about to be swept back into power. The Tamil Tigers, concerned that Gandhi would send Indian troops back to Sri Lanka (Singh had ordered them out the previous year), decided to strike first.

There was no shortage of volunteers. The Tiger cult around their headstrong leader Vilupillai Prabhakaran was as strong as ever, and young Tamil recruits flocked to his banner, eager to embrace the austere, fanatical mindset of a Tiger. Each young terrorist embraced their AK-47 rifle as their most precious belonging and strictly followed the rule that it should never touch the ground. They sat through long hours of indoctrination that covered everything from grisly photographs of Tamils tortured and butchered by the Sri Lankan army to the glories of the Tamil kings of the Chola dynasty, who had conquered Sri Lanka in the eleventh century.

Every Tiger carried a cyanide pill around their neck in the event of capture – by 1991, it was estimated that at least six hundred Tigers had ended their own lives this way. But their first job was to kill the enemy. Kanthi, a young girl recruit with the Tigers, told a journalist in 1991: 'I don't mind dying so long as I can kill a few Sri Lankan soldiers first.'

Apart from a burning desire to die before she got old, Thenmuli Rajaratnam, known to her friends as Dhanu, was about as far removed from traditional teenage preoccupations as a seventeen-year-old could get. She didn't care about clothes, music or parties. She couldn't remember the last time she'd had to study for a test. And as for boys, well, forget it. Dhanu's chances of a normal life were shaky from the day she was born in Tamil Tiger territory in northern Sri Lanka. It was her rape at the age of fourteen and her family's slaughter by Indian soldiers that forced her to put aside thoughts of anything much but death.

Dhanu was not alone. Every time there was a call for suicide-mission volunteers, more than fifty young guerrillas applied. So many, in fact, that Prabhakaran created a martyrs' lottery. Everyone's name was put in a tombola drum and swirled around. Then, as the nervous young girls fiddled with the capsule of cyanide powder hanging from their necks, the Commander pulled out two names, read them out and the two joyful winners were carried on their comrade's shoulders. In May 1991, Dhanu's luck was in.

On the night of 21 May 1991, Dhanu was caught on camera as she approached forty-six-year-old Indian Prime Minister Rajiv Gandhi, cradling a sandalwood-flower garland as she strolled towards the greeting area in the Indian temple town of Srierumbudur near Madras. Dressed in robes of green and orange, her long hair held back from her youthful, pretty face, she was the picture of innocence.

Beneath her sari, Dhanu was wearing a brace of the kind usually associated with victims of back pain. But the back of the girdle was packed with sticks of cyclotrimethylenetrinitramine, a powerful plastic explosive used for demolition work, and about ten thousand two-millimetre steel balls. A power pack, two switches and the necessary circuitry were in front. One switch initiated the circuitry and the other activated the bomb. As soon as Dhanu saw Gandhi emerge from his car, she flicked the switch activating the circuitry. The plan was for her to place the garland over Gandhi's head and then flick the ignition switch as she bent down to kiss his feet.

Over two hundred people had already been killed in violent clashes during the election campaign, but Gandhi felt safe in Srierumbudur which was in Southern India, a Congress Party stronghold. The Prime Minister stepped out of his touring car and greeted the crowd of well-wishers. Though the itinerary had been hastily drafted, the town was electric with late-night festivities and a throng of ten thousand had turned out to welcome Gandhi. He made his way towards the temporary speaker's platform flanked by VIP and press enclosures, with a barricaded space for photographers in front.

Gandhi had been campaigning with little protection, in contrast to how things had been during his time as prime minister. His mother's assassination had made his vulnerability all too clear. For years he had worn a bulletproof vest and surrounded himself with security so tight that opponents had begun to ridicule him. Two weeks earlier, on 5 May, he had told a crowd: 'I used to campaign like this when I was Secretary-General of the Congress in 1984, but when I was Prime Minister I was hijacked by the system. There is still a threat, of course; it hasn't come down. But there is no choice. Either you campaign or you look after your security.'

Gandhi knew he was taking a risk. He had survived an assassination attempt in 1986 when a man had fired a home-made pistol at him while he was laying a wreath at the monument to the assassinated Mahatma Gandhi.

A scattering of lightly armed police did little to stop Gandhi from wading straight into the crowd before taking his place at the end of a red-carpeted greeting queue. People ran forward and started placing garlands over his head. At 10.20 p.m. Gandhi smiled at Dhanu as she handed him the garland. As she started to bend down Gandhi spotted the bomb. He dived forward, trying to grab the young assassin's arms.

A huge blast hit Gandhi in the face, blowing half of it away; it ripped into and scorched his torso, mutilating him beyond all recognition. Dhanu's head was blown clean off her shoulders: it sailed through the air and landed in the photographers' area. Her face remained unmarked. Nearby, a policewoman lay dead with both her legs severed, next to six of her colleagues, and a mortally wounded photographer lay on his back, his camera still in his hands.

Altogether, sixteen people were killed.

In the atrocity's immediate aftermath, Gandhi supporters on streets across India wanted to strike back but lacked clear-cut targets for their fury. Some chanted slogans blaming the CIA and called for an attack on the US embassy. Others randomly pointed to V.P. Singh one minute and the ultra-nationalist Bharatiya Janata Party the next.

Sonia Gandhi, forty-four, and her nineteen-year-old daughter Priyanka flew to Madras on an Indian Air Force plane to claim Rajiv's body. The rest of India was in shock. By government order, shops and offices remained closed, and security forces patrolled the capital. Voting, which had started the day before, was postponed for a month. In the wake of the assassination, twenty-six more people died in violent clashes. A week of national mourning was proclaimed, and Gandhi's body was laid to rest in state in Teen Murti House, the spacious dwelling that had been the residence of the colonial armed-forces chief under the British Raj.

With one blow, the fortunes of eight hundred and forty-four million people became hostage to a terrible uncertainty. Rajiv was the last standard-bearer of the Nehru–Gandhi line. Natwar Singh, a former deputy in Gandhi's Cabinet, said: 'What has this country of Buddha and Mahatma Gandhi come to? We were an example to the world. Now we are a warning.'

The desperation of the hour was vividly illustrated by the Congress Party's nomination of Gandhi's Italian-born and determinedly apolitical widow Sonia to the party presidency. Her polite refusal, returned within a day of the offer, forced the party to look within for the first non-descendant of Nehru, the first Prime Minister of India who had taken control of the country in 1947.

When the elections were eventually held, the Congress Party was swept back into power and eventually the country was placed in the safe hands of P.V. Narasimha Rao who successfully steered India through several crises over the next five years – he also ensured that Indian troops did not return to Sri Lanka.

The investigation into the crime got an early breakthrough when the film of the dead photographer was developed and Dhanu was identified as the bomber. From the photos, police calculated that five co-conspirators were present who were there to ensure that Dhanu went through with the assassination. One of them had survived. 'Nalini', a thirty-three-year old stenographer who later gave birth to her daughter in prison, proved to be the most vital link for the Special Investigation Team (SIT). Her signed confession gave the investigators all the evidence they needed to pursue those responsible.

The Tamil Tigers issued a press release denying any involvement but now the SIT had a name. A man called Sivarasan, known as 'One-Eyed Jack', had organised the operation, recruiting a nine-member team. Then, four days after the assassination, a radio operator from the Sri Lankan National Intelligence Bureau and an officer at the Department of Cryptology managed to decode a sudden flurry of radio messages that had been exchanged between Sivarasan and fellow Tigers in Sri Lanka. On 25 May Sivarasan was asked by a counterpart: 'Is the photo of Anbu (Dhanu) identifiable?' Names and locations were retrieved and an operation was mounted to capture One-Eyed Jack and the rest of the accomplices before they tried to leave India.

The SIT were given more time when a boat that the Tigers had sent to pick up Sivarasan sank in the sea off India's southern coast. After running from one hideout to another, Sivarasan and his co-conspirators took shelter in a hideout on the outskirts of Bangalore. At seven p.m. on 19 August 1991 the SIT and the commandos of the National Security Guard stormed the house. But by the time they got to them, the assassins were all dead. Sivarasan had shot himself in the head as he bit down on a cyanide capsule.

This was by no means the end of the Tamils' suicide bombing. Two years later Ranasinghe Premadasa, the Prime Minister of Sri Lanka, was blown up by a Black Tiger as he attended a May Day parade. By 2002, the Black Tigers accounted for around a third of all suicide attacks in the world.

Twenty-nine

Lady Macdeath

Assassinations are sometimes the sparks that start much larger events; the shootings of Shlomo Argov and Archduke Franz Ferdinand both kick-started long wars, for example. The following assassination was also a spark that lit a fire, a fire that had been carefully prepared by the victim's wife and which would claim the lives of hundreds of thousands of people.

A tiny fertile and hilly dot in the centre of Africa, Rwanda is home to rainforests, moors and savannah, interspersed with mighty, jagged volcanic mountains that tear into the clouds. The rocky escarpments, home to rare mountain gorillas (of Diane Fossey fame), act as boundaries between towns and small settlements where eucalyptus trees and banana plantations thrive in the rich soil.

In the spring of 1994 Rwanda, with the world's highest birth rate (each woman bore an average of 8.6 children; out of every one thousand children, 189 died before reaching five years of age), was the most densely populated country in Africa (eight million people). It was also on the brink of disaster. A drought that had plagued most of East Africa threatened almost half a million Rwandan lives and an on-and-off civil war – that had so far cost fifty thousand lives – between the majority ruling Hutus (roughly eighty-five per cent) and the minority Tutsis (fourteen per cent – there is a tiny minority of Pygmies as well) was threatening to reignite.

*

The first Tutsis who migrated to central Africa with their cattle, probably from the Nile, were tall and slim, with thin lips, high foreheads and aquiline noses. Though a minority, the Tutsis ruled the short, stocky Hutus, a farming people of Bantu ethnicity, under a medieval system known as *buhake*, offering protection in return for a share of Hutu crops and services. Eventually *buhake* became synonymous with servitude.

The Germans who colonised Rwanda in the late nineteenth century brought with them the philosophy of eugenics, which the Tutsis embraced. With the help of the Belgians who took control of Rwanda at the end of the First World War they created an apartheid-like system, collecting taxes from the Hutus, using forced-labour polices and introducing identity cards while the Tutsis were favoured in matters of education, commerce, government and security.

In 1959 the Hutus successfully revolted in a civil war that cost one hundred thousand lives, and by the time Rwanda gained its independence in 1962 they were firmly in control. The slaughters, which included the cutting-off of Tutsi feet to 'cut them down to size', prompted the English philosopher Bertrand Russell to call them 'the most horrible and systematic human massacre we have had occasion to witness since the extermination of the Jews by the Nazis'. Instead of abolishing the apartheid system, the Hutus simply swapped places with the Tutsis.

In 1994, the ruler of Rwanda was a Hutu, fifty-seven-year-old Juvenal Habyarimana, an aristocrat who had governed uninterruptedly since 1973. After graduating from school, he briefly studied medicine before entering the army's Officer Academy in Kigali in January 1960, graduating top of his year in December 1961. He rose rapidly through the ranks to become Army Chief of Staff in 1963 before entering the government in 1965 as Minister for the National Guard and the Police. He took power in a coup in 1973 after falling out with President Kayibanda and ruled in a virtual dictatorship.

Habyarimana, a monomaniacal strongman, bred a cult of personality by holding mass tribal-like ceremonies where dancers would perform spectacular routines, chanting his name for hours at a time while he watched from his throne, typically wearing a Western suit and dark glasses.

Habyarimana was re-elected on 19 December 1989 for a third term in office (he was the only candidate). In October 1990 (shortly after globe-trotting Pope John Paul II visited the deeply Catholic country) civil war broke out when the Tutsi Rwanda Patriotic Front (RPF) tried to overthrow Habyarimana. The war ended with a peace accord signed at Arusha, Tanzania, on 4 August 1993. Habyarimana was sworn in again as president on 5 January the following year, which marked the first stage of the peace accords setting out the creation of a transitional authority in Rwanda, including representatives of the RPF.

Habyarimana did all he could to stand in the way of the formation of a new democratic government in which the Tutsis would have a voice. Boutros Boutros-Ghali, then Secretary-General of the UN, told Habyarimana that unless he accepted the conditions of the peace accords, he would withdraw the UN peacekeepers and terminate UNAMIR (United Nations Assistance Mission for Rwanda) mission, which was costing the UN about half a million pounds per day. Habyarimana knew that there would come a point where he would have to cave in and, at a peace conference in Tanzania on 5 April 1994, he pledged to make all efforts to restore peace. But extremists within his government had other ideas.

The root of Habyarimana's power lay with his wife, Agathe Kanziga, a real Lady Macbeth figure. Kanziga came from an even more powerful aristocratic family than did her husband. Her network of in-laws was called the *Akazu* (the little house), a sort of sinister Mafia-type organisation, with a Cabinet, sometimes referred to as the *clan de madame*. They were the muscle behind the extremist Hutu power network. They also controlled the economy and the militia.

By 1993 the *Akazu*, determined to hold on to power, had put in place all the elements necessary for the genocide that would appear spontaneous and uncontrolled to outsiders: a propaganda machine that operated first through the press and national radio and later through a supposedly private radio station, *Radio Télévision Libre des Mille Collines* (RTLM); the organisation of militia groups, the most notorious of which was the thirty thousand-strong *Interahamwe* (those who attack together) – unemployed and uneducated youths recruited for £2 a day to help the army and presidential guard carry out massacres; supplies of arms and ammunition that had been distributed clandestinely and a network of committed administrative, military, and political leaders who were ready to lead the attack on the Tutsi minority.

All that remained was for the *clan de madame* to provide them with a good enough reason to begin the slaughter: it would have to be a truly catastrophic incident that would make the Hutu fear they were under attack. Kanziga had prepared the perfect event: the assassination of her husband.

As President Juvenal Habyarimana's private Falcon 50 jet (a gift from French Prime Minister Jacques Chirac) flew over Kigali on its return from Tanzania, soldiers on the ground busied themselves with a rarely used anti-aircraft weapon mounted on the back of a truck. The men took so long to get the missile ready for launch that the aircraft was already over Kigali and almost out of sight by the time it was fired.

The pilot fought for control of the aircraft as it dived towards the outskirts of the city before spotting a clear patch of open ground where he could attempt to crash-land: the gardens of Habyarimana's presidential palace. As Habyarimana's wife watched from the palace windows, the aircraft plunged nose first into the ground, just next to an ornamental pond. The plane exploded, lighting up the palace. Both Habyarimana and his neighbouring Head of State, Burundi's Cyprien Ntaryamira, were killed.

The next day, those close to Habyarimana, speaking on RTLM, immediately blamed the RPF for his death. Those in the villages outside Kigali did not need RTLM to tell them what was coming. As they travelled to the nation's shrinking rivers in search of fresh water, they watched as initially the blood, then the corpses of men and older boys, slain first as they tried to protect their wives, daughters and mothers, drifted past. A few minutes later came the bodies of the women, pulled from their hiding places and cut down. Finally came the dead babies who had been tossed in alive to drown on the journey downstream.

Bodies and body parts drifted by for half an hour or so – the time it took to wipe out a village, carry the inhabitants' bodies to the river's edge and throw them in. Then the waters cleared for a while, until the carcasses of more men and boys drifted into view. As village after village was cleared of Tutsis, the products of the massacres first congested and then poisoned the drought-stricken rivers of Rwanda.

In Kigali, guided by government troops, gangs of young thugs with clubs, machetes and spears rampaged through the capital, at first choosing their targets selectively, matching addresses with names on lists they carried. Then, exhilarated by their thoroughness, they began killing anyone they felt like killing. While the government-sponsored radio station RTLM exhorted 'Kill the Tutsis or they will kill you,' the organised gangs of marauders went street by street doing just that.

Hutu civilians were forced to murder their Tutsi neighbours by military personnel. Participants were often given incentives, such as money or food, and some were even told that they could appropriate the land of the Tutsis they killed.

Government-appointed Tutsis were among the first targets. After presidential guards surrounded the house of Prime Minister (and Tutsi) Agathe Uwilingiyimana, ten Belgian soldiers, part of the 2,400-member UN peacekeeping force charged with enforcing the truce between the government and the rebels, spirited her away. But the Hutu guards pursued them, disarmed the UN troops and assassinated the Prime Minister.

The Hutu guards were then told by their leaders that the Belgians, the best-trained and best-equipped troops in the UNAMIR force, had been complicit in the assassination of Habyarimana. The guards took the Belgians back to their barracks, cut their Achilles tendons so that they couldn't run away, and embarked on a horrific orgy of torture that only ended with the ten men choking to death on their own genitalia.

Two days after her husband's assassination Agathe Kanziga and thirty members of her *Akazu*, including the director of RTLM, were airlifted out of Rwanda by French troops. The French government then gave her 230,000 francs from a budget allocated for 'urgent assistance for Rwandan refugees'.

Seeing the situation in Rwanda deteriorating rapidly, Lieutenant-General Roméo Alain Dallaire pleaded for logistical support and reinforcements of two thousand soldiers for UNAMIR; he estimated that a total of four thousand well-equipped troops would give the UN enough leverage to put an end to the killings.

The UN Security Council refused, influenced by the new US President Bill Clinton (who had taken power from George H. Bush in 1992 after the latter reneged on his famous 'Read my lips. No . . . new . . . taxes' promise). America had been recently stung by a disastrous aid mission to Mogadishu in Somalia and, unlike the Congo, Rwanda held no strategic or mineral importance for the US.

Five days later Belgium withdrew its troops, as the extremists had hoped they would, and began exerting pressure on other members of the Security Council to remove the entire peacekeeping force. On 21 April the Security Council decided to remove all but two hundred and sixty of the UNAMIR soldiers who were then protecting some twenty thousand persons at risk, many of them Tutsi. Dallaire consolidated his contingent of Canadian, Ghanaian, Tunisian and Bangladeshi soldiers in urban zones and focused on providing areas of 'safe control'. His actions saved the lives of twenty thousand Tutsis.

Relief workers tried desperately to help where they could, but the fervour of the butchery grew too powerful, and people were dying too fast. Prison inmates were ordered to collect the corpses piling up in every corner of the capital. They came with caterpillar tractors and shovelled the bodies into mass graves, sometimes thousands at a time.

Without water or electricity and afraid to venture out for food, civilians huddled in their homes listening to the screams as the militia moved from house to house, slaying whomever they found. If one militiaman spotted a Tutsi family emerging from hiding and trying to flee, he blew his whistle and his comrades sealed off any escape.

The mayor of the southern town of Butare, married to a Tutsi, was offered a choice by Hutu peasants: he could save his wife and children if he gave up his wife's family – her parents and her sister – to be killed. He made the deal.

Seven Tutsi pastors, hiding in their Adventist church along with hundreds of members of their congregation, had been told that the Hutu militia would massacre them the next day. They wrote a letter to the president of the Adventist Church. 'Dear leader, we hope that you're well in these times that are so trying. We wish to inform you that tomorrow we will be killed with our families . . . we hope that you will intercede on our behalf and try to help us at this time, as a man of influence, as the president of the church, to go and talk to the mayor, to try and help stay the authorities who are planning to kill us.' The letter was successfully delivered to the Church president who then helped to organise their massacre – he was a Hutu.

The population grew so desperate that in a single twenty-four-hour period a quarter of a million people streamed across the border into Tanzania, creating an instant city, the second largest in the country. Sanitation was impossible: typhoid, dysentery, cholera were all menacing the refugees, especially the children. Malarial mosquitoes swarmed above the swamps. The dry cough of pneumonia and tuberculosis rasped through the camps.

One Red Cross doctor commandeered a partly built breeze-block structure and roofed it with blue plastic sheeting to make a hospital. More than seventy patients with bullet wounds and a hundred others with horrendous machete gashes arrived at the surgery each day.

Once the genocide began, the Tutsi RPF renewed its military offensive against the genocidal Hutu government, and managed to defeat the Hutu army in a series of bloody battles. In an incredible role reversal, two million Hutus fled from the vengeance of the RPF.

Fearing that these refugee movements would destabilise the whole region and by now horrified by the continued slaughter, the UN decided on 17 May to send an expanded peacekeeping force, UNAMIR II, to Rwanda. Because of bureaucratic delays at the UN and the lack of political will among most member states, the new force did not begin to arrive until August. Boutros Boutros-Ghali castigated the United Nations members, in particular its most powerful member and main financier, the United States, for its slowness in helping. 'During the Cold War, [the US was] ready to have its bombers flying twenty-four hours a day, which cost you one billion dollars a day. But [now] UN members will not agree to spend fifty million dollars to send troops on a mission to avoid conflict.'

By the time UNAMIR II started to touch down in Kigali, the RPF had already defeated the genocidal government. The new crisis was one not of war but of starvation and disease which killed fifty thousand predominantly Hutu refugees who had fled to neighbouring Zaire.

The genocide had lasted for a hundred days, beginning with the assassination of Habyarimana on 6 April. Between eight and ten thousand people were murdered each day – eventually more than ten per cent of the population. And with 3.2 million people turned into refugees, it was by far the biggest mass exodus in Africa's tragic history.

On 8 November 1994, the UN Security Council set up an International Criminal Tribunal for Rwanda, but the search for justice was a long and arduous one. About five hundred people were sentenced to death, while another 125,000 accused of aiding the genocide were held in overcrowded prisons. The impossibility of conducting 125,000 individual murder trials made any sort of justice unlikely. In February 2007, France rejected Agathe Kanziga Habyarimana's appeal for political asylum, stating that they now believed, thanks to a French investigation led by terrorism expert Jean Louis Bruguiere, that she was at the heart of the regime responsible for her husband's assassination and the ensuing genocide. If her appeal fails then she will be expelled from France, although not to Rwanda where she faces the death penalty – this is against French law. If she is forced to leave then French officials will have to find a country prepared to take her.

Thirty

Top Secret: The Exceptional Case Study

President Bill Clinton later described the US inaction in Rwanda as 'the biggest regret of my administration'. Classified documents made available through the Freedom of Information Act show that the Cabinet and almost certainly the President had been told of a planned 'final solution to eliminate all Tutsis' long before the slaughter reached its peak. The CIA's national intelligence daily, a secret briefing circulated to Clinton, the then Vice-President Al Gore, and hundreds of senior officials, included almost daily reports on Rwanda throughout the genocide.

In 1998 Clinton made his excuses for not acting quickly enough or immediately calling the crimes genocide: 'It may seem strange to you here, especially the many of you who lost members of your family, but all over the world there were people like me sitting in offices, day after day after day, who did not fully appreciate the depth and speed with which you were being engulfed by this unimaginable terror.'

Something else that President Clinton didn't appreciate in 1994 was the danger he was in from several lone assassins. Clinton, who as a young man had shaken the hand of President Kennedy five months before his assassination (an event that inspired young Bill to enter politics) once jokingly moaned: 'I haven't had one single attempt on my life since becoming President – all the great ones have faced an assassin, why not me?'

In 1994 his wish came true – seven times. It was a record-breaking year. On 12 September at 1.49 a.m., a Cessna airplane crashed into the south wall of the White House, killing the pilot, Frank Eugene Corder, but injuring no one else. On 29 October, Francisco Martin Duran fired twenty-nine rounds from a rifle when he thought he saw President Clinton standing among a group of men on the White House lawn. He was wrestled to the ground by two civilians before being arrested and sentenced to forty years in prison.

Then, in December 1994, there were five attacks mounted on the White House while Clinton was present. On the morning of 17 December four shots were fired from a 9mm handgun at Clinton's bedroom. On 20 December an individual wielding a knife ran towards the White House – Secret Service officers shot him dead. The next day, a man who had previously been identified as being a probable threat to the President breached the Southwest Gate of the White House but was soon captured. Two incidents occurred on 23 December. In the morning a Secret Service officer recovered a 9mm handgun from a 'suspicious individual' near the White House. Later the same day, a man parked his car next to the South Lawn of the White House and ran from the vehicle, leaving the motor running. As the man sprinted away, officers approached him. He told them that the car contained a bomb, a statement that turned out to be untrue.

This series of attacks on the White House by a bunch of disturbed lone would-be assassins led to a Security Review. Gradually the review grew to become an in-depth analysis of the role of the Secret Service as well as a detailed examination of all of the assassination attempts on US presidents that had occurred over the previous twenty years. The extreme sensitivity of the material contained in the ensuing Classified Report meant that only two copies were ever printed. Some of the information that the Review gathered was deemed so sensitive that it was in fact never printed and was reported to President Clinton only via oral briefings. The contents list many dozens of attempts on the lives of presidents which the public has never been – nor is ever likely to be – told about.

In addition to the Classified Report, the Secret Service conducted its own secret eight-year study of assassinations and attempted assassinations on US presidents and other public figures which was concluded in August 2000. The classified study, called *The Exceptional Case Study Project*, began after several close calls, which have been kept secret for a number of reasons. (All sorts of unrelated but classified and sometimes embarrassing facts tend to emerge in assassination investigations and the report reveals just how vulnerable the President really is.) Fortunately permission has been given to relate some of them here and to reveal for the first time the Secret Service's own findings about lone-wolf assassins.

The American Secret Service (the agency entrusted with the President's life) receives around five hundred or so lone-wolf threats each month. The Intelligence Division of the Secret Service examines each threat and decides which ones are potentially serious (usually somewhere between twenty-five and forty per month) and then field agents are despatched to investigate the individual/s involved, who are known as QI (Quarterly Investigation) subjects. Secret Service agents have established ongoing relationships with suspects across the US, sometimes arranging counselling or psychiatric care; a key factor in preventing the lone assassin from striking. A psychotherapist often helps agents analyse the potential assassin's delusions in an attempt to discover whether they are likely to carry out an attack.

During the early 1980s, the Secret Service successfully prevented four 'close-call' assassination attempts, not including that of Hinckley. (For example, in 1984 David Mahonski, who had made threats against President Reagan, was under surveillance by both the FBI and the Secret Service when he charged the White House with a sawn-off shotgun – sharpshooters disabled him and he was arrested. On the day that Reagan was sworn in for his second term, Robert Latta managed to enter the White House carrying an overnight bag while posing as a member of the Marine Band – he remained in the Executive Mansion for fifteen minutes before he was captured.) Many would-be assassins have struck dozens of times against American Presidents since then.

One of the cases featured 'JD', who struck not long after Hinckley, in 1982. Until he had a breakdown, JD was an ambitious medical student. While at medical school he began hearing voices: voices which he believed were aliens. The aliens gave him a choice: kill children or assassinate the President. If he didn't, they would poison him. JD got hold of a .38 and began stalking President Reagan disguised as a detective. Agents tried to get hold of JD for three years but his transient, cash-only life made finding him very difficult. He robbed several banks to cover his costs, changing cars and weapons so often that he was never linked to more than one robbery. JD didn't fire a single shot during the robberies; he claimed he was able to 'instil such fear' into the cashier that they would do anything he wanted. JD was picked up with his gun at a Presidential appearance, the details of which the Secret Service are not prepared to reveal. However, they do say that JD was unable to shoot the President because he was unable to penetrate the close protection team.

As part of their training, agents are shown a film of JD being interviewed. It's important for them to understand that assassins can often look and behave no differently from other people. It's also vital to realise that while the logic behind someone's decision to assassinate the President might be very obviously flawed, the logic in their strategy of the act of planning and carrying out the assassination is usually pretty flawless. Although JD, for example, was clearly mentally unbalanced he planned very carefully for the attack: 'I bought the suit, the shoes,' he told the agents. 'And bought a trench coat and had a hair cut. And then, I went north up above Flint, [Michigan] because I was looking for a location where I could test fire the gun.' This paradox is seen time and again in lone assassins in America and across the world, throughout history, from Tsafendas in South Africa to Peter Kocan in Australia, whose story is described on page 338.

For the *Exceptional Case Study Report* (ECSP), agents

interviewed eighty-three people who had come close to assassinating a US president or prominent US figure over the past fifty years. Among those they spoke to were Arthur Bremer, Mark Chapman and John Hinckley. Based on these interviews, agents are now taught that their gunman is probably suicidal and convinced that he has nothing to lose after suffering a set of negative experiences: emotional reversals, financial reversals, unhappy family situations and sometimes child abuse. They tend to see assassination as an acceptable way and possibly a successful way to resolve whatever desperation, whatever problem they are struggling with.

Agents asked Mark Chapman whether, if John Lennon had died a few days earlier – for example, in a car accident – would he, Chapman, have stalked someone else? 'I can't answer that question,' said Chapman. 'I don't know. I was so bonded with John Lennon at that point . . . I'd probably be crushed . . . I don't know what I would have done.' Although many lone assassins seem to switch targets, they almost always create an imaginary bond with their intended victim.

Attacks on public officials are not impulsive actions. They typically occur after weeks or months of planning. Understanding this 'pathway to attack' is the key to stopping assassins before they strike. Mounting an attack on a prominent person requires a number of preparatory decisions and activities; most assassins execute similar plans and often share similar motives. A potential assassin must choose a target, learn where the target is going to be, choose and secure a weapon, survey security, develop an attack plan, and consider whether and/or how to escape.

Although not every ECSP attacker and near-attacker engaged in all these activities and behaviours, most engaged in several of them. Not one of the assassins ever sent a direct threat to their intended target. Most, however, told someone close to them something about their plans. Many spent months or years planning. Some tried to learn about previous assassins. A few wrote to their predecessors. Many switched targets.

Lone-wolf assassins rarely show remorse. They are, however,

generally interested in explaining their acts and claiming to have played a historic role – fame and immortality appear to be their primary motivation. They are engaged primarily in psychodrama rather than political drama. It makes no difference to them whether their victim belongs to the left or the right. Arthur Bremer, who crippled George Wallace, previously considered killing Wallace's political opposite George McGovern. John Hinckley Jr stalked President Carter during the 1980 campaign until he realised that Carter was going to lose the election. Lee Harvey Oswald shot at General Edwin Walker, a right-wing fanatic, before killing President Kennedy. Giuseppe Zangara, who took aim at President Franklin D. Roosevelt in 1933 (accidentally killing the mayor of Chicago) said he would just as soon have killed Herbert Hoover.

Marina Oswald, the Russian wife of Lee Harvey, told reporters: 'He want to be popular, so everyone know who is Lee Harvey Oswald.' Oswald's mother, Marguerite, emanated maternal pride in her son's action: '. . . And let me tell you this: Mr Johnson should also remember that I am not just anyone, and that he is only President of the United States by the grace of my son's action . . . I am an important person. I understand that I will go down in history too.'

Sirhan Sirhan felt he had surpassed himself by killing Robert F. Kennedy and was happy to die, knowing that the world knew who he, Sirhan, was: 'They can gas me, but I am famous: I have achieved in one day what it took Robert Kennedy all his life to do.' At his first parole hearing Mark Chapman said that he had shot John Lennon to gain attention, 'to steal John Lennon's fame'. He said: 'In some ways I'm a bigger nobody than I was before because, you know, people hate me.' John Hinckley Jr told psychologists: 'I was desperate in some bold way to get . . . attention.'

Giuseppe Zangara went quietly to the electric chair but lost his composure when he saw that no photographers were there to record the scene. Lynette 'Squeaky' Fromme's attempt to shoot President Gerald Ford was equivalent to a little girl stamping her foot. Fromme, a disciple of the infamous killer Charles Manson, said:

'When people around you treat you like a child and pay no attention to the things you say, you have to do something.' Her gun was grabbed by a Secret Service agent before she could fire it at the President. And although Sara Jane Moore, who tried to shoot Ford less than three weeks later, cried 'I'm no Squeaky Fromme!' she also wanted attention, saying during her trial: 'I knew I was rapidly reaching a point that all avenues of taking action were being closed off . . . there comes a point when the only way you can make a statement is to pick up a gun.' Fortunately, although Moore picked up a gun, she was unable to shoot straight thanks to the prompt action of the man standing next to her, a Vietnam veteran who deflected the pistol.

The diarist Arthur Bremer was clearly after fame: 'If I killed him wearing a sweatty tee-shirt some of the fun and Glamore would definently be worn off . . . I won't even rate a TV enteroption in Russia or Europe when the news breaks – they never heard of Wallace. If something big in Name flares up I'll end up at the bottom of the 1st page in America. The editors will say "Wallace dead? Who cares." '

Rigoberto Lopez envisioned glorious tyrannicide and a martyr's death when he shot the seventeen-stone dictator of Nicaragua, Anastasio 'Tacho' Somoza, dead. He was convinced that his poems and letter of confession would go down in his country's history.[25]

When Valerie Solanas was asked why she shot Andy Warhol, her response was: 'I have lots of reasons. Read my manifesto and it will tell you who I am.' James Earl Ray imagined living abroad and writing a book about his shooting of Martin Luther King. Almost all the lone assassins who attempted to kill a US President

[25] Lopez's poetry never achieved the immortality he hoped for, but in the days following Somoza's death, a newspaper offered a hundred and forty dollars for the best verse of homage to the dead dictator. The winning entry was fourteen lines of flowery verse ('Renowned paladin and cavalier/Glory of America!'). Nicaraguans, by and large, read it with little interest, but here and there a face lit up with malicious appreciation. *Novedades*'s editors ran the poem for several days - until they too noticed that the first letters of the fourteen lines spelled out the name of Tacho's assassin: Rigoberto Lopez.

studied the methods of their predecessors. (They also read the literature: *The Day of the Jackal* by Frederick Forsyth has been found in the possession of several famous lone wolves and, as reported earlier, one group of ETA terrorists even went to see the film of the book while planning to take out Prime Minister Luis Carrero Blanco.)

One would-be assassin who eventually wrote a book based on his experience was Peter Raymond Kocan. Kocan, who shot Australian Labour Party Leader Arthur Calwell at point-blank range (Calwell survived), said: 'I wanted to make myself feel real' and claimed that he was a disaffected youth who had slipped through the net. 'That's the tragedy,' he argued. 'If some sort of genuine help had turned up, things might have been different.' Kocan's advice to someone in a similar state of mind would be: 'Don't panic and don't despair, because time takes care of a lot of things.' But advice alone isn't enough. 'Something has to enter deeply in their life,' he said. In his case, it was discovering literature. As Arthur Bremer told the judge the day he was sentenced: 'Looking back on my life, I would have liked it if society had protected me.'

Although most lone assassins tend to be in their twenties, there are some notable exceptions. Seventeen-year-old Marcus Serjeant tried to shoot Queen Elizabeth II during the Trooping the Colour ceremony near Buckingham Palace in 1982. Flanked by Prince Charles and Prince Philip, the Queen fought to control her horse as the young assassin fired a series of shots before he was wrestled to the ground by guardsmen and police. Serjeant said he wanted to kill the Queen 'to be famous'.

Seventy-three-year-old Richard Pavlick was older but no wiser. The pensioner's 1960 attempt to blow up his car within range of John F. Kennedy came from a bizarre personal hatred, coupled with the fact that people weren't taking his complaints seriously. He had hoped, however, that he would find fame in his death, not in his failure. Pavlick was about to detonate his home-made bomb as the President left church but became 'morally squeamish' when he saw that JFK's wife and children were with him. After his arrest, he told police: 'In a way, I'm glad it's turned out the way it has. But I don't like the publicity.'

Byron de la Beckwith, the assassin of Medgar Evers, was a racist with a starved ego, the sad end of the line of a family who could still recall their former glory days and their friendship with a president.

Both Dimitrios Tsafendas and Samuel Byck were medically insane but they also wanted attention, someone to address their problems; in their confused mental state, they had no idea from where it could come. Byck hoped to become a hero in his death, an avenger of his family break-up and failure in business which he blamed on Nixon. The fact that he wrote letters explaining his motives to a hodgepodge of celebrities and intellectuals showed how he needed the world to understand what he had done. Tsafendas spent several years in and out of countless institutions on what seemed to be the careless whim of psychiatrists before he finally struck out in a way that would guarantee him lifelong confinement in a mental institution and the attention that he felt he needed.

For some reason, lone assassins tend to be predominantly American. This may be at least in part due to Americans' ease of access to guns (which are by far the assassin's weapons of choice). In 1968, psychiatrist Robert Coles remarked: 'Every psychiatrist has treated patients who were thankful that guns were not around at one time or another in their lives.' All the lone assassins described here had easy access to, or already owned, guns. Most were young, male and white, failures and drifters, unloved and unloving. Often they were sexually dissatisfied and had little contact with women. Ordinary murderers often come from violent homes or were violent as youngsters. But lone-wolf assassins are deceptively calm, even passive. They are ordinary, shy, well behaved, often mousy loners, whose efforts to control themselves succeed – until their internal pressures explode in an assassination attempt.

Most lone-wolf assassins seem to have been the equivalent of 'model prisoners' in their own families, dominated by an overbearing, financially successful parent. (Hinckley, Bremer, Wallace, Sirhan, Moore, Fromme all had overly dominant fathers.) They tend to be unable to express themselves or let out their normal aggressive and sexual feelings. When the demons inside finally burst through, an ordinary victim would not be sufficient to satisfy their twisted impulses. The target has to be as far above the average citizen as the parent was above the assassin-son.

Many of the killers and would-be killers studied in this book zigzagged from city to city, stalking their targets, often drawing close, then pulling away, expressing in their frantic movements a personality threatened with disintegration. Oswald travelled to the Soviet Union, New Orleans and Mexico; Chapman moved from Tennessee to Atlanta to Honolulu and New York; Bremer and Hinckley both got together whatever money they could and criss-crossed the USA, chasing their destiny.

Lacking in self-esteem, many created new identities, weaving themselves into heroes and celebrities – Bremer, for example, imagined himself as the son of actress Donna Reed. Sara Jane Moore thought of herself as a magazine cover-girl. The film *Taxi Driver* wove together many themes found in the lives of American assassins. In it, a taxi driver (played by Robert De Niro), obsessed with shooting a political candidate and protecting a young prostitute (Jodie Foster), beset by aggressive urges as well as sexual ones (coded in the film as a pure-hearted defence of a prostitute), finds an acceptable resolution: he spares the candidate and instead shoots the girl's pimp and one of her Johns, thus symbolically killing his lust and emerging in his own eyes as something of a hero.

De Niro's character was based on Bremer who in the run-up to his assassination attempt tried and failed to emotionally and sexually bond with a young prostitute. After seeing the film, Hinckley became obsessed with Jodie Foster: after Foster understandably refused his confused advances, Hinckley wrote her a letter saying that he was going to assassinate Reagan as proof of his love for her. Unfortunately for Reagan, there was to be no pimp to turn Hinckley into a 'hero'.

Interestingly, the profiles of these assassins match the profiles of spree killers (people who go on a sudden murderous rampage).

Several lone wolves considered spree killing as an option. Bremer toyed with the idea of hijacking an armoured truck, parking it at a busy intersection and then shooting as many people as possible from its slit windows. Hinckley considered a mass shooting on the Yale campus and in the US Senate. Oswald considered becoming a serial sniper, Sara Jane Moore talked about going on a 'shooting spree' and Neo-Nazi Joe Franklin was already a serial sniper who shot up to three people at a time before he attacked Larry Flynt.

American spree killers often threaten, try to, or make it known that they would like to assassinate the President of the United States. According to the wife of spree killer James Huberty, her extremely bitter husband was a potential assassin. Huberty raged against both Presidents Carter and Reagan during his 1984 rampage at a San Ysidro McDonald's where he killed twenty-one people. (He blamed Carter especially for the loss of his job and investments.) Twenty-three-year-old Mark Essex, who shot nineteen people from a hotel rooftop in 1973, wanted to assassinate President Richard Nixon and had written 'Kill pig Nixon and all his running dogs' on his bedroom wall.

Several factors decided the actions that these people ultimately took. Getting a gun was no problem; it was getting close to the President that proved difficult logistically (Bremer was unable to penetrate Richard Nixon's ring of security), sometimes financially, sometimes because of the time it would take and the distance that needed to be covered. But it also depended on the speed of an assassin's mental breakdown and the growth of their rage.

The fact that lone-wolf assassins are such misfits, failures who are so utterly the antithesis of what is perceived to be the professional assassin, gives impetus to conspiracy theories, credible and fantastic alike – and everybody seems to have one. In the aftermath of Hinckley's attempted assassination of Reagan, a fourteen-year-old pupil at a junior high school in Washington DC was asked for her view of the assassination attempt. She thought for a moment and said: 'It is a plot by Vice-President Bush to get into power. If Bush becomes President, the CIA would be in charge of the country.' It seems incredible that a man like Hinckley, lonely, physically weak, mentally unbalanced, socially incompetent, unintelligent – the complete opposite of the President of the United States – could possibly conceive and execute a plan to assassinate arguably the most successful and powerful person in the world.

The same, of course, goes for Lee Harvey Oswald, Arthur Bremer, Sirhan Sirhan and James Earl Ray but, with little proof to support them, only circumstance and conjecture, such speculations have now been discounted. Ray, for example, retracted his original confession when he found that the initial interest in him melted away and spent the next thirty years misleading investigators by crying conspiracy for which no proof exists.

The lone-wolf assassin is, then, generally male, in his twenties, a drifter, unremarkable and well behaved. He is likely to be shy and inarticulate, sexually frustrated, dominated by a successful parent and unable to sustain a relationship. Their shyness masks an overly inflated ego: in the lone wolf's mind he is a hero with a great destiny. In reality he is in need of some psychological help (although it is important to note that the vast majority of assassins do not have a mental disorder such as schizophrenia). His apparent ordinariness is misleading; it allows him to blend into a crowd, the perfect cover for such an operation. He is likely to keep a diary or write letters and have easy access to guns. He will generally choose targets by fame and importance rather than by politics and beliefs.

Lone-wolf assassins (and spree killers) need to make a statement, to be taken seriously. What they want is a truly spectacular public event, an act so vile, so out of proportion, that it and they will be remembered as most momentous public events have been since 1963. They are taking a shot at the title, reaching for a notorious immortality.

Thirty-one

The Enemy Within

While in 1995 the Secret Service were toasting their success at keeping US presidents, especially the current incumbent, safe since 1981, a lone assassin, in what turned out to be one of the most depressingly straightforward assassinations of the late twentieth century, struck in an attack which had devastating consequences for the Middle East Peace Process, something that Bill Clinton had fought so hard to achieve.

On 13 September, 1993, as Prime Minister Yitzhak Rabin stepped on to the White House lawn, he was wrestling with a difficult conundrum. That morning, he had already achieved the impossible, but now he was seconds away from the unthinkable – shaking the hand of Yasser Arafat, a man who had dedicated much of his life to planning, financing and inspiring hundreds of attacks on Jewish men, women and children.

Rabin's reluctance was clear and he wore a painful grimace as President Bill Clinton raised his arms to the two men's shoulders as if to physically push them into an embrace. Rabin took Arafat by the hand. 'Of all the hands in the world, it was not the hand I wanted or even dreamed of touching,' he said later. As it was, that handshake, as difficult as it may have been, marked his place in history and won him (along with Arafat) the Nobel Prize for Peace the following year.

Two years later, in a rare moment of elation, the normally reserved Rabin tucked a paper with the lyrics to *Shir Ha-Shalom*, the Song of Peace, into his breast pocket. He had just sung along with 250,000 people who had come to Kings of Israel Square in the heart of Tel Aviv to celebrate and support his fight for peace. 'There are enemies of the peace process, and they try to hurt us,' he had told the crowd. 'But violence undermines democracy and must be denounced and isolated...there is no painless way forward for Israel, but the way of peace is preferable to the way of war.'

To his people, Rabin was either a hero for bringing peace to the Middle East or a traitor for giving land away to the Palestinians. Yigal Amir, a 25-year-old right-wing Jewish militant definitely believed Rabin belonged in the latter category. Amir, a quiet, modestly-mannered law student, was one of eight children raised in an Orthodox family in the town of Herzliyya, north of Tel Aviv. The only thing that got him riled was the subject of peace with the Arabs and he mixed with members of the right-wing group called *Eyal*, also known as the Fighting Jews. He repeatedly told friends that he felt he had to do something to stop the peace process; he believed that if he killed Rabin, then peace with Palestine would die with him.

His friends dismissed Amir's words as an empty threat. But Amir had already tried twice; once at a ceremony at a sacred memorial to the Holocaust (Rabin cancelled the visit at the last moment after an Islamic Jihad suicide bomb at an Israeli bus station) and again at a highway dedication, but was unable to penetrate the Prime Minister's security detail.

On the night of 3 November 1995, Amir took out his 9mm Beretta from among his few treasured possessions (which included a copy of Frederick Forsyth's *The Day of the Jackal*) and loaded it with a combination of dumdum bullets that had been made by his brother. He tucked the pistol into his belt, covered it with his shirt and boarded a bus to the Kings of Israel Square. Once there, he found that the security was so bad that he was able to access the VIP parking area; even a Shin Bet (Israel's counter-terrorism unit) agent who spotted him assumed he was a plain-clothes detective. Yigal, with his skullcap tucked into his back pocket, small, slight and curly-haired, was obviously not an Arab, so posed no threat. Only two weeks previously, Rabin had said: 'A Jew will never kill another Jew' and most Israelis believed it.

When the rally ended, Rabin, along with Deputy Prime Minister Shimon Peres, walked off the podium and down a stairway leading to a sheltered area where an armoured Cadillac awaited him. Peres and his bodyguards continued on their way past Yigal Amir, standing hidden in the shadow of a stairwell.

Rabin, meanwhile, turned back to say a few words to the organisers of the event, telling them that it was one of the happiest days of his life. Back on the main stage, the security team congratulated themselves on a job well done, relieved that Islamic radicals had not attacked the rally. Meanwhile Rabin was descending the stairs to the exit where hundreds of supporters, mostly teenagers, were shouting 'Peace, peace' and 'We're with you.' The PM waved at them and started down the stairs with four bodyguards behind him and one up front. His wife, Leah, was following behind at a slightly slower pace as her husband took the final few steps towards the open door of his car.

As Rabin reached the door, Amir, now only three paces away from the PM's left, raised his Beretta and ran right up to Rabin's back and fired three times from point-blank range, yelling at the same time: 'It's nothing, they're not real bullets! They're blanks. It's not real!' Rabin turned towards his assailant and pitched forward, only to be scooped up by his nearest bodyguard – who had been hit in the shoulder by the third bullet – and forced into the back of the Cadillac which immediately screeched away.

Amir was bundled against a wall by police officers, disarmed and marched off; one officer had his arm firmly hooked around the assassin's throat. The attack had happened so quickly that no one was sure if Rabin had been injured.

Inside the car Rabin's driver shouted: 'Prime Minister, are you hurt?'

'Yes, yes,' the PM replied.

'Where does it hurt you?'

'In my back, it's not so bad.'

At that point, Rabin fell unconscious. While his bodyguard tried to give him first aid, the driver, who had not been briefed on the best escape routes, tried to find his way to Ichilov Hospital. Dodging the crowds that had spilled out from Freedom Square added precious seconds to the journey. As he tried to make the final right turn into the hospital he was slowed by a police roadblock. The hospital had not yet been alerted and only a lone security guard was there to greet them. The bodyguard and the driver lifted Rabin out of the car as the security guard went to fetch a stretcher and together they crashed through the hospital doors screaming: 'The prime minister is hurt! Come and help him!' The doctors came running.

Like so many political leaders, Rabin had always refused to wear a bulletproof vest and so the hollow-point dumdum bullets had torn his chest apart. One ruptured his spleen; the other severed major arteries in his chest and shattered his spinal cord. By the time the doctors started to try and repair the damage, Rabin's heart had already pumped air into his brain, causing irreparable damage. Nine minutes later, he was dead.

Yigal Amir might have acted alone but he had many supporters, not all of them Jewish militants. Mohammed Zahhar, a leader of the terrorist organisation Hamas, said: 'He [Rabin] practised all forms of violence against us. I'm joyful because he was punished.' And in Beirut the Hizbollah television station showed film of locals celebrating 'the death of the Zionist criminal Rabin', as a news anchor described him to viewers. When the station – *Al Manar* (The Lighthouse) – showed footage of an Israeli TV journalist weeping, the anchor laughed out loud.

The assassination dealt a terrible, humiliating blow to Shin Bet. Its head, known only by his Hebrew initial *Kaf*, acknowledged a complete security breakdown as Rabin had descended from the podium at the end of the peace rally. Though close to twenty protective agents were present, Rabin was not cocooned within a ring of bodyguards facing in and out, nor was his back adequately shielded. No one had prevented Amir from hanging around the parking area where Rabin's car had been waiting. Although Shin Bet knew that Rabin had received death threats, they did not noticeably tighten their procedures at the giant public rally.

Many conspiracy theories were floated after the assassination, most of them involving Shin Bet. But an official investigation revealed that while the security service's performance had been very inferior, there was no evidence to support a plot. Amir repeatedly and proudly told investigators that he had acted alone, claiming that he had 'received instructions from God to kill Prime Minister Rabin'. On 27 March 1996 a three-judge panel found twenty-five-year-old Yigal Amir guilty of the murder of Yitzhak Rabin and sentenced him to life in prison. Amir responded by shouting, 'The State of Israel is a monstrosity!'

Amir was probably satisfied with what he accomplished by his assassination of Rabin. The peace process faltered under Shimon Peres and then vanished entirely when, after his security services failed to prevent a series of terrorist attacks, Peres lost the 1996 general election to Benjamin Netanyahu, who opposed the peace negotiations. Only when Netanyahu lost the 1999 election to Ehud Barak was hope renewed that peace might yet be won. But as Barak's government collapsed in 2001 there was good reason to doubt that the peace process instigated by Rabin and Arafat would ever be completed.

Thirty-two

Operation Certain Death

This is the story of what was probably the boldest assassination attempt by an organised squad since the young would-be assassin Saddam Hussein struck in Baghdad in 1953. It is an amazing story, partly because the target was Hussein's son and the action took place in the same city close to the same street in which the country's history had been changed forty-three years earlier. The assassins were desperate, totally committed to their cause, and they knew that this operation would mean certain death. But as with many such attacks things took an unpredictable turn, leading to a terrifying series of murders.

The golden Porsche sped down Baghdad's most exclusive street, a thoroughfare lined with fashionable shops and bars The expensive car's driver was unaware that four adrenalin-fuelled assassins armed with AK-47s, pistols and grenades were waiting to terminate him with extreme prejudice.

Five hundred metres away, assassin Salman Sharif knew that he was probably only a few minutes from death. He checked his watch. It was just after seven p.m. on 12 December 1996. From where he was sitting in a busy ice-cream parlour he could see his accomplices standing by their parked car, eating ice cream. The AK-47s, two spare magazines and six grenades in a sports bag were on the passenger seat. Sharif peered over the top of his paper. Hidden among the shoppers in Baghdad's most exclusive street were expertly trained, heavily armed bodyguards and undercover policemen, all of whom were ready to die trying to protect the man in the golden Porsche. He had to be careful.

Sharif slipped his hand into his jacket pocket and released the safety catch of his gun. Months of planning had led to this moment: it would be their only chance to eliminate one of the most evil, most feared men in the world. He had to focus and get the job done. Whatever happened after Sharif and his comrades had emptied their weapons' magazines didn't matter – the utter destruction of their target was more important than their own survival.

Twenty-seven-year-old Sharif did not look like an assassin. Wearing inconspicuous clothes, large spectacles and affecting a shy attitude, he resembled a primary schoolteacher. A Shiite Muslim who had suffered from lifelong persecution by the ruling Baath Party, Sharif had leaped at the chance to join the armed resistance group while still a student in the small, impoverished desert town of Shatra in 1990.

When the Americans invaded Iraq in 1991, Sharif joined the Shiite uprising, and helped take control of Shatra, expecting the support of the United States Army. But none came. The Shiites held off the Iraqi army for three weeks until, low on ammunition and near starvation, they were overwhelmed.

Sharif escaped capture and fled to the safety of the marshes near Basra, where those resistance fighters lucky enough to have evaded the wrath of Saddam Hussein formed the 15 Shaaban movement, named after the day of the Shiite uprising (Shaaban is the name of one of the twelve lunar months on the Islamic calendar, as is Ramadan).

Sharif lived constantly on the run for the next five years, leading one of his movement's secret mobile base-camps, which was built at each new location using dry reeds. They frequently moved camp to escape detection by the Iraqi Army, travelling by canoe through the thick marsh vegetation from one reed hut to another.

Then, in 1996, 15 Shaaban changed tack. Instead of trying to kill regional Baath Party leaders and local officials, they decided to aim at the heart of the regime, targeting its most senior leaders. The idea, explained Hussein Hamza, leader of 15 Shaaban (which has since transformed itself into a political party), was 'to weaken the regime, to undermine its foundations and to create a state of chaos. And we wanted to encourage people to rise up against the government.'

Sharif was given a key role. Hamza asked him to take control of the group's Baghdad cells and handed him a list of targets. Top of the list was Uday Hussein. Sharif wasn't surprised. Uday was hated and feared by everybody: he was the obvious target.

Born in 1964, Uday was Saddam's eldest and favourite son. He was also an ultra-violent sadist and totally deranged psychopath with limitless funds and almost no legal restraints. He was the playboy from hell. Uday had an insatiable appetite for beautiful women, all of whom would emerge from his chambers physically and emotionally scarred – if they could still walk at all.

Ala Bashir was the Hussein family's personal physician from 1983 until 2003, when he escaped from Iraq. He would often have to patch up the abused women whom Uday left in his bed each morning: 'Several times I treated female party-goers who came to my clinic having been knifed, disfigured by burning cigarettes.'

Those women who failed to please Uday had the word 'shame' branded on their buttocks. According to Latif Yahia, who was Uday's body double for five years, a fifteen-year-old deaf girl was raped first by Uday and then by his security guards. When she tried to communicate to her family what had happened Uday had her executed. He also almost beat to death a children's TV presenter before having his bodyguards throw her from his helicopter into a lake.

In another incident, while in a drunken rage and waving a new toy, a Jackhammer 'Terminator' pump-action shotgun, Uday shot two uncles and killed three innocent party-goers at an Iraqi yacht club. 'Friends' who displeased him were either dropped into an empty swimming pool full of ferocious Alsatians or, if they were lucky, got to spend a few weeks in the one-and-a-half-metre-cubed concrete cells he had specially built for this purpose.

Uday ran Iraq's Olympic committee in much the same style. At the entrance to his first-floor offices in the Football Association, he kept a seven-foot-tall Iron Maiden. The inside was stained with blood and the nails were worn blunt. Athletes who were not up to Uday's gold-medal standards were beaten with iron bars, caned on the soles of their feet and chained to walls where they were left to stay in contorted positions for days. He also ordered them dragged across pavements until their backs were bloody, then dunked in sewage to ensure that the wounds became infected.

Yahia will never forget witnessing Uday's torture of an Iraqi boxer who had been knocked out in the first round of a Gulf States competition. He was beaten, electrocuted, and sliced with a cut-throat razor before being taken to the basement of the Olympic building to be shot.

In 1988, Uday killed his father's valet with a specially adapted German-made nightstick combined with a stiletto blade and an electric cattle-prod. After this, Saddam sent his troublesome son to Switzerland where he stayed with Saddam's half-brother, Barzan Al-Tikritti, who looked after the Hussein family billions and bought weapons for the Iraqi army.

Uday was almost immediately expelled by the Swiss government after threatening to stab someone in a restaurant: he was in a bad mood after gambling away five million dollars of his father's money in a French casino. Saddam Hussein welcomed Uday back to Iraq as if nothing had happened and made him Head of the Olympic Committee and one of his myriad security organisations.

Needless to say, Uday's sudden death would be met with great celebration, especially as Saddam's own popularity was at an all-time low. Not since the social and economic downturn of the 1980s had the Iraqis found themselves in such straitened circumstances. Although the country had stabilised, the past sixteen years had seen two wars, internal strife and UN sanctions which had drained the people of their energy. Poverty, hunger, sickness and prostitution were rife.

It was not long after he arrived in Baghdad that Sharif heard of Uday's regular Thursday-night trawls for pretty girls in Mansour, an upscale part of town where he was notorious for forcing young women to accompany him back to one of his palaces. For the next two months Sharif strolled along the crowded streets of Mansour each Thursday evening, the night before the Muslim weekend, and, sure enough, every Thursday at about seven p.m. Uday would kerb-crawl along the main drag. This would be by far the best chance for Sharif to assassinate Uday, especially as the dictator's son preferred to pick up women without his bodyguards. Plus, although Uday could afford limitless sports cars, he never considered fitting them with bulletproof windows.

By keeping his eyes open and by making friends with some of the neighbourhood shopkeepers, Sharif learned which of the street peddlers were regime informers, which traffic policemen were really secret-police officers, which buildings housed government offices, and which of the regular passers-by wandering up and down the pavement were actually security men. He didn't tell anyone about his plan until he was a hundred per cent certain that it was feasible. Eventually he travelled south, slipped into the marshes, and presented his findings to the 15 Shaaban movement's leadership. They gave him the go-ahead.

Sharif selected three competent men who would make up the hit squad under his leadership. 'The team members were very happy: they said they felt lucky to have been chosen for such an operation even though it meant certain death. Everybody from all sides, all political and religious groups in Iraq hated Uday,' said Hamza. They rented a safe house in Baghdad, bought a getaway car, and smuggled guns and grenades up from the marshes into the capital.

One of the team, known by his code name Abu Zahrar, would drive the getaway car. Sharif, who went by the name Abu Ahmed, would give the go-ahead signal and would shoot any bodyguards who might be accompanying Uday, or any undercover officers in the street. Abu Sadeq and Abu Sajad would carry out the actual assassination.

On the appointed day, seven o'clock found the hit men eating ice cream on the pavement outside one of Mansour's best known ice-cream parlours, keeping their eyes skinned for their target. Half an hour passed. Another half-hour. No Uday. After waiting a little longer, the adrenalin draining from their veins, the would-be assassins went home. The following Thursday, the same thing happened. And the next Thursday. And the next.

After five weeks of waiting impatiently at his marshy headquarters for news, Hamza sent an envoy to Baghdad with a coded message calling off the operation. Such a long delay carried with it the risk of exposure. Sharif begged for one more chance. His request was granted.

The following week, at just after seven p.m., Sharif's heart jumped as he spotted Uday's golden Porsche slowing to a crawl only a hundred metres away from where he was sitting. As Uday began his Thursday hunt for fresh women, Sharif got up, his eyes scanning for any escort vehicles: there appeared to be none. The hit was on.

Abu Sadeq and Abu Sajad climbed out of the car, wiped ice cream from their hands and opened the bag containing the weapons. Abu Zahrar drove the car a few yards into the shadows, picking a spot from where he could exit in almost any direction. Sharif felt his pistol one more time and moved into position.

The car crawled along the road; Uday was in no hurry. Sharif strained his eyes trying to see whether there were any security guards inside. About thirty metres away, the car stopped; a man leaped out of the passenger seat and ran towards them. Sharif signalled quickly to his men to stay calm and hold back; they hadn't been spotted.

It was in fact a brilliant piece of luck. Uday had sent his security guard on ahead to check for girls. The Porsche started its crawl again and as it drew alongside Sharif peered inside, confirmed that Uday was there and gave the signal. Abu Sadeq and Abu Sajad pulled their weapons from the bag and let rip, emptying their fifty-bullet magazines at five paces. The windows shattered and the car stalled as Uday's body bounced and jerked in the driver's seat, bullets pulverising bone, ripping flesh, spraying the interior with blood.

Sharif stood behind the shooters, his pistol drawn. No security man had responded. No police. No militia. People were screaming and running away; the street was emptying fast. Sharif looked into the car and saw Uday's bloodstained broken body slumped to his right. He shouted 'Let's go!' They threw down their weapons, leaped into the getaway car and roared off. Nobody had shot back at them. Nobody followed them.

Elated, they reached their safe house, where they slept the night. The next morning they took the bus to Nasariyah and then a connecting bus to Suq-ash-Shuyukh, on the edge of the marshes. By nightfall they were back in the safety of their base. They couldn't believe it. They had successfully assassinated Saddam's son. 'We never imagined it would be so easy,' Sharif said later. 'We thought we had been sent to our deaths.'

But they were wrong in their belief that they had killed Uday. The man who had climbed out of the Porsche to look for girls was not Uday's bodyguard but his friend Al-Sahr. He ran back to Uday, pulled him out of the car and got him into a taxi to Bin Sina hospital (the private hospital for the presidential family with twenty beds and two well-equipped operating theatres) where Ala Bashir worked.

When Uday arrived he was close to death – his blood pressure was almost zero. The doctors counted seventeen bullet entry points. One had missed his heart by a few millimetres but most of the shots had hit his right thigh. He pulled through the first emergency operation but remained in constant mortal danger because of a lack of modern equipment. Infections and a whole variety of complications including pulmonary thrombosis threatened to strike at any moment. But then Dr Bashir enlisted the help of a French medical team who flew over just in time to catch a five-centimetre thrombosis in Uday's groin, which would otherwise have certainly proven fatal.

There were other problems. A CT scan of Uday showed signs of brain damage. As Dr Bashir put it, it was 'difficult to gauge the extent of any damage to the brain; he was already insane . . . he appeared significantly more short-tempered and aggressive towards those around him than before the attempted assassination.' A series of lengthy operations left Uday impotent, with a crippled leg and a bullet in his spine. But he had survived. It took him a few months, but with the aid of a specialist Cuban medical team Uday was walking again. And now he was ready to exact revenge.

At first, in the marshes in the next few days following the assassination attempt, Hamza, the leader of 15 Shaaban, listened to Voice of America radio and other international stations and chuckled as Iraq pundits speculated about an attempted coup. 'Lots of other parties claimed responsibility for the attack, but we didn't,' he recalled. 'We wanted the regime to think it came from its own ranks.'

The assassins couldn't believe that their target had survived. Uday Hussein had clearly been saved by a combination of their poor marksmanship and his own astounding luck. Confronted with all the blood and the obvious damage to Uday's body – and with little time to check – Sharif had mistakenly assumed that Saddam's eldest son was beyond help. He could have made sure by shooting him in the head but he hadn't. Sharif took comfort from the fact that at least Uday was now impotent and the other Husseins and the world had been shown that they were vulnerable.

But Uday was determined to have vengeance.

Two months later, a member of 15 Shaaban who knew about the plot was arrested in Jordan in connection with another affair and was handed over to the Iraqi secret police. Under torture, he broke. By August 1998, eighteen months after the assassination attempt, Saddam's security men had arrested Abu Sajad. He too broke under torture and now the authorities had the details of the other members of the team.

Uday's revenge, as might be expected, was vicious and total. Sharif's seven brothers and his father were rounded up: his mother was told later to collect their bodies from the Baghdad morgue. Abu Sadeq's father and three of his brothers were executed. Abu Sajad and his father suffered the same fate. Security men bulldozed all the families' houses and confiscated all their property. In December 2003 an Iraqi hit squad tracked down Abu Sadeq, who was living in exile in Iran, and killed him.

Sharif, the only surviving member of the original assassination team, remained in the marshes until the US-led invasion in March 2003. He has now returned to Shatra which he has helped transform into a bustling clean town that, by Iraqi standards, is thriving. Sharif recently buried the repatriated body of Abu Sadeq (real name: Abbas Majeed Abid Maktoub) in a ceremony attended by members of the 15 Shaaban, whom he describes as his 'family'. He still insists that the operation was worth the price his comrades and their families paid. 'When you weigh up the pros and cons, the advantages are bigger,' he argues. 'It is not easy for a man to sacrifice his family: nobody would do it unless it was for a noble cause. But I think my family was ready for that sacrifice. I inherited my sense of sacrifice from them. It was the way I was brought up.'

In a footnote to the story of this failed assassination, Ali al-Sahr (the man who saved Uday's life by dragging him into a taxi and getting him to hospital) tried to escape to Jordan in the autumn of 2002 but was stopped at the border post. Uday called him over to the Olympic Committee HQ and told him: 'You'll try again, and like other friends who've cleared off, no doubt you'll blab. I'll have to make sure that won't happen.' A few days later Uday sent a gang of his paramilitary Fedayeen militia to al-Sahr's home. There, in front of his wife, children and neighbours, they cut out his tongue.

Thirty-three

Three in the Head

The year 1998 saw an upturn in the number of journalists who were assassinated. In the tiny African republic of Burkina Faso, journalist Norbert Zongo was killed after his newspaper began investigating the torture and murder of a driver who had worked for the brother of President Blaise Compaore. His burned body was found along with those of his brother, a chauffeur and his companion. Nobody was ever prosecuted for his assassination.

In Canada, Sikh journalist Tara Singh Hayer, who was confined to a wheelchair from a 1988 attempt on his life, was shot to death after he got out of his car in his garage at home on 18 November. The motive was widely suspected to have been his investigation into the 1985 Air India bombing which killed three hundred and twenty-nine people (including sixty children under the age of ten) on a flight from Canada to India. Until 11 September 2001, the Air India bombing was the single deadliest attack involving aircraft. The subsequent investigation, trials and prosecution took twenty years and cost £66.5 million; only the bomb-maker was prosecuted. Hayer had obtained evidence that, had he lived, would have convicted one of the bombers. The Babbar Khalsa cell (an extremist Sikh terrorist group) was held responsible for the atrocity.

In Tajikistan, Otakhon Latifi, a journalist turned politician, was shot in the head at point-blank range as he left his apartment on the morning of 22 September. He had spent the previous six years trying to unite his homeland and curb organised crime. Towards the end of the twentieth century, assassinations had become fairly common in Russia and the former Soviet States. As the Soviet Union steadily broke up throughout the 1990s, criminal gangs sought to exploit the unstable situation in breakaway republics such as Chechnya, Armenia, Georgia, the Ukraine, Uzbekistan and Tajikistan and took advantage of the lawlessness to build empires from drug, diamond and people smuggling as well as the forced takeover and sale of businesses.

In boom-time Russia, life was the only commodity getting cheaper. There was no shortage of assassins: hundreds of ex-soldiers turned mercenary and were easily hired for two hundred pounds a hit (equivalent to a non-commissioned officer's yearly pay). Many are still employed by criminal gangs to take out journalists and politicians who threaten to expose or end their enterprises.

Out of all Russia's cities, St Petersburg was where organised gangs had most control by 1998. Powerful crime syndicates, such as the *Tambov*, were allied with local politicians and held tremendous sway over the city – after all if a bribe wouldn't do, there were plenty of killers for hire. That year, more than seven hundred attempted and actual assassinations took place, mainly of prominent businessmen, along with several media moguls and a handful of politicians. A leading Russian parliamentarian, Viktor Novosyolov, who was left paralysed and wheelchair-bound by a 1993 attack, was targeted by two hit men who placed a bomb on the roof of his car as he waited at a set of traffic lights. The blast took off his head and the assassination was never solved.

St Petersburg was also home to the 1990 would-be assassin of Soviet President Mikhail Gorbachev, Alexander Shmonov, who spent five years in a mental asylum after a botched bid to shoot the Russian Premier (he was caught waving his pistol some distance from his target). By 1998, he had bounced back and was planning to run in the elections for Russia's lower parliamentary house, the Duma. 'I know people have a negative attitude towards terrorists today, but I have a strong programme,' he insisted. Mad, maybe, but Shmonov wasn't any crazier than many of the other characters in the colourful cast battling for a place in the Duma in the following year's elections – including a pair of cosmonauts, a feminist author, an accused contract killer, a wrestling champion, Stalin's grandson and the inventor of the infamous Kalashnikov assault weapon.

Also fighting for her place in the Duma was Galina Starovoitova who, perhaps more than any other journalist or politician, had made a large number of enemies in her long political fight against crime and corruption. The former journalist and People's Deputy of the Soviet Union always made sure to change her travel plans at the last minute. But as she travelled home to St Petersburg, Russia's most criminalised city, she and her trusted aide Ruslan Linkov failed to spot the two men carefully shadowing them.

Fifty-two-year-old Starovoitova was the most active and well-known politician in St Petersburg and her popularity always assured her a seat in the Duma. She was a tireless advocate for human rights, an outspoken defender of democracy and an aggressive opponent of anti-Semitism, corruption and political extremism.

Born in the Urals to a Belorussian father and a Russian mother, Starovoitova gained her first degree from the Leningrad College of Military Engineering in 1966 and an MA in social psychology from Leningrad University in 1971. In 1980, she gained a doctorate in social anthropology from the Institute of Ethnography at the USSR Academy of Sciences, where she worked for seventeen years. She moved into politics under the tutelage of Nobel Peace Prize-winner Andrei Sakharov and eventually became one of Premier Boris Yeltsin's closest aides. They fell out over the Chechen war which Starovoitova rightly predicted would be futile. In the 1995 Duma election she won a seat and was a leading member of the Russian parliament.

In the summer of 1998 Starovoitova announced her plans to run for governor of Leningrad after Vladimir Zhirinovsky, Head of the Liberal Democratic Party of Russia (a man who counted Saddam

Hussein as a 'dear friend' and whose party campaigned for the return of a dictator-led Stalinesque system of rule), said he would make a bid for the post.

Starovoitova lived in an apartment on the Griboyedov Embankment, a well-to-do neighbourhood (apartments sold for twenty thousand pounds) right at St Petersburg's heart. As she walked up the steps to the building's lobby, escorted by Linkov, two young mercenaries skipped up the steps behind them. One, Vitali Akishin, was an ex-soldier, the other, Yuri Kolchin, was a former employee of Russian Military Intelligence (GRU) working for the *Tambov* organised-crime gang.

Linkov just had time to see the man clearly before the first shot hit him in the neck. As Kolchin kept lookout Akishin marched up to Starovoitova and fired twice into her head with a silenced handgun at point-blank range. After she had fallen, the assassin leaned down and fired a third shot, true to the old Mafioso hit-man motto 'three in the head, you know they're dead'. As Linkov lay gasping for air, the assassin strode over to him, checked his gun, levelled it at his head and fired.

Within hours of her brutal murder, Starovoitova was being hailed as a hero and a brave voice of democratic decency in Russia. At her funeral, attended by ten thousand mourners as well as by the cream of the country's liberal politicians, there was a collective sense of outrage. Coming on the heels of a burst of depressing public statements by another member of parliament, including claims that the Russian security services were being used for freelance assassinations – along with allegations of corruption levelled against Premier Boris Yeltsin – the killing reminded everyone of the dark side of Russian politics. And it reignited the old debate about how Russia should be ruled: could liberal democracy work, or was a more authoritarian hand needed?

The media pummelled the government. Corruption, unsolved murders, open demonstrations by neo-Nazis and anti-Semites meant just one thing, the newspaper *Izvestiya* declared in a typical front-page editorial: 'It means that in Russia today there is no state; it is dead.'

News of Starovoitova's assassination made it to the front pages of the international press; it was even suggested that she should be nominated for the Nobel Peace Prize. (But the Nobel committee doesn't award posthumous prizes – Mahatma Gandhi would have won in 1948 had he not been assassinated that year.) Tens of thousands of people (including three former prime ministers) queued to pay their respects and a mountain of flowers piled up beside her grave.

Officials declared that solving the case would be a matter of national honour. President Boris Yeltsin himself said he would take personal control over the investigation, hailing Starovoitova as one of his 'closest companions and assistants' and vowing that the 'contractors and executors of the murder will be found and severely punished'.

On President Boris Yeltsin's insistence, the case was to be directed from Moscow by the FSB (the agency that replaced the KGB, which had been dismantled after the aborted 1991 coup against Mikhail Gorbachev). The newly appointed head of the FSB at that time was a little-known former KGB mid-level spy who began his career in government as St Petersburg's first director of the Committee on Foreign Economic Relations, where co-workers nicknamed him the 'Grey Cardinal' for his Vatican-like mastery of back-room intrigue.

His name was Vladimir Putin.

Linkov woke up in a hospital bed a few days later. As he gradually came round and woozily recovered his memories, he noticed that someone was sitting by the bed, holding his hand. As Linkov's eyes focused he blinked in disbelief. It was Vladimir Putin, head of the FSB. 'It's all right,' Putin said. 'It's all going to be all right.' Linkov wanted to laugh. 'What a funny dream,' he thought before passing out again.

The next time he woke, his doctor immediately told him what he already guessed: that he was a very lucky man. The bullet had ricocheted off his skull, leaving a nasty wound, but his brain was still intact. It was the bullet in the neck that had nearly cost him his life, but he would recover. As he was about to leave, the doctor paused and asked: 'Did you know that Vladimir Putin came to see you?'

Amnesty International, as well as virtually every other human-rights organisation and supporter of democracy, deplored the decision to let the FSB handle the investigation, given the notorious history of its predecessor. At the time the FSB was facing credible allegations that it was involved in assassinations – most notably that it had tried to assassinate the tycoon Boris Berezovsky. (An assassination that ex-FSB agent Alexander Litvinenko – who was given a lethal dose of radiation in London in 2006 – claimed he was ordered to carry out.)

Berezovsky was able to influence any Russian election (he owned dozens of Russia's most popular TV channels, radio stations, magazines and newspapers). The alleged plot to kill him took place before Putin headed the agency – and the new head of the FSB displayed characteristic cunning when he became a strategic friend of the media mogul whose media support would be crucial in winning him the Russian Presidency.

Putin appeared truly concerned over Starovoitova's killing. And he was. They had been good friends early on in their careers. Promises were made that the assassins would be caught. Raids were carried out, over seven hundred people were interviewed, weapons were seized and several times announcements were made of a breakthrough. Weeks went by and then months but still no arrests were made.

Linkov believed that Putin – who, as already mentioned, had once had close relations with Starovoitova – was sincerely trying to solve the crime, but 'didn't seem to have control over his bureaucracy'. It seems inconceivable, given the phenomenal reach and resources of the FSB, that Putin could not have found out who had Starovoitova killed and why.

But most Russians were not surprised that the case remained unsolved. Assassinations continued in St Petersburg. Fuel boss Pavel Kapysh was killed on 16 August when his car was attacked with rocket-propelled-grenade and automatic-rifle fire. The city's Legislative Assembly Deputy Speaker, Viktor Novosyolov, was killed by a bomb on 20 October; one of his assistants was shot and killed in his home two days later. Yet another seven hundred politicians, businessmen and journalists met similar fates in St Petersburg in the following months: their murders demanded fresh attention as memories of the old ones faded away. One year after Starovoitova's assassination, only one hundred mourners gathered at a special ceremony to commemorate her life.

Besides, during her political career she had made so many powerful enemies that it was impossible for Putin to investigate them all to his satisfaction. Starovoitova was investigating two very senior politicians' ties to organised crime. She was also investigating the General Prosecutor's Office, which she accused of corruption.

Starovoitova had even angered Putin's FSB with her active support of retired navy captain and environmentalist Aleksandr Nikitin, who stood accused of espionage for revealing the truth about the Russian North Sea Fleet's handling of nuclear waste (Nikitin was eventually cleared).

Eight months after the start of the investigation, Yeltsin made Putin Prime Minister. Then, with the help of Berezovsky's media machine, Putin took the presidency from Yeltsin in 2000 and applied pressure on the FSB to restart the investigation.

In June 2005, in an unexpected breakthrough, Kolchin and Akishin were captured and interrogated. They confessed. They were convicted of Starovoitova's murder and were sentenced to twenty and twenty-three years imprisonment respectively.

Putin continued to chip away at the case and eventually arrested six members of the Liberal Democratic Party of Russia for conspiring to arrange the assassination of his old friend.

Thirty-four

A Bloodbath in Parliament

In Armenia on 27 October 1999 there were signs of genuine progress in the long-paralysed talks with Azerbaijan over the disputed territory of Nagorno-Karabakh. Vladimir Putin had just visited to offer his congratulations to the Armenian negotiators and United States Deputy Secretary of State Strobe Talbott had joined Armenian Prime Minister Vazgen Sarkissian for a working breakfast before flying back to the United States. Local elections, which had won praise from international observers as the freest yet, had just been held.

Armenia had hoisted its nationalist flag and claimed independence the day before Mikhail Gorbachev resigned as Communist leader, back on 23 August 1991, in the wake of an attempted Communist coup and Boris Yeltsin's ascension to the Presidency. Before then little had been heard from the small Russian state, apart from when a terrible earthquake in 1988 claimed over fifty thousand lives. For a former Russian state, Armenia seemed to be a fairly stable country.

Vazgen Sarkissian wasn't short of enemies, however. Prior to becoming Prime Minister, the former physical education schoolteacher had been Armenia's Defence Minister since 1992. He controlled his own private army, the *Yerkrapah* (Defenders of the Homeland) which he unleashed on people he disliked within Armenia, especially political opponents, human-rights activists and members of religious minorities, who suffered brutal attacks in 1995 after Sarkissian appealed on TV for people to tell him where insurgents were hiding. He later told the *Yerkrapah* that they had saved the country from the 'plague of religious sects'.

Despite the purges conducted by the *Yerkrapah*, Armenia had remained relatively stable in recent years and the people looked to the future with some enthusiasm. But not everyone was happy; in particular, a rather excitable former Armenian radio talk-show host and journalist called Nairiu Hounanian. In the autumn of 1999, he told anyone who would listen that bloodshed was necessary to improve life in Armenia. His friends listened politely but no one took him seriously, except for one . . . and his brother and uncle.

At five p.m. on 27 October 1999, four gunmen in long coats and carrying Kalashnikov assault rifles stormed past dozing security guards into the Armenian parliament during a live televised Q&A session being led by Sarkissian. Daytime TV viewers watched in stunned amazement as Hounanian positioned himself directly in front of Sarkissian, shouted, 'Enough of drinking our blood' and lifted his rifle, adding, 'This is a coup!'

Vazgen Sarkissian looked his assassin dead in the eye and calmly replied: 'Everything is being done for you and the future of your children.' Hounanian paused and looked around the parliament before turning back to Sarkissian. The gunman raised his rifle and fired a bullet through the Prime Minister's head.

More than fifty MPs cowered behind their desks while the coup's leader shouted towards the cameras: 'We're going to punish the authorities for what they did to the nation!' A second gunman then marched up behind the Speaker of the Parliament, Karen Demirchian, from behind, placed his gun at the base of Demirchian's head and shot him dead, spraying blood over dozens of people in front of him in the chamber.

At this point the TV coverage was cut, leaving shocked TV viewers wondering what it was that Sarkissian had done that merited his assassination. After the cameras went off, the gunmen shot and killed Deputy Speakers Yuri Bakhshian and Ruben Miroian, Energy

Minister Leonard Petrosian, senior economic official Mikhail Kotanian, and lawmakers Genrikh Abramian and Armenak Armenakian. Thirty more were injured as the men marched around the room's perimeter, firing indiscriminately into the chamber.

For over eighteen hours, the terrorists held what remained of the nation's government hostage as the Armenian President, Robert Kocharian, bravely entered the building to negotiate directly with the gunmen. But despite intensive talks Hounanian's motive remained unclear. As the *Yerkrapah* prepared to storm the parliament building, the attackers (no doubt aware that they were not likely to survive such a confrontation) let it be known that they were prepared to surrender peacefully if they were granted some TV airtime in return. Kocharian agreed.

By now, coverage of the event was being transmitted across much of Russia and millions watched as the wild-eyed Hounanian told viewers: 'Under your very eyes, during the past several years, our country was being tormented and has turned into a country that everyone wants to leave. Our fathers and grandfathers, who had built this country by their own sweat and blood, drag out a half-starved and wretched existence today. Thousands of our children cannot go to school because they cannot buy textbooks and shoes. The economy has collapsed, social insecurity has increased greatly, and we're facing the danger of losing our statehood.'

Although many people agreed with what Hounanian had to say, they also believed that the government was doing everything in its power to improve its lot (which included befriending the United States who were in the process of granting them seventy million dollars in aid as part of a recent US policy designed to befriend the former Soviet States, a Cold War Two strategy that had already been especially effective in Georgia). After making his speech, Hounanian and his companions surrendered peacefully.

During his trial, Hounanian tried unsuccessfully to enter the race for president. Along with his fellow gunmen, he was later sentenced to life imprisonment. Vazgen Sarkissian was succeeded by his thirty-eight-year-old younger brother Aram, a man who had no interest in politics and who ran a cement factory in the town of Ararat. It was primarily a symbolic stand-in for his murdered brother and he was replaced in May 2000 by former *Yerkrapah* member Andranik Markaryan.

Fortunately, although the country was economically weak, Armenia was stable enough to cope with this transition and, with America's help, has since gone on to become one of the most financially secure of the former Soviet States.

This was a remarkable comeback for a nation that had suffered one of the world's worst genocides, losing one million people – half its population – to wholesale slaughter by the Turkish army which began on 24 April 1915. The genocide was caused by longstanding racial disharmony on the Turkish–Armenian border and the false accusation by the Turks that the Armenians had sided with the Russians in the First World War. And on the seventy-seventh anniversary of the Armenian atrocities, genocide returned to Europe, an occurrence which, until then, had been to most people unthinkable.

Thirty-five

The Final Solution

On 24 April 1992 Arkan and his Tigers came to Bijeljina, a medium-sized town in the north-eastern corner of Bosnia–Herzegovina. About sixty men got out of the bus: many of them were 'weekend' mercenaries, former football hooligans turned into a bloodthirsty militia. They were all in uniform and were armed with AK-47s. They lined up for Arkan's inspection. Arkan, real name Zeljko Raznatovic, a youthful-looking forty with a striking resemblance to Hollywood actor Kevin Spacey, emerged from a 4x4 and told his Tigers: 'Get ready – we are going to liberate this city of Muslim fundamentalists.'

The men split up into groups of ten to fifteen and moved through the streets in different directions. One group reached a mosque and marched inside, pulled down the Muslim flag and posed for a photo with a terrified eighteen-year-old Muslim youth. They joked and made fun of him as he struggled to get away. Eventually he broke free and they let him go, laughing at him as he ran to the back of the mosque. It was a dead end. Two mercenaries followed and shot him in the back.

The militiamen crossed to the other side of the street and pulled a man out of a house. His wife came out of the house as well – she was screaming. They shot the man, and she tried to help him by putting her hand over his wound. They shot her as well. An old woman came out of the house and an overweight Tiger who was wearing Ray-

Bans executed her with a short burst from his sub-machine gun. Some other mercenaries marched inside and a few moments later screaming was followed by a crash as a man was thrown out of a third-floor window and into the street. 'Ray-Bans' shouted up to the soldiers in the house to be careful, that they could have killed somebody on the ground by throwing that guy through the window. As he talked he kicked the still-conscious man where he lay and dragged him back into the house to be beaten and executed.

In the days that followed, as Arkan and his Tigers butchered their way through Bijeljina, houses, shops, and businesses owned by Bosniaks were ransacked and burned, and hundreds of people were murdered. Bodies were loaded onto trucks and driven down to the Drina River and tipped in. There were no lists: nobody kept count of who or how many were killed. In the 1991 census, Bijeljina was fifty-nine per cent Serb and thirty-four per cent Muslim. After the war, Bijeljina was 98.75 per cent Serb.

Arkan was the most notorious of the Serbian paramilitary chiefs who operated in the Bosnian War, which was fought between March 1992 and November 1995 and began after the collapse of Communism in Yugoslavia.

War had erupted after two of the Federal Republics, Slovenia and Croatia, declared their independence – and, subsequently, war upon each other. Then, as another republic, the multi-ethnic Bosnia–Herzegovina (Croat, Serb and Muslim), declared its independence too Serbia and Croatia fought over its control. The ultimate aim of the Bosnian Serb nationalist leaders was the creation of a 'Greater Serbia' – an ethnically homogeneous area inhabited exclusively by ethnic Serbs.

No one profited more from the killing frenzy than Arkan and his Tigers. (Officially known as the Serb Volunteer Guard, they were originally formed by the members of the Red Star football club, of which Arkan was president – at various times between 1992 and 1995 the Guard had between 200 and 10,000 members.) Since the Tigers were paid mainly in what they could steal, theft provoked many atrocities. Arkan reportedly had a price list for 'liberating' a town: between half a million and one million pounds, plus all the loot from the police station and bank, plus right of passage for thirty cars, plus everything else that his men could carry. The Tigers' plunder attracted 'weekend warriors' from Belgrade's underworld who would pillage for profit. Arkan also became one of Serbia's richest men by busting UN sanctions and awarding himself lucrative oil and gas concessions in Serbian-held Bosnia and Yugoslavia.

Born in 1952 in Slovenija, Zeljko Raznatovic was a delinquent teenager whose father – a senior air force officer in Communist dictator Tito's military – asked if the Yugoslav security services could put him to work. Raznatovic became a professional hit man for the Yugoslav Interior Ministry, assassinating Croatian nationalists in other parts of Europe who were considered enemies of the state.

A convicted armed robber and quasi-Houdini, Raznatovic escaped from prisons in Belgium, Holland, Germany, Switzerland and even from a Swedish courtroom where he was being tried. (This last-mentioned escape was reportedly made with the help of the Yugoslav security service.) One of the fake passports he was issued by the Yugoslav security services was said to be in the name Arkan, which he adopted as a nickname.

After the war in Bosnia, Croatia and Kosovo, Arkan was secretly indicted by the UN's International Criminal Tribunal for the Former Yugoslavia in the Hague for a variety of war crimes, including ethnic cleansing. By then he had taken on a new existence in Serbia where he was widely regarded as a patriotic hero and whose populace refused to believe that he had used murder as part of his military doctrine. He was also Serbia's premier celebrity. In 1995, wearing a First World War Serbian general's uniform, the forty-two-year-old warrior married the nation's most popular singer – twenty-one-year-old Svetlana Velickovic, aka Ceca, the queen of *turbofolk* (a terrifyingly kitsch fusion of Serb traditional music and 1980s rock) who was dressed in a *Gone With the Wind*-style wedding dress bought in Rome. During the ceremony Arkan, using a double-barrelled shotgun, shot an apple off a thirty-three-foot pole (on his sixth attempt) atop his bride-to-be's house while Borislav Pelevic, former Tiger commander and best man, threw banknotes over the happy couple, as is the local tradition.

It was one of the great social events of Belgrade in recent years; in a country starved of celebrity the couple had become Serbia's Posh and Becks. They appeared regularly on Serbia's TV talk shows where Ceca informed her audience that she had now switched to wearing Armani but would go back to Versace 'if he improved', while Arkan dealt with the important political issues of the day.

Arkan was the king of 'True Glitz', as the locals described it, and was variously accompanied by an odd entourage of mobsters, police, sports stars, starlets, politicians and businessmen. One *New York Times* reporter declared: 'It was as if Al Capone had merged with General George S. Patton and then married Madonna, moving into the semi-respectable, tacky elite of Serbia, with its openings and fashion shows, all the while doing favours for and being protected by the police and important politicians.'

Arkan also devoted himself to sports – he turned second-division Obilic into the country's premier football team and provided funding for kick-boxing tournaments. He distributed free bread to the poor from bakeries he owned and actively supported a popular children's charity.

Arkan had invested his looted spoils in Serbian banks, gasoline smuggling, illegal gambling and secret casinos; he also made money by hiring out his Tigers as hit men and made plans to become a candidate in the presidential elections scheduled for autumn 2000, forming a new political organisation, the far-right Party of Serbian Unity. His strong ties to the police and military services, as well as the fanatical support he got from ruthless ex-Tigers (officially disbanded in 1996) who patrolled his luxury marble mansion, meant he was untouchable. Those close to him were not, however, and Serbia's secret police began a ruthless process of eliminating those closest to Arkan: dozens of his most devoted friends, trusted soldiers and business partners were bumped off in an attempt to weaken his control over Serbia.

To say that many people wanted Arkan dead would be a dramatic understatement – everyone from NATO commanders to corrupt businessmen, rival nationalist politicians and even the owners of rival football teams had wanted him killed at some point. None more so, however, than the former President of Serbia and Yugoslavia, Slobodan Milosevic.

Milosevic was one of the great losers of history. He failed to hold Yugoslavia together; he then failed to build in its place a Greater Serbia. He started four wars and lost three. He was responsible for the extermination of a quarter of a million innocent people in Bosnia and Croatia, for the European revival of concentration camps and massacres, for the displacement of millions in Bosnia, Croatia and Kosovo and for his country's impoverishment.

In the spring of 1999, NATO belatedly intervened in the Kosovo War, forcing Serbia to surrender after seventy-eight days and nights of continued bombing, which cost the lives of five thousand soldiers and two thousand civilians. Within twenty-four hours of entering Kosovo, British and German troops found mass graves of thousands of victims of ethnic cleansing at five villages. The world watched horrified, hardly able to believe that, for the first time since the Second World War, a genocide had taken place in Europe. By the end of the week another fifty mass-grave sites had been discovered.

In May 1999 Milosevic was indicted by the UN's war-crimes tribunal, charged with war crimes and crimes against humanity. While there was no shortage of witnesses willing to testify to the genocidal behaviour of the Serbian troops, the tribunal had to prove that Milosevic had 'command responsibility' for the atrocities committed in Croatia and Bosnia. There was precious little or no evidence to support this.

But no one knew more about Milosevic's policy towards genocide than Arkan, who had also been indicted by the tribunal (but remained free). In 1999, Arkan instructed his lawyers to start exploring ways in which he might surrender and give testimony against Milosevic and other war criminals in exchange for leniency. The UN was very interested in Arkan's proposition. If Arkan testified against Milosevic, then the former president would be convicted.

As soon as Milosevic learned of Arkan's betrayal (while in prison awaiting trial, Milosevic had a team of agents in Belgrade helping him, often sending him information from the files of the secret police), he gave a top-secret order for the 'urgent removal' of Arkan in June 1999 to one of his henchmen, who hired fellow gangster Dragan Nikolic, known as *Gagi*, who then brought in his first cousin Milan Duricic and former best man Dobrosav Gavric – a twenty-five-year-old-policeman on sick leave and a former Tiger. For four months, they followed Arkan, looking for an opportunity.

At five p.m. on 15 January 2000 Arkan's navy-blue armoured Chevrolet Blazer SUV, registration number BG-19-99, screeched to a halt outside Belgrade's Intercontinental Hotel. With Arkan was a lone bodyguard, his wife and their two young children, Veljko, four, and Anastasija, two. As Arkan, dressed in an Armani suit, strode into the busy hotel lobby with the glamorous Ceca, heads turned. The hotel had happy memories for the stellar couple: it had played host to their half-million-pound wedding celebrations.

Gavric went unnoticed as he followed through the door and sat at a table just behind Arkan, who was meeting Milenko Mandic, a business manager, and Dragan Garic, a police inspector. (The details of the subject of the meeting were never revealed.) Gavric waited for a few minutes, until he thought Arkan's bodyguard had relaxed slightly, drew his CZ99 service pistol and shot Arkan three times in the back of the head. Gavric then shot and killed both Garic and Mandic before they could react (probably because they knew him) and ran for the hotel doors.

Zvonko Mateovic, Arkan's bodyguard, returned fire, hitting Gavric as he ran. The assassin fell to the floor but turned and continued to fire back, hitting a woman in the chest (she survived) before Duricic came to his rescue and tried to drag him out into a waiting car. But by that time the heavily armed police were waiting for them outside. Gavric and Duricic surrendered. Ceca and the children were unhurt.

To Mateovic's amazement, Arkan was still alive he pleaded with the police officers to take him in their car. They refused, claiming that the law forbade them from transporting wounded civilians in a police vehicle. Instead, they radioed for an ambulance. Mateovic ran outside with Arkan over his shoulder and quickly commandeered a car, threw Arkan into the back and sped to the nearest hospital. Doctors tried resuscitation for over one hour, but Arkan was declared dead at 6.50 p.m.

Gavric survived, albeit paralysed from the waist down. In October 2006, Gavric, Nikolic and Duricic were sentenced to thirty years. Unfortunately, Gavric and Duricic weren't in court to hear their sentences; they had been freed some weeks earlier after having served the maximum time permissible on remand under Serbian law. At the time of writing they are still being hunted by police. Five of their accomplices were jailed for between three and five years. Another three men, including a senior politician close to Milosevic, were set free after the chief witness against them, former police boss Vojislav Jeki, was shot dead in a Belgrade café in May 2006.

Arkan's best man, Borislav Pelevic, took over the leadership of the Party of Serbian Unity and capitalised on the public outpouring of grief after Arkan's assassination to win fourteen seats in the Serbian elections held in December 2000, far more than was expected. The following year, the Hague tribunal chief prosecutor Carla Del Ponte presented Yugoslav authorities with a warrant for Pelevic's arrest for war crimes. He was also charged with 'being a part of a group engaged in violence'. So far, Pelevic has not been arrested. Slobodan Milosevic escaped justice by dying of a heart condition a few weeks before his trial was due to end on 11 March 2006. In June 2006, the Supreme Court of Serbia revealed that they had uncovered evidence that he had ordered the assassinations of several people, including Arkan.

7 March 1999 was the end of an era as Sydney Gottlieb, the CIA's one-time 'Black Sorcerer', peacefully passed away at the age of eighty, having spent a career supposedly protecting the USA. In

reality he had caused its inhabitants more harm than good. His poisons were used more in tests on innocent people in the US than on any enemy power. Meanwhile, his most famous target, seventy-four-year-old Fidel Castro, was still in rude health despite a constant stream of assassination attempts. But Castro's survival had cost Cuba dearly.

The Cuban people suffered half a century of political, economic, technological and military blockades by the most powerful country in the world. After the collapse of the Soviet Union in 1991, Cuba was left without markets and without a source of supplies of food, fuel, raw materials and many other essential products: the average Cuban's daily caloric intake of 3,000 was reduced overnight to 1,800 calories. But, as ever, at the end of the century Castro remained defiant as he prepared to give a speech at a Panamanian university on 18 November 2000.

If a team of four assassins had had anything to do with it, it would have been his last public appearance. They travelled from El Salvador on false passports with more than thirty kilos of C4 plastic explosives. Their aim was to plant them in the university hall and detonate them as Castro arrived. The enormous blast would have killed hundreds of students along with Castro and various Panamanian dignitaries. But the Cuban secret service uncovered the plot and the men were arrested at their hotel in Panama. One of the men arrested was the terrorist Luis Posada, a seventy-year-old Cuban exile and former CIA operative who had been trying to kill Castro ever since the Bay of Pigs.[26]

[26] Posada had a remarkable career as a terrorist. He had escaped from prison in Venezuela in 1985 where he had been incarcerated after the bombing of a Cuban airliner in 1976 in which seventy-three people died. He also claimed responsibility for a string of hotel bombings in Havana during which eleven people were injured and one Italian businessman was killed. Inexplicably, he was pardoned in 2004 for the attempted assassination of Castro and he fled to America where he was arrested on immigration charges but was bailed. He currently lives in Miami. US President George Bush has repeatedly stated that no nation should harbour terrorists, and yet while the Venezuelan government has demanded that the US hand this convicted terrorist back to them so that he can serve the rest of his sentence, the American authorities have, so far, done nothing to facilitate this.

*

Castro was unperturbed by these events and went ahead with all his scheduled appearances. Referring to the assassination attempt, he told an enthusiastic crowd of university students: 'Throughout my life I have received all kinds of threats. We have to count not only the plots organised by the CIA, the acquisition of bombs or elephant rifles, a pen that shot a poisoned dart, a mask that produces who knows what fungus, and others. This time I was simply lucky, and that is not something I take credit for. But it does not matter if I fall; what matters is that the flag remains high, that the idea continues, and that the fatherland lives.'

This, one can only assume, is the wish of all those who live with the threat of assassination: that although their life may be suddenly cut short, their legacy is strong enough to survive without them.

Thirty-six

The Statistics of How to Kill

In the weeks following Robert Kennedy's death, President Lyndon Johnson established the National Commission on the Causes and Prevention of Violence. A special task force was created, made up of eminent psychologists and sociologists, to investigate the rising tide of violence in America, with particular regard to assassination. The report, published in 1970, was called *A Staff Report to the National Commission on the Causes and Prevention of Violence*. The introduction, written by Harrison E. Salisbury of the *New York Times* read: 'Hundreds of thousands of words. Staggering man-hours of investigation. Painstaking analysis. Learned research. Hypotheses. Statistics. Frequency charts. Historical parallels. Everyone has been consulted – the illiterate accidental witness and the psychiatrists, the behavioural scientists, the high priests of our technological times.'

The eight-hundred-page report concluded: 'We have shown that the level of assassination corresponds to the level of political turmoil and violence in general. In comparison to other nations, the United States experiences a high level of political violence and assassination events. The present level of assassination and political turmoil, however, is no greater than at times in the past. Violence to achieve political goals is a thread which runs throughout the history of the United States.'

Those 'staggering man-hours of investigation' and 'painstaking analysis' had resulted in a rather obvious statement: violence in the US is historic and traditional and assassination is a natural part of it. The report failed to answer the most obvious and important questions: Who are the assassins? Why do they decide on such a desperate act? What factors decide when they will strike and how?

Surprisingly, there has been little research into the patterns of assassination and this is the first attempt to examine all the significant assassinations across the world from 1950–2000 in an effort to better understand the phenomenon.[27]

In a nutshell, a typical assassination is most likely to occur between six p.m. and nine p.m. (31.7 per cent of cases) on a Friday (20.7 per cent) in October (19.5 per cent), with a high likelihood that the assassin, most likely aged between 21 and 30 (45.1 per cent), either on their own (25.6 per cent) or as a member of a small conspiracy (28 per cent) or terrorist group (26.8 per cent), will use a gun (53.9 per cent, a weapon which has a 63 per cent rate of success) and will possibly escape the scene and may never be apprehended (38.9 per cent). It will occur where the target is making a public appearance (26.9 per cent) or at their home (29.3 per cent).

The fact that so many assassinations take place at the end of the week and in the early evening (see Figs. 1, 2, 3 and 4 in the Appendix) suggests that this is when targets are at their most vulnerable. Friday night is typically a time for relaxing – perhaps for a head of state this might mean attending an informal public function where security cannot be as tight as normal – or even a night off (for example, Olof Palme was assassinated on a Friday night as he left a cinema). Over 32 per cent of heads-of-state targets were attacked on a Friday, with most assaults occurring later in the week, between Wednesday and Friday (62.8 per cent).

The fact that very few assassinations of heads of state occur in the summer months May to July (see Fig. 6) clearly suggests that the summer break, perhaps leading to a reduction in public appearances and the number of publicised trips on government business, reduces

[27] For those interested in examining the full data set, please see www.assassinology.org

the chance of assassination. For heads of state, September, October and November are by far the most dangerous months as the business of government gets into full swing (see Fig. 6). The evenings are darker too (for most of the political globe), increasing the possibility of success by adding the cover of darkness between six and nine p.m., when the target is often in transit between their well-protected place of work and arrival at their well-guarded home. (Overall, 22 per cent of attacks were executed while the target was in transit.)

Over 40 per cent of heads of state are attacked while they are making a public appearance (see Fig. 9) while for non-heads of state it is the home that is most dangerous (see Fig.10). This is understandable – a lack of witnesses and security staff, little chance of police or have-a-go-hero intervention and the confinement of the target, who may be asleep, are all attractive factors to an assassin.

It is surprising to discover that two-thirds of assassins manage at least to escape the immediate scene of the crime and that only one-third of those who manage to escape are eventually captured (see Fig. 7). Obviously, the capture of the assassin is instrumental in solving the crime and the security services are often criticised for their failure to apprehend assassins who were in the immediate vicinity – the cases of Palme, Moro, Uday Hussein, Luther King and Evers are just a few of many.

As for motivation, the main reasons for assassinations are:

1. Regime change 26 per cent
2. Bring to attention a personal or public problem 24.6 per cent
3. Destroy a rival organisation 10.1 per cent
4. Cause war 7.4 per cent
5. Make money 1.4 per cent
6. Silence a witness or an influential negotiator 13 per cent
7. End war 2.8 per cent
8. Protect a regime from change 4.3 per cent
9. Revenge 4.3 per cent

If the assassination is successful then there is an 80 per cent probability that the perpetrator's aims will have been advanced (see Fig. 12). In 47.7% cases of unsuccessful assassinations the perpetrators can expect a negative outcome as a result but in most cases (52.3%) there will be no change (see Fig.13). By the end of the nineteenth century it was thought that assassination was an outdated anarchist tool, but its use gradually rose throughout the first half of the twentieth century. Since 1950 assassination has become an everyday fact of life, an effective political tool that has frequently altered the fate of nations, affecting national economies, liberties and politics while placing millions of lives in peril, proving that, more often than most people realise, one murder can change the world.

Appendix
THE STATISTICS OF HOW TO KILL
(All data is in percentages)

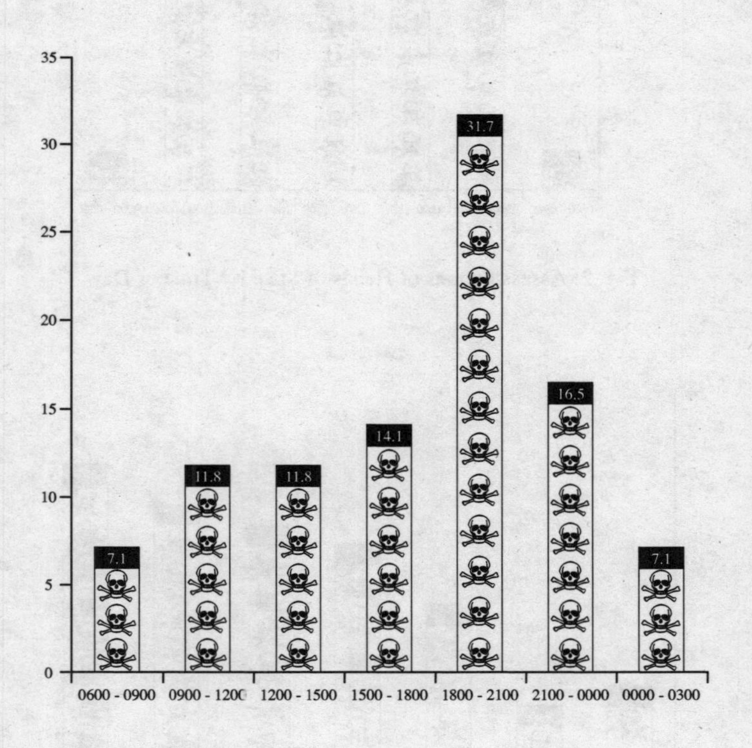

Fig. 1: All Assassinations by the Time of Day

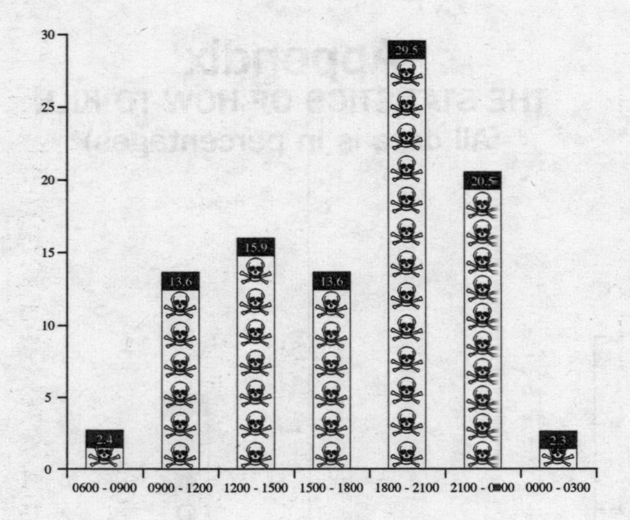

Fig. 2: Assassinations of Heads of State by Time of Day

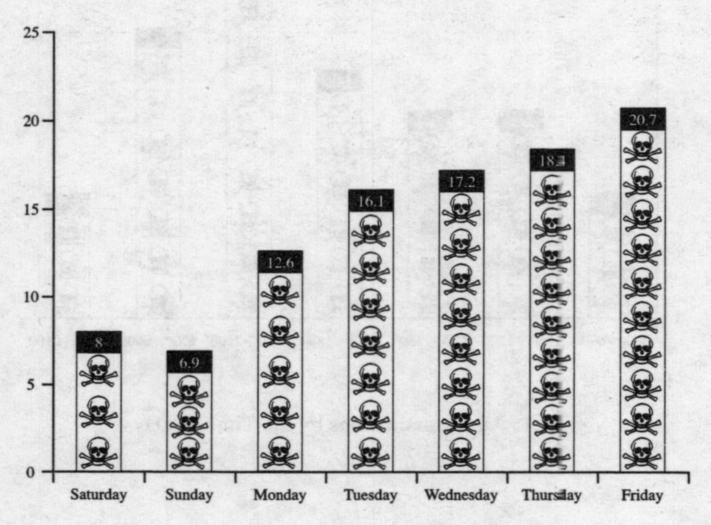

Fig. 3: All Assassinations by Day

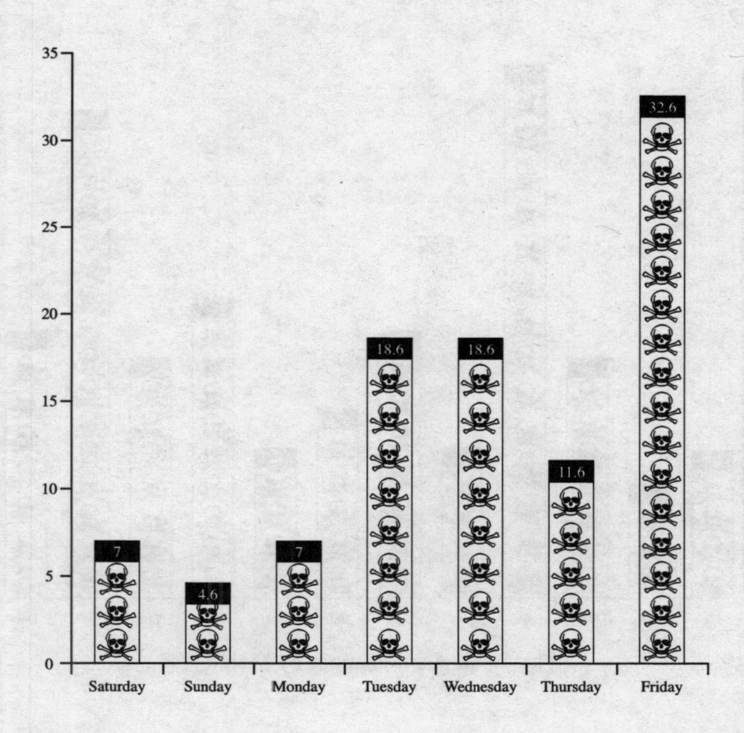

Fig. 4: Assassinations of Heads of State by Day

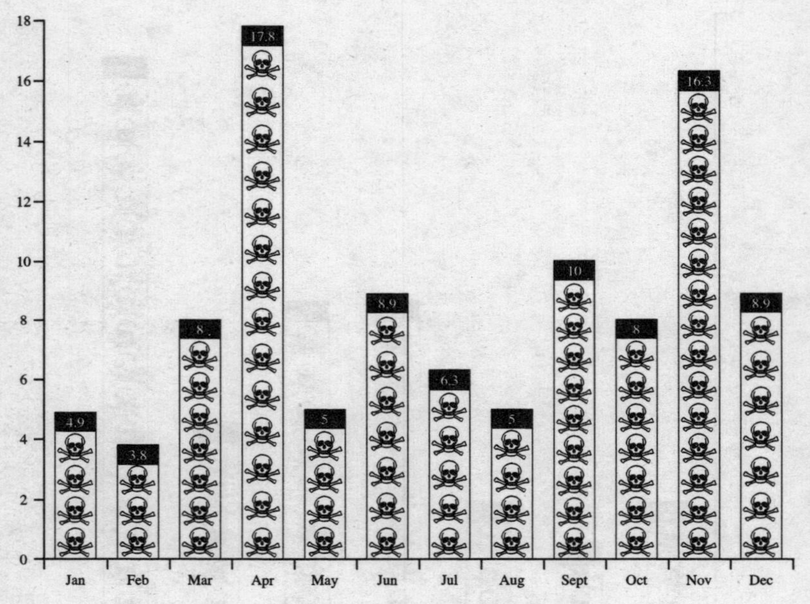

Fig. 5: All Assassinations by Month

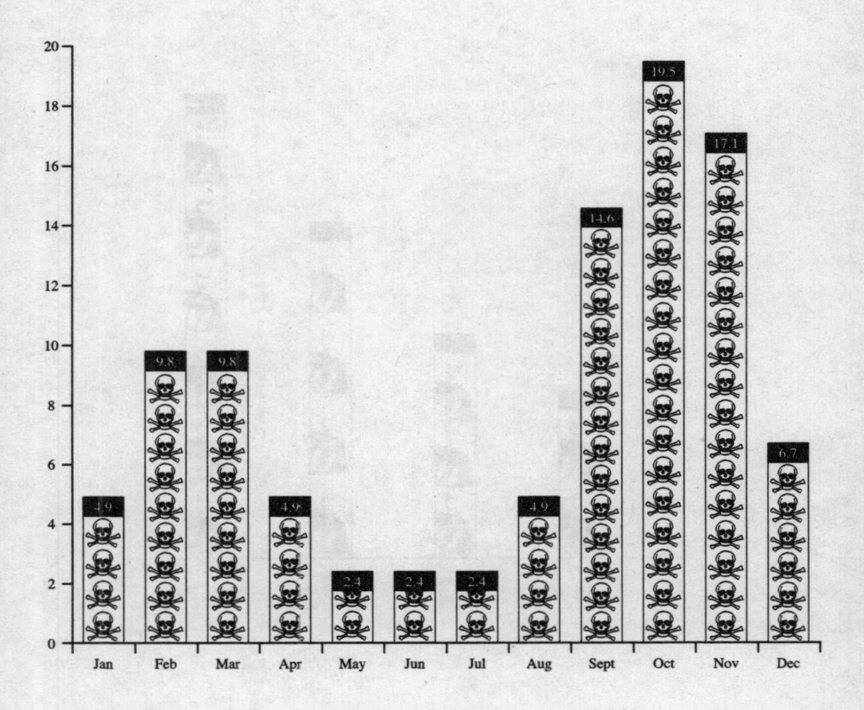

Fig. 6: Assassinations of Heads of State by Month

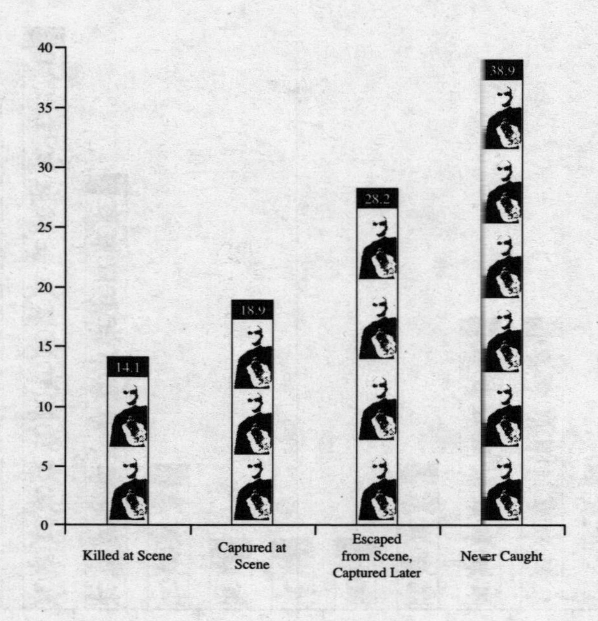

Fig. 7: Fate of Assassins in all Assassinations

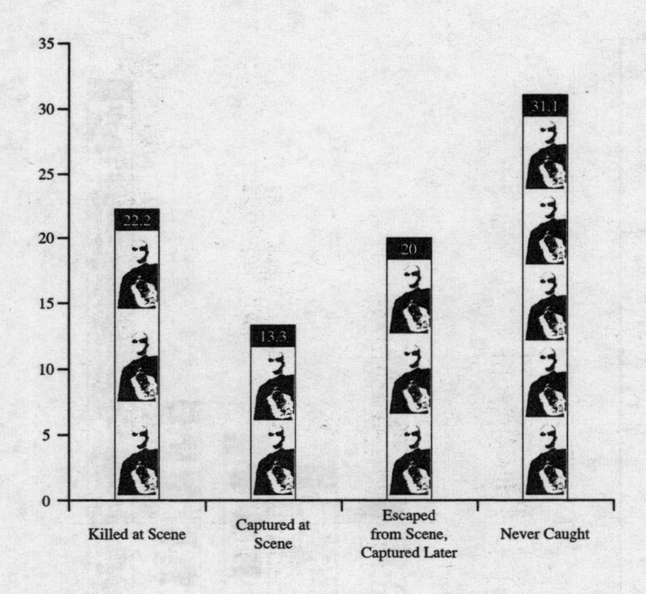

Fig. 8: Fate of Assassins of Heads of State

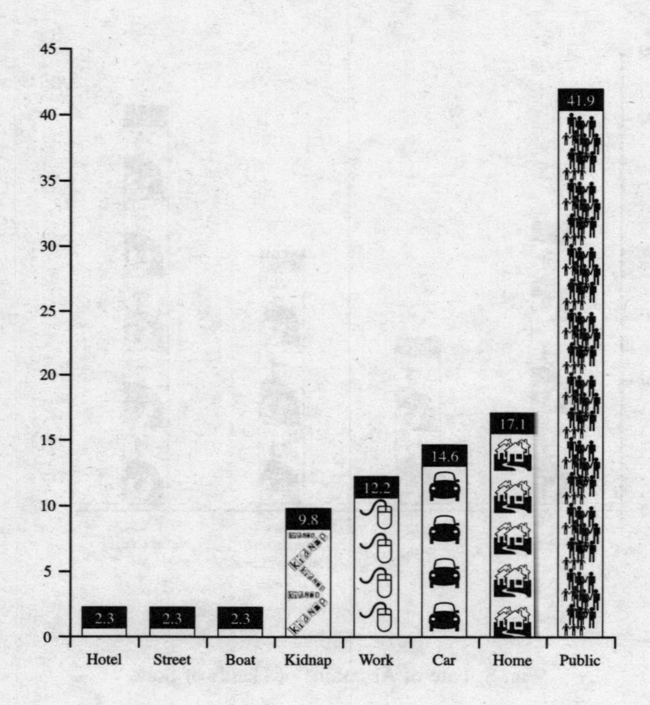

Fig. 9: Assassinations of Heads of State by Location

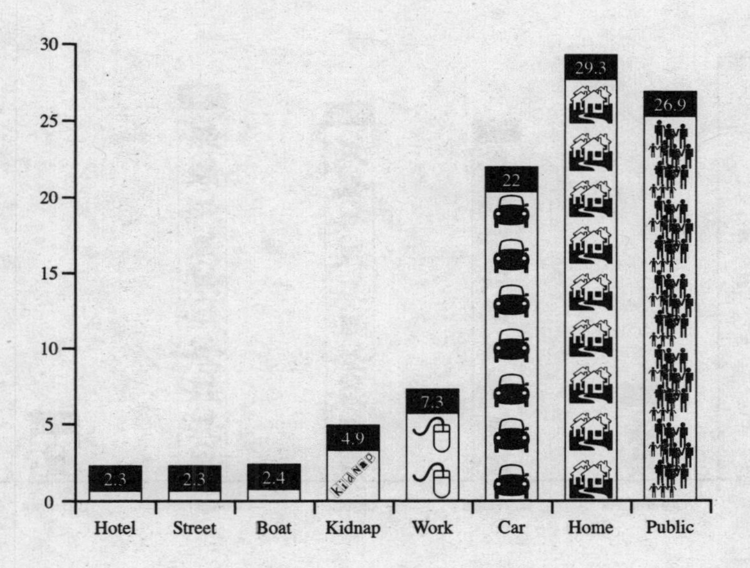

Fig. 10: All Assassinations by Location

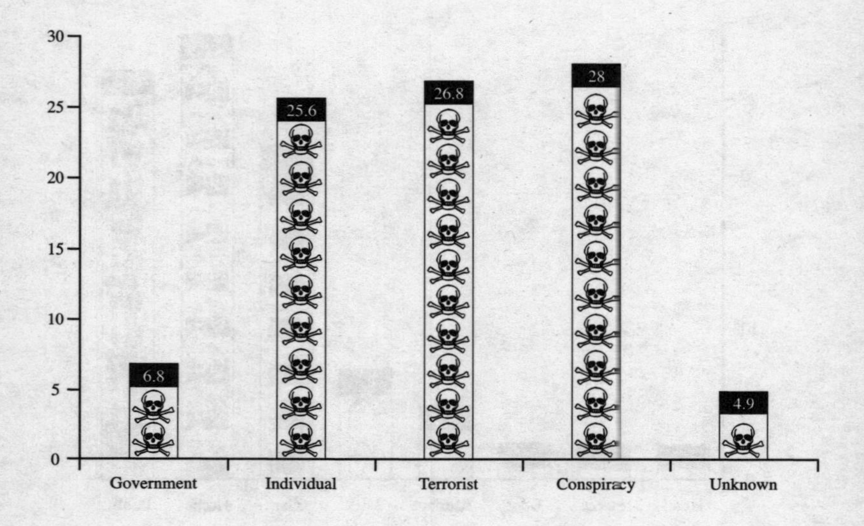

Fig. 11: All Assassinations by Perpetrator
(No difference between Heads of State and this group)

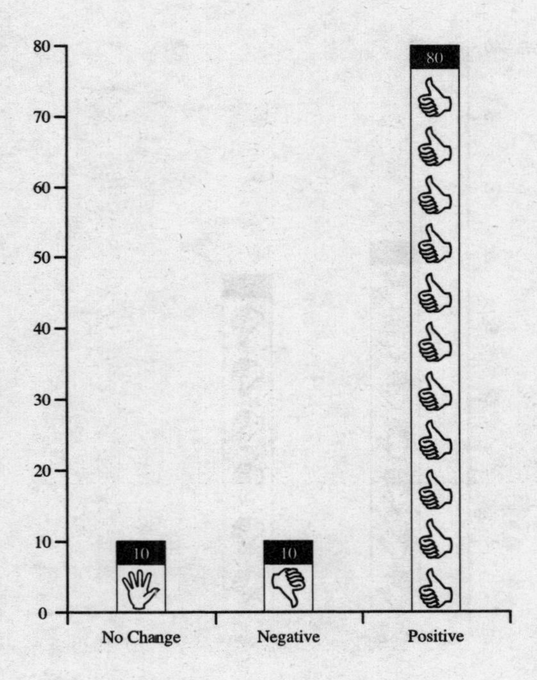

Fig. 12: Effects of the Successful Assassination of Heads of State on Killer's Aims

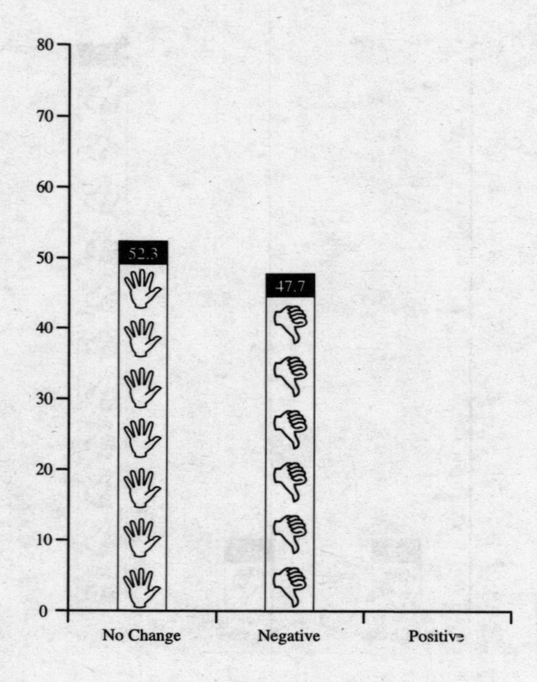

Fig. 13: Effects of Unsuccessful Assassination of Heads of State on Killer's Aims

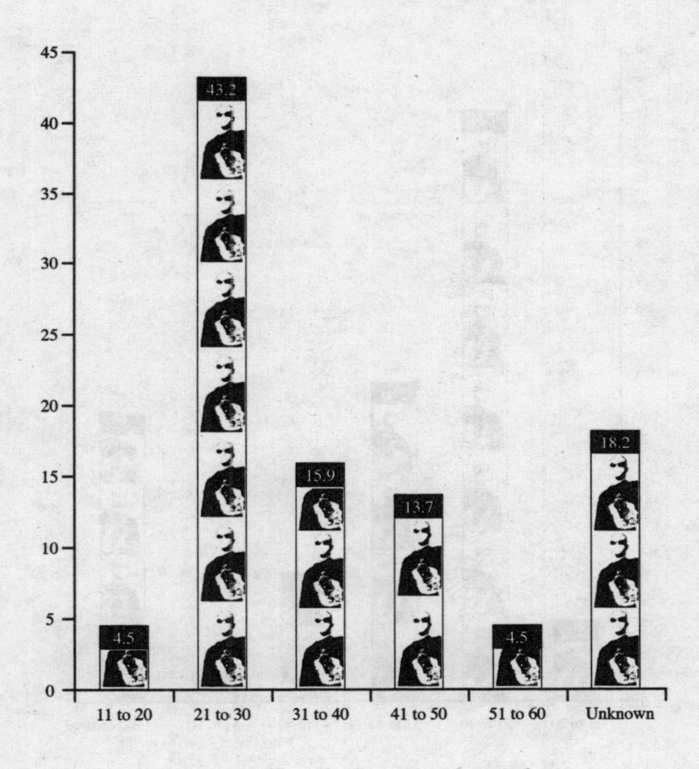

Fig. 14: Assassins by Age for Heads of State

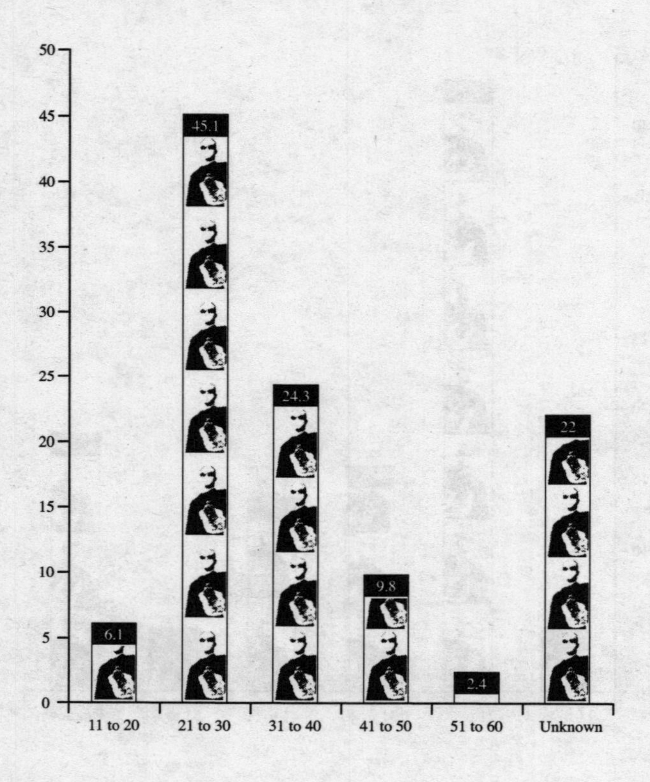

Fig. 15: Assassins by Age for All

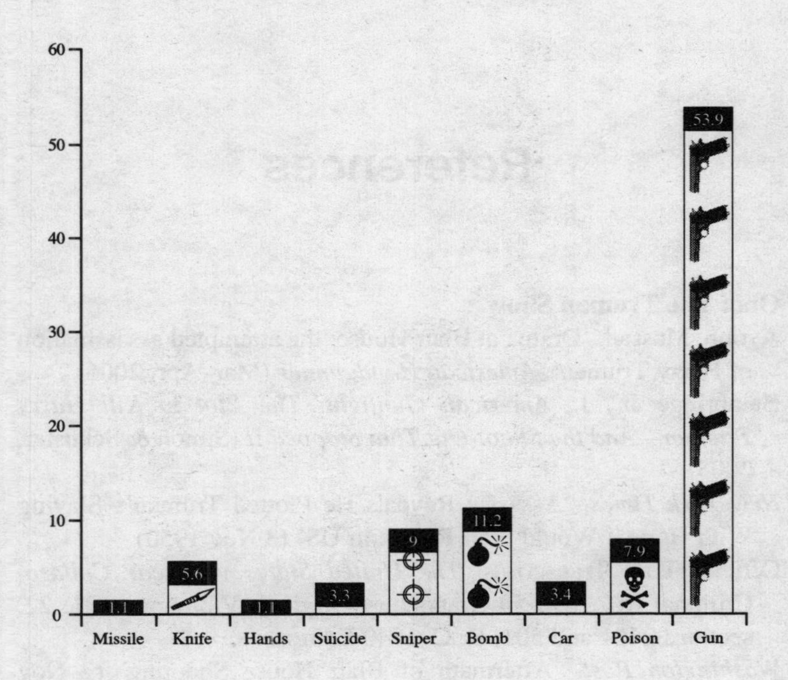

Fig. 16: Assassinations by Weapon
Guns have a 68.3 per cent success rate

References

One: The Truman Show

Ayoob, Massad, 'Drama at Blair House: the attempted assassination of Harry Truman', *American Handgunner* (Mar–Apr, 2006)

Bainbridge Jr., J., *American Gunfight: The Plot to Kill Harry Truman – And the Shoot-Out That Stopped It* (Simon & Schuster, 2005)

New York Times, 'Assassin Reveals He Plotted Truman's Slaying With Hope it Would Start Revolt in US' (3 Nov 1950)

Official Trial Transcripts, *The United States v. Oscar Collazo*, Criminal No. 1690-50 Grand Jury Original, Violations Title 22, sections 2401 and 501, D. C. 1940 Edition

Washington Post, 'Aftermath of Blair House Shooting' (2 Nov 1950)

For more details on Leslie Coffelt and photos of his funeral, see: http://www.arlingtoncemetery.net/lcoffelt.htm

Two: Stalin's Last Supper

Brent, Professor Jonathan and Naumov, Vladimir, *Stalin's Last Crime: The Plot Against the Jewish Doctors* 1948–1953 (HarperCollins, 2003)

Conquest, Robert R., *The Great Terror: A Reassessment*, (Oxford University Press, New York and Oxford, 1990)

Franchetti, Mark, 'Beria's Executioner Hizhnyak Gurevich', *The Times* (4 Jan 1998)

Kenyon, Brig. Gen. Lloyd Everett, interviewed by Bell, Chris R., *My*

Army Recollections [sound recording] (Reel 8, Side 1) an off-the-record briefing including an account of the death of Beria.

Knight, Amy W., *Beria: Stalin's First Lieutenant* (Princeton University Press, 1995)

Pravda, *Vicious Spies and Killers under the Mask of Academic Physicians* (13 Jan 1953) *Pravda*, *Announcement; Ministry of the Internal Affairs of the USSR* (4 Apr 1953)

Rapoport, Yakov, *The Doctors' Plot of 1953*, translated by N.A. Perova and R.S. Bobrova (Harvard University Press, Cambridge MA, 1991)

Rodina, *The Archives of the Central Committee*, Document 1502, pp. 62–63, Top Secret File (4 Jul 1992)

Three: Saddam's First Kill

United Press International, 'Saddam Key in Early CIA Plot' (11 Apr 2003)

Wolf, Paul, *Rise of the Baath Party in Iraq, 1959–1962* – online resource which includes first-hand reports made by CIA operatives and embassy staff in the days following the assassination, as well as interviews with Kassem. http://www.icdc.com/~paulwolf/iraq/baath.htm

Four: The Black Sorcerer

Counterpunch, *CIA's Sidney Gottlieb: Pusher, Assassin & Pimp. US Official Poisoner Dies* http://www.counterpunch.org/gottlieb.html

Foster, Sarah, *Meet Sidney Gottlieb – CIA dirty trickster He's the target of more than one lawsuit* WorldNetDaily.com (19 Nov 1998) http://www.worldnetdaily.com/news/article.asp?ARTICLE_ID=16807

Hersh, Seymour M., *The Dark Side of Camelot* (HarperCollins Publishers Ltd, 1998)

Jacobs, John, 'The Diaries Of a CIA Operative', *Washington Post* (5 Sept 1977)

Marks, John, *The Search for the Manchurian Candidate: CIA and Mind Control* (W W Norton & Co Ltd, 2004)

Streatfield, Dominic, *Brainwash: The Secret History of Mind Control*, (Hodder & Stoughton Ltd, 2006)
Time, 'Of Dart Guns and Poisons' (29 Sept 1975)

Fidel Castro

Bohning, Don, *The Castro Obsession: U.S. Covert Operations Against Cuba, 1959–1965* (Potomac Books, 2005)
CIA targets Fidel: secret 1967 CIA Inspector General's report on plots to assassinate Fidel Castro (Ocean Press, New York, NY, USA 1996)
Coltman, Leycester, *The real Fidel Castro* (Yale University Press, 2003)
Escalante, Fabian, *638 Ways to Kill Castro* (Ocean Press, 3 Jan 2007)
Escalante, Fabian, *The Secret War: CIA Covert Operations Against Cuba, 1959–62* (Ocean Press, 1995)
Lorenz, Marita, *One Woman's Extraordinary Tale of Love and Espionage from Castro to Kennedy* (Thunder's Mouth Press, Nov 1993)
United States Congress House Committee on the Judiciary Statement of Information: Hearings Before the Committee on the Judiciary, House of Representatives (1974)

Five: Hearts of Darkness

Patrice Lumumba

Africa Within, *Patrice Lumumba's last letter to his wife after his arrest*: http://www.africawithin.com/lumumba/last_letter.htm
Boateng, Osei, *The Diabolical Job* (*New African* 1 Sep 2001) http://www.africasia.co.uk/archive/na/01_09/cover3.htm
Castro, Silvio, 'The Assassination of Lumumba' (*Tricontinental Magazine* #146) http://www.nigerdeltacongress.com/articles/assassination_of_lumumba.htm
De Witte, Ludo, *The Assassination of Lumumba* (Verso Books, New Ed edition, 30 Sept 2002)
DiEugenio, Jim, 'Dodd and Dulles vs. Kennedy in Africa' (*Probe*

Magazine,Jan–Feb 1999, Vol. 6 No. 2)

Parliamentary Committee of Inquiry in charge of determining the exact circumstances of the assassination of Patrice Lumumba and the possible involvement of Belgian politicians

The full 1,000 page report of the committee is available in French at: http://www.lachambre.be/commissions/LMB/indexF.html

Links to a summary, introduction, and conclusions in English, in Word or PDF formats, can be found at the same site.

Time, 'The Medieval Pattern' (7 Nov. 1960)

Time, 'Change of Venue' (27 Jan. 1961)

Time, 'The U.S. Can Take Care of Itself' (Feb 24, 1961)

Weissman, Stephen R., 'Opening the Secret Files on Lumumba's Murder' (*Washington Post*, 21 Jul 2002)

Dag Hammarskjold

BBC news, *UN assassination plot denied* (19 Aug 1998) http://news.bbc.co.uk/1/hi/world/africa/154384.stm (World: Africa)

Burger, Marlene, 'CIA and MI5 linked to Hammarskjöld death' (*Electronic Mail & Guardian*, 28 Aug 1998) http://southmovement. alphalink.com.au/southnews/980829-truth.html

Pease, Lisa, 'Midnight in the Congo: The Assassination of Lumumba and the Mysterious Death of Dag Hammarskjold' (*Probe Magazine* Mar–Apr, 1999, Vol. 6 No. 3)

Reuters, 'Letters Say Hammarskjold Death Western Plot' (19 Aug 1998) http://www.globalpolicy.org/secgen/pastsg/murder.htm

Tutu, Desmond, Chairperson Of The Truth And Reconciliation Commission 'Notes For Media Briefing By Archbishop', Issued by: Truth and Reconciliation Commission (19 Aug 1998) http://www.info.gov.za/speeches/1998/98820_0x1539810364.htm

Six: The Mississippi Conspiracy

Brown, Jennie, *Medgar Evers* (Melrose Square Pub. Co., 1994)

Jackson, James E, *At the funeral of Medgar Evers in Jackson, Mississippi: A Tribute in Tears and a Thrust for Freedom*

(Publisher's New Press, 1963)
Klopfer, Susan, *Domestic Spying? It happened in Mississippi not so long ago* http://neshobanews.blogspot.com/2005_12_01_neshobanews_archive.html
Massengill, Reed, *Portrait of a Racist: The Man Who Killed Medgar Evers?* (St Martin's Press, 1994)
New York Times, 'Byron De La Beckwith Is Guilty' (8 Feb 1994)
Sovereignty Commission Online: http://www.mdah.state.ms.us/arlib/contents/er/sovcom/
Facts about Mississippi Sovereignty Commission http://www.mdcbowen.org/p2/bh/badco/missSov.htm
Vollers, Maryanne, *Ghosts of Mississippi: The Murder of Medgar Evers, The Trials of Byron de la Beckwith, and the Haunting of the New South* (Little, Brown, 1995)
Time, 'Life & Death in Jackson' (21 Jun 1963)
Time, 'Strife & Strides' (28 Jun 1963)
Time, 'More Strife & More Strides' (5 Jul 1963)
Time, 'A Little Abnormal' (5 Jul 1963)

Seven: JFK Reloaded

Ayton, Mel, 'The Warren Commission Report: Forty Years Later it still stands up' http://hnn.us/articles18059.html (Oct 2004)
Benson, Michael, *The Encyclopaedia of the JFK Assassination* (Checkmark Books, 2002)
Fetzer, James, H., (editor), *Assassination science: experts speak out on the death of JFK* (Catfeet Press, 1998)
McAdams, John, http://mcadams.posc.mu.edu. The clip of conspiracy author Josiah Thompson accidentally debunking his own book can be found at http://mcadams.posc.mu.edu/dealey.htm, arguably the best and certainly the most rational and useful website which examines the JFK assassination.
Thompson, Josiah, *Six Seconds in Dallas: A Micro-Study of the Kennedy Assassination* (Bernard Geis/Random House Inc, 1967)
President's Commission on the Assassination of President John F. Kennedy. The Official Warren Commission Report on the

Assassination of President John F. Kennedy, etc. (Doubleday & Co, 1964) www.jdtippit.com

Eight: By Any Means Necessary

Time, 'Death and Transfiguration' (5 Mar 1965)
X, Malcolm, *The Autobiography of Malcolm X* (Penguin Modern Classics, 2001)
X, Malcolm, *By Any Means Necessary* (Pathfinder, 1992)

Nine: The Monstrous Tapeworm

Marsh, Rob, *Famous South African Crimes* (Struik Publishers) Available for free download http://www.africacrime-mystery.co.za/books/fsac/index.htm#download
Woerden, Henk van, *A mouthful of glass* (Granta, 2000)

Ten: Murder in Memphis

Ayton, Mel, *The Martin Luther King Jr. Assassination: What Really Happened?* http://www.crimemagazine.com/05/martin lutherking,0612-5.htm
Branch, Taylor, *At Canaan's Edge: America in the King Years, 1965–68* (Simon & Schuster Ltd, 2006)
Huie, William Bradford, *He slew the dreamer: my search with James Earl Ray for the truth about the murder of Martin Luther King* (W. H. Allen, 1970)
McMillan, George, *The making of an assassin : the life of James Earl Ray* (Little, Brown and Company, 1976)
Posner, Gerald L., *Killing the dream: James Earl Ray and the assassination of Martin Luther King, Jr,* (Little, Brown, 1999)
Recordings of the Memphis police radios in the wake of the assassination: http://register.shelby.tn.us/mlk/index.php?album =Audio+Files

Eleven: The Route of Most Danger

Ayton, Mel, *The Unaffiliated Terrorist* (FrontPageMagazine.com, May 16, 2005)

Clarke, James W., *Defining Danger: American Assassins and the New Domestic Terrorists* (New Brunswick, 2006)
Dallek, Robert *John F Kennedy: An Unfinished Life* (Penguin Books, 1 Jul 2004)
House Select Committee on Assassinations, US House of Representatives Ninety-Fifth Congress second session, 2 Jan 1979 (US Government Printing Office, Washington, 1979)
Klaber, William and Melanson, Philip H., *Shadow Play* (St Martin's Press, 1997)
Moldea, Dan E., *The killing of Robert F. Kennedy: an investigation of motive, means, and opportunity* (W. W. Norton, 1995)
Schlesinger, Arthur Meier, *Robert Kennedy and his times* (Deutsch, 1978)

Twelve: Something Bold and Dramatic

Bernstein, Carl and Woodward, Bob, *All the President's Men* (Simon and Schuster, 1974)
Bremer, Arthur H., *An Assassin's Diary* (Harper's Magazine Press, 1973)
Portrait of an Assassin: Arthur Bremer http://www.pbs.org/wgbh/amex/wallace/sfeature/assasin.html
Carter, Dan T., *The Politics of Rage: George Wallace, the Origins of the New Conservatism, and the Transformation of American Politics* (Louisiana State University Press, 1996)
Leek, Sybil and Sugar, Bert R., *The Assassination Chain* (New York: Corwin Books, 1976)
US National Archives, *The White House Tapes* (15 May 1972)

Thirteen: Spain's First Astronaut

Bell, Bowyer, J., *Assassin: Theory and Practice of Political Violence* (Transaction Publishers, 2005)
El Mundo, 'I killed Carrero Blanco's assassin' (21 Dec 2003)
Forest, Eva, *Operation Ogro: The Execution of Admiral Luis Carrero Blanco* (New York Times Book Co., 1975)
Rosen, Phillip Marguiles, *ETA: Spain's Basque Terrorists (Inside*

the World's Most Infamous Terrorist Organizations) (Rosen Publishing Group, 2004)

Woodworth, Paddy, *Dirty War, Clean Hands: ETA, the GAL and Spanish Democracy* (Yale Nota Bene, Nov 2002)

Fourteen: Operation Pandora's Box

9/11 Commission Report, page 537 www.9-11commission.gov/report/911Report.pdf

Federal Airlines Authority Report, *Troubled Passage: The Federal Aviation Administration During the Nixon–Ford Term 1973–1977* (1987)

Fifteen: Bite of the Cobra

CBS Evening News, *Interview with Christine Surma*, Wednesday, 26 Mar 1975 5.45 p.m. Vanderbilt Television News Archive TVN Record Number 239219

New York Times, 26 and 27 Mar 1975

Time, 'The Death of a Desert Monarch' (7 Apr, 1975)

Sixteen: Terror in Rome

Drake, Richard, 'The Aldo Moro Murder Case in Retrospect' (*Journal of Cold War Studies* Vol. 8, No. 2, Spring 2006, pp. 114–125)

Katz, Robert, *Days of Wrath: The Ordeal of Aldo Moro, the Kidnapping, the Execution, the Aftermath* (Doubleday, May 1980)

Katz, Robert, *The Man Who Killed Aldo Moro* http://www.theboot.it/aldo_moro_op-ed.htm

Moretti, Mario, 'Red Brigades: An Italian Story' (Reporters Without Borders Annual Report, 2004)

Sciascia, Leonardo, 'The Moro Affair' (*New York Review of Books*, 2004)

Seventeen: The Umbrella of Death

Hamilton, Jack and Walker, Tom, 'Dane named as umbrella killer' (*Sunday Times* 5 Jun 2005)

Hristov, Hristo, *Kill the Tramp: Bulgarian and British State Policies Related to the Case of Georgi Markov* (CIELA Soft and Publishing AD, Sofia 2005)
Markov, Georgi, *The Truth That Killed* (Weidenfeld and Nicolson, 1983)
Time, 'Another Odd Bulgarian Death' (16 Oct 1978)
Time, 'From Vegetables to Dirty Tricks, Bulgaria Gives its All' (14 Feb 1983)
Walsh, Nick Paton, 'Markov's Umbrella Assassin Revealed' (*Guardian*, 6 Jun 2005)

Eighteen: The Serial Assassin

The photos of President Jimmy Carter's battle with the swamp rabbit can be found at http://www.narsil.org/politics/carter/killer_rabbit.html
Associated Press, *Imprisoned Racist Admits to 2 Killings in '80* (21 Aug 1990)
Associated Press, *Man Details How He Shot a Black Leader* (Apr 9, 1996)
Blair, William G., 'Slayer a suspect in 13 more deaths', (*New York Times*, 25 Mar 1984)
Fein, Robert A. and Vossekuil, Brian, 'Assassination in the United States: An Operational Study of Recent Assassins, Attackers, and Near Lethal Approachers' (*Journal of Forensic Sciences*, Volume 44, Number 2, Mar 1999)
Hickey, Eric W., *Encyclopaedia of Murder and Violent Crime* (SAGE Publications, Aug 2003)
New York Times, 'Larry Flynt's Assailant Has Left a Trail of Bigotry and Murder' (16 Feb 1997)
New York Times, 'Suspect Indicted in Flynt Case' (13 Jun 1984)
Powell, Jody, *The Other Side of the Story* (William Morrow & Co, 1986)
Reuters, 'White Supremacist Named in 5th Killing' (12 Nov 1994)
Severo, Richard, 'Former Klansman Indicted in Bombing of a Synagogue' (*New York Times*, 8 Mar 1984)

Voyde Harrelson/Judge John Wood

Contreras, Guillermo, 'Chagra is set free early' *(San Antonio Express News,* 31 Dec 2003)

Moore, Jim, *Very Special Agents: The Inside Story of America's Most Controversial Law Enforcement Agency* (University of Illinois Press, 2001)

Smith, John L., *Of Rats and Men: Oscar Goodman's Life from Mob Mouthpiece to Mayor of Las Vegas* (Huntington Press, 2003)

Nineteen: You Talkin' to Me?

John Lennon

Jones, Jack, *Let me take you down: inside the mind of Mark David Chapman, the man who shot John Lennon* (Virgin, 2001)

Time, 'A Lethal Delusion' (22 Dec 1980)

Time, 'The Last Day in the Life' (22 Dec 1980)

Ronald Reagan

Abrams, Herbert L., *The President Has Been Shot: Confusion, Disability and the 25th Amendment in the Aftermath of the Attempted Assassination of Ronald Reagan* (Stanford University Press, 1994)

Associated Press, Bush Son Had Dinner Plans With Hinckley Brother Before Shooting (31 Mar 1981)

Caplan, Lincoln, *The insanity defense and the trial of John W. Hinckley, Jr.* (Godine, 1984)

Clarke, James W., *On being mad or merely angry: John W. Hinckley, Jr., and other dangerous people* (Princeton University Press, 1990)

FBI Files, *President Ronald Reagan Assassination Attempt: John Hinckley Jr.*

796 pages of FBI files summarising the investigation conducted in the first several days after the 30 Mar 1981 assassination attempt on President Ronald Reagan, archived on CD-ROM, available from http://www.paperlessarchives.com/reagan_assassination _attempt.html

Mossman, John, Family 'Destroyed' By Assassination Attempt (Associated Press, 1 Apr 1981)

Lerman, David, 'Judge rules Hinckley can continue visits to parents' home' (*Minneapolis–St. Paul Pioneer Press* 21 Aug 2006)

Virginia Gazette, *Hinckley in Home Visits* (3 Feb 2006)

Webster, Tarpley Griffin, and Chaitkin, Anton, *George Bush: The Unauthorized Biography* (Progressive Press, 2004)

Weinberger, Caspar, *In the Arena* (Regnery Publishing Inc, 2003)

Wiese, Arthur and Downing, Margarte, 'Bush's Son Was To Dine With Suspect's Brother' (*Houston Post*, Mar 31 1981)

Twenty: The Pope Must Die

Anadolu News Agency, *Daughter of Agca's Victim: Pope's Attitude Hurt Us* (14 Jan 2006)

Campbell, Matthew, 'Family demand justice over Agca's forgotten murder' (*Sunday Times* 15 Jan 2006)

Griffiths, Emma, *Italian investigation concludes Pope assassination attempt a Soviet Plot* (ABC News Correspondents Report, Sunday 12 Mar 2006) http://www.abc.net.au/correspondents/content/2006/s1589402.htm

Henze, Paul, *The plot to kill the Pope* (Macmillan, 1985)

Penner, Martin, 'Soviet spies "controlled" would-be papal assassin' (*The Times*, 3 Mar 2006)

Associated Press, *Panel concludes Russia was behind assassination attempt on pope* (2 Mar 2006)

West, Nigel, *The Third Secret: The CIA, Solidarity and the KGB's Plot to Kill the Pope* (HarperCollins, 2001)

Twenty-one: Z-Squad Incorporated

Bell, Terry, *Unfinished Business: South Africa, Apartheid and Truth* (Verso Books, 2003)

Cape Times, 'Orders to kill: New inquest on UDF killings' (9 Mar 1992)

Pauw, Jacques, *In the heart of the whore: the story of apartheid's death squads* (Southern Book Publishers, 1991)

Pauw, Jacques, *Into the heart of darkness: confessions of apartheid's assassins* (Jonathan Ball, 1997)

Truth and Reconciliation Committee, *Hearing on the death of Griffith Mxenge* http://sahistory.org.za/pages/sources/docs/1997_TRC-hearing-mxenge-murder.htm

Time, 'South Africa Probing the Hit Squads' (18 Dec 1989)

Vrye Weekblad, *Bloedspoor van die SAP* [Bloody Trail of the SAP] (1 Nov 1989)

Vrye Weekblad, 'At last proof of the Third Force' (30 Oct 1992)

Twenty-two: Death at the Dorchester

Follain, John, *Jackal: The Secret Wars of Carlos the Jackal* (Orion, 1999)

Joffe, Lawrence, 'Shlomo Argov Obituary: Israeli diplomat whose shooting triggered the invasion of Lebanon' (*Guardian*, 25 Feb 2003)

Yallop, David A., *To the ends of the earth: the hunt for the jackal* (Corgi, 1994)

Melman, Yossi, *The Master Terrorist: The True Story Behind Abu Nidal* (Mama Books, 1986)

Seale, Patrick, *Abu Nidal: A Gun for Hire* (Hutchinson, 1992)

Steinberg, Matti, *The Radical Worldview of the Abu Nidal Faction* (Jerusalem Quarterly 48, pp88–104)

Time, *An Israeli Ambassador is shot, and Jerusalem strikes back* (Jun 14, 1982)

Time, 'Ten Minutes of Horror' (6 Jan 1986)

Twenty-three: Three Weeks in October

Jerzy Popieluszko

Boyes, Roger, *The priest who had to die* (Gollancz, 1986)

Sikorska, Grazyna. *A martyr for the truth: Jerzy Popieluszko* (Fount, 1985)

Sikorska, Grazyna, *Jerzy Popieluszko: victim of communism*, (Catholic Truth Society, 1999)

Margaret Thatcher

Brown, Paul, et al *Cabinet survives IRA hotel blast* (*Guardian*, 13 Oct 1984)

Wilson, Jamie, *Brighton bomber thinks again Special report: Northern Ireland* (*Guardian*, 28 Aug 2000)

Indira Gandhi

Anandaram, S., *Assassination of a Prime Minister as It Happened* (Vision Books, Mar 1994)

Gupte, Pranay, *Vengeance* (W W Norton, 1986)

Shourie, Arun, *The Assassination & After* (Roli Books International, 1985) http://www.time.com/time/community/transcripts/1999/082599ustinov.html

Time, 'Slaughter at the Golden Temple' (18 Jun 1984)

Time, 'Death in the Garden' (12 Nov 1984)

Time Transcripts, 'Telephone interview with Peter Ustinov' (25 Aug 1999)

Twenty-four: The Stockholm Takedown

Bondeson, Jan, *Blood on the snow: the killing of Olof Palme*, (Cornell University Press, 2005)

Cooper, H. H. A., *The murder of Olof Palme: a tale of assassination, deception and intrigue, with appendix : the assassination of Anna Lindh, Swedish Foreign Minister* (Edwin Mellen Press, 2003)

Hansen, Dan, *The crisis management of the murder of Olof Palme: a cognitive-institutional analysis* (Swedish National Defence College, 2003)

Hasselbohm, Anders, five articles written by this Swedish journalist, translated into English by The Norwegian Council for Africa (originally written for *Aftonbladet* 1994–95)

Freeman, Ruth, *Death of a statesman: the solution to the murder of Olof Palme* (Hale, 1989)

Nicoll, Ruaridh, *The maverick, the mole and the ant. Which South African agent killed Sweden's Olof Palme?* (*Observer*, 6 Oct 1996)

Rodney, Derek, *Super-spy Craig Williamson involved in Swedish assassination* (*Star* on-line, 27 Sep 1996)

Sapa-AFP, 'Palme's alleged assassin denies involvement' (30 Sep 1996)

Sapa-AFP, 'Palme's killer in Turkey' (4 Oct 1996)

Sapa-Ap, 'Sweden had allegations of SA involvement in Palme's death' (26 Sep 1996)

Sapa-AFP, *Swedish police aim to follow Palme murder trail to South Africa* (1 Oct 1996)

Smith, Alexandra Duval, *15,000 Leads to nowhere* (*Guardian*, Feb 25 1993)

Jo'burg Sapa, 'Williamson speaks to Swedish investigators' (19 Oct 1996)

Independent, 'Ex-soldier is named as Palme's assassin' (30 Sep 1996)

Searchlight, 'On the trail of Palme's assassins. The finger points South,' (Nov. 1996)

Twenty-five: A Very Modern Conspiracy

Associated Press: *Detlev Rohwedder fatally shot in his home* (2 Apr 1991)

Brockmann, Stephen, 'Living where the wall was: what still divides the Germans', *Commonwealth* (24 Sept 1993)

Hart-Lansberg, Martin, *Korea: Division Reunification and US Foreign Policy* (Chapter Eight: 'The Economic and Social Costs of German Absorption'), *Monthly Review Press* (1 Dec 1998)

Kinzer, Stephen, '*German Far Left Dogs New Agency*', *New York Times* (5 Apr 1991)

Maier, Charles S., *Dissolution: The crisis of communism and the end of East Germany* (Princeton University Press, 1999)

McAdams, A. James, *Germany Divided: From the Wall to Reunification* (Princeton University Press, 1994)

Morrissey, Michael D., *Alfred Herrhausen: Terrorist Victim?* (Jun 1990) http://www.prouty.org/letter7.html

http://127.0.0.1:4664/cache?event_id=62915&schema_id=2&q=rohwedder&s=eogVPIjQGoJEE8w8EmaSXjK7z_o

Reuters, 'German Gains In Privatizing' (19 Mar 1991)
Reuters, 'Post Is Filled In Germany' (15 Apr 1991)
Reuters, 'Rowhedder Murder May Shake Confidence in Germany' (2 Apr 1991)
Time, 'A Global Fire Sale' (22 Apr 1991)
Time, 'Terrorism Target for the Red Army Faction' (11 Dec 1991)
We (German News English Edition), *Clue in Treuhand-head Rohwedder's 1991 murder*, (16 May 2001)
Wisnewski, Gerhard, *Das RAF-Phantom: Wozu Politik und Wirtschaft Terroristen brauchen*, Knaur (31 Jan 1997)
Zepp-LaRouche, Helga, *Unmasking the Secret War*, *Executive Intelligence Review* (10 Dec 2004)

Twenty-six: Dr Strangelove's Supergun

Adams, James, *Bull's Eye: The Assassination and Life of Supergun Inventor Gerald Bull*, (Times Books, 1992)
CBC, *Dr Gerald Bull: Scientist, Weapons Maker, Dreamer* – excellent multimedia history from the CBC archives at http://archives.cbc.ca/IDD-1-74-626/people/gerald_bull/
Grant, Dale, *Wilderness of mirrors: the life of Gerald Bull* (Prentice-Hall Canada, 1991)
Lowther, William, *Arms and the man: Dr Gerald Bull, Iraq and the supergun* (Macmillan, 1991)
Malone, William Scott et al, 'Guns of Saddam: America Shrugged While Gerald Bull Designed the Ultimate Cannon and Sold It to Iraq' (*Washington Post*, 10 Feb 1991)
PBS Frontline, 'The Man Who Made The Supergun' (12 Feb, 1991) http://www.pbs.org/wgbh/pages/frontline/programs/transcripts/911.html
Thomas, Gordon, 'Mossad – The World's Most Efficient Killing Machine' (9 Dec 2002) 12-9-2 http://www.rense.com/general32/ruth.htm

Twenty-seven: The Karate Death-Chop

Iran Focus, 'Iran's former intelligence chief a wanted man' (11 Nov 2006) http://www.iranfocus.com/modules/news/article.php?storyid=9192

Iran Focus, 'Iran's New president has past mired in controversy' (25 Jun 2006)

http://www.iranfocus.com/modules/news/article.php?storyid=2605

Iran Focus, *Exclusive: Photo shows Iran's Ahmadinejad as hostage-taker of US diplomats* (28 Jun 2005)

Time, *The Tehran Connection* (21 Mar 1994)

Twenty-eight: One-Eyed Jack

Dalal, Ramesh. *Rajiv Gandhi's assassination: the mystery unfolds* (UBSPD, 2001)

Indian Express Newspapers, 'Cracking the code' (5 Feb 1998)

Sarin, Ritu, 'Confessions of an accomplice' *Indian Express Newspapers* (7 May 1991)

Sharma, Rajeev, *Beyond the tigers: tracking Rajiv Gandhi's assassination* (Kaveri Books, 1998)

Swamy, Subramanian. *The assassination of Rajiv Gandhi: unanswered questions and unasked queries* (Delhi: Konark Publishers, 2000)

Time, 'Sri Lanka's Tamil Tigers' (16 Sep 1991)

Time, 'How Sri Lanka's Rebels Build a Suicide Bomber' (12 May 2006)

Twenty-nine: Lady Macdeath

Dallaire, Romeo, *Shake Hands with the Devil: The Failure of Humanity in Rwanda* (Arrow, 2005)

Frontline PBS, 'The Triumph of Evil', on-line interview with Philip Gourevitch

http://www.pbs.org/wgbh/pages/frontline/shows/evil/interviews/gourevitch.html

Gourevitch, Philip, *We Wish to Inform You That Tomorrow We Will be Killed With Our Families* (Picador, 2000)

Human Rights Watch, 'Leave None to Tell the Story: Genocide in Rwanda 1999' (Jun 1999) http://www.hrw.org/reports/1999/rwanda/

Human Rights Watch, 'Rearming with Impunity: International Support for the Perpetrators of the Rwandan Genocide', Human Rights Watch Report, vol. 7 no. 4 (May 1995)

Human Rights Watch, Democratic Republic of Congo, 'What Kabila is Hiding: Civilian Killings and Impunity in Eastern Congo, A Human Rights Watch Report', vol. 9 no. 5(A) (Oct 1997)

Thirty: Top Secret – The Exceptional Case Study

Fein R., Vossekuil B., *Preventing attacks on public officials and public figures: a Secret Service perspective,* in *The Psychology of Stalking: Clinical and Forensic Perspectives* pp. 175–91, (Academic Press, 1998)

Fein R., Vossekuil B., *Protective Intelligence and Threat Assessment Investigations: A Guide for State and Local Law Enforcement Officials* (A Research Report Monograph), National Institute of Justice, Office of Justice Programs, US Department of Justice (1998)

Hoffman J.L., 'Psychotic visitors to government offices in the National Capitol', *American Journal of Psychiatry*, 99:571–5 (1943)

Loci, T., 'Duran convicted of trying to kill the President', *Washington Post* (5 Apr 1995)

Loci, T., 'Man charged with Clinton assassination attempt', *Washington Post* (18 Nov 1994)

Loci, T., 'Tourist tells how shooter was tackled,' *Washington Post*, (23 Mar 1995)

Meloy J.R., James D.V., Franham FR, et al, 'A research review of public figure threats, approaches, attacks, and assassinations in the United States', *Journal of Forensic Science*, 49:1–7 (2004)

Public Documents of the White House Security Review: The 29 Oct 1994 Shooting. White House Security Review (1995)

Rothstein, D. A., *Presidential assassination syndrome*. Archives of General Psychiatry 11:245–54 (1964)

Shore D, Filson C, Davis T, et al, 'White House cases: psychiatric patients and the Secret Service', *American Journal of Psychiatry* 142:308–12 (1985)

Thirty-one: The Enemy Within

Associated Press, 'Video of Rabin's assassination broadcast' (16 Feb 1996)
Reuters, 'Jailed Rabin assassination accomplice punished again' (27 Apr 2006)
Time, 'A Majority Of One' (13 Nov 1995)
Time, 'Man Of Israel' (13 Nov 1995)
Time, 'Soldier Of Peace' (13 Nov 1995)
Time, 'Thou Shalt Not Kill' (13 Nov 1995)
Yoram, Peri, *The Assassination of Yitzhak Rabin* (Stanford University Press, 2000)

Thirty-two: Operation Certain Death

Bashir, Ala, *The Insider: Trapped In Saddam's Brutal Regime* (Abacus, 2005)
Sada, General Georges, *Saddam's Secrets: How an Iraqi General Defied and Survived Saddam Hussein* (Integrity Publishers, Mar 2006)
Soloway, Colin, *Uday's Home Movies* Newsweek Web Exclusive Jun 2 http://www.msnbc.msn.com/id/3068268/site/newsweek/
Yahyá, Latif, *The devil's double: the true story of the man forced to be the double of Saddam Hussein's eldest son* (Arrow, 2003)

Thirty-three: Three in the Head

Politics can be murder. The NIS Observed: An Analytical Review, Volume IX Number 01 (23 Jan 2004) http://www.bu.edu/iscip/digest/vol9/ed0901.html
Moscow Times, 'Starovoitova Slaying Commemorated' (23 Nov 1999)
St Petersburg Times, 'Starovoitova: Soon To Be Forgotten?' (26 Nov 1999)

BBC News, *Reward for information in Starovoitova murder* (26 Nov 1998)

Whitmore, Brian, *The Strange Investigation Of Galina Starovoitova's Murder*, *PRISM*, Volume 5, Issue 2 (29 Jan 1999)

BBC News, 'Clinton: Starovoitova murder assault on democracy' (26 Nov 1998)

BBC News, 'Prominent Russian reformist Starovoitova assassinated' (20 Nov 1998)

BBC News, 'Russia loses an icon' (21 Nov 1998)

BBC News, 'Russia mourns murdered' MP (24 Nov 1998)

BBC News, 'Russian media reviles killers' (24 Nov 1998)

BBC News, 'Six held over Russian politician's killing' (6 Nov 2002)

BBC News, 'The death of democracy' (4 Dec 1998)

Thirty-four: Bloodbath in Parliament

Afrikian, Gayane, 'Chamber of horrors – "Only bloodshed will clean out these bastard"' *Independent* (29 Oct 1999)

Afrikian, Gayane, 'Day murder came to the Armenian parliament' *Independent* (Oct 28, 1999)

Agence France Presse, 'Armenian Gunmen surrender' (28 Oct 1999)

Agence France Presse, 'Clinton: Sarkissian assassination "real blow"' (27 Oct 1999)

Agence France Presse, 'Sarkissian the strongman' (27 Oct 1999)

Agence France Presse, *Yeltsin expresses 'profound indignation'* (27 Oct 1999)

Corley, Felix, 'Obituary – Vazgen Sarkissian', *Independent* (29 Oct 1999)

'Shooting in the Armenian Parliament' (Internews, Oct 27 1999) http://www.internews.am/projects/archive/events/english/main1.htm

Thirty-five: The Final Solution

Agence France Presse, 'Zeljko Raznatovic Killed' (16 Jan 2000)

Amnesty International, 'Living for the Day – Forcible Expulsions

from Bijeljina and Janja' (1994)
BBC Online, 'Arkan, death of a warlord: Special report' (20 Jan 2000) http://news.bbc.co.uk/1/hi/world/europe/611826.stm
Evening Standard, 'War Criminals who may be Charged with Balkan Atrocities' (16 Feb, 1993)
Human Rights Watch, 'The Take-Over Of Bijeljina And Janja' (May 2000)
Human Rights Watch, 'War Crimes in Bosnia–Hercegovina' (Aug 1992)
Mueller, John, *The Banality of 'Ethnic War'* International Security, Vol. 25, No. 1, pp. 42-70 (Summer, 2000)
Vreme News Digest Agency, *Arkan: From Bijeljina to Infamy* (Jun 7, 1997)

General

Amnesty International, 'Political killings by governments' (Amnesty International, 1983)
Camellion, Richard, *Assassination: theory and practice* (Paladin Press, 1977)
Clarke, James W., *American assassins: the darker side of politics* [Rev. ed., with new preface] (Princeton University Press, 1990)
Cooper, H. H. A., *On assassination* (Paladin Press, 1984)
Elliott, Paul, *Assassin!: the bloody history of political murder* (Blandford, 1999)
Kirkham, James F., Levy, Sheldon G., Crotty, Willam J., *Assassination and political violence: a report to the National Commission on the Causes and Prevention of Violence*, (U.S. Government Printing Office, NCCPV Staff Study Series, 8, 1969)
Laucella, Linda, *Assassination : the politics of murder* (Lowell House, 1999)
McKinley, James, *Assassination in America* (Harper and Row, 1977)
Melanson, Philip H. *The Secret Service : the hidden history of an enigmatic agency* (Carroll & Graf Publishers, 2002)

THE DEFINITIVE HISTORY CONTINUES online at the author's unique website www.assassinology.org which features ongoing investigations as well as the latest assassination news and research from around the world, including articles on assassination prevention. There are also links to many of the sources for *How to Kill*.

Index